D0288526

Political concepts

WITHDRAWN

Learning Resources Center
Collin County Community College District
SPRING CREEK CAMPUS
Plano, Texas 75074

MANCHESTER
UNIVERSITY PRESS

JA
66
P614
2003

$24.95

Political concepts.

Political concepts

edited by
Richard Bellamy
and
Andrew Mason

Manchester University Press
Manchester and New York
distributed exclusively in the USA by Palgrave

Copyright © Manchester University Press 2003

While copyright in the volume as a whole is vested in Manchester University Press, copyright in individual chapters belongs to their respective authors, and no chapter may be reproduced wholly or in part without the express permission in writing of both author and publisher.

Published by Manchester University Press
Oxford Road, Manchester M13 9NR, UK
and Room 400, 175 Fifth Avenue, New York, NY 10010, USA
www.manchesteruniversitypress.co.uk

Distributed exclusively in the USA by
Palgrave, 175 Fifth Avenue, New York,
NY 10010, USA

Distributed exclusively in Canada by
UBC Press, University of British Columbia, 2029 West Mall,
Vancouver, BC, Canada V6T 1Z2

British Library Cataloguing-in-Publication Data
A catalogue record for this book is available from the British Library

Library of Congress Cataloging-in-Publication Data applied for

ISBN   0 7190 5908 9 *hardback*
          0 7190 5909 7 *paperback*

First published 2003

11 10 09 08 07 06 05 04 03   10 9 8 7 6 5 4 3 2 1

Typeset in Photina
by Northern Phototypesetting Co. Ltd, Bolton
Printed in Great Britain
by Bookcraft (Bath) Ltd, Midsomer Norton

Contents

Notes on contributors   *page* vi

Introduction   *Richard Bellamy and Andrew Mason*   1

1   Liberty   *Ian Carter*   4

2   Rights: their basis and limits   *Catriona McKinnon*   16

3   Social justice: the place of equal opportunity   *Andrew Mason*   28

4   Political obligation   *Rex Martin*   41

5   Nationalism and the state   *Ciarán O'Kelly*   52

6   Crime and punishment   *Emilio Santoro*   65

7   Welfare and social exclusion   *Bill Jordan*   77

8   Legitimacy   *Alan Cromartie*   93

9   Democracy   *David Owen*   105

10   The rule of law   *Richard Bellamy*   118

11   Public and private   *Judith Squires*   131

12   Community: individuals acting together   *Keith Graham*   145

13   Multiculturalism   *Jonathan Seglow*   156

14   Gender   *Terrell Carver*   169

15   Green political theory   *Andrew Vincent*   182

16   International justice   *David Boucher*   196

17   Just war   *Anthony Coates*   211

Bibliography   225

Index   239

Notes on contributors

Richard Bellamy is Professor of Government at the University of Essex. His many publications include: *Modern Italian Social Theory: Ideology and Politics from Pareto to the Present* (1987), *Liberalism and Modern Society: An Historical Argument* (1992), *Liberalism and Pluralism: Towards a Politics of Compromise* (1999) and, as co-editor, *Constitutionalism in Transformation; European and Theoretical Perspectives* (1996), *Citizenship and Governance in the EU* (2001) and the forthcoming *Cambridge History of Twentieth Century Political Thought.*

David Boucher is a Professorial Fellow in the School of European Studies, Cardiff University. His books include *Texts in Context* (1985), *The Social and Political thought of R. G. Collingwood* (1989), *Political Theories of International Relations* (1998), *British Idealism and Political Theory* (with Andrew Vincent, 2000) and, as co-editor, *The Social Contract: From Hobbes to Rawls* (1994) and *Social Justice: From Hume to Walzer* (1998).

Ian Carter teaches Political Philosophy at the University of Pavia, Italy. His research interests include the concepts of freedom, equality and rights, action theory and value theory. He is the author of *A Measure of Freedom* (1999), editor of *L'idea di eguaglianza* (2001) and co-editor (with Mario Ricciardi) of *Freedom, Power and Political Morality. Essays for Felix Oppenheim* (2001).

Terrell Carver is Professor of Political Theory at the University of Bristol. He has written many books and articles on Marx, Engels and Marxism, and has re-translated Marx's *Later Political Writings* (1996) and published *The Postmodern Marx* (1998). In the area of gender studies and sexuality he has published *Gender is Not a Synonym for Women* (1996), 'A Political Theory of Gender: Perspectives on the Universal Subject' (in *Gender, Politics and the State*, 1998), and two articles: 'Theorizing Men in Engels's *Origin of the Family*' (*Masculinities*, 1994) and '"Public Man" and the Critique of Masculinity' (*Political Theory*, 1996). Most recently he has been co-editor of *Politics of Sexuality: Identity, Gender, Citizenship* (1998), and his current project in this area is a substantial study for Manchester University Press, *Men in Political Theory.*

Anthony Coates is Lecturer in Politics at the University of Reading. His publications include *The Ethics of War* (1997), 'The New World Order and the Ethics of War' in Holden, B. (ed.), *The Ethical Dimensions of Global Change* (1996) and, as editor, *International Justice* (2000).

Alan Cromartie is Lecturer in Political Theory at the University of Reading. He has published on Hobbes, Harrington and early modern constitutionalism. At present he is working on *The Constitutionalist Revolution*, a study of the causes of the English civil war.

Keith Graham is Professor of Social and Political Philosophy at the University of Bristol, and has held visiting research fellowships at the universities of Manchester, St Andrews and London. His books include *The Battle of Democracy* (1986), *Karl Marx: Our Contemporary* (1992), *Practical Reasoning in a Social World* (2002) and, as editor, *Contemporary Political Philosophy: Radical Studies* (1982).

Bill Jordan is Professor of Social Policy at Exeter and Huddersfield Universities and Reader in Social Policy at the University of North London. His recent books include *A Theory of the New Politics of Welfare* (1998), and (with Franck Duvell) *Irregular Migration* (2002).

Rex Martin is Professor of Philosophy at the University of Kansas and was Professor of Political Theory and Government in the University of Wales Swansea. His books include *Rawls and Rights* (1985) and *A System of Rights* (1993).

Andrew Mason is Professor of Political Theory at the University of Southampton. He is the author of *Explaining Political Disagreement* (1993), *Community, Solidarity and Belonging* (2000) and editor of *Ideals of Equality* (1998).

Catriona McKinnon is Lecturer in Political Philosophy, Department of Politics, University of York. She has published papers on the role of self-respect in liberal justification, and on liberal constructivist approaches to justificatory values. She is co-editor (with Iain Hampsher-Monk) of *The Demands of Citizenship* (2000), author of *Liberalism and the Defence of Political Constructivism* (2002) and edits the journal *Imprints*, a journal of analytical socialism.

Ciarán O'Kelly teaches Political Theory at the University of Reading. He has research interests in nationalism and liberal/social democratic political thought.

David Owen is Reader in Politics at the University of Southampton. He is the author of *Maturity and Modernity: Nietzsche, Weber, Foucault and the Ambivalence of Reason* (1994), *Nietzsche, Politics and Modernity: A Critique of Liberal Reason* (1995) and editor of *Sociology after Postmodernism* (1997).

Emilio Santoro is Professor of Philosophy and Sociology of Law at the University of Florence. His publications include: *Carcere e società liberale* (1997), *Autonomia individuale, Libertà e diritti* (1999; English translation forthcoming by Kluwer), *Common Law e Costituzione nell'Inghilterra moderna* (1999). He is currently working on the links among market, discipline and liberal order.

Jonathan Seglow is Lecturer in Politics at Royal Holloway, University of London. He has research interests in a variety of issues in contemporary political philosophy, including, social justice, toleration, altruism, as well as multiculturalism and the politics of recognition.

Judith Squires is Senior Lecturer in Political Theory in the Politics Department at the University of Bristol. She is author of *Gender in Political Theory* (1999), and is the editor of several collections including *Feminisms: A Reader* (1997), *Cultural Readings of Orientalism: Secular Criticism and the Gravity of History* (1997), *Cultural Remix: Theories of Politics and the Popular* (1995), *Space and Place: Theories of Identity and Location* (1993) and *Principled Positions: Postmodernism and the Rediscovery of Value* (1993).

Andrew Vincent is Professor of Political Theory at the University of Sheffield. His many publications include: *Philosophy Politics and Citizenship* (with Raymond Plant, 1984), *Theories of the State* (1987), *Modern Political Ideologies* (1992 and 1995), *A Radical Hegelian* (with David Boucher, 1995) and *British Idealism and Political Theory* (with

David Boucher, 2000). He has also edited *The Philosophy of T.H. Green* (1986) and *Political Theory: Tradition and Diversity* (1998). His most recent book is *Nationalism and Particularity* (2002). He is currently joint editor of the journal *Collingwood and British Idealism Studies* and associate editor of the *Journal of Political Ideologies*.

Introduction

Richard Bellamy and Andrew Mason

All political argument employs political concepts. They provide the building blocks needed to construct a case for or against a given political position. Is development aid too low, income tax too high, pornography violence against women, or mass bombing unjust? Any response to topical questions such as these involves developing a view of what individuals are entitled to, what they owe to others, the role of individual choice and responsibility in these matters, and so on. These views, in their turn, imply a certain understanding of concepts like rights, equality and liberty, and their relationship to each other. People of different political persuasions interpret these key concepts of politics in different ways. This book introduces students to some of the main interpretations, pointing out their various strengths and weaknesses.

Older texts on political concepts sought to offer neutral definitions that should be accepted by everyone, regardless of their political commitments and values.[1] Unfortunately, this task proved harder than many had believed. For example, a common argument of this school was that it was a misuse of the term 'freedom' to suggest that people who lacked the resources to read books were unfree to read them. What one ought to say was that such people were unable to read them. Individuals were only unfree to read books if they were legally prohibited or physically prevented from doing so. However, as Ian Carter shows in his chapter, this is not an issue that can be settled by attending to actual linguistic practice, no matter how carefully. Most theorists do distinguish between freedom and ability, but many dispute the view that a lack of resources is necessarily a matter of inability rather than unfreedom. For instance, some people would argue that the uneven distribution of such resources typically results from unjust social arrangements that could and should be rectified and as such has implications for judgements about the extent of a person's freedom. States can provide free education and libraries, say, rather than leaving the provision of schooling and books solely to the market. They contend that deliberately withholding such public provision would constitute a form of coercion, similar in kind to state censorship. In this dispute, disagreement over the correct use and meaning of freedom is firmly related to differences in people's normative and social theories. It is these differences rather than straightforwardly linguistic ones that lead them to diverge in their views of whether individuals acting in a free market could ever coerce others, and so on. Though all parties in this debate might agree that being free is different to being able, some may still detect a lack of freedom where others only see inability.

These sorts of disagreements about the meanings of terms have led many commentators to argue that political concepts are 'essentially contestable'.[2] According to this view, it is part of the nature of these concepts to be open to dispute, and disagreements over their proper use reflect divergent normative, theoretical and empirical assumptions. Even so, these theorists would still maintain that competing views represent alternative 'conceptions' of the same 'concept'. In other words, in spite of their disagreements about how the concept might be defined, they are nonetheless debating the same idea. As a result, it also makes sense to compare different views and to argue that some are more coherent, empirically plausible and normatively attractive than others. With differences of emphasis, all the contributors to this volume broadly adopt this approach. Some, like Rex Martin, Richard Bellamy, David Owen and Catriona McKinnon, contrast two or more different views in order to defend a particular account. Others, like Andrew Vincent, Ciarán O'Kelly and Alan Cromartie, explore difficulties in all accounts. Still others, like Andrew Mason and Anthony Coates, explore a particularly important conception of a given concept, indicating both its appeal and problems. In some cases, as in Bill Jordan's and Emilio Santoro's chapters, the authors concentrate on the theoretical presuppositions of current policies that are guided by a particular understanding of a concept. In others, as in David Boucher's and Jonathan Seglow's chapters, authors compare how different conceptual underpinnings might generate different policy recommendations.

No book will cover all political concepts, and this one is no exception. While aware of many regrettable, if inevitable, omissions, we have attempted to include a broad range of the main concepts employed in contemporary debates among both political theorists and ordinary citizens.[3] Each concept tends to relate to the others in various ways but not all the authors would agree how they do so.[4] Consequently, we have not grouped the chapters into sections. However, the first three chapters tackle the principal concepts employed to justify any policy or institution, the next seven can be roughly related to the main domestic purposes and functions of the state, the following four concern the relationship between state and civil society, and the final three look beyond the state to issues of global concern and relations between states. While not an exhaustive survey therefore, we have tried to offer a wide selection of the concepts used to discuss most dimensions of politics.

Notes

1 Two well-known examples of this genre are T.D. Weldon, *The Vocabulary of Politics* (Harmondsworth, Penguin, 1953), and F. Oppenheim, *Political Concepts: A Reconstruction* (Oxford, Blackwell, 1981).
2 The classical account of this thesis is W.B. Gallie, 'Essentially Contested Concepts', *Proceedings of the Aristotelian Society*, 56 (1956), pp. 167–98. A text that employed this thesis to analyse various concepts, including freedom, is W.E. Connolly, *The Terms of Political Discourse* (Oxford, Blackwell, 1974).
3 For a more historical approach, see R. Bellamy and A. Ross, *A Textual Introduction to Social and Political Theory* (Manchester, Manchester University Press, 1996).
4 Students interested in looking at how the main contemporary political philosophers have related these concepts to each other might care to consult W. Kymlicka's excellent *Contemporary Political Philosophy* (Oxford, Oxford University Press, 2001, 2nd edn).

1
Liberty

Ian Carter

Introduction

Imagine a woman is driving a car through town, and she comes to a fork in the road. She turns left, but no one was forcing her to go one way or the other. Next she comes to a crossroads. She turns right, but no one was preventing her from going left or straight on. There is no traffic to speak of and there are no diversions or police roadblocks. So she seems, as a driver, to be completely free. But this picture of her situation might change quite dramatically if we consider that the reason she went left and then right is that she is addicted to cigarettes and is desperate to get to the tobacconists before it closes. Rather than driving, she feels she is being driven, as her urge to smoke leads her uncontrollably to turn the wheel first to the left and then to the right. Moreover, she is perfectly aware that turning right at the crossroads means she will probably miss a train that was to take her to an appointment she cares about very much. The woman longs to be free of this irrational desire that is not only threatening her longevity but is also stopping her right now from doing what she thinks she ought to be doing.

This story gives us two contrasting ways of thinking of freedom. On the one hand, one can think of freedom as the absence of obstacles external to the agent. You are free if no one is stopping you from doing whatever you might want to do. In the above story the woman appears, in this sense, to be free. On the other hand, one can think of freedom as the presence of control on the part of the agent. To be free, you must be self-determined, which is to say that you must be able to control your own destiny in your own interests. In the above story the woman appears, in this sense, to be unfree: she is not in control of her own destiny, as she is failing to control a passion that she herself would rather be rid of and which is preventing her from realising what she recognises to be her true interests. One might say that while on the first view freedom is simply about how many doors are open to the agent, on the second view it is more about going through the right doors for the right reasons.

1 Negative and positive freedom

Isaiah Berlin, the English philosopher and historian of ideas, called these two concepts of freedom 'negative' and 'positive'. The reason for using these labels is that in the first case freedom seems to be a mere *absence* of something (i.e., of 'obstacles', 'barriers', 'constraints' or 'interference from others'), whereas in the second case freedom seems to require the *presence* of something (i.e., of 'control', 'self-mastery', 'self-determination' or 'self-realisation'). In Berlin's words, we use the negative concept of freedom in attempting to answer the question 'What is the area within which the subject – a person or group of persons – is or should be left to do or be what he is able to do or be, without interference by other persons?', whereas we use the positive concept in attempting to answer the question 'What, or who, is the source of control or interference that can determine someone to do, or be, this rather than that?'[1]

It is useful to think of the difference between the two concepts in terms of the difference between factors that are 'external' and factors that are 'internal' to the agent. While the prime interest of theorists of negative freedom is the degree to which individuals or groups suffer interference from external bodies, theorists of positive freedom are more attentive to the internal factors affecting the degree to which individuals or groups act autonomously. Given this difference, one might be tempted to think that a political theorist should concentrate exclusively on negative freedom, a concern with positive freedom being more relevant to psychology or individual morality than to political theory. This, however, would be premature, for among the most hotly debated issues in political theory are the following: *is* the positive concept of freedom a political concept? Can individuals or groups achieve positive freedom through political action? Is it possible for the state to promote the positive freedom of citizens on their behalf? And, if so, is it desirable for the state to do so? The classic texts in the history of western political thought are divided over how these questions should be answered: theorists in the classical liberal tradition, like Constant, Humboldt, Spencer and Mill, are typically classed as answering 'no' and, therefore, as defending a negative concept of political freedom; theorists that are critical of this tradition, like Rousseau, Hegel, Marx and T.H. Green, are typically classed as answering 'yes' and as defending a positive concept of political freedom.

In its political form, positive freedom has often been thought of as necessarily achieved through a collectivity. Perhaps the clearest case is that of Rousseau's theory of freedom, according to which individual freedom is achieved through participation in the process whereby one's community exercises collective control over its own affairs in accordance with the general will. Put in the simplest terms, one might say that a democratic society is a free society because it is a self-determined society, and that a member of that society is free to the extent that he or she participates in its democratic process.

For liberals, on the other hand, Rousseau's idea of freedom carries with it a danger of authoritarianism. Consider the fate of a permanent and oppressed minority. Because the members of this minority participate in a democratic process characterised by majority rule, they might be said to be free on the grounds that they are members of a society exercising self-control over its own affairs. But they are oppressed, and so are surely unfree. Moreover, it is not necessary to see a society as democratic in order to see it as 'self-controlled'; one might instead adopt an organic conception of society, according to which the collectivity is to be thought of as a living organism, and one might believe that this organism will only act rationally, will only be in control of itself, when its various parts are brought into line with some rational plan devised by its wise governors (who, to extend the metaphor, might be thought of as the organism's brain). In this case, even the majority might be oppressed in the name of liberty.

Such justifications of oppression in the name of liberty are no mere products of the liberal imagination, for there are notorious historical examples of their endorsement by authoritarian political leaders. Berlin, himself a liberal, and writing during the cold war, was clearly moved by the way in which the apparently noble ideal of freedom as self-mastery or self-realisation had been twisted and distorted by the totalitarian dictators of the twentieth century – most notably those of the Soviet Union – so as to claim that they, rather than the liberal West, were the true champions of freedom. The slippery slope towards this paradoxical conclusion begins, according to Berlin, with the idea of a 'divided self'. To illustrate: the smoker in our story provides a clear example of a divided self, as there is the self that wants to get to the appointment and there is the self that wants to get to the tobacconists. We now add to this that one of the selves – the respecter of appointments – is a 'higher' self, and the other – the smoker – is a 'lower' self. The higher self is the rational, reflecting self, the self that is capable of moral action and of taking responsibility for what she does. This is the 'true' self, since it is what marks us off from other animals. The lower self, on the other hand, is the self of the passions, of unreflecting desires and irrational impulses. One is free, then, when one's higher, rational self is in control and one is not a slave to one's passions or to one's 'merely empirical' self. The next step down the slippery slope consists in pointing out that some individuals are more rational than others, and can therefore know best what is in their and others' rational interests. This allows them to say that by forcing people less rational than themselves to do the rational thing and thus to realise their 'true' selves, they are in fact 'liberating' them from their merely empirical desires. Occasionally, Berlin says, the defender of positive freedom will take an additional step that consists in conceiving of the self as wider than the individual and as represented by an organic social 'whole' – 'a tribe, a race, a church, a state, the great society of the living and the dead and the yet unborn'. The 'true' interests of the individual are to be identified with the interests of this whole, and individuals can and should be coerced into fulfilling these interests, for they would not resist coercion if they were as rational and wise as their coercers. 'Once I take this view', Berlin says, 'I am in a position to ignore the actual wishes of men or societies, to bully, oppress, torture in the name, and on behalf, of their "real" selves, in the secure knowledge that whatever is the true goal of man ... must be identical with his freedom.'[2]

Those in the negative camp try to cut off this line of reasoning at the first step, by denying that there is any necessary relation between one's freedom and one's desires. Since one is free to the extent that one is externally unprevented from doing things, they say, one can be free to do what one does not desire to do. If being free meant being unprevented from realising one's desires, then one could, again paradoxically, reduce one's unfreedom by coming to desire fewer of the things one is unfree to do. One could become free simply by contenting oneself with one's situation. A perfectly contented slave is perfectly free to realise all of her desires. Nevertheless, we tend to think of slavery as the opposite of freedom. More generally, freedom is not to be confused with happiness, for in logical terms there is nothing to stop a free person from being unhappy or an unfree person from being happy. The happy person might *feel* free, but whether they *are* free is another matter. Negative theorists of freedom therefore tend to say not that having freedom means being unprevented from doing as one desires, but that it means being unprevented from doing whatever one *might* desire to do.

Some positive theorists of freedom bite the bullet and say that the contented slave is indeed free – that in order to be free the individual must learn, not so much to dominate certain merely empirical desires, but to rid herself of them. She must, in other words, remove as many of her desires as possible. As Berlin puts it, if I have a wounded leg 'there are two methods of freeing myself from pain. One is to heal the wound. But if the cure is too difficult or uncertain, there is another method. I can get rid of the wound by cutting off my leg'. This is the strategy of liberation adopted by ascetics, stoics and Buddhist sages. It involves a 'retreat into an inner citadel' – a soul or a purely 'noumenal' self – in which the individual is immune to any outside forces.[3] But this state, even if it can be achieved, is not one that liberals would want to call one of freedom, for it again risks masking important forms of oppression. It is, after all, often in coming to terms with excessive external limitations in society that individuals retreat into themselves, pretending to themselves that they do not really desire the worldly goods or pleasures they have been denied. Moreover, the removal of desires may also be an effect of outside forces, such as brainwashing, which we should hardly want to call a realisation of freedom.

Because the concept of negative freedom concentrates on the external sphere in which individuals interact, it seems to provide a better guarantee against the dangers of paternalism and authoritarianism perceived by Berlin. To promote negative freedom is to promote the existence of a sphere of action within which the individual is sovereign, and within which she can pursue her own projects subject only to the constraint that she respect the spheres of others. Humboldt and Mill, both defenders of the negative concept of freedom, usefully compared the development of an individual to that of a plant: individuals, like plants, must be allowed to 'grow', in the sense of developing their own faculties to the full and according to their own inner logic. Personal growth is something that cannot be imposed from without, but must come from within the individual.

Critics, however, have objected that the ideal described by Humboldt and Mill looks much more like a positive concept of freedom than a negative one. Positive freedom consists, they say, in exactly this 'growth' of the individual: the free individual is one that develops, determines and changes her own desires and interests autonomously and 'from within'. This is not freedom as the mere absence of obstacles, but freedom as self-realisation. Why should the mere absence of state interference be thought to guarantee such growth? Is there not some 'third way' between the extremes of totalitarianism and the minimal state of the classical liberals – some non-paternalist, non-authoritarian means by which positive freedom in the above sense can be actively promoted?

Much of the more recent work on positive liberty has been motivated by a dissatisfaction with the ideal of negative liberty combined with an awareness of the possible abuses of the positive concept so forcefully exposed by Berlin. John Christman, for example, has argued that positive freedom concerns the *ways* in which desires are formed – whether as a result of rational reflection on all the options available, or as a result of pressure, manipulation or ignorance. What it does not regard, he says, is the *content* of an individual's desires.[4] The promotion of positive freedom need not therefore involve the claim that there is only one right answer to the question of how a person should live. Take the example of a Muslim woman who claims to espouse the fundamentalist doctrines generally followed by her family and society. On Christman's account, this person is positively unfree if her desire to conform was somehow oppressively imposed upon her through indoctrination, manipulation or deceit. She is positively free, on the other hand, if she arrived at her desire to conform while aware of other reasonable options and she weighed and assessed these other options rationally. There is nothing necessarily freedom-enhancing or freedom-restricting about her having the desires she has, since freedom regards not the content of these desires but their mode of formation. On this view, forcing her to do certain things rather than others can never make her more free, and Berlin's paradox of positive freedom would seem to have been avoided. It remains to be seen, however, just what a state can do, in practice, to promote positive freedom in Christman's sense without encroaching on any individual's sphere of negative freedom. An education system that cultivates personal autonomy may prove an important exception, but even here it might be objected that the right to negative liberty includes the right to decide how one's children should be educated.

Another group of theorists has claimed that Berlin's dichotomy leaves out a third alternative, according to which freedom is not merely the enjoyment of a sphere of non-interference – as it is on the negative concept – but the enjoyment of certain conditions in which such non-interference is guaranteed.[5] These conditions may include the presence of a democratic constitution and a series of safeguards against a government wielding power arbitrarily and against the interests of the governed. As Berlin admits, on the negative view of freedom, I am free even if I live in a dictatorship just as long as the dictator happens, on a whim, not to interfer with me. There is no necessary connection between negative freedom and any particular form of government. On the alternative view sketched here – often called the 'republican' concept of freedom – I am free only if I live in a society with the kinds of political institutions that guarantee non-interference resiliently and over time. The republican concept allows that the state may encroach upon the negative freedom of individuals, enforcing and promoting certain civic virtues as a means of strengthening democratic institutions. On the other hand, the concept cannot lead to the oppressive consequences feared by Berlin, because it has a commitment to liberal-democratic institutions already built into it. It remains to be seen, however, whether the republican concept of freedom is ultimately distinguishable from the negative concept, or whether republican writers on freedom have not simply provided good arguments to the effect that negative freedom is best promoted, *on balance and over time*, through certain kinds of political institutions rather than others.[6]

2 Freedom as a triadic relation

The two sides in Berlin's debate disagree over which of two different concepts best deserves the name of 'freedom'. Does this fact not denote the presence of some more basic *agreement* between the two sides? How, after all, could they see their disagreement as one about the definition of 'freedom' if they did not think of themselves as in some sense *talking about the same thing*? In an influential article,[7] the American legal philosopher Gerald MacCallum put forward the following answer: there is in fact only one basic 'concept of freedom', on which both sides in the debate *converge*. What the so-called 'negative' and 'positive' theorists disagree about is how this single concept of freedom should be interpreted. Indeed, in MacCallum's view, there are a great many different possible interpretations of 'freedom', and it is only Berlin's artificial dichotomy that has led us to think in terms of there being two.

MacCallum defines the basic concept of freedom – the concept on which everyone agrees – as follows: a subject, or 'agent', is free from certain constraints, or 'preventing conditions', to do or be certain things. Freedom is therefore a 'triadic relation' – that is, a relation between *three things*: an agent, certain preventing conditions, and certain doings or becomings of the agent. Any statement about freedom or unfreedom can be translated into a statement of the above form by specifying *what* is free or unfree, *from* what it is free or unfree, and what it is free or unfree *to do or be*. Any claim about the presence or absence of freedom in a given situation will therefore make certain assumptions about what counts as an agent, what counts as a constraint or limitation on freedom, and what counts as a purpose that the agent can be described as either free or unfree to carry out. Let us return to the example of the driver on her way to the tobacconists. In describing this person as either free or unfree, we shall be making assumptions about each of MacCallum's three variables. If we say that the driver is *free*, what we shall probably mean is that an agent, consisting in the driver's empirical self, is free from external (physical or legal) obstacles to do whatever she might want to do. If, on the other hand, we say that the driver is *unfree*, what we shall probably mean is that an agent, consisting in a 'higher' or 'rational' self, is made unfree by internal, psychological constraints to carry out some rational, authentic or virtuous plan. Notice that in both claims there is a negative element and a positive element: each claim about freedom assumes *both* that freedom is the *absence* of something (i.e., preventing conditions) *and* that it is the *presence* of something (the doings or beings that are unprevented). The dichotomy between 'freedom from' and 'freedom to' is therefore a false one, and it is misleading say that those who see the driver as free employ a 'negative' concept and those who see her as unfree employ a 'positive' one. What these two camps differ over is the way in which one should interpret each of the three variables in the triadic freedom-relation. More precisely, we can see that what they differ over is the *extension* to be assigned to each of the variables.

Thus, those whom Berlin places in the 'negative' camp typically conceive of the agent as having the same extension as that which it is generally given in ordinary discourse: they tend to think of the agent as an individual human being and as including all of the empirical beliefs and desires of that individual. Those in the so-called 'positive' camp, on the other hand, often depart from the ordinary notion, in one sense imagining the agent as more extensive (or 'larger') than in the ordinary notion, and in another sense imagining it as less extensive (or 'smaller'): they think of the agent as having a greater extension than in ordinary discourse in cases where they identify the agent's 'true' desires and aims with those of some collectivity of which she is a member; and they think of the agent as having a lesser extension than in ordinary discourse in cases where they identify the 'true' agent with only a subset of her empirical beliefs and desires – i.e., with those that are rational, authentic or virtuous. Second, those in Berlin's 'positive' camp tend to take a wider view of what counts as a constraint on freedom than those in his 'negative' camp: the set of relevant obstacles is more extensive for the former than for the latter, since negative theorists tend to count only external obstacles as constraints on freedom, whereas positive theorists also allow that one may be constrained by internal factors, such as irrational desires, fears or ignorance. Third, those in Berlin's 'positive' camp tend to take a narrower view of what counts as a purpose one can be free to fulfil. The set of relevant purposes is *less* extensive for them than for the negative theorists, for we have seen that they tend to restrict the relevant set of actions or states to those that are rational, authentic or virtuous, whereas those in the 'negative' camp tend to extend this variable so as to cover any action or state the agent might desire.

On MacCallum's analysis, then, there is no simple dichotomy between 'positive' and 'negative' freedom; rather, we should recognise that there is a whole range of possible interpretations or 'conceptions' of the single concept of freedom.[8] Indeed, says MacCallum, a number of classic authors cannot be placed unequivocally in one or the other of Berlin's two camps. Locke, for example, is normally thought of as a staunch defender of the negative concept of freedom, and he indeed states explicitly that '[to be at] liberty is to be free from restraint and violence from others'.[9] But he also says that 'liberty' is not to be confused with 'licence', and that 'that ill deserves the name of confinement which hedges us in only from bogs and precipices.[10] While Locke gives a more 'negative' account of 'constraints on freedom', he seems to endorse a more 'positive' account of the third freedom-variable, restricting this to actions that are not immoral and to those that are in the agent's own interests. This suggests that it is not only conceptually misleading, but also historically mistaken, to divide theorists into two camps – a 'negative' one and a 'positive' one.

3 Constraints on freedom

To illustrate the range of interpretations of the concept of freedom made available by MacCallum's analysis, let us now take a closer look at his second variable – that of 'constraints on freedom'.

We have seen that for those theorists Berlin places in the 'negative' camp, only obstacles external to the agent tend to count as constraints on her freedom. We should now note that these theorists usually distinguish between different kinds of external obstacle, restricting the range of obstacles that count as constraints on freedom to those that are brought about by other agents. For theorists who conceive of 'constraints on freedom' in this way, I am only unfree to the extent that *other people* prevent me from doing certain things. If I am incapacitated by natural causes – by a genetic handicap, say, or by a virus or by certain climatic conditions – I may be rendered *unable* to do certain things, but I am not, for that reason, rendered *unfree* to do them. Thus, if you lock me in my house, I shall be both unable and unfree to leave. But if I am unable to leave because I suffer from a debilitating illness or because a snow drift has blocked my exit, I am nevertheless free, or am at least not unfree,[11] to leave. The reason such theorists give, for restricting the set of relevant preventing conditions in this way, is that they see freedom as a *social* relation – a relation between persons.[12] Freedom as a non-social relation is more the concern of engineers and medics than of political and social theorists.

In attempting to distinguish between 'natural' and 'social' obstacles we shall inevitably come across grey areas. An important example is that of obstacles created by impersonal economic forces. Do economic constraints like recession, poverty and unemployment merely incapacitate people, or do they also render them unfree? One way of supplying a clear answer to this question is by taking an even more restrictive view of what counts as a constraint on freedom, and saying that only a subset of those obstacles brought about by other persons counts as a restriction of freedom: those brought about *intentionally*. In this case, impersonal economic forces, being brought about unintentionally, do not restrict people's *freedom*, even though they undoubtedly make many people *unable* to do many things. This last view has been taken by a number of market-orientated libertarians, including, most famously, Friedrich von Hayek, according to whom freedom is the absence of coercion, where to be coerced is to be subject to the arbitrary will of another.[13] Critics of libertarianism, on the other hand, typically endorse a wider conception of 'constraints on freedom' that includes not only intentionally imposed obstacles but also unintended obstacles for which someone may nevertheless be held responsible,[14] or indeed obstacles of any kind whatsoever.[15] Thus, socialists have tended to claim that the poor in a capitalist society are unfree, or are 'less free', than the rich, in contrast to libertarians, who have tended to claim that the poor in a capitalist society are no less free than the rich. Socialists typically assume a broader notion than libertarians of what counts as a 'constraint on freedom', though without necessarily embracing anything like Berlin's 'positive' notion of freedom.[16]

If we take an even closer look at the different notions of 'constraint on freedom' employed, we can see that there are in fact two different dimensions along which one's notion of a constraint might be broader or narrower. A first dimension is that of the *source* of a constraint on freedom – in other words, what it is that *brings about* a constraint on freedom. We have seen, for example, that some include as 'constraints on freedom' only obstacles brought about by human action, whereas others also include obstacles with a natural origin. A second dimension is that of the *type* of constraint involved. We have seen, for example, that some include only coercion or physical barriers as relevant types of preventing factors, whereas others want to include as 'constraints on freedom' more subtle forms of influence, including not only external constraints but also internal ones such as those brought about through ideological manipulation. To see the difference between the two dimensions of source and type, consider the case of 'internal' constraints. An internal constraint is a 'type' of constraint, defined by reference to its location 'inside' the agent. It is a category that covers various psychological phenomena such as ignorance, irrational desires, illusions and phobias. Such a constraint can be caused in various ways: for example, it might have a genetic origin, or it might be brought about intentionally by others, as in the case of brainwashing or manipulation. In the first case we have an internal constraint brought about by natural causes; in the second, an internal constraint intentionally imposed by another. Given the independence of these two dimensions, one might want to combine a narrow view of what counts as a source of a constraint with a broad view of what types of obstacle count as constraints, or vice versa. The two dimensions are represented as in Table 1.1, where a narrower notion of constraints is one that restricts freedom-limiting factors to those located towards the top left-hand corner of the table, whereas a broader notion is one that includes more factors located towards the right or towards the bottom of the table.

To illustrate the independence of these two dimensions, consider the case of the unorthodox libertarian Hillel Steiner.[17] On the one hand, Steiner has a much *broader* view than Hayek of the possible *sources* of constraints on free-

Table 1.1

Sources of constraint	Types of constraint		
	The physical impossibility of action	The difficulty or costliness of action	Internal factors (e.g., phobias, compulsions, irrationality, ignorance)
Intentional human actions			
Actions for which humans are morally responsible			
Human causes			
Natural causes			

dom, extending that notion as far as the third row in Table 1.1: he does not limit the set of such sources to intentional human actions, but extends it to cover all kinds of human cause, whether or not any humans intend such causes and whether or not they can be held morally accountable for them, believing that any restriction of such non-natural sources can only be an arbitrary stipulation, usually arising from some more or less conscious ideological bias. On the other hand, Steiner has an even *narrower* view than Hayek of what counts as a *type* of constraint, restricting this to the left-most column in Table 1.1: for Steiner, an agent only counts as unfree to do something if it is *physically impossible* for her to do that thing. Any extension of the constraint variable to include other types of obstacle, such as those brought about by coercive threats, would, in his view, necessarily involve a reference to the agent's desires, and we have seen that for those liberals in the 'negative' camp there is no necessary relation between an agent's freedom and her desires. Consider the coercive threat 'your money or your life!'. This does not make it impossible for you to refuse to hand over your money, only much less desirable for you to do so. If you decide not to hand over the money, you will of course be killed. That *will* count as a restriction of your freedom, because it will render physically impossible a great number of actions on your part. But it is not the issuing of the threat that creates this unfreedom, and you are not unfree until the threat is carried out. For this reason, Steiner excludes threats – and with them all other kinds of imposed costs – from the set of obstacles that count as freedom-restricting.

Steiner's account of the relation between freedom and coercive threats might be thought to have counter-intuitive implications, even from the liberal point of view. Many laws that are normally thought to restrict 'negative' freedom do not physically prevent people from doing what is prohibited, but deter them from doing so by threatening punishment. Are we to say, then, that these laws do not restrict the freedom of those who obey them? A solution to this problem may consist in saying that although a law against doing some action, x, does not remove the freedom to do x, it nevertheless renders physically impossible certain *combinations* of actions that include doing x and doing what would be precluded by the punishment. There is a restriction of the person's *overall* freedom – i.e., a reduction in the overall number of act-combinations available to her – even though she does not lose the freedom to do any specific thing taken in isolation.[18]

Conclusion

We began with a simple distinction between two concepts of freedom, and have progressed from this to the recognition that freedom might be defined in any number of ways, depending on how one interprets the three variables of agent, constraints, and purposes. Might Berlin's concepts of 'negative' and 'positive' freedom nevertheless still be of some use? Perhaps, in the sense that the concept of self-mastery or self-direction implies a presence of control that may not be adequately captured by MacCallum's explication of freedom as a triadic relation. If one thinks of freedom as involving self-direction, one has in mind an 'excercise concept' of freedom, as opposed to an 'opportunity concept'.[19] On an excercise concept, freedom consists not merely in the *possibility* of doing certain things (i.e., in the lack of constraints on doing them), but in actually *doing* certain things in certain ways – for example, in realising one's true self or in acting on the basis of rational and well-informed decisions. MacCallum's triadic relation does not really capture this 'excercise' element in the concept of freedom as self-direction. The importance of this concept continues to be dicussed in contemporary political philosophy, though normally under the rubric of 'personal autonomy'. Mac-Callum's framework has nevertheless tended to dominate in contemporary discussions about the nature of 'constraints on freedom', about the relation between an agent's options and her desires or values, and about whether and how an agent's specific freedoms can be aggregated so as to make sense of the liberal political prescription that people enjoy 'maximal' freedom or 'equal' freedom.

Notes

1 I. Berlin, 'Two Concepts of Liberty', in I. Berlin, *Four Essays on Liberty* (Oxford, Oxford University Press, 1969), pp. 121–2.
2 Berlin, 'Two Concepts of Liberty', pp. 132–3.
3 Berlin, 'Two Concepts of Liberty', pp. 135–6.
4 J. Christman, 'Liberalism and Individual Positive Freedom', *Ethics*, 101 (1991), pp. 343–59. On the positive concept of freedom see also C. Taylor, 'What's Wrong with Negative Liberty', in A. Ryan (ed.), *The Idea of Freedom* (London, Oxford University Press), reprinted in D. Miller (ed.), *Liberty* (Oxford, Oxford University Press, 1991); J. Christman (ed.), *The Inner Citadel: Essays on Individual Autonomy* (Oxford, Oxford University Press, 1989).

5 Q. Skinner, *Liberty before Liberalism* (Cambridge, Cambridge University Press, 1998); P. Pettit, *Republicanism: A Theory of Freedom and Government* (Oxford, Oxford University Press, 1997).

6 This criticism is made in I. Carter, *A Measure of Freedom* (Oxford, Oxford University Press, 1999), ch. 8; and in M.H. Kramer, *The Quality of Freedom* (Oxford, Oxford University Press, 2003), ch. 2.

7 G.C. MacCallum, jr, 'Negative and Positive Freedom', *Philosophical Review*, 76 (1967), pp. 312–34, reprinted in D. Miller (ed.), *Liberty* (Oxford, Oxford University Press, 1991). The real origin of the idea of freedom as a triadic relation is F. Oppenheim, *Dimensions of Freedom: An Analysis* (New York, St. Martin's Press, 1961). However, Oppenheim did not use this relation to identify a 'core concept' on which all agree.

8 On the distinction between 'concepts' and 'conceptions' see J. Rawls, *A Theory of Justice* (Oxford, Oxford University Press, 1971), p. 5. On its application to freedom, see T. Gray, *Freedom* (London, Macmillan, 1991), ch. 1.

9 J. Locke, *Two Treatises of Government* (first published 1698), ed. P. Laslett (Cambridge, Cambridge University Press, 1967), *Second Treatise*, s. 57.

10 Locke, *Second Treatise*, ss. 6 and 57 respectively.

11 Some theorists think that if am not free to do x then I am unfree to do x. Others deny this, saying that one might be neither free nor unfree to do x. See, respectively, H. Steiner, 'Freedom and Bivalence', in I. Carter and M. Ricciardi (eds), *Freedom, Power and Political Morality. Essays for Felix Oppenheim* (London, Palgrave, 2001); Kramer, *The Quality of Freedom*, ch. 2.

12 On this point see in particular F. Oppenheim, *Political Concepts: A Reconstruction* (Oxford, Blackwell, 1981), ch. 4.

13 F.A. von Hayek, *The Constitution of Liberty* (London, Routledge and Kegan Paul, 1960), ch. 1.

14 D. Miller, 'Constraints on Freedom', *Ethics*, 94 (1983), pp. 66–86; K. Kristjánsson, *Social Freedom: The Responsibility View* (Cambridge, Cambridge University Press, 1996).

15 This appears at times to be the view of A. Sen. See, for example, his *Inequality Reexamined* (Oxford, Oxford University Press, 1992).

16 G.A. Cohen has claimed that the poor are less free than the rich even on a libertarian conception of freedom. See his 'Capitalism, Freedom and the Proletariat', in D. Miller (ed.), *Liberty* (Oxford, Oxford University Press, 1991), and Cohen's *Self-Ownership, Freedom and Equality* (Cambridge, Cambridge University Press, 1995), ch. 2.

17 H. Steiner, *An Essay on Rights* (Oxford, Blackwell, 1994).

18 On the distinction between overall freedom and specific freedoms, and on whether and how overall freedom might be measured, see Carter, *A Measure of Freedom*. The measurability of overall freedom has recently been much discussed by economists and social choice theorists. See, for example, R. Sugden, 'The Metric of Opportunity', *Economics and Philosophy*, 14 (1998), pp. 307–37.

19 The distinction between an opportunity concept and an excercise concept of freedom comes from Taylor, 'What's Wrong with Negative Liberty', p. 177.

2

Rights: their basis and limits

Catriona McKinnon

Introduction

Rights appear in every plausible theory of justice and dominate contemporary political rhetoric. Critics, as a matter of course, raise two objections to this proliferation of rights talk. First, they argue that no clear justification exists for rights. As a result, every political issue can be turned into a demand for rights. This inflation of rights claims has devalued the currency of rights to the point of worthlessness. Second, they object that rights encourage individualistic and anti-social behaviour. People stand on their rights to avoid obligations to others. Such attitudes are justified when society makes unreasonable demands on people. But they can also appear at odds with, or indifferent to, such necessary social virtues as compassion, civility and charity. This chapter addresses these two standard criticisms. Section 1 explores two approaches to rights – the interest-based (IB) approach, and the obligation-based or Kantian view. Both are shown to offer coherent justifications that can avoid turning all political concerns into a matter of rights. Section 2 then compares the ways they relate to other social duties. It shall be argued that only the Kantian approach fully escapes the second criticism by positively requiring that we supplement rights with other social virtues. As such, it is to be preferred over the IB approach.

1 Interest-based and Kantian approaches

Contemporary political theorising starts by accepting that a diversity of religious, moral and philosophical outlooks is a permanent fact about societies which is not to be regretted. Given this pluralism, rights-theorists cannot invoke theological premises in their justification of rights, and without these premises the claim that rights are natural is mysterious and metaphysically suspect. The most promising approaches to rights which eschew such thinking are the IB and Kantian approaches.

The IB approach has it that a person has a right to x when his or her interest in x is sufficiently important for other people to be held under a duty to provide him or her with x, or not prevent his or her pursuit of x. Rights are systematised by principles of justice specifying the nature of these rights, and the priority they have in relation to one another. Two prominent advocates of the IB approach are Jeremy Waldron and Joseph Raz. Waldron claims that, 'An individual has a right to G when the importance of his interest in G, considered on its own, is sufficient to justify holding others to be under a duty to promote G'.[1] For Waldron, rights protect a person's important interests not only in liberal freedoms, but also in socio-economic goods.[2] For Raz, rights protect persons' interests in securing well-being.[3]

By contrast, on the Kantian view duties of justice constitute the basis of rights, and these duties, rather than interests, are morally basic. Duties of justice are systematised by principles of justice which specify the content of rights, and their relationship to other social values. The Kantian view is that a person A has a right to x if and only if all other people have an obligation to provide A with x, or not to prevent A from having x, and this obligation is derived from the categorical imperative (CI). Kant argued that all moral obligations are derived from one supreme moral principle, the CI, which asks each of us to 'Act as if the maxim of your action were to become through your will a universal law of nature' (a maxim is a subjective principle of action, or the purpose of an action). Kant classified obligations deriving from the CI as perfect or imperfect. If a maxim cannot be *conceived* of as a universal law of nature without contradiction then we have a perfect duty not to act according to that maxim; Kant's famous examples of perfect duties are the avoidance of suicide and false promising.[4] If a maxim cannot be *willed* as a universal law of nature without contradiction then we have an imperfect duty not to act according to that maxim; Kant's examples are developing one's talents and charitable giving.[5] The difference between perfect and imperfect duties is that the latter contain a greater degree of latitude with respect to their performance than the former. For example, if I have a perfect duty not to make false promises then I must never make a false promise at any time, but if I have an imperfect duty of beneficence to give to charity this need not mean that I must put money in every charity tin I come across, although the pattern of my giving behaviour, and possibly my character, must be of a certain type. Kant thought that only certain perfect duties – duties of justice – should serve as the input to a theory of justice. Kant's fundamental principle of justice ensures a right to equal freedom for every citizen.[6]

The desiderata of a theory of rights according to which these two approaches will be considered are as follows:

1 An account of the basis of rights should allow for an interesting debate with respect to the content of rights. Having established a basis for rights, it should then be a further question whether people only have rights to non-interference by others, or whether in addition they have substantial, 'welfare' rights to things like food, shelter, medical care and education.[7] Unless questions about the basis and content of rights are kept separate, no debate

SPRING CREEK CAMPUS

about the content of rights is possible among those who agree on the basis of rights, let alone among those who disagree about the basis of rights.

2 A theory of rights should generate concomitant duties in a way that is sensitive to the context of the rights-holder. That is, a theory of rights should allow that what is demanded of people in order that Alison's right to X in circumstances C is met might differ from what is demanded of people in order that Bob's right to X in C is met. The duties which correlate with rights should not be taken to demand uniform courses of action across time and space.

3 A theory of rights should allow for a distinction between universal rights and special rights. Universal rights are had by every person with the characteristics providing a basis for rights; special rights are had by a person in virtue of something that distinguishes him or her from other persons. The most common example of a universal right is the right to non-interference: in various ways it is argued that all persons share something according to which they have this right. The most common example of a special right is a right created by contract: for example, spouses have particular rights against one another in virtue of the contract they make with one another in marriage. The distinction between universal and special rights is fundamental to law and jurisprudence, and should be accommodated and explained by a theory of rights.

4 A theory of rights should make possible the construction of rights-respecting institutions from scratch. That is, a theory of rights should guide us to political action even in the absence of institutions that encode these rights in law. Unless this is the case, rights are impotent as tools for political change.

Let me compare the IB account and the Kantian account in terms of how they satisfy these desiderata.

1 *Basis/content distinction.* The IB approach can, but need not, support a conception of substantial 'welfare' rights beyond more traditional rights to things like liberal freedoms, equality before the law, private property, and a vote. The concept of an interest is flexible enough for it to be an open question whether rights extend beyond non-interference. Interest-based theorists such as Jeremy Waldron support a view of rights as extending to welfare rights, but not all IB theorists insist on this point.[8]

Prima facie, the elasticity of the concept of an interest makes the IB account more attractive than the Kantian account with respect to the basis/content distinction. It might be thought that Kant's classification of duties of giving to others as imperfect – and thus not matters of justice – unacceptably narrows the scope of rights so as to include only libertarian rights to freedom and non-interference. However, there are interpretations of Kant's theory of rights which address this worry. For example, Onora O'Neill argues that the commitment of all practical reasoners to principles which could also serve as principles of practical reason for other agents yields a substantive account of justice whereby persons have both rights to non-interference and welfare rights.[9] On her interpretation, principles of justice must protect individuals against systematic or gratuitous injury, either through direct attacks upon them, or through damage to the social and natural fabric of the world. Thus, principles of justice protect individuals from more than the interference by others with their freedom; individuals are also injured when they are prevented from obtaining food, deprived of shelter or denied an education. When this form of injury is systematically inflicted – as might be the case in famine situations, societies in which the homeless form a class, or in societies marked by mass illiteracy – political institutions distributing rights to food, shelter, and education are demanded by justice.

2 *Context sensitivity.* The IB approach is context sensitive: the demands placed on person A by person B's important interest in x will not be the same as the demands placed on person C if A and C stand in different relations to B. In Jeremy Waldron's terms, each interest-based right will generate waves of duties for people differentially placed with respect to rights-holders. For example, the right not to be tortured imposes a duty on all people not to torture one another, but it imposes extra 'duties of enforcement' on government officials to investigate and prosecute torturers, 'duties of rescue' on those in a position to save torture victims and, perhaps, 'duties of communication' on journalists and educators.[10] Once we have identified an important interest, and established a person's right to have that interest satisfied, we can trace the waves of duty to their various holders and set up political and legal institutions and procedures to ensure that these duties are performed.[11]

Similarly, the Kantian approach makes the duties associated with rights sensitive to the context in which both rights and duties appear. Discharging a duty of justice which is politically manifested in the right of hungry people to food may, in some contexts, demand simply that hungry people are not interfered with in their planting and harvesting of crops. But in other contexts, when planting and harvesting is not possible, it might require the active provision of food for hungry people and, perhaps, action to make planting and harvesting possible in the future. Duties the performance of which are sensitive to context in the sense of external circumstances will also be sensitive to the ways in which people are differentially situated with respect to rights-holders. The actions which qualify as the performance of a duty to provide hungry people with food will be different for a genetically modified (GM) foods executive than for a citizen of a state which has eradicated hunger among its people. The GM foods executive will have duties to be honest about the extent to which use of GM seeds may make a population dependent on GM companies in the future; the citizen of an affluent state will have duties to lobby his or her government to apply pressure to GM foods companies to make such matters clear to their customers; both have a duty to pay taxes which contribute towards foreign aid programs.

3 *Universal and special rights.* It is clear how an IB approach can give an account of universal rights: once an interest shared by all people has been identified as being of sufficient importance to provide the basis for a right, we can claim that all people have a duty to help/not hinder one another in the pursuit of this interest. For example, the important interest every person has in not being assaulted straightforwardly means that each person has a duty not to assault another person, in which case all people have the right not to be assaulted.

It might seem that the IB account cannot so easily accommodate special rights, because it is hard to see how an interest can be sufficiently important to ground a right unless it is an interest that all people share, in which case the interest grounds a universal right. The way in which an IB approach might accommodate special rights can be seen in Joseph Raz's account of the rights created by promise-making. Raz claims that every person has an interest 'to be able to forge special bonds with other people'.[12] This shared interest (a) grounds the universal right to make promises from which the right to make a particular promise is derived, and (b) grounds the universal right to have promises made to us kept. Given that the second of these universal rights can only be exercised when a person has had a promise made to him or her, we can derive from it special rights to have this particular promise kept, even if what it is that is promised is not itself in our interests. Interest-based approaches can account for special rights by deriving them from higher level universal rights, and linking the exercise of the universal right to a particular set of circumstances which are not common to all people.

Kantian accounts have an in-built distinction between universal and special rights. Special rights, like those which correlate with promise-related and contract-based duties are duties of justice because principles of false promising and intentional contract breaking cannot be adopted by all practical reasoners. When a person has created a special relationship between himself or herself and another person through the making of a contract, then the other has special rights against him or her that he or she perform his or her side of the contract. In addition to special rights correlating with duties created by particular relationships, the CI procedure yields universal rights to reciprocal non-interference with the freedom of others. When a person adopts a principle of interfering with certain freedoms of others while denying that others ought to interfere with his or her own enjoyment of the same freedoms, he or she makes himself or herself an exception to the principle of reciprocal non-interference, which shows that his or her principle is not adoptable by all practical reasoners.[13]

4 *Building rights-respecting institutions.* Onora O'Neill argues that the Kantian approach is superior to the IB approach with respect to this desiderata

because the Kantian approach makes it easy to identify the counterpart-obligation holders for universal rights to liberty, or special rights attaching to particular relationships. If everyone has a right to liberty, then everyone has an obligation not to interfere with the liberty of others. In the same way, those with an obligation to respect special rights can be identified by considering the relationship characterised by the special right; for example, those who have a duty to respect a person's special rights arising out of a contract can be determined by discovering who the parties to the contract were.

O'Neill claims that although universal and special rights require institutional structures for their enforcement – courts, a penal system, a police force – they can nevertheless be pressed in the absence of these structures, which are not necessary for the identification of counterpart-obligation holders. But she claims that the same is not true of universal welfare rights to goods and services. Unless and until counterpart-obligations are distributed by institutions, it makes no sense to talk of welfare rights at all. It is important to note that O'Neill is not making the relatively uncontroversial point that institutional structures make the identification of counterpart-obligation holders for welfare rights more easy. Rather, her point is the stronger one that without the institutional identification of such obligation holders, welfare rights do not exist.[14] Thus, on O'Neill's account, and in the absence of institutional structures designed to ensure the satisfaction of welfare rights, it will not do to say that a given person has 'a right to relief against the whole world',[15] or to answer the question 'Who has the obligation to supply food to all those who need it?', with, 'All of us'.[16] When the language of universal welfare rights is used in the absence of structures which create counterpart-obligation holders – as is the case with United Nations (UN) Declaration of Human Rights – the expectations of putative rights-holders will be inflamed and disappointed: 'The perspective of rights provides a perilous way of formulating ethical requirements since it leaves many possible obligations dangling in the air.'[17] O'Neill claims that the priority given to obligations in Kantian approaches avoids this problem. The obligations with which her Kantian approach starts include obligations not to injure others by depriving them of important goods and services. Even if people with these obligations do not know to whom exactly these obligations are owed, they can nevertheless 'make the construction of institutions that allocate tasks and identify claimants the first step towards meeting their obligations'.[18]

O'Neill's argument does not succeed as a criticism of the IB approach. This is because the identification of interests as important enough to warrant holding others to be under a duty to promote the interest does not require institutional structures. Jeremy Waldron claims that conceiving of rights as generated by interests gives us enough grounds to start to think about how to distribute concomitant duties to promote or support that interest through political and legal institutions and processes. That is, the interest-based account of rights allows us to detect the presence of rights in the absence of legal or other structures which specify who has a duty to ensure that the right is met.[19]

This means that, 'I can say . . . that a child in Somalia has a right to be fed, meaning not that some determinate individual or agency has a duty to feed him, but simply that I recognize his interest in being fed as an appropriate ground for the assignment and allocation of duties'.[20]

Recognising that another person has an important interest in food, shelter or education does not require institutions of law or international political conventions. The fact that we recognise that a person A has such an interest in x is sufficient for us to attribute to A certain rights to x, which means that we can begin to build institutions to distribute the counterpart-obligations to provide A with x, which we acknowledge to exist when we attribute a right to x to A. On the IB account, when we accept the rights-claims people make we also accept an obligation to put in place structures which ensure that that right is met by distributing its counterpart-obligations. But this seems on a par with the Kantian approach which moves from obligations through institutions to political rights.

The IB approach and the Kantian approach are evenly matched according to desiderata 1–4. In the remainder of this chapter I want to focus on the extent to which commitment to each theory of rights gives us grounds for choosing between different and competing conceptions of the good society, and for arguing that people ought to work to create this society. I shall argue that with respect to this question, the Kantian approach is superior to the IB approach.

2 Beyond justice?

Let me start by considering the Kantian approach to the good society question. O'Neill and other Kantians point out that there are many 'social virtues' – for example, charity, civility, solidarity, compassion – which are not a part of justice, and to which people do not have rights, yet which we have an obligation to develop and which have non-justice related value.[21] The Kantian approach can make sense of duties to work towards these valuable aspects of society with its tripartite division of morally good actions.

1 *Perfect duties of justice* are required and are the basis upon which rights are attributed to people.
2 *Imperfect social duties* do not have correlate rights but are nevertheless required: for example, we have a duty to act charitably, but not everyone has the right to charity from us.

3 Finally, there are *supererogatory acts* which it is good to perform, but which we do not have a duty to perform (for example, acts of heroism or great self-sacrifice).

By creating conceptual space between perfect duties and supererogatory actions the Kantian approach allows that we have some social obligations to which no rights correlate. The Kantian approach thus has the resources to explain why we ought to work towards a rights-respecting compassionate, civil, fraternal society rather than a rights-respecting heartless, aggressive, self-seeking society: we have imperfect, non-justice related, duties of compassion, civility and fraternity.

O'Neill argues that, in general, pure rights-based approaches lack the resources to address the good society question because they only address the obligations people have to perform those actions necessary for the respect of rights; the performance of all other actions, or the cultivation of certain dispositions, however laudable, is on these accounts non-obligatory.[22] There are two ways of taking this criticism. First, it might be claimed that rights-based approaches lack an account of why a just and good society is better than a just and bad society. Second, it might be claimed that rights-based approaches cannot explain why people in a just society ought to work to make that society good. With respect to the IB approach, this criticism bites only in its second sense. The problem with the IB approach is not that it is necessarily indifferent between visions of the good and bad just society. The good just society can be endorsed over the bad just society in virtue of its supererogatory value, assuming that IB theorists can give an account of supererogatory value. Rather, the criticism is that on the IB approach people only have obligations to perform actions necessary for the protection of certain important interests, but there are social virtues not related to the protection of such interests which characterise the good society and which, we would want to say, people ought to cultivate. The problem is that supporting judgements about the goodness of societies by reference to their supererogatory values leaves it unclear why people ought to work to create this value in their societies. If the value of a good society is supererogatory, then presumably action fit to create this value is also supererogatory. But supererogatory action is non-obligatory, in which case we cannot say of people who do not work to create the good society that they ought to do so. The Kantian approach avoids this problem because its account of the value of a good just society is given in terms of the performance of actions which are obligatory, albeit imperfectly so.

Let me assess the force of this criticism against Waldron's version of the IB approach. With respect to the social virtue of charity, Waldron claims that 'the welfare state functions . . . as a clearing house for . . . imperfect obligations [of charity]'.[23] Although Waldron makes room for the concept of imperfect duty, this does not yield an answer to the good society question which resembles the

Kantian answer. This is because, according to Waldron, some important interests generate imperfect duties *which correlate with rights*: an interest in, say, food
is sufficiently important to hold others to have imperfect duty of charity
towards the hungry and, therefore, for the hungry to have rights to have this
interest satisfied.[24]

Waldron's incorporation of imperfect duty into the typology of value of the
IB approach might straightforwardly be taken to address the question of the
good society question by being extended to cover social other social virtues like
fraternity, civility and kindness. However, this extension dissolves the distinction between the just and the good society, and so should be avoided. If it is
claimed that persons' important interests in being treated fraternally, civilly
and kindly generate imperfect duties to be fraternal, civil and kind, then what
Waldron claims about the imperfect duty of charity applies *mutatis mutandis* to
these other imperfect duties: people have rights that others treat them fraternally, civilly and kindly. But if people can claim the performance of imperfect
duty as a matter of right, then rights take up all the space of value-judgements
about the nature of a society. The claim implies that all societies are either just
or unjust, and that there is no possibility of a society which is just but not good
(as in, for example, Kant's 'nation of devils').[25]

It is clear that Waldron does not hold this view. For him, people have rights
to perform actions that are 'stupid, cowardly, tasteless, inconsiderate, destructive, wasteful, deceitful, and just plain wrong, as well as actions that are wise,
courageous, cultured, compassionate, creative, honest, and good'.[26] Rights do
not take up all the space of value-judgements. But in that case, duties to create a good society must be understood in terms of something other than the
promotion of/non-interference with persons' important interests, otherwise
such duties would generate rights, and judgements about the goodness of a
society would be equivalent to judgements about its justice. The IB theorist has
two options for fleshing out this understanding of imperfect duties to create a
good society.

First, it might be claimed that imperfect duties characterising the good society are not generated by interests at all, in which case the question of their correlation with rights does not arise on the IB approach. The problem with this
approach is as follows. Any account of justice fit for conditions of pluralism will
explain why people who reject justice nevertheless have an obligation to be just:
it will have authority for such people. If the account of imperfect duties to create the good society is derived from the same source as the account of justice
which it accompanies, then it will have the same authority as this account. This
is the case with the Kantian approach: obligations of justice and imperfect
social obligations are both derived from the CI, and have their authority in
virtue of this derivation. In contrast, if the authority of imperfect social obligations is divorced from the authority of duties of justice – as is the case in the
approach under consideration – then we are owed an independent account of
the grounds on which imperfect social obligations have their authority. Perhaps

such an argument can be made. However, given the difficulty philosophers have faced in coming up with accounts of justice which are plausibly authoritative in conditions of pluralism, we are entitled to some scepticism here.

A different approach for the IB theorist is to claim that imperfect social obligations are derived from interests, but that these interests are not important enough to hold others to be under duties to help/not hinder their pursuit, and so do not correlate with rights. Here, duties of justice and imperfect social obligations share their authority in virtue of being derived from the same source: interests. If an argument can be made to show that, regardless of how they differ on moral, religious, or philosophical questions, all people ought to help/not hinder one another in the pursuit of their interests, then both duties of justice and imperfect social obligations have authority in pluralism. What distinguishes them is the importance of the interests from which they are generated, which affects whether performance of the duties can be enforced in law through the allocation of rights to people.

The key claim of this approach is that social obligations are generated by interests which are of less importance than interests generating rights. The problem is how to make an argument for this claim. Consider some standard imperfect social obligations: toleration, kindness, charity. Is it the case that persons' interests in being treated with toleration, kindness or charity are less important than their being assured freedom of speech, association or market participation through the allocation of rights? Of course, freedom of speech, association and market participation are very important goods necessary for human flourishing. But the idea that these goods can be ranked above toleration, kindness and charity is unattractive, for two reasons. First, ranking strategies require the employment of some overarching standard or master-good according to which all goods can be compared, such as utility. But in conditions of pluralism appeal to such a master-good in political justification is problematical. Second, even if the problems associated with appeal to a master-good can be avoided, the way in which particular goods are ranked will be a matter of disagreement among people committed to a just and good society in conditions of pluralism. These problems make it best to avoid such ranking strategies.

The Kantian approach retains the distinction between duties of justice and imperfect social obligations without ranking the goods to which these duties relate. On the Kantian view, these obligations are distinguished according to how maxims expressing purposes contrary to the realisation of these goods fare when subjected to the CI procedure: a person has a duty of justice not to act on any maxim which cannot be conceived without contradiction, and an imperfect duty not to act on any maxim which cannot be willed without contradiction. But this does not mean that the goods protected by duties of justice are more important than the goods, protected by imperfect duties. All it means is that the way in which these goods are realised differs.

Conclusion

Given that the IB approach and the Kantian approach perform equally well according to the four desiderata outlined earlier, should the fact that the Kantian approach performs better with respect to the good society desideratum lead us to prefer this approach? A hard-nosed response would be to deny that the good society desideratum is appropriate as a touchstone for comparing the approaches. A hard-nosed person might respond that a theory of *justice* is just that; it is no criticism of such a theory that it does not provide answers to questions about the good society, and so there is no reason to prefer a Kantian approach to rights over an IB approach. The problem with this response is that it makes theories of justice rather mean and cold-blooded creatures. Conceptions of justice which have in the past inspired people have offered substantive accounts of the content of justice, but have also suggested ways of thinking about what a good society might be like once justice is achieved. They have offered visions of transformed social relations, improved characters, more fulfilling work and more exciting art and culture, and they have done this without collapsing the distinction between the just society and the good society. Without pretending to argues this point, I think it would be a great loss if such visions disappeared from the landscape of justice-talk. For anyone who agrees, the Kantian approach to the basis of rights is preferable to the IB approach.

Notes

I would like to thank Richard Bellamy, Andy Mason, Matt Matravers, Sue Mendus and Onora O'Neill for their written comments. Thanks are also due to the Chinese Academy of Social Sciences for an invitation to present this paper at their International Conference on Political Philosophy in Beijing in April 2001, and to the British Academy for a grant to attend the Conference.

1 J. Waldron, 'Can Communal Goods be Human Rights?', *Liberal Rights: Collected Papers 1981–1991* (Cambridge, Cambridge University Press, 1993), p. 359.
2 See J. Waldron, 'Liberal Rights: Two Sides of the Coin', *Liberal Rights: Collected Papers 1981–1991* (Cambridge, Cambridge University Press, 1993), p. 11.
3 See J. Raz, 'On the Nature of Rights', *Mind*, 93 (1984), pp. 207–8.
4 I. Kant, *Groundwork of the Metaphysic of Morals (The Moral Law)*, tr. H.J. Paton (London, Unwin Hyman, 1948), p. 85, 422/54–5.
5 Kant, *Groundwork of the Metaphysic of Morals*, pp. 85–6, 423/55–7.
6 'Every action which by itself or by its maxim enables the freedom of each individual's will to co-exist with the freedom of everyone else in accordance with a universal law is *right*'. I. Kant, 'The Metaphysics of Morals', in *Kant's Political Writings*, ed. H. Reiss (Cambridge, Cambridge University Press, 1970), p. 133.
7 An example of the former conception is R. Nozick's conception of rights as 'side-constraints'; *Anarchy, State, and Utopia* (Oxford, Basil Blackwell, 1974), pp. 26–53. An example of the latter is the UN Declaration on Human Rights.
8 See Waldron, 'Liberal Rights: Two Sides of the Coin', p. 11.
9 O'Neill's version of Kant's CI procedure '*demands* that practical reasoning follow

principles that are thought of as *adoptable* or *followable* by all for whom it is to count as reasoning'. O. O'Neill, *Towards Justice and Virtue: A Constructive Account of Practical Reasoning* (Cambridge, Cambridge University Press, 1996), p. 57.

10 See J. Waldron, 'Rights in Conflict', *Liberal Rights: Collected Papers 1981–1991* (Cambridge, Cambridge University Press, 1993), pp. 203–25, 212–13.

11 Context sensitivity is also a feature of Raz's IB approach. See Raz, 'On the Nature of Rights', pp. 199–200.

12 Raz, 'On the Nature of Rights', pp. 201–4.

13 Of course, there are questions here about how principles of interference are described by those who adopt them. For example, take a person who defends a principle of reciprocal non-interference with sexual freedom, but wants to ban homosexual sex in virtue of his or her principle of reciprocal interference with ungodly practices. Does this person make an exception of himself or herself in virtue of holding the second principle? Much depends on the account we give of the correct exercise of judgement in the formation of maxims, and in the relationships that persons take to hold between their maxims. For a good discussion, see B. Herman, *The Practice of Moral Judgement* (Cambridge, MA, Harvard University Press, 1993).

14 See O'Neill, *Towards Justice and Virtue*, p. 132. See also O. O'Neill, 'Women's Rights: Whose Obligations?', *Bounds of Justice* (Cambridge, Cambridge University Press, 2000), pp. 97–114.

15 Waldron, 'Liberal Rights: Two Sides of the Coin', p. 16.

16 C. Jones, *Global Justice* (Oxford, Oxford University Press, 1999), p. 94.

17 O'Neill, *Towards Justice and Virtue*, p. 134.

18 O'Neill, *Towards Justice and Virtue*, p. 135.

19 See J. Waldron, 'Introduction', in J. Waldron (ed.), *Theories of Rights* (Oxford, Oxford University Press, 1984), pp. 1–20, 10–11.

20 Waldron, 'Introduction', p. 10.

21 O'Neill, *Towards Justice and Virtue*, p. 143.

22 As O'Neill puts it, 'Nothing shows why indifference or self-centredness should not be life-projects for liberals, providing, of course, that others' rights are respected'; *Towards Justice and Virtue*, p. 144.

23 Waldron, 'Liberal Rights: Two Sides of the Coin', p. 17.

24 It is not clear why Waldron feels the need to appeal to an imperfect duty of charity in order to generate rights to food. Why not argue that the interest people have in food is sufficiently important to hold all others to be under a perfect duty to promote this interest, and that the state acts as a clearing house for the discharge of this perfect duty? Indeed, on O'Neill's Kantian approach, key socio-economic rights like the right to food are generated by duties of *justice* because the provision of food is necessary if gratuitous and systematic injury to the hungry is to be avoided.

25 Kant states that, 'As hard as it may sound, the problem of setting up a state can be solved even by a nation of devils (so long as they possess understanding)'. 'Perpetual Peace', in *Kant's Political Writings*, ed. Hans Reiss (Cambridge, Cambridge University Press, 1970), pp. 93–130, 112.

26 J. Waldron, 'A Right to Do Wrong', *Liberal Rights: Collected Papers 1981–1991* (Cambridge, Cambridge University Press, 1993), pp. 63–87, 85.

3

Social justice: the place of equal opportunity[1]

Andrew Mason

Introduction

Most liberals believe that equality of opportunity requires sought after occupations to be allocated to the best-qualified candidates, and institutions to be designed to ensure that everyone has fair access to qualifications. They suppose that equality of opportunity so conceived has sufficient weight that it cannot legitimately be sacrificed to promote overall welfare. Although liberals pay lip-service to this ideal of equality of opportunity and seek to enshrine it in legislation and public policy, it is hard for them to carve out the right role for it within their theories. On the one hand, they want to show that a commitment to equality of opportunity is compatible with respecting personal liberty, especially in the face of those who insist that enforcing it threatens individual rights, including the right of parents to raise their children as they see fit so long as they do not harm them. On the other hand, they want to show that equality of opportunity is an *independent* principle of justice, not simply an efficient way in most circumstances of allocating jobs and educational places that is consistent with what justice requires.

John Rawls's account of fair equality of opportunity in *A Theory of Justice* provides a good illustration of the difficulties involved here. It is a sophisticated attempt to defend the idea that equality of opportunity is an independent principle of justice, the enforcement of which takes second place to respect for individual rights. I propose to explore Rawls's account in some depth in order to bring out both its strengths and its weaknesses. I shall begin by briefly presenting, for the uninitiated, the main elements of his theory. Those already familiar with it should go straight to section 2. There I defend Rawls's principle of fair equality of opportunity against two objections, including the challenge that implementing it in full would require abolishing the family. In section 3, however, I take the offensive, maintaining that it is unable to provide a secure justification for the idea that equality of opportunity is an independent principle of justice. In the final section of the chapter I try to diagnose why contemporary theories of justice, influenced as they are by Rawls's work, have difficulty in accommodating this idea.

1 The basic elements of Rawls's theory

Let me introduce the basic elements of Rawls's theory as they were presented in *A Theory of Justice*, for it is here that Rawls gives the most sustained treatment of equality of opportunity.[2] He begins from the idea of society as a co-operative venture for mutual advantage. He claims that, so understood, a society requires principles of justice because it needs some way of determining how the various benefits and burdens of social co-operation should be distributed. In the face of widespread disagreement over which principles of justice should govern our major institutions, Rawls draws upon the social contract tradition in order to develop a method which he hopes can secure agreement on a particular conception of justice.

Rawls's guiding idea is that the principles which should be adopted are those which rational persons, concerned to further their own interests, would agree upon in an initial position of equality. In order to model this initial position, he employs a device he calls the veil of ignorance, behind which people are presumed to be ignorant of various facts about themselves, such as their class or status, race and wealth, and their conception of the good, i.e., their views about what is of value and importance in life. This veil of ignorance is intended to secure a kind of impartiality or neutrality: if people are in ignorance of these facts, they cannot seek to benefit themselves by arguing for principles that are congenial to, say, their class, race or conception of the good.

Although they are behind a veil of ignorance, the parties are to make certain assumptions. First, each is to assume that they have some conception of the good, even though they do not know its content. Second, each is assumed to be rational, and because they are rational they are assumed to want the means to realise their conception of the good, whatever its content. Since things like liberty and opportunity, wealth and income, and self-respect are likely to make it easier for a person to realise his own conception of the good, it is assumed that persons in the original position will want as much of them as possible. Rawls calls these the primary goods.

Rawls argues that persons in this initial or original position of equality, behind the veil of ignorance, will choose two main principles. According to the first principle, each person is to have an equal right to the most extensive basic liberty compatible with a similar liberty for all. Basic liberties include political liberty, freedom of speech and assembly, liberty of conscience and freedom of thought, freedom of the person along with the right to hold personal property and freedom from arbitrary arrest and seizure. The second principle comes in two main parts. According to it, social and economic inequalities are to be arranged so that they are open to all, which Rawls develops into the principle of fair equality of opportunity, and so that they are to the greatest benefit of the least advantaged, which he calls the difference principle. He argues that when entertaining the possibility of conflict between these principles, the parties in the original position will rank the first principle above the second, and the principle of fair equality of opportunity above the difference principle.

Although the original position is the centrepiece of Rawls's theory as it was originally presented, he also gave a further argument for both the principle of fair equality of opportunity and the difference principle that is sometimes referred to as 'the intuitive argument'. This starts from the premise that distributive shares should not be influenced (at least in any systematic way) by factors arbitrary from the moral point of view, and concludes that the difference principle, constrained by the principle of fair equality of opportunity, is what is needed to achieve this outcome.

This is the briefest possible sketch of Rawls's theory of justice. The next two sections will explore his account of fair equality of opportunity in more depth and consider some difficulties it faces.

2 Fair equality of opportunity defended against two objections

Rawls begins his discussion of equality of opportunity by endorsing the idea that careers should be open to talents in the sense that everyone should have 'the same legal rights of access to all advantaged social positions'.[3] Minimally this must imply that there should be no legislation requiring discrimination and no legislation requiring different treatment of different groups. Rawls does not say anything more to clarify the notion of 'careers open to talents' and as a result it is amenable to different interpretations. But I assume that careers would not be genuinely open to talents if selectors chose to exclude certain groups from consideration, for otherwise that would make the notion consistent with an informal system of apartheid. Even if selectors are not legally obliged to do so, they must by and large practice non-discrimination if there is to be equality of opportunity. The idea that careers should be open to talents is perhaps not equivalent to the idea that the best-qualified candidates should be selected for advantaged social positions but it is a close relative of it.[4]

Rawls argues that the principle of careers open to talents is insufficient for fair equality of opportunity by appealing to the major premise in what I referred to earlier as the intuitive argument. In his view this principle is insufficient because it permits 'distributive shares to be improperly influenced by . . . factors . . . arbitrary from a moral point of view'.[5] He argues that a principle of fair equality of opportunity can correct for this by requiring that positions be open to all not only formally, but also in such a way that each has a fair chance of attaining them.[6] He treats this as equivalent to the idea that 'those who are at the same level of talent and ability, and have the same willingness to use them, should have the same prospects of success regardless of their initial place in the social system, that is, irrespective of the income class into which they are born'.[7]

In order to assess Rawls's account of fair equality of opportunity, let me begin by considering two influential objections. The first objection maintains that what Rawls seeks to achieve from fair equality of opportunity – that is, equal life chances for those similarly endowed and motivated – could be secured simply by randomly reassigning babies to different parents at birth.[8] Indeed, as Brian Barry points out, if equality of life chances at birth were a sufficient condition for fair equality of opportunity, then a caste system which randomly reassigned babies shortly afterwards would qualify.[9] This is surely enough to refute the idea that equality of life chances is a sufficient condition of fair equality of opportunity.

To suppose that Rawls is advocating that idea, however, is to ignore one of the two elements of fair equality of opportunity. He is clear that careers must be open to talents and that would immediately rule out a caste system. This does not wholly defeat the objection, however. There are many possible social systems in which the best-qualified candidates are appointed to advantaged social positions but where economic class, say, still strongly influences one's chances of success. According to Rawls's conception of fair equality of opportunity, it would appear that in these systems equal opportunity could be achieved simply by randomly reassigning babies at birth, and this is surely an unpalatable conclusion.

But I think Rawls can also respond to this point. His guiding idea is that people should not be systematically disadvantaged by morally arbitrary factors; that result could not be achieved simply by randomly reassigning babies at birth. If one's life chances were a function of the family to which one happened to be reassigned, they would be deeply affected by morally arbitrary factors. Fair equality of opportunity obtains only when similarly endowed and motivated individuals have an equal chance of success *because* morally arbitrary disadvantage has been avoided or received compensation.

The second objection I shall consider maintains that fair equality of opportunity can be realised only by abolishing the family and that this is an unacceptable price to pay.[10] Similarly motivated and similarly endowed individuals will have unequal prospects of success so long as they experience different family environments. For example, some parents may value educational achievement, and encourage their children in this direction, while others do not. Rawls recognises this difficulty but his response to it is weak.[11] He moves from the claim that 'the principle of fair equality of opportunity can be only imperfectly carried out, at least as long as the institution of the family exists' to the claim that '[i]t is impossible in practice to secure equal chances of achievement . . . for those similarly endowed and motivated',[12] and from there to the conclusion that all we can do is mitigate the morally arbitrary effects of 'the natural lottery' by implementing the difference principle. But if fair equality of opportunity requires abolishing the family, Rawls needs to give us some reason for not doing so. It is not enough for him to reply that fair equality of opportunity can never be fully realised in practice, for the objection is that it could be more fully realised by abolishing the family.[13]

Does Rawls have the resources to construct a better response to the argument that fair equality of opportunity, as he understands it, would require abolishing the family? He could point out that in his theory the basic liberties take priority over fair equality of opportunity and then argue that these basic liberties entail that people be allowed to form families. This would require him to add to his list of basic liberties, for they do not as they stand appear to justify a right to raise one's children. He could then concede that, strictly speaking, fair equality of opportunity would require abolishing the family but maintain that this is ruled out by the priority given to the (conditional) liberty to raise one's children.

This line of argument is not without difficulty, however. In his later work Rawls employs a conception of citizens as reasonable and rational, which requires them to possess two moral powers, namely, the capacity for a sense of justice, and the capacity to form and revise a conception of the good. The basic liberties are then conceived as 'essential social conditions for the adequate development and full exercise of the two powers of moral personality over a complete life'.[14] Yet, as Véronique Munoz-Dardé points out, it is not obvious that a right to raise one's children, of the kind which would be required to justify something akin to the traditional family, is an essential condition for the adequate development and full exercise of the two moral powers that Rawls identifies.[15] The best case which can be made here is that even if the family is not strictly an essential condition for the adequate development of these two powers, in practice over time other institutions, such as compulsory state provision of childcare of various kinds, would be likely to fare worse in developing these powers than some suitably constrained form of the family, given the dangers of vesting the state with that amount of power in the upbringing of children.[16]

3 The independent role of equality of opportunity in Rawls's theory of justice

In the process of answering objections to Rawls's account of fair equality of opportunity, I have argued that it needs to be understood in the context of his overall theory, and I have emphasised that it consists of two elements – the idea of careers being open to talents and the idea of equal chances of success for those with the same level of endowments and motivation to use them. Both of these points introduce difficulties of their own, however.

For a start, there are potential conflicts between the principle that careers should be open to talents and the idea that similarly endowed and motivated individuals should have equal chances of success.[17] Suppose that employers tend to devalue women. As a result of discrimination women's life chances may be less good than the life chances of men with similar talents and motivation. Given the complexity of selection decisions, sexism may operate in subtle and even unintentional ways, and as a result it may be hard to detect or prevent.[18] For example, it may be hard to know when gender stereotypes, such as the idea that women are less committed to their careers, are active in selection decisions. So in some circumstances the most effective means of promoting equal chances of success for similarly endowed and motivated men and women in the long term may be to enforce a quota system by means of the law. As a result, promoting equal life chances would entail abandoning the idea that equality of opportunity requires careers to be open to talents, at least when that is understood (in the way that Rawls does) to require the same legal rights of access to advantaged social positions.

If careers being open to talents and equal life chances for the similarly endowed and motivated are *each* necessary conditions of fair equality of opportunity, it follows that in some circumstances equality of opportunity may be impossible to achieve in practice. Given Rawls's aspiration to provide us with a theory in which conflicts within and between principles are resolved by priority rules, he at least owes us an account of which of these two necessary conditions should take priority when they come into conflict. The point cuts deeper than this, however. When we reflect upon the issue of which of these two elements should take priority in Rawls's theory, it starts to become unclear why he should give the idea of careers being open to talents any independent role at all.[19] What drives his account of fair equality of opportunity is the idea that the distribution of advantaged social positions should not be affected by morally arbitrary factors, and that idea is cashed out in terms of equal chances of success for those with the same level of talents and abilities and willingness to use them. But if equal chances of success for people thus situated is what really matters for fair equality of opportunity, then the idea of careers being open to talents appears to play at best a derivative role. In most circumstances holding careers open to talents may be the best means of ensuring that those with the same level of capabilities and willingness to use them have the same chances of success. But when that goal could be better realised by giving individuals different rights of access to advantaged social positions, then fair equality of opportunity would appear to require us to abandon our commitment to it.

Just as within Rawls's account of fair equality of opportunity the independence of the principle of careers open to talents is problematic, so too in his theory as a whole it is hard to justify the independent role of the account of fair equality of opportunity. Let me explain.

Recall that the difference principle says that inequalities are permissible if they are to the greatest benefit of the worst off group. The effect of giving the principle of fair equality of opportunity priority over the difference principle is to insist that equal opportunity, so understood, cannot legitimately be sacrificed for greater material benefits for the worst off group.[20] But why should we suppose that the principle of fair equality of opportunity ought to be ranked above the difference principle? Rawls does not explicitly present his reasoning but hints that the same line of argument which justifies giving the principle of liberty priority over the difference principle will also justify giving fair equality of opportunity priority over the difference principle.[21]

The argument he gives for the priority of liberty appeals to the device of the original position: when a person knows in the original position that society has reached a point where everyone's basic needs can be met, it is rational for him to give priority to liberty.[22] It is rational for someone in the original position to assume that once his basic needs have been met, the basic liberties will be more beneficial for pursuing his own conception of the good, whatever that turns out to be, than, say, greater wealth or income. Even if this is a good argument for the priority of liberty,[23] it is hard to see how the analogous argument in relation to opportunity is supposed to work. The original question in effect resurfaces in a new form: why is it supposed to be rationally required from the standpoint of the original position to refuse to trade off access to advantaged social positions in favour of greater wealth and income *if* the basic liberties are in place? Rawls is implicitly treating access to advantaged social positions as more important than other primary goods such as wealth and income, the distribution of which is to be governed by the difference principle. But why should we suppose that access to these positions is of such importance to justify ranking the principle of fair equality of opportunity above the difference principle in a way that disallows trade-offs?

Rawls develops his argument for the priority of liberty in a way that might seem to promise an explanation of why he thinks the principle of fair equality of opportunity should take priority over the difference principle. He argues that in a just society the basis of self-respect for all is secured by the public affirmation of equal citizenship, which requires enshrining the basic liberties in public institutions.[24] Might it be argued in a parallel way that the basis for self-respect for all can be secured only if the principle of fair equality of opportunity is also enshrined in society's basic institutions? It is hard to see how this position could be sustained. Rawls faces a dilemma. Either the social basis of self-respect can be secured simply by institutionalising the principle of equal liberty or it cannot. If it can, then the social basis of self-respect does not require institutionalising the principle of fair equality of opportunity. On the other hand, if the social basis of self-respect cannot be secured simply by institutionalising the principle of equal liberty, the question immediately arises of why we should think it will be best secured by enshrining the principle of fair equality of opportunity and giving it lexical priority over the difference principle. For once we have moved away from the assumption that the principle of equal liberty suffices, it is hard to see how we could justifiably rule out the possibility that the basis for the self-respect of the worst off group might sometimes be better secured by giving priority to the difference principle rather than the principle of fair equality of opportunity in matters of institutional design.[25] Why is access to advantaged social positions, understood in Rawls's terms, supposed to be so much more important for securing self-respect than making the worst off as well off as it is possible for them to be in terms of their share of wealth and income?

Rawls does present a further reason for thinking that access to advantaged social positions is of particular importance. He points out that they may be valuable not just as a means of securing material goods but also as a means of securing rewarding jobs and hence self-realisation:

> if some places were not open on a fair basis to all, those kept out would be right in feeling unjustly treated even though they benefited from the greater efforts of those who were allowed to hold them. They would be justified in their complaint not only

because they were excluded from certain external rewards of office such as wealth and privilege, but because they were debarred from experiencing the realization of self which comes from a skilful and devoted exercise of social duties. They would be deprived of one of the main forms of human good.[26]

The idea that access to advantaged social positions is important for this reason is plausible but it is of limited help in justifying the priority of fair equality of opportunity over the difference principle. At best it warrants the conclusion that access to these positions should be given special weight. But that could be done in two ways, neither of which requires there to be an independent principle of equality of opportunity, ranked above the difference principle. First, freedom of occupation could be treated as a basic liberty, to be protected by the first principle of justice, the principle of liberty. Second, access to advantaged social positions could be added to the list of primary goods that the difference principle is supposed to cover.[27]

Consider the first of these suggestions. Rawls himself seems to treat freedom of occupation as a basic liberty in his more recent book *Political Liberalism*.[28] But he accepts that freedom of occupation can be secured without the principle of fair equality of opportunity being satisfied.[29] Freedom of occupation, when it is conceived as a negative liberty in Rawls's preferred way, in effect as the absence of state-directed labour, does not seem to require equal chances of success for the similarly endowed and motivated. (Nor does it seem to require careers to be open to talents, as Rawls conceives it, for there are ways of regulating access to jobs which fall short of a policy of state-directed labour but which nevertheless mean that people do not have the same legal rights of access to them. An enforced quota system of the kind described earlier would be an example.)

Consider the second proposal, that access to advantaged social positions might be included in the list of primary goods that the difference principle covers. As Rawls deploys the difference principle, it is primarily concerned with the distribution of wealth and income but there is no reason in principle why it could not be extended to cover opportunity, if opportunity (conceived as having a genuine chance of occupying advantaged social positions that enable self-realisation) were regarded as a separate primary good. In practice, of course, this would raise various difficult questions concerning the relative weight to accord to wealth, income and opportunity. But these difficulties are not resolved by insisting that opportunity is much more significant than wealth and income, which in effect is the assumption behind ranking the principle of fair equality of opportunity above the difference principle.

The difference principle, reformulated in this way, would still have implications for the distribution of advantaged social positions. If institutions are to ensure that members of the worst off group are as well of as possible (in terms of their shares of opportunity, wealth and income), these positions must be distributed in such a way that the talents and powers of individuals are utilised to good effect. Although this does not in any straightforward way imply the principle of fair equality of opportunity, it lends some limited support to it. For designing institutions in such a way that those with the same level of talents and abilities, and willingness to use them, have the same chances of success is, in most circumstances, likely to benefit the worst off group considerably in terms of the opportunities and income and wealth they enjoy.

The suspicion that Rawls's theory lacks the resources to explain why the principle of fair equality of opportunity should be given an independent role is reinforced by considering an incoherence from which that principle appears to suffer. Rawls's move from careers open to talents to fair equality of opportunity is driven by the idea that the distribution of advantaged social positions should not be affected by factors that are arbitrary from the moral point of view. Yet fair equality of opportunity permits access to positions to be affected by natural endowments (i.e., those talents and abilities, or parts of them, which are due to one's genetic inheritance) which Rawls also accepts are arbitrary from the moral point of view. Therefore, if he is to be fully consistent it seems he must concede that fair equality of opportunity, properly thought out, requires all persons to have an equal chance of occupying advantaged social positions, irrespective of natural endowment.[30] If Rawls's theory were implicitly committed to the idea that advantaged social positions should be distributed in such a way that people's natural abilities have no bearing on who gets them, it would be hard to imagine a notion that is more fundamentally at odds with our intuitive understanding of equality of opportunity.

Rawls is aware of this problem. In response he seems to argue that the best solution in practice is to allow unequal natural endowments to affect access to advantaged social positions in the way the principle of fair equality of opportunity does, while adjusting the extrinsic rewards accruing to these positions so that inequalities in the distribution of these rewards are limited in accordance with the difference principle.[31] In the context of Rawls's theory, however, this response appears flawed. It would seem that extrinsic rewards are being offered to those with less natural talent as a way of compensating them for their relative lack of access to the goods intrinsic to advantaged social positions.[32] Yet surely it is precisely this kind of compensation that is supposed to be disallowed by ranking the principle of fair equality of opportunity above the difference principle. If compensation of this kind is permitted, again there seems to be no reason to give the principle of fair equality of opportunity any independent role. The opportunity to occupy advantaged social positions could be treated as a primary good, which, along with wealth and income, is to be distributed by the difference principle.

4 Can appointing the best-qualified candidates be defended as an independent principle of justice?

From within Rawls's framework it is hard to see why equality of opportunity should be given any independent role. This is a problematic conclusion which must raise doubts about the framework itself. For once we embrace this conclusion, the justification of fair equality of opportunity, and indeed of a practice of appointing the best-qualified candidates to advantaged social positions, becomes contingent upon its role in making the worst off group as well off as possible (judged in terms of some appropriate metric which gives weight to income, wealth and opportunity). The point here is not that this way of justifying equality of opportunity will allow exceptions to the idea that the best-qualified candidates should be appointed to advantaged social positions. Exceptions to this principle may be justified, as indeed defenders of affirmative action programmes argue. The problem is rather that this principle seems to have independent weight in our thinking about justice, even if does not express a strict requirement of justice. Rawls's principle of fair equality of opportunity held open the possibility of being faithful to this deeply rooted intuition but it cannot be if we must regard it as derived using empirical premises from some suitably expanded version of the difference principle.

The difficulty Rawls faces in giving the principle that selectors should appoint the best-qualified candidates an independent role as a principle of justice arises, at least in part, because the two most obvious ways of trying to justify this principle are unavailable to Rawls, revealing the gulf between his theory and ordinary intuitions.

It is sometimes held that the best-qualified candidate for an advantaged social position *deserves* to be appointed to it, at least if there is fair access to qualifications.[33] But this kind of defence is ruled out by Rawls, for he believes that it is impracticable to reward desert. In his view people's achievements are due not only to their own efforts but also their fortunate circumstances, such as the supportive family into which they were born or their inheritance of various talents. Rawls appears to assume that people deserve to be rewarded only for their efforts; therefore tracking desert would require us to disentangle these different components which he maintains is impossible in practice.[34] Even if Rawls were wrong and we could disentangle the different components, the idea that the best-qualified candidates deserve to be appointed would be hard to justify if we employ his conception of desert, for a person's qualifications are due in part to factors beyond her control such as her natural endowments and social circumstances.

Other writers, such as George Sher, have tried to defend the idea that appointing the best-qualified candidates is an independent principle of justice by appealing to the notion of respect for persons as agents. He writes:

> When we hire by merit, we abstract from all facts about the applicants except their ability to perform well at the relevant tasks. By thus concentrating on their ability to perform, we treat them as agents whose purposeful acts are capable of making a difference in the world . . . [S]electing by merit is a way of taking seriously the potential agency of both the successful and the unsuccessful applicants.[35]

When someone is hired because they are the nephew of the director, or because they are members of disadvantaged groups, or when hiring them will bring about better overall consequences for society, the potential agency of the applicants – successful or not – is ignored and they are not accorded respect as rational agents: candidates are treated 'as mere bearers of needs or claims, as passive links in causal chains, or as interchangeable specimens of larger groups or classes'.[36] Sher regards this argument as grounded in the idea of desert but I think it is better conceived as appealing directly to the idea of respect for persons.

A defence of this kind (though in my view much stronger than one which appeals to the idea of desert) is unavailable to Rawls for it relies upon a contestable notion of respect for persons, which, even if it can be given more defence, will remain contentious. The idea that a theory of justice should appeal to premises which are widely shared and weak figured prominently in *A Theory of Justice*, and was reformulated in *Political Liberalism* in terms of the requirement that principles of justice should not be defended by appealing to comprehensive moral doctrines. Now Rawls supposes that the fundamental purpose of political philosophy in a democratic society is to devise a theory that could become the object of an overlapping consensus between those who subscribe to widely different comprehensive moral doctrines. Appealing abstractly to ideas of respect for persons in the way that Sher does in order to defend the appointment of the best-qualified candidates to advantaged social positions is poorly adapted to this role.

The discrepancy between, on the one hand, Rawls's account of equality of opportunity and the role he gives it within his theory of justice and, on the other hand, our intuitions about equality of opportunity does not show that we should reject the former. But I hope that I have clarified the choice facing liberal theorists. They must either reject key elements of Rawls's theory (such as the conception of desert he employs and his claim that it is impracticable to reward desert) or acknowledge that the idea of appointing the best-qualified candidates for advantaged social positions can be given no independent justification.

Notes

1 I would like to thank Richard Bellamy, John Horton and audiences at Manchester and Reading for their helpful comments.
2 For Rawls's discussion of equality of opportunity, see J. Rawls, *A Theory of Justice* (Oxford, Oxford University Press, 1971), pp. 72–5, 83–90.
3 Rawls, *A Theory of Justice*, p. 72. Advantaged social positions include positions which are in themselves rewarding as well as those which merely carry material benefits or prestige. (This becomes important later when I consider Rawls's argument for ranking the principle of fair equality of opportunity above the difference principle.) Some dispute is possible over exactly what is covered here but jobs of all varieties are clearly included.
4 For example, Rawls appears to think that to say positions are open to all means that they must be accessible to all: Rawls, *A Theory of Justice*, p. 61. But see T. Pogge, *Realizing Rawls* (Ithaca, NY, Cornell University Press, 1989), p. 165.

5 Rawls, *A Theory of Justice*, p. 72.
6 Rawls, *A Theory of Justice*, p. 73.
7 Rawls, *A Theory of Justice*, p. 73.
8 J. Fishkin, *Justice, Equal Opportunity, and the Family* (New Haven, CT, Yale University Press, 1983), p. 57.
9 B. Barry, 'Equal Opportunity and Moral Arbitrariness', in N. Bowie (ed.), *Equal Opportunity* (Boulder, CO, Westview Press, 1988), p. 32.
10 A. Flew, *The Politics of Procrustes* (London, Temple Smith, 1981), pp. 55–6.
11 Rawls, *A Theory of Justice*, pp. 511–12, 74.
12 Rawls, *A Theory of Justice*, p. 74.
13 See V. Munoz-Darde, 'Is the Family to be Abolished Then?', *Proceedings of the Aristotelian Society*, 72 (1998), pp. 37–55.
14 J. Rawls, *Political Liberalism* (New York, Columbia University Press, 1993), p. 293.
15 See Munoz-Darde, 'Is the Family to be Abolished Then?', p. 41.
16 Munoz-Darde, 'Is the Family to be Abolished Then?', pp. 48–9.
17 See also R. Arneson, 'Against Rawlsian Equality of Opportunity', *Philosophical Studies*, 93 (1999), p. 81.
18 See L.W. Sumner, 'Positive Sexism', *Social Philosophy and Policy*, 5 (1987), esp. pp. 213–14.
19 This issue is also explored in Arneson, 'Against Rawlsian Equality of Opportunity'.
20 Rawls, *A Theory of Justice*, pp. 302–3.
21 See Rawls, *A Theory of Justice*, p. 301.
22 Rawls, *A Theory of Justice*, pp. 542–3.
23 See H.L.A. Hart, 'Rawls on Liberty and its Priority', in N. Daniels (ed.), *Reading Rawls* (Oxford, Blackwell, 1975), esp. pp. 249–52, for some doubts about this argument. See Rawls, *Political Liberalism*, lecture VIII, esp. pp. 310–24, for Rawls's response.
24 See Rawls, *A Theory of Justice*, s. 82.
25 See Arneson, 'Against Rawlsian Equality of Opportunity', pp. 104–5.
26 Rawls, *A Theory of Justice*, p. 84.
27 See Arneson, 'Against Rawlsian Equality of Opportunity', pp. 98–9.
28 See Rawls, *Political Liberalism*, pp. 228, 230, 308. See also Rawls, *A Theory of Justice*, p. 275; B. Barry, *Theories of Justice: A Treatise on Social Justice, Vol. I* (Hemel Hempstead, Harvester Wheatsheaf, 1989), pp. 398–400.
29 Rawls, *Political Liberalism*, p. 228.
30 See Barr, 'Equal Opportunity and Moral Arbitrariness'.
31 See Rawls, *A Theory of Justice*, pp. 74–5.
32 Of course, offering a job to a person who lacks the natural talent or ability to secure the goods of self-development to which it allows access would be pointless. But under a Rawlsian regime of fair equality of opportunity there would be many who had the capacity to secure such goods but who failed to succeed in competitions for the positions from which they could be obtained simply because they had less natural talent than those who succeeded.
33 For a sophisticated recent defence of this idea, see D. Miller, *Principles of Social Justice* (Cambridge, MA, Harvard University Press, 1999), ch. 8.
34 See Rawls, *A Theory of Justice*, p. 312.
35 G. Sher, 'Qualifications, Fairness, and Desert', in N. Bowie (ed.), *Equal Opportunity* (Boulder, CO, Westview Press, 1988), pp. 119–20.

36 Sher, 'Qualifications, Fairness, and Desert', p. 123. Sher's approach here is an exten-
    sion of one which maintains that selection for advantaged social positions should be
    done on the basis of relevant reasons. See B. Williams, 'The Idea of Equality', in his
    Problems of the Self (Cambridge, Cambridge University Press, 1973).

4
Political obligation

Rex Martin

Introduction

'Political obligation' is a broad notion and covers many things. Some have said, for example, that the citizen has an obligation or duty to vote. Others have claimed that citizens may have a duty to serve their country and possibly even to fight in its defence. Most people who talk of political obligation, however, have one thing in particular in mind: the citizens' duty to obey the laws in their own country.

The issue I want to discuss in this chapter is whether people do in fact have good and justifiable reasons for complying with laws that go beyond mere fear of punishment, and, if so, whether they are *bound* or obligated by those reasons to comply.

1 One main argument for a duty to obey the law: consent

Socrates had to decide whether to disobey an *unjust* but legal decision; the remarkable thing is that he decided to obey, for what he thought were sound reasons, in circumstances that would cost him his life. Socrates believed people had a *moral* duty to obey the law. It is a very strict duty based on an agreement they have made.[1]

What is distinctive about the agreement argument Socrates assented to (in the *Crito*) is that it puts the issue in terms of justice or morality. In our own political tradition there is an argument somewhat like the Socratic one; it stresses not the morality of keeping agreements but, rather, the connection between a legitimately constituted government, on the one hand, and a citizen's duty to obey the valid laws issued by such a government, on the other. This obligation is a strict one; it attaches to all laws and can be overridden, if at all, only in exceptional cases.

In this theory, usually associated with Hobbes and Locke in particular, a contract (sometimes called 'consent to government') is said both to authorise a government to make laws and to bind subjects to strict obedience. Actually the theories of Hobbes and Locke are not quite so simple as this.

Locke argues that, at a certain point (that is, upon reaching the age of adult-hood and then by staying on, more or less voluntarily, in the face of an unexer-cised right of emigration), people become members or parts of a particular body politic. The main function of any such body is to create a constitution or form of government and, presumably, there is a consensus (what Locke calls a major-ity) among the citizens as to where – that is, in what institutions – the main powers of government (legislative, executive, etc.) have been lodged. Indeed, Locke says, if there were not this consensus the body politic would come apart, would simply disintegrate, and could only be held together by obvious and clearly improper force. Now, from these two facts (that one is a member of a body politic and that there is a consensually based constitutional government for it) it follows for Locke, as a matter of logic, that each citizen (each member of a political society so organised) is strictly bound to obey the laws duly issued by such a constitutional government. Or it follows from these two facts plus one other – if laws were not obeyed people would in effect have returned to the unwanted state of nature – that each member has the strict obligation in ques-tion. One has, in short, not consented (contracted, promised) in so many words to obey the laws; rather, one has consented to be a member of a body politic and from that fact, plus one or two others, it follows logically that the citizen has a strict duty to obey laws duly issued. One is thus obliged *as if* one had in fact expressly consented to obey.[2]

The doctrine of consent in Hobbes is, perhaps, simpler. Hobbes argues that all subjects of all governments consent in one and the same fundamental way. They simply 'stand aside' from their own exercise of natural rights (from the right to do anything they are physically able to do); thus each subject has indi-vidually consented (or, in effect, promised) permanently but conditionally to waive that exercise in deference to the exercise of that same right (the right to do anything) by the government. Hence, the subjects consent to be under the sovereign's will and are obliged to comply with it, whatever it is, in all or almost all cases.[3]

For the 'contract' theorists, just as for Socrates's idea of an agreement, the relationship of citizens to the government and its laws is construed on an anal-ogy with some non-political undertaking, like promising, agreeing, consenting or signing a contract, which is obligation-creating in character. It is the fact of agreement or the act of consent that *grounds* the obligation to obey the law in all these theories.

I can see two main problems with this overall approach. First, there is the problem of what counts as consent. Second, there is the problem of whether consent so conceived can really bind people to obey all, or almost all, valid laws simply because these laws were issued in the correct way by a legitimate or effective government.

What counts as consent? All of the theorists count mere residence, permanent residence, during adulthood. Hobbes adds the interesting twist that a resident could even bow one's head and go on living under a conqueror, on pain of death if such 'consent' were not given, and that would count fully as consent. Many people are reluctant to think that mere continued residence should count, especially under the condition Hobbes envisioned, as having exactly the force of an explicit and solemn promise.

Some have said that voting in a free election should so count. Well, so voting might commit you to accepting the outcome of the election, we might grant. But why should it commit you to accepting, being obliged to accept, all the laws issued by those elected? Some of those laws might be foolish or unconstitutional, or even wicked. Suppose you voted on the losing side. Your candidate did not win. You voted that way because you did not want a certain bad law passed. And now the candidate you voted *against* has, along with others, supported that very law. Or suppose it was a really wicked law, like the US law in the 1850s which required runaway slaves to be recaptured and returned to their owners, and you were a voter in the state of Massachusetts who did not like the idea of such a law and who had voted for a candidate who opposed it, a candidate who was then elected but whose vote against this law was then defeated in the next meeting of the national legislature. These examples suggest that it goes a bit far to say that simply by voting in a general election you are committed to accepting this law, and are obliged to obey it.

But what about an explicit and solemn promise, a full-bodied agreement to accept all valid laws and to be bound by them? Would that work? Not too well. Most citizens have never consented or contracted, in a way that can be regarded as really counting, to obey the laws of the country in which they reside. For example, not everyone (certainly not every citizen) has engaged in a meaningful act of consent in Britain or America or Canada; in fact, relatively few people there have done so. Therefore, if full-bodied actual consent is required, the contract theory cannot account for an obligation to obey the law in such countries.

One could always reply: well, if everyone had freely and explicitly promised to obey the laws in their own country (in a solemn oath of some sort), *that* would surely count. We could still ask, even if such a promise counted as consent, whether such explicit consent would or could *bind* those who had taken that oath, could *oblige* them, to obey all the valid laws of the land simply because they were the country's laws. Is the strict obligation to obey laws grounded merely in the bare existence of consent to do so or is it grounded in whatever good reasons (excluding fear of punishment, of course) one might have for so consenting in the first place?

Clearly, if we simply cited the reasons (but without an act of explicit consent by the people involved) then we no longer have actual consent as the ground of obligation, contrary to what the contract theory requires.[4] Suppose, though, we cited both the fact of an explicit and widespread agreement in a given country and good reasons for making such an agreement. One could still question whether the fact of explicit consent really added anything to these reasons.

Consider. If we regard our obligation to obey our country's laws as a moral obligation (as did Socrates in the *Crito*), then we probably also believe that most or very many of these laws have a good moral content (such as do the laws that prohibit murder, kidnap, rape or physical assault). But would not the prohibitions in such laws (given their good moral content) control our conduct, morally speaking, even if they were not set down in law? By the same token, they would also control our conduct, morally speaking, even if we had never explicitly and solemnly promised to obey the laws of the land.

The matter becomes more complicated when we consider laws that are morally indifferent. I would think a question of *moral* obligation could arise in such cases only where what the law required (for example, the payment of income taxes) could be shown to be necessary or substantially important to the government's continuing ability to encourage people's compliance with those laws that do have a morally good content.

When we come to wicked laws (laws with a bad moral content, like the Fugitive Slave Law mentioned earlier, or Nazi laws against the Jews) I think the matter changes considerably from what it was in the two earlier cases (the case of laws with good moral content and the case of laws with morally neutral content). I do not think it possible to ground the *moral* precept of obedience to law on a foundation of indifference with respect to whether the laws are, in most cases and in the long run, of a morally good or at least a morally acceptable content. The moral presumption here is surely against evil laws, and this presumption will tell against any morally based obligation to obey such laws. In the analysis we have given, a promise to obey evil laws could not be morally justified and any such promise, even the promise to obey *all* laws (just and unjust), would not have obliging weight.

2 Another main argument for a duty to obey the law: benefit

Dissatisfaction with consent theory has led political theorists to consider other possible grounds of an obligation to obey law. What follows is perhaps the most commonly cited alternative.

It is often alleged that the receipt of benefits obliges one, as based on a proper sense of gratitude, to show appropriate responsive conduct. Some have said (as it was said, for example, in Plato's *Crito*) that when the benefit comes from the government, the appropriate responsive conduct is to obey the laws.

Of course, some benefits are 'open'; they come to everyone and one can hardly help but receive them (like breathing clean air as the result of anti-pollution measures). Sometimes benefits come, even though one actively tries to avoid them. (Many of my neighbours actively opposed the city building sidewalks, along our street, but now they use those pavements like anyone else.) But some benefits are positively sought (and accepted) or are at least voluntarily received, knowingly and willingly. These it might be said are the ones for which one clearly owes a duty of gratitude, and appropriate responsive conduct is owed to the benefactor.

The question is, though, Where these benefits are positively sought or voluntarily received from government, does one owe obedience to law as one feature (perhaps the main feature) of one's appropriate responsive conduct? Does one, indeed, have an obligation to obey *all* the laws on such a basis?

Consider the following example. A black student (age nineteen) in South Africa during the period of apartheid requests and receives admission to a state-run high school and some monetary aid (to cover costs and fees) from the local education authority, support that is paid for out of tax revenues. Suppose it is believed that the student might now owe a debt of gratitude, to be paid back in some sort of appropriate responsive conduct. But what conduct is appropriate? Contributing to state-supported education in the future (through donation of one's time or contributing financially to a scholarship fund) might well be. But it can hardly be alleged that one now is obliged, morally obligated, to support the government and obey all its laws (including the laws that maintain apartheid). The same could be said of a white student in similar circumstances. That student might be thought to be obliged to contribute to state-supported education in the future, but there is no good reason to say that this student, who has probably received more benefits overall than the black student, is morally obligated, any more than is the black student, to support the government and obey *all* its laws.

Indeed, we could vary the picture somewhat, to include important benefits people receive (but without assuming their voluntary acceptance). For instance, both our students (black and white) might have benefited greatly from public health measures (clean water, sanitation, vaccination and other disease control programmes). Would it follow from this that either is morally obligated to support the government and obey *all* its laws?

The basic point I am making, that there is no obligation to obey *all* the laws of the land in such cases, would probably hold even if the evil apartheid laws were completely removed from the picture. The fundamental question here is whether the appropriate responsive conduct, said to be owed in these two cases of education and public health, can reasonably be thought to include supporting the government and obeying all its laws. More to the point, if you were to run through a wide number of cases, of various benefits actively sought or voluntarily received from government or of important benefits merely received, and reach the same conclusion in each case, then you do not think gratitude for benefits received does ground an obligation for recipients to obey *all* the laws of their country.

Some have pointed to a special version of benefit theory, called fair play, to make the case for a duty to obey law. Here is the picture they present. People are engaged in a joint activity, a practice or an enterprise, that is widely beneficial (like conserving water in time of drought or reducing electricity use in the face of a brownout [a partial blackout]). The benefits of this activity can only be obtained if most people join in, but doing so carries certain costs for each of them (for example, I cannot water my lawn, you cannot wash your car).

Now let us say that I (a university student) am engaged in such a practice (in a scheme of things) in which others are doing something to benefit me (like paying their taxes) and I have voluntarily accepted these benefits; now it comes my turn, after a few years have passed, to pay taxes (for I have now entered the workaday world). Fair play theory alleges that I am obligated, by my participation in this practice (in particular, through my voluntary receipt of benefits and the costs to others of these benefits being provided), to do my share, to return in kind the benefits I have received, by paying my taxes. And this means complying with the tax laws. (To keep matters simple, let us suppose that these laws are not unfair.)

Technically, the obligation I owe, under fair play, is to the other participants in the joint activity. It can become an obligation to obey the law only indirectly, in so far as the activity itself is essentially or significantly involved with one's being law abiding.

This said, I cannot quarrel with the analysis just given. The question, though, is whether you or I have an obligation to obey *all* the laws (including future laws, some of which might be bad laws or even evil ones).

The same thought experiment I suggested earlier would work here as well, to help answer this question. The issue we are raising here is whether the appropriate responsive conduct, said to be owed in this one case of receipt of benefits from tax revenues raised and spent, can reasonably be thought to go beyond conformity to the tax laws to include supporting the government and obeying all its laws. Surely, it does not. And if we took each practice up in turn, one after the other, we would reach the same conclusion in each case. Thus, a person who had benefited from other people's obedience to laws against theft should obey those same laws, were the circumstance to arise. You owe it to these others, in fair play, so to act. But there would be no generalised duty, a duty that went beyond conformity to anti-theft laws, to obey *all* the government's laws.

Indeed, if you ran through a wide number of cases, envisioning people's participation in a variety of practices or joint activities (where they voluntarily received benefits in each of them) and lumped them all together, you might conclude that the persons involved should do their share, to pay back in kind the benefits they have received. This may well involve a duty to obey several, even many, laws. But none of this would mandate the conclusion that fair play (in the case of benefits voluntarily received by participants in a wide variety of practices) would ground an obligation for each of them to obey *all* the laws of their country. Obedience to some laws may not benefit everyone (and obedience to some laws might not benefit anyone).

The conclusions reached in our survey of fair play are, of course, strengthened when we consider that some laws may be evil (like the Nazi laws against Jews or the apartheid laws in South Africa) and that such evil laws cannot benefit literally everyone. And if any are benefited in such cases (as some would be by wicked laws, as were slave-owners in a slave system, for instance) there is no *moral* obligation, no obligation of fair play, even for them (let alone for the persons victimised by such laws) to obey all the laws of the land.

3 A preliminary conclusion and some materials for a new start

We have now canvassed some of the main arguments for a generalised duty, a duty of everyone, to obey all laws. The arguments based on consent, on gratitude for benefits, and on fair play have been looked at in turn and each has failed.

Some have concluded from this that there simply is no obligation, no *moral* obligation, for everyone to obey all laws in their own country. In fact, there may not be a standing obligation, for some at least, to obey any of the laws.[5] Others, looking at this same sample, have concluded that none of the standard arguments will work but these theorists have left open that another, radically different, approach might work. And some have even suggested the main lines of such an approach.[6] I tend to side with this second view, suitably qualified.

The theorists we have been criticising all treat the obligation to obey the law as primarily a *moral* one and thus the grounds they emphasise are distinctively moral grounds. These theorists are interested in *general* grounds for obeying law – grounds operative in all or almost all societies, grounds that could cover all laws or, conceivably, all persons – and they disdain reasons which are local or distinctive only of a particular society (or specific kind of system). But their analysis, by its very nature, creates a deep problem: they cannot show that the duties so generated – by reference to these general, distinctively moral grounds (such grounds as agreement or express consent or gratitude for benefits received or fair play) – can ever be duties of all people in a given country to obey all the laws there. Or so I have argued. The quest for such generality has proven to be a hopeless and unrewarding one.

A second feature of the standard approach also needs bringing out. The favoured grounds cited in this approach all have in common that they invoke some *voluntary* act on an agent's part. Typically, the agents are here said voluntarily to have consented or, alternatively, voluntarily to have received benefits or, as yet another alternative, to have knowingly participated in a practice or joint activity from which they have voluntarily received benefits of the very sort they're now being asked to provide in turn. The main point relied on in all these cases is the same: having an obligation implies that one has *voluntarily* taken on that obligation through some sort of (morally approvable) transaction.

This pronounced emphasis on voluntariness may be out of place. One can have duties that are not based on voluntary acts at all. For example, children (say teenagers) could have duties to their parents which are not based on voluntary transactions on the young persons' part; among the benefits they have received are many that were not voluntarily sought or voluntarily taken (for example, the enormous number of such benefits they received when they were infants or very young children). More to the point, it may be the relationship they are in, with their parents, that counts entirely (or for the most part) for the duties they have.

Consider now a parallel case. The requirements on people's conduct that the law imposes are often there because of the status these individuals have (as innkeeper or employer or, quite typically, as member and fellow citizen) in a given political society. The normative directions for conduct laid down in the law often come with the territory and are imposed simply by the rule-making actions of government officials. These requirements are, thus, unlike standard voluntary obligations in a number of important respects. They do not necessarily involve undertakings or determinate transactions that serve to bring a citizen specifically under a given requirement; they are not, in many typical cases, owed to definite or named individuals (but, rather, to all citizens); they are not imposed *because* the individual has been the actual beneficiary of the very way of acting which that individual is now being normatively directed to engage in, and so on. (This last point is in deliberate contrast with fair play.) We need, in short, to be able to discuss the duty one might have, to conform to such laws, without assuming that the duty is there on the basis of some voluntary undertaking or determinate transaction that has served to bring the citizen specifically under that requirement.

Another dimension to this important matter of voluntariness needs mention as well. Most people are in fact citizens or lifelong members of only one country during their entire lifetimes. They are born in that one country and they will spend their whole lives there. Many others have joined them, for reasons of their own, and have in effect cast their lots there; this we must grant. But we must be able to make a case for a duty to obey laws for this vast majority (those who were born there), if we are going to have any serious case for the claim that citizens have or may have a duty to conform to laws. We need, in short, to be able to discuss the duty one might have, to conform to laws in the country of their birth, without assuming that the duty is there and can only be there on the basis of some voluntary undertaking or determinate transaction that has served to bring the citizen specifically under that duty.[7]

One final point is worth making. People often talk about a duty to conform to law which is system specific. Here one's obligation to obey laws is not represented as a moral one at all; rather, it is thought to be based on some feature of the political system itself. Thus, someone might allege that in a democratic state the norms of democracy require that one accept democratically established law as law, as binding law, and be willing to comply with it so long as it remains in force.

The problem with taking a very general 'moral reasons' approach to political obligation (where we consider *only* moral reasons that would bind all people at all times and places to obey all the laws in their country) is not just that it would not work, a point I have already made, but also that it deflects attention from the notion of any sort of special obligation to laws *as laws*. It seems we should determine what it is about laws simply in so far as they are laws and about the specific political system in which they occur that might initially engender and justify such a duty. If we cannot do this, one might wonder if we are really talking about *political* obligation at all. We should, then, if we want to take seriously the issue of an obligation towards laws as such, make system-specific reasons our first line of attack in determining the grounds of one's obligation to obey the law.

Let me summarise the main themes, now, of our suggested new approach to assessing political obligation. First, we should emphasise the case of people who are born in a given country and are lifelong residents there. And we should not assume that any duty to obey laws, should there be one, is a duty voluntarily taken on or one involved in a transaction of some sort. Second, we would do well, at least as an initial step, to focus on specific features of the political system of the country in which these people reside, to see if these features give rise to any sort of duty to obey the laws there. And, finally, we should give up the quest for generality, of trying to find general reasons that would underwrite an obligation of all people at all times and places to obey all the laws in their country.

To follow out the new approach just suggested does not preclude us from asking moral questions. We can still ask whether a given system of political conceptions and institutions, in which the elements of political obligation have been established as embedded, can be morally approved. Or we can ask whether most laws generated by such a system can be morally approved. This is the same as asking whether a system-specific political obligation can be morally justified.

But the questions we are asking here can only be asked and answered in the order I have given. Without first showing that an obligation is owed to the laws qua laws and that such obligation can be given a system-specific justification, any programme for a moral justification of political obligation would seem to be off target. It could not tell us whether (or why) we have a duty to comply with laws simply in so far as they were laws. And this would be to miss the point of raising the issue *political* obligation in the first place. Or so I would argue.[8]

What we would be looking for, in carrying through this analysis, are reasons specific to a given political system that could bind people to conform with the laws, simply as laws, in such a system. If such a system actually exists to an appreciable degree in the country in which a group of people live, then we have found reasons that will bind such people to the laws there, merely in so far as these are duly enacted laws, or will bind them with respect to an important subset of these laws. In following out the lines of the new approach we might be able to come up with a definite and workable notion of political obligation.

We will not have time in the present study to carry through this analysis. What is important to see here is the basic approach we would be taking to it. But the analysis itself is something we must save for another day.[9]

Notes

1 For that part of the *Crito* which contains the Socratic arguments against disobedience to law, see Plato, *Five Dialogues*, tr. G.M.A. Grube (Indianapolis, IN, Hackett, 1981), pp. 52–6.

2 For the main points (body politic, constitutional consensus, avoidance of state of nature), see J. Locke, *Two Treatises of Government* (first published 1690) ed. P. Laslett, 2nd edn (Cambridge, Cambridge University Press, 1970), *Second Treatise*, s. 97; and also ss. 89, 95–6, 98–9. Locke's account of the powers of government is found in

Second Treatise, chs 11 and 12. Locke's discussion of *express* consent, that is, the permanent or standing consent of citizen-members, occurs in *Second Treatise*, ss. 116–18; and his further account of it and contrast with *tacit* consent, that is, the temporary consent of visitors etc., is found in *Second Treatise*, ss. 119–22.

3   I said that, in Hobbes's view, each subject has consented here permanently but *conditionally*. The condition is that the government (the sovereign) does not invade the subject's unmistakably vital interests. The vital interests Hobbes had in mind are the subject's avoidance of 'death, wounds, and imprisonment' at the hands of the government (for elaboration see T. Hobbes, *Leviathan*, ed. R.Tuck (Cambridge, Cambridge University Press, 1996), ch. 14).

4   The idea I have just suggested – that there might be good reasons for people to act *as if* they had explicitly consented – is sometimes called hypothetical consent. J. Rawls is often taken to have advocated such an approach in his *A Theory of Justice* (Cambridge, MA, Harvard University Press, 1999), ch. 3. (Rawls's book was initially published in 1971.) Here Rawls was discussing what would count as a reasonable agreement for people to make concerning the principles of justice that should govern the basic structure of their own society during their entire lives. See also J. Rawls, *Political Liberalism* (New York, Columbia University Press, 1996), pp. 273–4. For an important criticism of Rawls's contract theory of justice and for the whole 'hypothetical consent' approach, see Ronald Dworkin, 'Justice and Rights' (originally published in 1973), reprinted in Dworkin's *Taking Rights Seriously* (Cambridge, MA, Harvard University Press, 1978); see esp. pp. 150–8. There continue to be sophisticated defences of hypothetical consent (as conveying the best insight into traditional consent theory). Among those I particularly recommend are Thomas Lewis, 'On Using the Concept of Hypothetical Consent', *Canadian Journal of Political Science*, 22 (1989), and Cynthia Stark, 'Hypothetical Consent and Justification', *Journal of Philosophy*, 97 (2000).

5   John Simmons, in his book *Moral Principles and Political Obligations* (Princeton, NJ, Princeton University Press, 1979) discusses a number of such grounds: fidelity or consent (chs 3 and 4), fair play (ch. 5), Rawls's natural duty of justice (ch. 6) and gratitude or repayment (ch. 7); see also pp. 15–16, 54–5. Simmons reaches the conclusion I have identified in ch. 8 of his book; many anarchist theorists would, of course, echo this conclusion. The idea that a theory of political obligation must concern itself, in particular, with the obligation of people to obey the laws in *their own country* is one that Simmons has brought to the fore and emphasised; see Simmons, *Moral Principles and Political Obligations*, esp. pp. 31–5 and also 37, 43, 54, 64, 155–6.

6   John Horton, in his book *Political Obligation* (Atlantic Highlands, NJ, Humanities Press International, 1992), surveys these same grounds in chs 2 (on consent) and 4 (fair play and gratitude) and finds all of them wanting. His suggestion that we take a different basic approach is developed in the final chapter of his book (ch. 6). For a similar line of attack with a similar conclusion, see Ronald Dworkin, *Law's Empire* (Cambridge, MA, Harvard University Press, 1986), ch. 6.

7   The approach I have just outlined in this paragraph has been taken by several theorists. See, for example, Rawls, *A Theory of Justice*, s. 19 and ch. 6, esp. ss. 51–3; R. Martin, *A System of Rights* (Oxford, Clarendon Press, 1993), ch. 8; also J. Waldron, 'Special Ties and Natural Duties', *Philosophy and Public Affairs*, 22 (1993), and the chapters in Horton and in Dworkin cited in note 6. For criticisms of this approach, see Richard Dagger, 'Membership, Fair Play, and Political Obligation', *Political Studies*, 48 (2000).

8   For elaboration, see Martin, *A System of Rights*, ch. 1, also p. 186.
9   See Martin, *A System of Rights*, ch. 8, for a more detailed working out of the notion of political obligation (or allegiance, as I prefer to call it) of the sort I have here suggested.

5
Nationalism and the state

Ciarán O'Kelly

Introduction

This chapter is about national ties and how they are supposed to act as a glue that holds the state together in the eyes of its citizens. A nation-state, so the story goes, is one where all the people in the state are bound together by ties of national solidarity. The solidarity legitimates the state – it tells the citizens why they are members and why it is right for the state to exist. In theory the power of the state is really in the hands of the nation because the state is nothing more or less than the great national project.

National stories are told all over the world. Despite its sordid history, the South African state is legitimated as the project of the 'rainbow nation'. The Scots have a new parliament (though not quite a state) that represents the Scottish nation. The newly unified German state allows the nation to shape its destiny as one. East Timor is free from Indonesian domination, and the nation can now have its say. Of course, this is not the whole story. For example, national solidarity appears in a less benign light in the former Yugoslavia, where conflict has raged over national self-determination. When members of one nation live in another state, things often get unpleasant. Very many people have killed and died in the name of the nation, and states have disintegrated into bitterness and conflict as a result.

Nationalism can be very exclusive. Much of the thinking described in this chapter prizes a solidarity that is strong yet socially inclusive. In section 1 the issue of solidarity will be explained. Nationalists argue that solidarity derived from 'thin' concepts like 'justice' and 'utility' cannot bind people to their states. The only solidarity that works is one that appeals to strong affections for communities, in this case the nation. Conceptually, the sources of solidarity have either derived from ideas of ethnicity or from ideas of civic unity (section 2). The stories we tell are often either about common origins, or common social traditions. We may be members of the *Volk* or citizens of 'the land of the free'.

In section 3, three attempts to give civic nationalism the upper hand are outlined. The questions provoked by attempts to redeem civic nationalism concern the coherence and practicality of civic solidarity. Is it possible to have a strong solidarity that does not descend either into chaos or into ethnic cruelty? Can we say 'we' without presupposing some sort of common character? Civic nationalists think we can, and they argue for a renewal of nationalist thought. However, perhaps they are swimming against currents that are just too strong.

1 On solidarity

Some contemporary political theorists regard nationalism as an anachronistic vestige of less enlightened times, or as a distraction from the real issues of politics. For example, when asked the question 'what reasons do we have to identify with the state to which we belong?' they may answer that we have ties because states have pragmatic and tangible benefits, both economically and socially. Alternatively, they might say that we should not have primary ties to states at all, but should have ties to justice.

For example, Robert Goodin sees the state as having two roles. First, it forces people to '"internalise" externalities'.[1] The state ensures that people pay the real cost of their activities, including environmental and social costs. If citizens drive cars, they pay for roads and for the costs of the pollution that they create. The state co-ordinates the payment of these costs. Second, the state may be the primary agent of welfarism where, through any one of a number of political agendas, wealth is redistributed according to certain political criteria.[2] So, when we ask why we have ties to the state, the answer is that we are tying ourselves to the *usefulness* of the state.

By contrast, John Rawls emphasises justice. His theory is related to Goodin's in that he sees the state as having a redistributive and regulatory role.[3] The key to Rawls's understanding of the state is that it is not the starting point of his thinking. Institutions will provoke allegiance if people find them acceptable, and citizens will find them acceptable if they are just.[4] The formations of states, as manifested in the drawing of their boundaries, are thought by Rawls to be arbitrary. As such, the place of states in the political run of things is just not all that significant. The significant thing, again, is justice. What matters is the development of an 'overlapping consensus' on the habits and institutions by which people, who might otherwise diverge, can get along with each other.

Very many people have argued that the sorts of solidarity envisaged by Goodin, Rawls and others is too 'thin' to be meaningful. This criticism has often come from communitarians and multicultural theorists, who argue that political understanding must take account of the fact that individuals are strongly embedded in communities.[5] These communities shape individuals in ways that are politically significant. Community membership determines the 'thick' political conceptions that real people, not the abstractions of liberal theory, carry around with them.

As with communitarian and multicultural theory, nationalism emphasises the importance of community membership. Nationalists argue that ties grounded in the justice of institutions, or ties grounded in pragmatic calculation, are not strong enough to bind people to the state. Solidarity that is rooted in utility or justice as advocated by Goodin and Rawls, is not solidarity in any meaningful sense.

For nationalists, such a solidarity fails to do two things. It fails to describe the reasons why people have experienced solidarity in the past, in situations when their relationships with their states were neither hugely beneficial nor just in the senses that Goodin and Rawls hold. Such a solidarity also fails to tell us why people should regard a state as *theirs*. Justice, almost always universalist in intention, and pragmatic calculation, always contingent on benefits, cannot explain the feelings of ownership that French people have regarding the French state, or that Spaniards feel regarding the Spanish state.

A theory of nationalism explains the affection people feel for their state. Nationalists argue that the mutual affections of co-nationals are a positive part of political life. National affections help legitimate states, creating a sense of membership and ownership. National membership is the root of legitimate authority. The state can tell us what to do because the state is *our* national project.

2 The nation and the nation-state

Historically, constitutional democracy is linked to the nation-state. When absolute monarchs ruled states, states were regarded as legitimate in virtue of the authority of the king, who was thought to receive his authority from God. Solidarity had nothing to do with it. When kings were overthrown across Europe and in America, the question of legitimacy arose. One answer to this question was that authority should be defined, at least in part, by solidarity. Boundaries were conceived as being dependent on something other than political decisions. Boundaries of states reflected the territorial spread of nations.

In France, the link between nationalism and state power was enshrined in the Declaration of the Rights of Man and the Individual, adopted in August 1789. The declaration was to serve as the preamble to France's Revolutionary constitution of 1791 and was drawn from the constitutions of some American states, and from the philosophies of Locke, Voltaire and Rousseau. Article III states that 'The principle of all sovereignty resides in the Nation. No body or individual may exercise any power other than that expressly emanating from the Nation'. Article III was derived specifically from Rousseau's writing.[6]

There are two ways of thinking about the nation. When the thinkers of the French revolution thought of sovereignty as being vested in the nation, they meant that it was vested in the people born in France. However, the second wave of nationalism, beginning in the late nineteenth century, thought of the nation as a *Volk* – as a group tied by their shared nationhood, not by their being born in a certain state. In its first manifestation at the origins of the civic tradition, the nation was decidedly subordinate to the bourgeois state and attendant rights held by all the citizenry. The second wave was rooted in the romantic origins of pre-political groups. According to ethnic nationalists, the state was subordinate to the nation, because the nation was there first.[7]

2(a) *Civic nationalism*

As I said, in the civic tradition the nation was assumed to be more or less everybody in the state. Political structures were set up in line with the classical republican ideas of citizenship and discourse. However, a state like France was too big
to appeal to the sorts of strong solidarity that existed in medieval city-states,
where it was likely that everyone knew each other. The looser phenomenon of
national consciousness provided an appropriate story around which solidarity
could be built.

Quite literally, the state was deemed to be the national project. It belonged to
everyone, because everyone was involved in sustaining it. The appeal to nation
would present people with the interest and reference that overrode other, more
contingent concerns. Now, one could lose from the everyday rough and tumble
of the political world, and yet be given a reason to stay loyal. You might not have
your way in deciding the direction the ship of state was going to take, but you
were always part of the crew.

The civic national ideal also enshrined a concept of equality that had been
missing in the monarchical state. Not only were you part of the crew, but you
had as much right to be captain as everyone else. As such, the experience of
inequality was substantively different to the experience of inequality under
monarchism. Now inequality was thought of as a facet of merit, not of birth.
All members of the state were to be treated as equals without being equal in
merit. Success was linked to effort. The supposition that every member could,
through their own effort, climb to the top of the pile, was part of the basis for
people's nationalist affections. And if you were a loser, you could console your-
self, so the story went, by the knowledge that you were still a member of the
crew. 'Socially humiliated and discontented people find in the membership of
the nation a new sense of pride, a new dignity: "I am poor, but at least I am
American (or German or Italian)".'[8] You were still, so the story went, an author
of and participant in the great national project.

2(b) *Ethnic nationalism*

The second sort of nationalism chiefly developed across central and eastern
Europe. This nationalism was not based on the prior presence of a state or on the
need to legitimate a state. Instead it was based on groups that made claims to statehood. These groups appealed to the potent romantic brew of perceived cultural
and ethnic commonality to justify their uniqueness – the qualities that separated
them from their peers in whatever state they happened to find themselves in.

According to Hannah Arendt, the second wave of nationalism was substantially different from the first wave in that civic nationalism 'even in its
most wildly fantastic manifestations, did not hold that men of French origin,
born and raised in another country, without any knowledge of French language or culture, would be "born Frenchmen" thanks to some mysterious
qualities of body and soul'.[9] The new form of nationalism, or 'tribalism' as
Arendt called it, was characterised by a concentration on the nation as a set of

shared characteristics. The problem with this is that it was not confined to national borders, as civic nationalism was. So, pan-Germanism was an aspiration to unite the Germanic peoples of Europe, not a celebration of national achievement. This nationalism justified, and justifies, what we now call Balkanisation – the attempted division of territory along supposedly ethnic lines.[10]

The rise of ethnic nationalism and of imperialist racialism led to the sidelining in the more established nation-states of the republican traditions associated with civic nationalism. In France, where the republican tradition had been strong, the tone of statehood started to tend towards the authoritarian. Now the Dreyfusard appeal to 'the stern Jacobin concept of the nation based upon human rights – that republican view of communal life which asserts that (in the words of Clemenceau) by infringing on the rights of one you infringe on the rights of all'[11] fell on deaf ears. In Germany, where there was little in the way of a republican tradition, 'antirepublicanism was even more pronounced'.[12] The automatic right of state members to citizenship disappeared, and those who were deemed to be outside the nation were regarded as being beyond the protection of the state. Now, you were not of a place because you were born there. You were of a place because it was your home, your birthright.

The Jacobin tradition was usurped by the ethnic drives of the new nations, by people who drove their self-conceptions into increasingly narrow corridors and away from the democratic embrace of republicanism. Now we associate nationalism with racism, intolerance and ethnic hatred. The nation is largely, though not solely, the cause of the Balkan wars, of intolerance towards immigrants and of innumerable breaches of human rights. If we are interested in a moral world that reflects diversity, plurality and inclusion, we tend to fear nationalism's rise.

The problem is that, without denying the dangers of nationalism, very many people also recognise that the nation creates important social bonds. We cannot and should not ignore the nation, despite the cruelties associated with its ethnic manifestation. It is the root of solidarity in the nation-state that is still the primary focus of our political lives.

The contemporary nation-state is being squeezed, both from above and from below. The world we have inherited is made up of increasingly multi-ethnic societies, with stronger global institutions and changes in the nature of communications media, travel and education. As a matter of course, people make claims to sovereignty within state borders. People also make moral and legal appeals to institutions that exist beyond state borders. The nation-state is under pressure from all sides. Nevertheless, the weakening of the nation-state should not hide the fact that nationalism tapped, and still taps, directly into people's deepest affections. The nation is still a political issue. It has never gone away.

3 Transcending ethnic nationalism

Can we derive a notion of nationalism that does not hark back to the ethnic nationalisms of the late nineteenth and early twentieth centuries? Is it possible to hold nationalist sentiments without betraying a liberal or pluralist outlook? Some thinkers wish to preserve the legitimacy of states by restoring nationalism to its civic roots. The legitimacy of states, they argue, is under threat both from reactionary ethnic nationalists and from the dissolution of communities, as traditionally conceived. In a globalised world, the nation can play an important stabilising role. While ethnic nationalism is not desirable, neither is a situation where states cannot relate to their citizenries. Nationalists want to develop an agenda that will help reorientate people back to a relationship with their democratic states.

3(a) *Postnationalism*

Postmodernist thinkers 'hold this belief in common: that the project of modernity is now deeply problematic'.[13] As anti-dogmatists, they try to show how sets of concepts that had been accepted as similar or identical in the past are in fact separate. Their political conceptions tend to be oppositional. This is because of the inherently challenging nature of postmodern questions. Postmodernists present a challenge to perceived unity, and to accepted power. They challenge the supposed structures of the modern world.

In *Postnationalist Ireland*, Richard Kearney's self-proclaimed agenda is to separate into their constituent parts and varieties a series of nationalist concepts that have been assumed to be identical, or to be related. He argues that the relationship between citizens and the state, and indeed between each other, must be taken apart. Once this is done, people might derive value from nationalist ties without supposing that they should link national membership to ownership of the state. This can only be done if people understand that the basis of their ties is not real but 'imagined,' as Benedict Anderson put it – something that is not natural and has no implications beyond itself.[14] People must realise that their identities are not unitary and complete, but are disparate, heterogeneous and complicated.

The idea that national freedom should be equated with state authority will inevitably lead to instability. In the face of contrary feelings, the state cannot maintain the unity of a diverse population. We should acknowledge the different sources of legitimacy and identity. Authority can be based on these different sources. The ethnic nation is not the sole source of identity and of legitimation. If we want stability, authority must be dispersed above and below the nation-state: 'nations and states are of our own making and can be remade according to other images'.[15] If we understand the fact that our institutions are invented, then we will be willing to think about them creatively, and will reject the old dogmas.

Kearney replies to the question 'can citizens live by law alone?' in the negative. To try to 'cure' people of their communal ties would inevitably descend into totalitarian oppression. Instead, our communal expressions should find 'more appropriate forms'.[16] We should not hijack the state and turn it into a medium for the ethnos. Instead, we should recognise the things that hold us together as well as the things that keep us apart. The transcendence of ethnic nationalism lies in the recognition of the dubious grounds of ethnicity, both morally and historically. The post-nation is the self-knowing nation.

Margaret Canovan argues that Kearney's approach is problematic. The way we think about ourselves is not so clear. Following Arendt, she writes that 'politics is not a matter of moulding passive material. Free politics means action engaged in by plural actors, and no one can control or predict its outcome'.[17] The aspirations of postmodern nationalists may be too optimistic. Holders of identity may be too stubborn to develop the realisations that Kearney wants.

The arguments of postmodernists are far removed from the prevailing feelings of people. When it comes to identity, appearances may deceive. Post-modernism is, at best, ahead of its time. Indeed, as Canovan says,

> encouraging citizens to debate matters of common identity may generate more enlightened and cosmopolitan views, but it could just as well provide opportunities for populist mobilisation that might reinforce entrenched conceptions of 'us' and 'them,' or lead to re-imagined identities of an even less palatable kind. The increasing success, in Western Europe and elsewhere, of political parties hostile to immigration is a reminder of these possibilities.[18]

3(b) *Liberal nationalism*

In *On Nationality*, David Miller argues that liberalism and nationalism do not have to conflict. He starts from the premise that nations can provide people with a context for thick ethical outlooks – for concrete feelings of loyalty, bravery and the like, as opposed to thin, ethereal notions of justice and virtue. People's sense of value, or right and wrong, can come from the more concrete conceptions propagated by the nation. The nation also presents a rich foundation in our globalised, homogenous world. We should value the cultural depth that can be found amongst people who live their lives in rooted communities.[19] Nationalism provides us with a home. Nations exist to the extent that people believe they exist. The truth or falsity of those nationalist beliefs is not an issue.

The specific nation is 'strangely amorphous when we come to ask about the rights and obligations that flow from it':

> Whereas in face-to-face communities, especially perhaps those with defined objectives, there is a clear understanding of what each is expected to contribute towards the welfare of other members, in the case of nationality we are in no position to grasp the demands and expectations of other members directly, nor they ours.[20]

We may be able, Miller writes, to discern the national self-images of specific people. For example, Americans think of the USA as the 'land of the free.' Such images shape the way that people conceive of their national relationships. But Miller points out that such concepts have to do with political culture and not with national membership in the abstract. In the abstract sense, the nation has no specific moral qualities.

Nevertheless, the idea that people should

regard their nationality merely as historical accident, an identity to be sloughed off in favour of humanity at large, carries little appeal. If national identities are distasteful, or have distasteful aspects, it seems more reasonable to work from within, to get people to reassess what they have inherited, come to a new understanding of what it means to be German or Canadian, than to dismiss such identities from an external standpoint.[21]

In a way, Miller sees a potential for us to gain control over our national traditions, instead of regarding ourselves as passive products of our nations.

Miller argues that people within the state should be included even if they regard themselves as different to the main current of national identity. 'If a state houses a minority who for one reason or another do not feel themselves to be fully part of the national community, but who do not want or cannot realistically hope to form a nation-state of their own, then national identity must be transformed in such a way that they can be included.'[22] A plural society demands a pluralist nationalism. It is important to

> free the public sphere of symbols, practices and unstated assumptions that prevent the members of some groups from participating as equal citizens. I do not mean that the public sphere should become culturally neutral: it expresses the shared national identity of the citizens, and this must have some determinate content that varies from place to place. But national identities have always been in a state of flux, and the challenge now is to remake them in a way that is more hospitable to women, ethnic minorities and other groups without emptying them of content and destroying the underpinnings of democratic politics.[23]

Perhaps Miller, just like Kearney, is a bit optimistic. Can his argument propagate change? Certainly when we think of, say, German identity, we think of a transformation that is linked to the traumas of self-recognition in the wake of Nazism and the Holocaust. However, other identities have not been forced into such self-recognition or have refused such self-recognition. Changes in national identity may happen, but there is no guarantee that the politics of members will end up turning in one direction rather than the other. We may wish for nations to be nicer, but we cannot make our wishes come true.

Even in states that are supposed to be nationalist in the civic sense, like the USA, incidents of exclusion and repression are not uncommon. American nationalism may focus on the rhetoric of freedom, but it can also turn towards violence against foreigners or other outsiders. If we agree that identities are here to stay as part of the political landscape, then we have to admit that nobody knows how to control them. Nobody knows how to make nationalism nicer.

3(c) *Patriotism*

Miller and Kearney seek to renew nationalism. Patriots, on the other hand, regard themselves as focusing on a solidarity that can be distinguished from nationalism. They argue that nationalism cannot simultaneously guarantee stability and an acceptable ethical outlook. We cannot rely on national affections to come up with a political outlook that respects citizenship and equal liberties. Instead of directing our affections towards the nation we should direct them towards the legitimate democratic structures of the state.

Maurizio Viroli writes that

> the ideological victory of the language of nationalism has relegated the language of patriotism to the margins of contemporary political thought. And yet, when peoples become engaged in struggles for liberty, when they have to face the task of rebuilding their nations after experiences of war and totalitarian regimes, theorists are able to recover elements of the old language of patriotism under the predominant rhetoric of nationalism.[24]

Our civic tradition may be weak, but it is not dead.

Viroli argues that the 'patriotism of liberty' is neither nationalist nor universalist. Just like liberal nationalists, patriots do not seek to create homogeneity in cultural, ethnic and linguistic spheres. Neither do they expect us to engage solely with abstract universal concepts. Instead, patriots argue for a 'particularistic love' of 'common liberty and the institutions that sustain it'. They argue for

> love of the common liberty of a particular people, sustained by institutions that have a particular history which has for that people a particular meaning, or meanings, that inspire and are in turn sustained by a particular way of life and culture. Because it is a love of the particular it is possible, but because it is a love of a particular liberty it is not exclusive: love of the common liberty of one's people easily extends beyond national boundaries and translates into solidarity.[25]

Viroli has little to say about how such a love can be created, but he does point out that the patriotic tradition has been carried through centuries of political writing. Patriotism is the inclusive love of 'our' liberty.

Similarly, Jürgen Habermas argues in favour of 'constitutional patriotism', which is based on his sophisticated sociological theory, as presented in his two-volume *The Theory of Communicative Action*.[26] Habermas argues that, over time, social discourses become progressively more rational through the 'unforced force' of the better argument. Societal action rationalises as a result of open discourse concerning the reasons for action. Constitutional patriotism is a post-traditional phenomenon. Habermas argues that, in a post-traditional society, people have moved on from developing allegiance based on nationalist or other sentimental and mystical outlooks. Instead, they place their allegiance in the just political procedures of the state, based upon universalist and discursive principles.

Constitutional patriotism is a rational outlook because of the way that it has been decided. This marks it out from nationalism. The only thing that guarantees democratic rights is an explicit statement in a constitution. But that constitutional statement is nothing unless it is accompanied by an attachment to its moral standpoint. Habermas writes that

> the universalist principles of constitutional democracy need to be somehow anchored in the political culture of each country. Constitutional principles can neither take shape in social practices nor become the driving force for the dynamic

project of creating an association of free and equal persons until they are situated in the historical context of a nation of citizens in such a way that they link up with those citizens' motives and attitudes.[27]

As Attracta Ingram argues, it is part of the liberal state that it is unified by certain shared values and the institutional structures that carry them over time. The idea involves willingness to view people, for purposes of politics, as generic individuals rather than as members of this or that clan, tribe or nation'.[28] Ingram's point is that tight bonds can be created through ties to the political structures of the liberal state. The constitutional patriot's cause is obviously different to those of Kearney and Miller. Instead of looking to adjust nationalism, or to promote a kinder, gentler nationalism, Habermas wants to move away from nationalist feelings altogether. At least, that is, when it comes to thinking about politics.

Viroli does not want us to detach ourselves from the ties that we have. He is not asking us to remove ourselves from our deep communal structures.[29] Habermas's feelings about the benefits of such levels of commonality are somewhat open to question. It is difficult to know whether he wants us to forget national ties altogether or to associate our national ties with pride in our constitutional achievements.[30] Either way, neither thinker is suggesting that we completely rid ourselves of ties of birth. You do not become a citizen of your state by sitting an examination – you do so by being born there. The important thing is that we transcend the drive towards ethnic and cultural hegemony in our society. The patriotic drive, according to both Viroli and Habermas, is sufficient to tie us to our states. However, patriotism being sufficient for solidarity is less important than the fact that it is moral and rational in a way that nationalism is not.

That said, there is some doubt as to whether constitutional patriotism would create ties that are strong enough to bind people together in the way that a nation is supposed to. For example, we may take some pride in the institutions of the European Union, say the Convention on Human Rights, but that does not necessarily make us feel European in the same way that we feel British or Irish or French.[31] If patriotism does transcend ethnic nationalism, there is a risk that it will lead to the loss of solidarity in established states. That might mean greater instability, as people turn their political attention to levels above or below the nation-state.

Conclusion

In the introduction to this chapter, two questions were asked. First, is it possible to have a strong solidarity that does not descend either into chaos or into ethnic cruelty? Second, can we say 'we' without presupposing some sort of common character? Civic nationalists believe both questions can be answered affirmatively. However, there are problems with the various attempts to transcend ethnic nationalism, as surveyed in the first section. We might believe, somewhat optimistically, that nationalist ideas can be transformed. Kearney and Miller certainly believe this. Yet this strategy risks inadvertently legitimating old-style ethnic nationalism. If it is impossible to adjust nationalist ties in a way that rids us of the ethnic fixation, it might be safer to reject nationalism as a whole. Possibly any type of communal endeavour is exclusionary inasmuch as solidarity presupposes exclusion. The only inclusive solidarity may be a loose global solidarity. Instead of seeking a thicker solidarity, we could concentrate on the sort of concerns that Goodin and Rawls appeal to, as discussed in section 2. If this leads to the weakening and eventual dissolution of the nation-state, then so be it.

Of course, exclusion is not necessarily a problem in itself. The nation-state, whether we like it or not, is still the primary focus of political life. What civic nationalists and patriots want us to do is to realise that exclusion is an arbitrary thing. We should include all those who live inside our territories and simultaneously admit that the territory and its boundaries have no moral relevance. We may live in a nation-state, but that does not determine what our political actions will be. The problem with this view is that civic nationalism or patriotism may not be strong enough to create solidarity. Purely political solidarity may not be enough. National stories invest too much in common origin and the like to be open to adjustment in the direction of civic consciousness. Dangerous though it is, the ethnic nation may be more compatible with what people really need.

Yet, something does seem to be happening, certainly across the rich part of the world. To be sure, for some people the baby of social solidarity has been thrown out with the bath water of nationalism. Nationalism is irrelevant to them because they find all such bonds irrelevant. However, some others, without necessarily dropping national bonds altogether, express a more cosmopolitan sympathy with those who are not national members. Ideals of universal human rights are spreading globally, and within states. Very many people ignore nationalism when it comes to making decisions about the nature of sovereignty. It just does not figure in their ideas of right and wrong. They may maintain their pride in national achievements, whether cultural or political, but they do not think of the nation as the limit of their moral environment. Their moral environment is characterised by a multiplicity of considerations. While they want to get things right at home, they are also concerned that things are wrong elsewhere. And the fact that things are wrong elsewhere is seen as their business. People are not just civic nationalists – they also exist beyond nationalism.

Notes

1 R. Goodin, *Motivating Political Morality* (Oxford, Blackwell, 1992), p. 27.
2 R. Goodin, B. Headley, R. Muffels and H.K. Dirven, *The Real Worlds of Welfare Capitalism* (Cambridge, Cambridge University Press, 1999), p. 39f.
3 J. Rawls, 'Constitutional Liberty and the Concept of Justice', originally published in

1963, reprinted in J. Rawls (S. Freeman [ed.]), *Collected Papers* (Cambridge, MA, Harvard University Press, 1999), p. 90.

4 In *The Law of Peoples* (Cambridge, MA, Harvard University Press, 1999), p. 27f, Rawls develops the distinction between states and people, implying that peoples are groups interested in justice, while states are purely strategic entities.

5 See, for example, W. Kymlicka, *Multicultural Citizenship: A Liberal Theory of Minority Rights* (Oxford, Clarendon Press, 1995); M. Sandel, *Liberalism and the Limits of Justice* (Cambridge, Cambridge University Press, 1982); C. Taylor, 'The Politics of Recognition', in A. Gutman (ed.), *Multiculturalism: Examining 'The Politics of Recognition'* (Princeton, NJ, Princeton University Press, 1994, 2nd edn). See also the responses of J. Rawls, *Political Liberalism* (New York, Columbia University Press, 1993) and B. Barry, *Culture and Equality: An Egalitarian Critique of Multiculturalism* (Cambridge, Polity Press, 2001).

6 J.-J. Rousseau, *The Social Contract and Other Later Political Writings*, tr. V. Gourevitch (Cambridge, Cambridge University Press, 1998), p. 63.

7 On the differences between sorts of nationalism, see H. Arendt, *The Origins of Totalitarianism* (first published 1948) (London, Harvest, 1976), pp. 226ff, 267ff; A. Smith, *Nationalism and Modernity* (London, Routledge, 1998), pp. 125ff; E. Hobsbawm, *Nations and Nationalism since 1780* (Cambridge, Cambridge University Press, 1990), pp. 101ff.

8 M. Viroli, *For Love of Country – An Essay on Patriotism and Nationalism* (Oxford, Clarendon Press, 1995), p. 15.

9 Arendt, *Origins of Totalitarianism*, p. 226.

10 Supposed because ownership does not necessarily depend on who is in the majority in an area. It may just as well be the case that a certain group lays claim to an area because the group that lives there now are either the descendants of colonisers or because the ethnic group has a certain association to that piece of ground.

11 Arendt, *Origins of Totalitarianism*, p. 106. In 1894, Alfred Dreyfuss, a Jewish army officer, was arrested and falsely convicted of espionage in the wake of the Franco-Prussian war. With the complicity of the state and the press and despite the arrest of the real culprit, anti-Semitic officers tried to deny his innocence. They were challenged by Emíle Zola in his famous letter, 'J'Accuse'.

12 J. Isaac, 'A New Guarantee on Earth: Hannah Arendt on Human Dignity and the Politics of Human Rights', *American Political Science Review*, 90:1 (1996), p. 62.

13 H. Foster, 'Postmodernism: A Preface', in H. Foster (ed.), *Postmodern Culture* (London, Pluto Press, 1985), p. ix.

14 B. Anderson, *Imagined Communities* (London, Verso, 1991), p. 6f.

15 R. Kearney, *Postnationalist Ireland* (London, Routledge, 1997), p. 69.

16 Kearney, *Postnationalist Ireland*, p. 185.

17 M. Canovan, 'Patriotism is not Enough', *British Journal of Political Science*, 30:3 (2000), p. 430.

18 Canovan, 'Patriotism is not Enough', p. 430.

19 D. Miller, *On Nationality* (Oxford, Oxford University Press, 1995), p. 185f.

20 Miller, *On Nationality*, p. 68.

21 Miller, *On Nationality*, p. 184.

22 Miller, *On Nationality*, p. 188.

23 D. Miller, *Citizenship and National Identity* (Cambridge, Polity Press, 2000), p. 80.

24 Viroli, *For Love of Country*, p. 161.

25 Viroli, *For Love of Country*, p. 12.
26 J. Habermas, *The Theory of Communicative Action, Volume One – Reason and the Ratio-nalisation of Society*, tr. T. McCarthy (Boston, Beacon Press, 1984); J. Habermas, *The Theory of Communicative Action, Volume Two – Lifeworld and System: A Critique of Functionalist Reason*, tr. T. McCarthy (Boston, Beacon Press, 1987). Habermas is notoriously difficult, and should be approached with some caution. However, a number of clear and helpful introductions to the theory of communicative action are available. Try W. Outhwaite, *Habermas – a Critical Introduction* (Cambridge, Polity Press, 1994).
27 J. Habermas, 'Citizenship and National Identity', in J. Habermas *Between Facts and Norms: Contributions to a Discourse Theory of Law and Democracy*, tr. W. Rehg (first published 1990) (Cambridge, Polity Press, 1996), p. 499.
28 A. Ingram, 'Constitutional Patriotism', *Philosophy and Social Criticism*, 22:6 (1996), p. 12.
29 Viroli, *For Love of Country*, p. 3.
30 P. Markell, 'Making Affect Safe for Democracy? – On "Constitutional Patriotism"', *Political Theory*, 28:1 (2000), p. 57.
31 Canovan, 'Patriotism is not Enough', p. 421f.

6

Crime and punishment

Emilio Santoro[1]

Introduction

The prison populations of western countries have grown dramatically over the past few years. All developed democracies are building new prisons and increasing expenditure on law and order enforcement agencies, particularly police and prison officers. This trend has been accompanied by a proliferation of measures aimed at hindering or repressing any one who might disturb the peace, such as prohibitions or restrictions on begging, curfews for teenagers and the increased use of electronic controls, such as video surveillance in public places and on transport services. David Garland[2] has interpreted this situation as a 'hysterical denial' before the law enforcing agencies' self-confessed inability to control crime and their consequent resort to strategies that place ever more responsibility for crime prevention on citizens and increasingly delegate the policing of public places to private security firms. However, this thesis is too crude. In western democracies, the number and categories of people considered outlaws and suitable for imprisonment has risen at such a rate as to constitute a qualitative transformation of criminal policies. Both governments and public opinion appear to believe that current circumstances require a much broader institutionalisation of citizens than was previously considered acceptable.

Zygmunt Bauman[3] and Loïc Wacquant[4] have recently argued that the spread of security related policies is closely related to the neo-liberal programme first adopted by New Right governments in Britain and the USA, and which is now presented throughout the western world as the necessary (or inevitable) response to globalisation. They regard the criminalisation of poverty by western states as the paradoxical outcome of their weakened capacity for social intervention due to the erosion of their political sovereignty by global pressures. The marked expansion of social control and the barbarity of its methods ultimately result from an ideology that champions the omnipotence of global markets. This chapter explores the link between the weakening of states and this change in criminal policies, and outlines their implications for individual rights.

1 Criminal policy in the era of globalisation

Drawing on Max Weber's well-known thesis, Ernest Gellner[5] argued that the executive and legislative power of modern states rested upon three types of sovereignty: military, economic and cultural. Historically, the sovereignty of states cannot be separated from their capacity not only to defend their territories against challenges from other sources of order, both internal and external, but also to balance the accounts of the domestic economy and mobilise sufficient cultural resources to defend their individuality by giving their subjects or citizens a distinctive identity. Today the picture is quite different. The globalisation of financial markets is increasingly presented as an irresistible force with which states must comply, thereby relinquishing their hold on the regulation of the economy. This analysis of markets as irresistible has gone hand in hand with the ideology that the new world of mobile capital, where all state-created barriers have been removed, is bound to make everyone's life better.[6] It has become a commonplace that the control of the economic system by markets is of paramount importance for the well-being of humanity and the stability of the world's social arrangements. According to the ideology of globalisation, instead of the economy needing to be made compatible with a given scheme of social relations, society should be regulated to facilitate the operation of markets.

This approach drastically reduces the room for politics. Political activity, defined by Claus Offe as 'the capacity for making and implementing binding collective decisions',[7] has become a problem: the public discourse created by the ideology of global capitalism undermines the legitimacy of many choices that for over half a century have been traditionally acknowledged as the prerogative of states. In particular, the legitimacy of any state regulation of markets is being increasingly questioned: there is no longer a domestic market to regulate, the market is global and as such outside the state's power. Moreover, trust in spontaneous progress through the mechanism of the 'invisible hand' undermines any conception of the government's role in economic life. Deregulation, liberalisation, flexibility, the simplification of transactions in the labour and real estate markets, reduced taxation: all these factors tend to reduce state sovereignty to something merely nominal and to make its holder 'anonymous'. The trend is clear: the more the economy is taken out of political control, the less resources states have at their command and the less they can afford to exercise power – even when they are willing or supposed to do so.

As Bauman has emphasised,[8] the emergence of new small, weak and powerless sovereign states is consistent with economic and financial globalisation. Far from hindering the new world society of the free circulation of capital, goods and information, the birth of small politically independent territorial entities with very few resources is indeed functional to its development. In a situation where the border between what is 'internal' and what is 'external' to a state is continuously shifting, the only function which seems bound to remain definitely internal is that of policing the territory and its population. There seems to be a tendency to reduce state functions to their required minimum: namely, repressive power. Indeed, the new world order needs weak states for its preservation and reproduction: they 'can be easily reduced to the (useful) role of local police precincts, securing a modicum of order required for the conduct of business, but need not be feared as effective brakes on the global companies' freedom'.[9]

All the evidence indicates that the shift towards a judicial and prison management of poverty is more likely the more a government's economic and social policies are inspired by the neo-liberal 'privatisation' of social relations and the weakening of state welfare. 'Less state' in the social field, less economic intervention, apparently means 'more state' in the fields of law enforcement and policing: repressive justice policies are the counterpart of libertarian economic policies. Giving up the right to state welfare, let alone the right to employment (a non-temporary full time job with social security and a decent salary), is reflected in the obsession for reaffirming the 'right to security'. The increase in the resources devoted to maintaining public order compensates, above all symbolically, for the lack of legitimacy resulting from governments giving up economic regulation and the provision of social security.

2 From social contract to zero tolerance

From Cesare Beccaria in the eighteenth century to Hart and Rawls in the twentieth,[10] liberal theories of punishment have attempted to combine the general deterrence of crime with due retribution against actual criminals. In eighteenth-century theories, criminal law was regarded as an expression of the general will. As such, it was believed not to discriminate unfairly against any member of society or privilege any particular interest. According to social contract theory, the liberal state's monopoly of coercion was justified solely to protect those rights that reflected the rational interests of every individual. Its role was to ensure every one respected the rights of every body else. The criminal law was broken only by a small group of people who, unlike most citizens, were incapable of following their own rational will and distinguishing right from wrong. Those who committed crimes, especially re-offenders, thereby showed they were not rational and did not deserve their rights. They had not developed the required degree of self-control to deserve the benefits of the social contract. Individuals were fully responsible for their own actions, for they were supposed to be free to choose and directed by their own rational motives. Punishment was the means whereby an individual, who went astray out of myopia, was returned to the path of virtue. The law concentrated only on the crime, applying a strict code of retribution: the personal or social conditions leading an individual to commit a crime had no bearing on the sentence.

These early liberal theories of punishment assumed a conception of individuals as owning themselves and freely choosing and taking responsibility for their own conduct on the basis of a calculus of its personal and social consequences. This account of human agency came to provide both the underlying norm of the nineteenth-century liberal model of social order and the condition for its operation. Its 'actualisation' was to be achieved above all by a criminal policy that determined who and what to punish and how. As Foucault has emphasised, from the late eighteenth century in the USA and then little by little in Europe, it was realised that a stable liberal democracy required a set of institutions – penitentiaries as well as asylums, hospitals, schools and the like – capable of producing suitable citizens.[11] In particular, social control and criminal policy were deliberately aimed at reinforcing, and creating if necessary, the virtues of individual responsibility and self-discipline needed to cope with the impersonal social relations of the new urban and industrial environment. Deterrent criminal legislation, an efficient police force and a rigorous prison system that both stigmatised convicts and subjected them to a uniform, consistent and largely impersonal discipline, not only provided a practical means for controlling crime, but also reinforced a certain value system.

The deprivation of liberty was a revolutionary and apparently progressive approach to punishment, inspired by the values of the Enlightenment. It turned the traditional strategy of social defence upside down: changing the offender from an individual to be destroyed by death or torture to someone who remained an integral part of society, in spite of having broken its rules. Thus, punishment aimed at the criminal's reintegration into society. The key function of the 'penitentiary', it became the essence of the strategy of social control adopted following the advent of the capitalist mode of production. The penitentiary was viewed as the perfect instrument for turning the masses of former peasants migrating into the towns into industrial manpower. It became a place of forced socialisation and was structured according to the production model of the manufactory and, later, of the factory.[12] The penitentiary offered a theoretical and physical locus that allowed the liberal theory of punishment to be fully deployed. According to this theory, the best type of social defence required that the offender – the breaker of the social contract – paid damages to society through being deprived of a certain amount of liberty and subjected to discipline while serving his or her term. Only in this way could offenders be reintegrated into the texture of legal relations as docile subjects who no longer trespassed on property but were ready to earn a living by entering the market and selling their labour power.[13]

At the end of the nineteenth century, the framework of liberal criminal policy underwent a deep crisis. Liberal theories of order seemed unable to cope with the negative consequences of industrialisation. There emerged a widespread belief that the utilitarian account of agency, the unquestioned and vital basis of classical jurisprudence, should be abandoned. The metaphysics of interest, and hence of individual freedom and rationality, which was the premise of eighteenth-century economic and social theory, was replaced by the paradigm of the Positivist School. This model rejected the assumption that individuals possessed creativity and the ability to choose. Instead, it was premised on the idea that human beings had a given 'personality' or 'character' that could be scientifically known and manipulated. Criminals simply possessed deviant or pathological character traits.

In the twenty years following the Second World War, a new criminological approach arose focusing on different modes of social control. Primary instruments of social control (like the school, the family and the organisation of leisure), often directly managed by the state, were privileged over the secondary (notably prisons). The new strategy mostly addressed marginal non-criminalised individuals, such as the elderly, children, the unemployed and underemployed, immigrants and minority racial groups. Through financial and other forms of assistance, especially social welfare, the state tried to gain their acceptance of the existing social structure. An attempt was made to reduce imprisonment (both in prisons and asylums) as much as possible and to develop alternative strategies for controlling individuals, such as probation and parole for criminals and care in the community for the mentally ill.

During the 1970s this paradigm also underwent a crisis. Not only was prison perceived as an ineffective means of social control, but parole, community care, fines and the like also no longer seemed able to achieve their primary goal of re-educating offenders. In the concluding words of a well-known survey of the early 1970s literature, it was felt that 'nothing works'.[14] Early analyses of recidivism, which they regarded as the basic criteria for assessing the effectiveness of re-socialising measures, seemed to show that every strategy had failed. More generally, statistical evidence suggested that improving the living standards of the lower classes through state welfare did not in itself affect crime rates. These results led to a questioning of the aetiology of deprivation, that is, the theory associating deviance with subjective socio-economic disadvantage. A widespread perception emerged that a generalised improvement of economic conditions and a substantive enhancement of living standards had been unexpectedly followed by an increase in criminal activity. This view held true especially for that kind of criminality that had been thought to be closely related to social deprivation: street crime and petty offences.

The belief that evidence disproved a link between criminality and marginality ended up undermining the political legitimacy of both the pre-emptive and the re-educational strategies. This left a theoretical gap that still seems unbridgeable. For over two centuries every analysis of the failure and irrationality of the system of punishment had been made with a view to a proposed reform that would improve it. Such optimism has disappeared with the crisis of the notion of rehabilitation. Following the Second World War, this notion had provided the punishment of crime with both its goal and justification, legitimating it before public opinion. Now it seems to neither have a future nor make much sense.

As Castel has observed,[15] current criminal policies are radically different from traditional ones. Today, coping with deviance no longer means singling out deviant agents to be disciplined or otherwise 'taken care of'. The legitimacy of punishing is again a self-evident given and is totally severed from the possible 'positive' impact on individuals it was thought to have when penitentiaries first appeared. The demand, that was once prioritised, of institutions capable of sustaining and re-socialising their populations, seems to have become irrelevant. The policy of treatment or, more critically, disciplining, is now obsolete. Instead of being disciplined, the new poor, such as immigrants and marginalised people, and above all drug addicts, are merely contained and detained.

Punishment is no longer focused on rehabilitation but is simply a repressive measure designed to take the criminalised classes out of circulation. Its function is general prevention. It must act as a deterrent, with special prevention being limited to temporary detention. It is not intended to re-socialise but simply to incapacitate offenders – at least for a while. Punishment is mostly conceived of as a core set of physical material hindrances that make crime more difficult. A theory of preventing criminality, based on a view of criminals as socially, culturally, economically and biologically conditioned agents, has been supplanted by a discourse focusing almost exclusively on deviant behaviour and the environment within which it arises. The conception of agents as supple matter, developed by medical, psychiatric and criminological science as well as sociology, is likewise vanishing. Since agents are no longer seen as treatable transformable entities, their normalisation ceases to be the pivot of social control policies. The paradigm of these policies has changed: intervention in the space for action has emerged as the main strategy for preventing crime. Social control has been made independent of individuals and is associated with place, especially urban areas.

The most popular strategy of crime control of recent years has been the Zero Tolerance campaign promoted by the New York mayor, Rudolph Giuliani, and managed by the police chief, William Bratton. The theoretical bases of this criminal policy were laid by James Q. Wilson, perhaps the main authority of the New Right in criminology,[16] and George Kelling, a political scientist, in an article which appeared in 1982. The article's very title, 'Broken Windows'[17] suggests the authors' view that urban degradation, personal carelessness and criminality are closely related. According to their ecological-behaviourist account, when an urban environment is allowed to degrade, tolerating all sorts of spoiling, that environment will soon host real criminal forms of behaviour. The article's title derives from the example used to illustrate the theory. If someone is allowed to break a window in an abandoned building, without it being immediately replaced, all windows will soon be broken, thus triggering an escalation of illegal behaviour. Ultimately someone will trespass into the building, which in a short time will become a scene of vandalism. For Wilson and Kelling, urban degradation suggests a lack of attention by the authorities, thus encouraging the belief that illegal action can easily be taken, getting the community used to ever increasing levels of deviance and facilitating the emergence of criminal cultures.

The recipe against crime that this thesis is meant to suggest is clear: instead of the police simply trying to punish crimes after they have been committed, they should prevent them 'by protecting order'. Only by protecting order and shared values, providing a sense of membership of the community, can cities be naturally defended against the emergence of criminality. The main task of the police should be the repression of behaviour that, while being merely petty offences, are annoying and make citizens feel they live in a degraded city. In order to fight against criminality all 'broken windows' must be removed from citizens' sight, that is, rigorous repression must be used against those who draw graffiti on shutters and subway walls or beg in an aggressive or annoying way, street prostitutes, drunks and drug addicts staying in public places, tramps, etc. It is worth remarking that the two theorists of zero tolerance seem uninterested in either the 'reasons' for deviant behaviour (whether it expresses social distress or points to problems to be dealt with or whatever) or whether these phenomena can be really eradicated from society. In their view, it is only the prevention in public places of 'disruptive' behaviour that matters.[18]

The thesis of Wilson and Kelling can be read as a behaviourist version of what Hart,[19] in his polemics against Lord Devlin, Parsons and Durkheim, labelled the 'disintegration theory': namely, the theory that the task of criminal law, more than repressing and punishing harmful behaviour, is to defend social shared values. According to this theory, which rejects the separation of law and morals lying at the heart of liberal doctrine, failing to protect shared values by criminal punishment means that society – as Wilson and Kelling claim – runs the risk of disintegrating, losing its bonds, in another words, of becoming anomic. To the authors of 'Broken Windows', however, the values in need of protection are not the basic values of the social structure, those grounding the social contract in Locke's and Beccaria's theories: their protection is a by-product. What is to be secured directly is the external value of a clean and orderly environment for social interaction. Wilson and Kelling offer no criterion for distinguishing the permissible from the impermissible, orderly from disorderly public behaviour. This task is entrusted to the police, who are granted the status of the one legitimate interpreter of citizens' shared feelings.[20] Thus, the police come to express the genuine voice of a community scared of crime. It is up to them to repress behaviour that offends shared feelings. Whether this actually means that they offend legal rules, moral judgements or aesthetic beliefs is of no concern given the promise that this strategy guarantees security and the restoration of order.

3 Actuarial criminal policy and risk distribution

In the field of practice, this new approach to criminal policy means that a system focussed on individuals, the causes of their deviant behaviour and the possibility of their re-socialisation, is replaced with a system addressing whole social groups selected on the basis of the risk they pose to public security. Control strategies target not 'criminal' or 'deviant' individuals but 'categories of individuals' who ought to be the object of surveillance and deterrence. Individuals are only relevant to the extent that they fall under a category denoted by a probabilistic assessment of the risk created by its members. Paradoxically, the crisis of the welfare state and the success of libertarian policies have led to a criminal policy governed by the same governmental and disciplinary logic that had previously characterised the organisation of welfare.

The new criminal policies involve the state giving up its role as the agent of security: the right to security is replaced by a policy of the socialisation of risk designed to bring it within acceptable levels and mitigate its effects. Factors jeopardising public security are managed in the same way the welfare state approached social risks and unemployment, through a scheme of social insurance. Hence the label 'actuarial criminology', that highlights how the new types of social control are grounded on the sorts of calculations employed by the insurance industry.[21] This approach is based on a significant reconceptualisation of criminals: no longer are they either 'individuals inherently at risk' or 'in need of rehabilitation', they have become *'risk creating agents'*.[22]

The insurance strategy hinges upon economically effective techniques for the rational management of risk. At its heart is the elaboration of a system for pricing risk factors, so that the costs of possible accidents no longer fall on affected individuals but are redistributed among all the insured. Like the welfare state, actuarial criminology assumes that within each community there are randomly distributed risk factors that cannot be linked to any single individual but can be statistically related to certain groups of people.[23] Thus, the insurance strategy involves a probabilistic and statistical quantification of the types and levels of risk for different social groups. Each type of risk can then be priced according to its frequency and seriousness. However, whereas the welfare state sought to share costs through universal schemes of social insurance, actuarial criminology adopts the neo-libertarian logic of the insurance market and effectively charges people according to the categories and degrees of risk to which their group is prone. Though all citizens may pay in monetary terms for crime prevention, members of the more risk creating categories of people also have to pay in terms of freedom and opportunity regardless of their own actual propensity to crime. The very logic of insurance rules out any inquiry into the risk posed by an individual agent. The system operates on the basis of a classification of agents: while these classifications are unjust, they return a profit in terms of security.

Actuarial criminology does not deal with individuals but with risk factors, namely, statistical relations among heterogeneous factors that make it more or less likely that a crime may be committed. It deconstructs agents, replacing them with a list of circumstances that risk allegedly stems from. Dangerousness appears as a mysterious and paradoxical notion, for it is an individual's inherent quality and can only be proved after she has committed a crime. The attribution of dangerousness is always hypothetical, it is a more or less likely relation between present symptoms and certain prospective harmful events. Repetition, too, is something that cannot be predicted or can be predicted only with a high degree of uncertainty. Since deviants are almost always unpredictable, preventative measures are highly risky and hard to justify. Operators are often made to take action not in the light of objective data but out of the fear of being blamed for their inactivity should a deviant individual commit another crime. A conception of prevention confined to predicting a given occurrence appears archaic and unscientific. The goal of the new criminal policies is not to tackle an actual situation, dealing with and containing a given 'dangerous' individual, but the prevention of any possible occurrence of undesired behaviour. Prevention promotes suspicion to the scientific status of probability calculation. For an individual to be suspected, special outer symptoms of dangerousness are no longer required; it suffices to have those features security agencies count as risk factors, on the basis of statistical induction.

Possible 'injustices' resulting from the actuarial method are mentioned in the first document proposing a criminal policy of this kind in Europe: namely, the Floud Report,[24] drafted in England in 1981 during the Thatcher era. It acknowledged that any predictive judgement can make two mistakes: it may be a 'false positive' when it predicts an event that does not occur, or it may be a 'false negative' when it rules out in advance an event which does occur. The more 'false negatives', the less efficient the actuarial system and the less security it provides. 'False positives' always result in an unjust bias against the rights of an individual, whose prospective behaviour is not correctly predicted. For if a harmless person is imprisoned, a serious injustice is done with no benefit for public security. Not only is this risk cynically calculated, but it is candidly justified: new criminal policies are supposed to redistribute a burden of risk that the government cannot reduce and the best way of doing this is by the actuarial method.

This policy also may lead to sentences against two authors of the same crime being quite different in terms of the type and quantity of punishment inflicted. For the measure of punishment is not the offence but the presumptive indicators connected with the conduct, the circumstances of the crime, the groups the offender used to frequent: simply put, the class the offender falls into. For instance, according to the criteria of the new criminal policy, a 'pusher' of heroin from the Maghrib, an unemployed and homeless illegal immigrant, should be sentenced more severely, and be subjected to heavier cautionary measures, than an English cocaine 'seller' with a house and a family, who gives out cocaine at exclusive parties and takes it himself. For the former belongs to a dangerous class and this is sufficient grounds for differentiated punishment.

Thus, the rhetoric of unavoidable risks that need to be distributed in a socially acceptable way obscures that of equality which, following the Enlightenment, used to be one of the major legitimating grounds of punitive power. For actuarial criminology, individuals should be treated differently depending on the class they belong to. This approach is justified by the idea that the 'burden of risk' currently threatening everyone's life can only be dealt with at the level of whole categories of individuals. This argument seems to have become acceptable in nearly all western democracies: nobody seems to be asking whether classes of dangerousness are a ruse to cover up the revival of a census based

system of justice, or whether it is right to sacrifice equality, a principle the liberal tradition viewed for over two centuries as the main protection against
abuses of the power to punish. Instead of segregating undesirable people with
a view to their re-socialisation through more or less forcible correctional or
therapeutic treatment, the new forms of population management attach a
'social fate' to individuals by virtue of how far they meet the market standards
of competitiveness and profitability

A two-speed, dual society is appearing. There is the highway of people who
satisfy the harsh requirements of economic competition, and there is the mean
street of marginal people who are incapable of keeping pace. Such a dual society may be said to have always existed, but the distribution of individuals
between the two sectors used to be theorised as the outcome of chance, depending on events. It was thought to result from markets and an individual's capacity for adapting and reacting to their logic, for staying in or re-entering if
expelled. On the classical liberal view, criminal policy was the junction point of
this system, segregating those unable to re-enter and trying, at least in principle, to enable them to do so after an intensive 'treatment'. The classification of
people into classes defined by the statistical findings of epidemiological research
draws a different image of society as a homogeneous space with predefined circuits. Instead of an unknown wild land, marginality becomes itself an organised social zone for those people that, owing to their social characteristics,
appear to be unsuited to entering the circuit of economic competition.[25]

Conclusion

New criminal policies reflect what Peter Gloz[26] has called 'the two-thirds
society', where a significant quota of citizens is excluded from well-being, or the
'good life' and the political means for claiming it. Within welfare systems, the
circuits of political and economic exchange systematically differentiate
between interests protected by organisations with strong bargaining power,
interests defended by associations without a strategic position and, finally,
'widespread' interests lacking any effective protection. Moreover, for over
twenty years in Europe, and much longer in the USA, there has been the phenomenon of a mass migration of people from continental areas with high
demographic rates and scarce, if any, development, desperately seeking the
advantages of belonging to a 'prized' citizenship. This situation has led to a
mass of economically and politically very weak people who are de facto
excluded from the actual enjoyment of nearly every sort of right. As Galbraith[27]
has argued, the guarantee of rights for majorities, together with the need for
downsizing social security owing to the fiscal crisis of the state, has turned
affluent democracies into 'dictatorships of a satisfied class': the rich, the
wealthy, the affluent have always existed but, while in the past they were a
minority, they are now a majority. Therefore, they are no longer forced to defend
their privileges by promoting social mobility: they can afford immobility. Such

historical-social conditions have led in all western countries to the emergence of a what has been labelled an underclass,[28] a more or less extended social sub-class, often ethnically defined, deprived of legitimate access to available economic and social resources. It is depicted as dangerous and felt as a threat to urban security. There might be cynical joy in seeing how power finally drops the mask of the rhetoric of equality, but what we call (legal) civilisation is but a collection of masks everyone is supposed to wear, above all, the state leviathan.

Notes

1 I'm grateful to Richard Bellamy, Danilo Zolo, Monia Coralli, Francesco Vertova, Raffaella Tucci and Miriam Aziz for their comments on a previous version of this essay.

2 D. Garland, 'The Limits of the Sovereign State. Strategies of Crime Control in Contemporary Society', *British Journal of Criminology*, 4 (1987), pp. 445–71.

3 Z. Bauman, *Globalization: The Human Consequences* (Cambridge, Polity Press, 1998).

4 L. Wacquant, *Les prisons de la misère* (Paris, Raisons d'Agir, 1999).

5 E. Gellner, *Culture, Identity,and Politics* (Cambridge, Cambridge University Press, 1987).

6 A. Scott, 'Globalization: Social Process or Political Rhetoric?', in A. Scott (ed.), *The Limits of Globalization* (London, Routledge, 1997).

7 C. Offe, *Modernity and the State: East, West* (Cambridge, Polity Press, 1996), pp. vii, ix, 37.

8 Bauman, *Globalization*, p. 67.

9 Bauman, *Globalization*, p. 68.

10 C. Beccaria, *On Crime and Punishment and Other Writings*, ed. R. Bellamy (Cambridge, Cambridge University Press, 1995); H.L.A. Hart, *Punishment and Responsibility: Essays in the Philosophy of Law* (Oxford, Clarendon Press, 1968); J. Rawls, 'Two Concepts of Rules', *Philosophical Review*, 54 (1955), pp. 4–13.

11 M. Foucault, *Discipline and Punishment: The Birth of the Prison* (Harmondsworth, Penguin, 1977).

12 G. Rusche and O. Kirchheimer, *Punishment and Social Structure* (New York, Russell and Russell, 1968).

13 P. Costa, *Il progetto giuridico* (Milano, Giuffré, 1974), pp. 357–78.

14 R. Martison, 'What Works? – Questions and Answers about Prison Reform', *The Public Interest*, 35 (1974).

15 R. Castel, 'From Dangerous to Risk', in G. Burchell, C. Cordon and P. Miller (eds), *The Foucault Effect. Studies in Governmentality* (London, Harvester, 1991), p. 288.

16 Wilson at the beginning of the 1970s wrote *Thinking About Crime* (New York, Vintage, 1971), which became a sort of bible of New Right criminology. He was adviser for security for USA president Ronald Reagan.

17 J.Q. Wilson and G. Kelling, 'Broken Windows. The Police and Neighborhood Safety', *Atlantic Monthly*, March (1982).

18 A. De Giorgi, *Zero Tolleranza. Strategie e pratiche della società di controllo* (Roma, DeriveApprodi, 2000), pp. 106–7.

19 H.L.A. Hart, 'Social Solidarity and the Enforcement of Morals' (first published 1968), in H.L.A. Hart, *Essays in Jurisprudence and Philosophy* (Oxford, Clarendon Press, 1983), pp. 248–62.

20 In another article, in 1989, Wilson and Kelling write: 'Like it or not, the police are about the only city agency that makes house calls around the clock. And like it or not, the public defines broadly what it thinks of as public order, and holds the police responsible for maintaining that order'. Lord Devlin, the target of Hart's polemics, at least entrusted jurors with this 'defining' role (see P. Devlin, *The Enforcement of Morals* (Oxford, Oxford University Press, 1965)).

21 F. Ewald, 'Insurance and Risk', in G. Burchell, C. Cordon and P. Miller (eds), *The Foucault Effect: Studies in Governmentality* (London, Harvester, 1991); De Giorgi, *Zero Tolleranza*.

22 H. Kemshall, *Reviewing Risk. A Review of Research on the Assessment and Management of Risk and Dangerousness: Implications for Policy and Practice in the Probation Service* (Croydon, Report for the Home Office, Research and Statistics Directorate, 1996), p. 35.

23 Ewald, 'Insurance and Risk', p. 195.

24 J. Floud, W. Young, *Dangerousness and Criminal Justice, Cambridge Studies in Criminology XLVII*, ed. Sir L. Radzinowicz (London, Heinemann, 1981); a comment by the author, Jean Floud, was published under the same title as the 'Report' in the *British Journal of Criminology*, 22:3 (1982), pp. 213–28.

25 Castel, 'From Dangerous to Risk', pp. 294–5.

26 P. Gloz, *Manifest für eine neue europäische Linke* (Berlin, Wolf Jobst Siedler, 1985).

27 J.K. Galbraith, *The Culture of Contentment* (Harmondsworth, Penguin, 1993).

28 The notion of *underclass* was made the centre of recent criminological debate by W.J. Wilson, *The Truly Disadvantaged* (Chicago, University of Chicago Press, 1987). It has, however, illustrious ancestors such as E.H. Sutherland's theory of differential associations (*Criminology* (Philadelphia, Lippincott, 1924)), C.D. Shaw and H.D. McKay's ecological theory of social disorganisation (*Juvenile Delinquency and Urban Areas* (Chicago, University of Chicago Press, 1942)) and the theories of cultural conflict.

7
Welfare and social exclusion

Bill Jordan

Introduction

Political theory has recently responded to the central questions about redistributive welfare systems – their justification, and the institutional means for implementing them – raised by the political economy of the past twenty-five years. In the post-war period, the consensus around sustaining minimum standards of income, health, education and housing assumed an entitlement to such guarantees (social rights) by members born into national communities of fate (citizens). Rawls in turn built these assumptions into his theory of justice, which provided a liberal endorsement for social democratic policies.[1] His communitarian critics of the 1980s,[2] while lamenting the decline of family, associational and religious life, did not fundamentally question the nature of the political community itself, or the duties its members owed each other.[3]

Meanwhile in the real world, the political agenda was being set by libertarians,[4] with welfare states as their primary targets. In their emphasis on individual freedom, and the capacity of (global) markets to maximise this (while simultaneously optimising economic outcomes), they raised the possibility of self-governing communities of choice – selected by their members for the bundle of collective goods they offered and the tax rate this required. This challenge has provoked what might be called a post-libertarian liberalism, and a post-libertarian communitarianism, both of which attempt to supply political principles under which redistributive welfare provision for citizens can be justified. Yet as the work of Van Parijs and Etzioni respectively show, these analyses may not in practice be as irreconcilable as they appear at first sight to be. This chapter traces the transition from welfare to social exclusion sketched above, and the various theoretical responses it has elicited.

1 Communities of choice

The idea that political justice should deal in issues about the distribution of roles and resources, presupposes a political community which corresponds to an economic system for production and exchange. Within a closed system of co-operation, conceived as a kind of organism with interdependent parts, with each member's life chances affected by the actions of all others, it makes sense to ask questions about how burdens and benefits should distributed, and to apply a single system of rules to all members of this clearly bounded community. Both liberal political theory (from Mill to Rawls) and the neo-Hegelian, Progressive Catholic and communitarian traditions (from T.H. Green to Walzer) developed arguments for softening and embedding capitalism. The concept of social justice emerged in both at the start of the twentieth century,[5] and justified institutions for the democratic modification for market outcomes, on utilitarian, maximin or common good grounds.

Such ideas make less sense in a global economy, where citizens' life chances are strongly influenced by transnational forces, and where they often have investments in other countries, or are employed by international corporations or work abroad. In such a world, it is far harder to devise a coherent version of politico-economic membership, or to justify a system of redistribution. For example, if industrial capitalists are free to close factories in the UK or Germany, and reinvest in new plants in China or Poland (for the sake of global productive efficiency, from which all ultimately gain, and low-income Chinese and Polish workers gain immediately), who – if anyone – should compensate redundant British or German workers? Perhaps the Chinese or Polish governments might owe the British or German part of their economic gain, but there is no institutional mechanism for paying this. And, in any case, there are also British and German citizens working in China and Poland, but paying taxes on their earnings in the UK or Germany.

All these developments point towards a new version of social politics, very different from the consensus around welfare collectivism that prevailed in the post-war era all over the advanced capitalist world and in much of the developing one. In the 'golden age of welfare states',[6] it was taken for granted that citizens would look to nation-states for protection from the contingencies of the life cycle and the arbitrary outcomes of the labour market. The bigger and stronger the state, the more it was able to require capital and labour to submit to its redistributive plans, the more reliable was this protection, and the better the welfare dividend. But if states can no longer reliably offer this kind of protection, and if citizen-consumers can get better welfare returns in the global marketplace, then states must compete with each other to attract members and their resources, must tax and redistribute and provide only by agreement, and must clarify the terms of access and exit as well as those of voice.

Indeed, the institutional landscapes of almost all polities have been redesigned, to a greater or lesser extent, in the past twenty years to take account of this dynamic. The other side of the libertarian agenda, with its promotion of market freedoms, was the public choice programme, which reformed the public infrastructure as a space for rational economic action. Following the trail blazed by Tiebout,[7] whose model of governance postulated small cities competing for mobile residents in order to ensure the efficient supply of local collective goods, the theory of 'fiscal federalism' has been deployed to break up national monopolies over welfare provision and to establish competing authorities (or contracted commercial providers) for each of the social services.[8] In this new environment, voting with the feet – by moving to another jurisdiction – becomes the public choice equivalent of market preference and consumer sovereignty.

The declared aim of these approaches has been to hold down taxation and 'tame the Leviathan' of central government,[9] but their effects have been most strongly felt by the poor. The theory of 'clubs'[10] assumes that individuals have different incomes and tastes, and that the efficiency savings that come with mobility are best achieved when groups who share the costs of collective goods are homogeneous. 'The rich tend to want to be away from the poor, but the poor want to be in the same jurisdiction as the rich . . . There may be a tendency for zoning on the part of high-income groups to exclude the poor.'[11]

Some theorists have gone as far as to postulate self-governing, consensual territorial communities, with fully sovereign individual members (modelled on Locke's theory of moral autonomy, property, political authority and governance).[12] In practical terms, there is some evidence of the emergence of such 'private' communities, for instance in Israeli settlements, in 'gated communities' of white South Africans, and all over the U.S.A.[13] Although they still rely on central and local authorities to provide certain goods and services (usually defence and legal order), they offer applicants specific packages of collective amenities, including schools, health clinics, residential care homes and other facilities, provided they can pay the asking price for houses, and the service charges.

This raises important issues about the appropriateness of nation-states as political units under evolving global economic conditions. After all, the present system of nation-states finally came into being after intense competition between these and empires, city-states and city-leagues,[14] in the mid-seventeenth century. Nation-states adopted a concept of exclusive territorial sovereignty which was quite different from the versions prevailing in any of these other units. They succeeded because they were better able to create unified economies (with reduced transaction costs) to build legal systems, to mobilise their subjects for war and to empower each other through international treaties. None of these advantages may continue under present global conditions, though it will take a long time for the power of national political systems to break down.

Two aspects of national political authority are likely to be jealously guarded – control over entry by foreigners, and control over the redistribution of income. But even these might be adapted to be more consistent with the formation of communities of choice. On the one hand, nation-states might enable such communities to grant access to the workers they require, for efficient provision of the services members choose. Selective immigration by foreign workers (not granted welfare rights during their stay) could create a category of mobile employee that such communities might recruit at low cost. On the other hand, the state would retain responsibility for its increasingly totalitarian control over the lives of those citizens too poor (in terms of earning power) or too costly (in terms of health and welfare needs) to find a place in any community of choice. Hence the public sector could become, as it were, a 'community of fate'[15] for these outsiders, in which the regimes imposed by state officials would resemble the pre-war Poor Law, or (ironically) the conditions under state socialism, with compulsory labour as a condition for benefits, and little freedom for those receiving services.

So, a possible vision of a re-feudalised mid-twenty-first-century society emerges. Sovereignty has been divided between a number of authorities, all of which exercise some jurisdiction over the same territory. For most purposes and most citizens, the unit of membership and governance is the self-selecting and self-ruling community, which sets its own tax rates and determines its own form and level of public services. However, another authority (perhaps the nation-state) deals with the population who lack access to such communities, maybe through something like the Panopticon Villages foreseen by Jeremy Bentham.[16] *[margin note: liberalist thinker]* Finally, a supranational government deals with issues of migration, guaranteeing or supply of mobile workers between communities to staff essential services, and meet labour shortages. Of course, individuals might come under the jurisdiction of any of these at different periods of their lives. One pattern, for instance, might be a period as a migrant worker, which (if successful) would lead to entry into a self-governing community as a citizen, or (if unsuccessful) into the Panopticon sector as a pauper. *[margin note: Type of prison designed by Bentham. The prisoners can't tell if they are being observed or not]*

Such developments are foreshadowed in emerging political economy and social policy. The emphasis on conditionality and obligation for claimants and beneficiaries, and the popular pressure for increasingly tough enforcement, all point towards the Panopticon state. Meanwhile, European governments increasingly pursue a dual policy on immigration, presenting a Fortress front to asylum seekers (who are processed in camps, hulks or prisons), while actively encouraging migrants with skills required by their domestic economies, by giving them various forms of time-limited work permits. For example, the Irish government is currently running a television advertisement to recruit 50,000 workers in central Europe, and the UK minister for immigration has announced a spectacular U-turn on 'economic migration' (formerly a synonym for 'bogus asylum-seeking')[17] by stating:

> As with other aspects of globalisation, there are potentially huge economic benefits for Britain if it is able to adapt to the new environment. We are in competition for the brightest and best talents . . . Britain has always been a nation of migrants . . . Many immigrants, from all over the world, have been very successful here, bringing economic benefits to Britain as a whole . . . The evidence shows that economically driven migration can bring substantial overall benefits both for growth and economy.[18]

From an efficiency standpoint, such developments might have much to recommend them; but it is difficult to see how they can be justified from the perspective of equity. How do they stand up to scrutiny according to the criteria of social justice?

2 Social exclusion

As a response to the ideas and real-world developments identified in the previous section there have been attempts to redefine social justice as the basis for national welfare systems. Instead of a Rawlsian contract between all citizens guaranteeing social entitlements, these postulate contracts between the state and individual citizens, defining the responsibilities of each in welfare issues.[19] On the one hand, those who receive assistance or services of any kind are required to demonstrate either reciprocal efforts towards independence, or a 'genuine' incapacity. Such obligations rest ultimately on the duty not to burden one's fellow citizens unnecessarily,[20] by passing on costs that morally should be borne by the individual or family.[21] On the other hand, citizens have the right to expect the state to reach the quality standards and performance measures set by the commercial sector in its provision of benefits and services. Instead of shaping the market, by identifying the public goods undersupplied by commercial interests, and redistributing resources for the sake of equity, the state is required to submit itself to market disciplines, and to please 'the demanding, sceptical, citizen-consumer'.[22]

In many ways, these new approaches adapt to the opportunities for individual mobility and choice in a globalised environment. As a recent UK government policy document acknowledged:

> Society has become more demanding . . . First, confidence in the institutions of government and politics has tumbled. Second, expectations of service quality and convenience have risen – as with the growth of 24-hour banking – but public services have failed to keep up with these developments; their duplication, inefficiency, and unnecessary complexity should not be tolerated. Third, as incomes rise, people prefer to own their homes and investments.[23]

Already, the UK government has been forced to look abroad for staff to meet these demands. The largest occupational group recruited from overseas under its new policies, noted above, has not been computer experts but nurses,[24] while teachers and social workers also figure prominently. The state itself, like the communities of choice it contains, must attract temporary workers who are not citizens in order to supply public services.

However, the most significant shift has been in policies for 'activation' of working-age claimants, changing benefits systems 'from safety nets to trampolines'.[25] Pioneered in the USA, the UK, Australia and New Zealand, these have now been adopted in almost all European countries, including those with such entrenched social protection systems as Denmark and the Netherlands.[26] Theorists in turn have used the idea of social exclusion to advocate an approach to social justice that sees increased labour-market participation as the key to equal citizenship, in the face of mass long-term unemployment, and the emergence of a significant 'underclass' of 'welfare dependents'.[27] As Anthony Giddens puts it: 'the new politics defines equality as inclusion and inequality as exclusion . . . inclusion refers in its broadest sense to citizenship, to the civil and political rights and obligations that all members of society should have . . . It also refers to opportunities and to involvement in the public space'.[28] He goes on to suggest that 'exclusion is not about gradations of inequality, but about the mechanisms that act to detach groups from the social mainstream'.[29] This implies that welfare systems should focus on restoring them to employability and employment. 'The cultivation of human potential should as far as possible replace "after the event" redistribution';[30] hence the aim is, as the New Labour government puts it, to 'rebuild the [welfare] system around work and security. Work for those who can, security for those who cannot'.[31] Inclusion consists in equipping claimants for a competitive labour market, and reforming the tax-benefit system to 'make work pay'.

This shift reflects the success of libertarian theories in changing the social policy agenda of the 1980s and early 1990s, when the welfare state's 'rigidities' and 'barriers' came to be seen as the problem to be addressed, and its version of equality dismissed as a 'mirage' (now in Gordon Brown's words 'a socialist nightmare'). In the Anglo-Saxon countries it implies that, redistributive systems should focus on 'hardworking families with children' through tax credits,[32] targeted on the working poor, and leave them to work their own way out of poverty and exclusion. However, this addresses only one part of the dynamic by which citizens are relegated to the margins of society or the care of the state.

A fundamental tenet of the New Labour orthodoxy is that individuals and households must be free to exercise choice over welfare goods, and to improve their relative position through their own efforts. Equality of opportunity (a key New Labour value) implies social and residential mobility for the sake of efficiency and equity. But such mobility does not follow random patterns; citizens in pursuit of 'positional advantage'[33] move to more favoured residential districts, with better public facilities, and cluster around the best schools, health clinics, care homes and hospitals. In this way, society organises itself (through citizens 'voting with their feet') into homogeneous districts, where residents of like incomes congregate. Through residential polarisation of this kind, communities of choice make up the mainstream of society, while those unable to move, because they cannot afford the housing costs, remain in impoverished communities of fate on the margins (inner city ghettos or outer city social housing estates).

Furthermore, in the UK the Thatcher–Major reforms of the social services facilitated these developments. Under such new arrangements as the devolution of budgets to local units and the purchaser-provider split, schools, hospitals and care homes have an interest in attracting high-yield, low-cost pupils, patients and residents, and excluding low-yield, high-cost ones.[34] Thus even public sector health and welfare facilities reinforce the tendency for the highest income citizens to gain exclusive membership of the best (private) social service amenities, while strategic action by middle-income groups produces a public sector hierarchy (or league table) closely corresponding to the income levels of service users. In this way, state-funded services come to operate as 'clubs',[35] with strong professional interests in exclusionary practices; New Labour funding and regulatory systems tend to strengthen these pressures, and give even greater opportunities and incentives for citizens (including government ministers) to seek those schools or hospitals within the state sector that produce the best outcomes, even when this involves high transport or other transaction costs. At the other end of the scale, a fund-holding general practitioner practice in a deprived area of Edinburgh was recently advised by a firm of consultants it employed to devise the most efficient primary care strategy for its neighbourhood to get rid of all its current patients, and attract some better-off ones.

Exclusions of this kind cannot be overcome by national policies focused on increasing labour-market participation. The logic of collective action operates in such a way that, in the absence of the restraints on such strategic action as were exercised under post-war welfare states, citizens will group together in narrower mutualities for the sake of the shared benefits they can produce. These interdependencies are necessarily exclusive, because their benefits stem from the sharing of costs among members, and rely on each member making the necessary contribution to the association.[36] And interdependencies are formed because of members' common interests in gaining positional advantage over, or extracting 'rents' (monopolistic gains) from, those who remain outside the charmed circle of their exclusive interactions. Policies which promote low-skilled work do nothing to challenge these forms of exclusion; rather, they subsidise members of communities of choice to employ outsiders from communities of fate in service roles. This is recognised in the UK government's assessment of its measures to tackle unemployment in deprived neighbourhoods (the Employment Zones and Action Teams). They are 'identifying suitable vacancies in neighbouring areas and bringing the two together'. Additionally, they are tackling barriers to employment, including funding for transport to enable people to access nearby vacancies.[37] In other words, residents of poor districts will be required to work in more affluent ones, to serve the needs of communities of which they are not, and probably never will be, members. This is not inclusion.

Furthermore, the institutional and financial changes that have allowed (or encouraged) public sector schools, hospitals and care homes to operate as 'clubs' further reinforce these disadvantages. The economic theory of clubs[38] holds that members act together to internalise some of the costs of their association, and to externalise others by ensuring that they are borne by outsiders. Poor people not only endure the highest risks and costs connected with such social ills as pollution, the degeneration of urban infrastructure, housing squalor and social disorganisation; they also receive the worst in education, health care and social services, because higher-income groups act to attract most funding and the best professional staff for their facilities.

However, poor people have not been passive or acquiescent as these processes unfolded; they have developed individual, group and community strategies of resistance to offset their disadvantaged position. Research has shown how they countered the insecurities of the labour market (casualisation, falling wages, deteriorating conditions) and the means-tested benefits system (the delays and disentitlements of an increasingly complex and conditional process) by combining off-the-books work for cash with long-term claiming.[39] By deploying the covert 'weapons of the weak',[40] male networks exchanged information, traded in contraband or illicit drugs,[41] or resorted to petty crime and hustling, while female networks supplied informal order and mutual support.[42] In these ways, communities of fate evolved their own forms of collective action, at odds with those of mainstream society, filling the vacuum in their districts left by the withdrawal of the market and the state.

3 Theories of social justice

The libertarian challenge to liberal and communitarian political theorists over welfare and social exclusion is to reconstruct a convincing version of social justice – one which retains the appealing aspects of individual autonomy, but deals with its undesirable social consequences. Both schools of thought have started from a critique of the part played by *rights* in libertarian accounts of justice, where individuals are entitled to do what they want not only with themselves, but with 'whatever external objects they own by virtue of an uninterrupted chain of voluntary transactions starting from some initial unrestricted private appropriation of objects previously unowned'.[43]

In the communitarian response, this critique argues that rights must always be balanced by responsibilities in any adequate account of a just society. The analysis draws on interactions within families, informal groups and voluntary associations, in which reciprocal exchanges are the stuff of co-operation for the common good. This is, of course, to be expected, since communitarians recommend that these should be the basic units of society, with the public authority acting only when they prove insufficient. As Etzioni puts it: 'First, people have a moral responsibility to take care of themselves . . . the second line of responsibility lies with those closest to the person, including kin, friends, neighbours and other community members . . . As a rule any community ought to be expected to do the best it can to take care of its own.'[44]

On the face of it, this corresponds to the emergence of communities of choice, and justifies their exclusivity in terms of the voluntary nature of their collective provision. Since active participation in the meeting of social needs is a requirement of this version of social justice, such communities promote the good society. Like other communitarians, Etzioni focuses on the advantages of civil society organisations running schools and care facilities in each locality. However, this implies that both welfare provision and social inclusion fall within the province of moral obligation, binding individuals to particular groups through specific shared values, and moving them to contribute to the good of all.

But in the real world of communities of choice, such needs as education, health and social care are usually met by paid staff, and already in many cities public service professionals are single, short-term immigrants, recruited because indigenous staff with families cannot afford to live there on their pay. And communitarians are also remarkably coy about the coercion involved in welfare-to-work measures, which form the other part of recruitment to much low-paid social care work. In spite of the fact that his language of 'rights and responsibilities' was already being widely used in the USA and elsewhere to justify compulsion of claimants, Etzioni made no mention of this issue in *The Spirit of Community*. Instead, he resistricted himself to comments like, 'all people, no matter how disadvantaged or handicapped, should take some responsibility for themselves',[45] and 'honourable work contributes to the commonwealth and to the community's ability to fulfil its tasks'.[46]

In later work, Etzioni has suggested that we all have a duty not to burden our fellow citizens unnecessarily, and that this moral duty should be enforced by the state – but that claimants should not be cut off from benefits altogether.[47] Both the coercion of claimants to take employment, and the recruitment through these means of forced workers to meet social needs, seem to violate the principles of self-ownership and voluntary co-operation from which the benefits of community are supposed to stem.

The liberal response attacks the libertarian account of justice by pointing out that it is not only when rights are violated that freedom is restricted. Both internal and external endowments influence a person's range of choices, as do economic exploitation and political domination, even when these stem from circumstances which libertarians would deem 'rightful'. Hence Van Parijs concludes that 'any restriction of the opportunity set is relevant to the assessment of freedom'.[48] He goes on to argue that 'real freedom is not only a matter of having the right to do what one might want to do, but also of having the means for doing it',[49] and that 'real freedom-for-all . . . is all there is to social justice'.[50]

In order to fulfil the condition that each member of society should have the greatest possible opportunity to do what he or she might want to do, Van Parijs proposes an unconditional income for all (basic income), irrespective of their willingness to work, and at the highest sustainable level, subject to everyone's formal freedom.[51] Although most of this would be provided in cash, a 'significant fraction' would be supplied in kind, where it was 'unanimously wanted and cheaper to deliver free of charge'.[52] He justifies the substantial redistribution that all this would require by treating the 'job assets' of labour-market insiders as 'employment rents', gained at the expense of outsiders, thus standing on its head the notion of a moral obligation to take paid work.[53]

Although the basic income proposal by no means commands general support among liberals, it nonetheless has attracted considerable interest among political theorists. Van Parijs's analysis is post-libertarian, in the sense that it does not postulate a society that is a system of social and economic co-operation, nor is his concept of social justice based on reciprocal obligations among members. However, the justification for redistribution does rest on the notion of a *society* that is bounded. For instance, in rebutting the libertarian version of justice, Van Parijs points out that, in a society consisting of an island owned by one person, and where it was too expensive or difficult for other residents to leave, the former could exploit and dominate all the latter.[54] Lack of exit options define injustice in this case.

But one of the problems of social justice in a globalised environment is that some of the inhabitants of any real-world society would be able to leave it at relatively low cost, whereas others would not (either because they lacked the resources, or because of strong interdependencies with other residents). This is how the distinction between communities of choice and fate arises. Furthermore, the exit option open to owners of capital limits the scope for redistribution. Critics of the basic income proposal point out that, unless the level of income paid is sufficient for subsistence, the scheme loses many of the advantages for social justice claimed by Van Parijs. A small basic income would still leave those with low earning power open to exploitation, and would not give employers incentives to use their services efficiently. Without a strong state (by implication, one whose legitimacy rests on either a system of co-operation beneficial to all, or a moral consensus favouring the chosen principle for redistribution) the necessary contributions could not be collected – and the case for paying benefits to all without a requirement to work runs counter to popular moral intuitions.

Conclusions

In practical social policy terms the choice between conditional welfare-to-work approaches and the unconditional basic income principle is not as stark as the above analysis might suggest. The new politics of welfare in the USA and the UK is essentially concerned with an impasse that had developed during the Thatcher–Reagan years.[55] Poor people were unwilling to give up their strategies of combining benefits claims with various kinds of informal economic activity, and taxpayers were unwilling to contribute more to assist the poor until they gave them up. Welfare-to-work schemes reassure the latter that their taxes are focused on deserving claimants, while trying to give the former better incentives to take formal work.

But in the longer term, there is still an unresolved problem of how to include (that is, share the costs of sustaining) citizens whose labour power is not required for the economic efficiency of the productive unit. This 'surplus population' has constituted a thorny problem in political thought since Malthus;[56] if some citizens' needs fall as costs upon the rest of the community, even during their 'working' years, how then can their continuous maintenance be justified? The traditional solution – that they should be the responsibility of their families

– is scarcely viable when, as Malthus and others among his contemporaries[57] recognised, such individuals tend to be members of larger-than-average family units, all of whom made claims upon the public purse (the 'workless' households of New Labour hagiography).[58]

The new politics of welfare addresses this problem by investing in the human capital of this sector of the population (increased spending on education and training) and through the systematic subsidization, via tax credits, of its employment. The fact that this policy has not been wholly successful (despite consistent falls in unemployment) is advertised in the recruitment of overseas labour for important economic tasks – not only in high-tech sectors, or even just in health, education and social care, but also for such mundane tasks as fruit and vegetable picking.[59] The same trends can be seen all over the developed world. For example, in Germany, which spends DM45 billion on retraining unemployed people for labour market each year, there is increasing recruitment of central European guest workers for a similar range of tasks; and in the Czech and Polish republics, Ukrainians and Russians are imported to do manual work that citizens are now unwilling to take at the wages presently on offer. In other words, even in countries with extensive unemployment, neither compulsion nor retraining provides the most efficient means of supplying the labour power for performing society's necessary tasks.

This in turn poses a question about the most efficient and equitable division of labour in social reproduction work.[60] How much of it should be done by means of paid services and formal employment, and how much on an unpaid, informal basis, in families, kinship groups and neighbourhoods? Feminist theory (of citizenship and power relations)[61] is understandably suspicious of any tendencies to relegate such tasks to the private sphere, where women have traditionally been exploited and dominated by men.[62] But it asserts the importance of the politics of difference,[63] the relevant difference here being a preference for the informal and moral economy of care, or at least the right to choose how to combine access to the public sphere with participation in society's nurturing, civilising and socialising activities, outside formal employment.

Two problems are likely to present themselves sooner rather than later to governments of a New Labour stripe. The first is the problem of efficiency associated with social reproduction work, which forms an ever-growing sector of employment in advanced economies, but whose tasks (for instance, care of elderly and disabled people) are not susceptible to productivity improvements.[64] Although the success of Third Way programmes has been closely linked with expanding (often part-time and female) employment,[65] there must be limits to the extent to which this growth is consistent with the efficient use of labour power, especially when a large proportion of such work requires subsidisation through tax credits.

The second is linked to the latter point; eventually, the inexorable rise in the rates of credits paid (or tax-free earnings allowed) to individuals in low-paid work will come to equal the value of the (price-linked) benefits paid to those outside the labour market, despite the latter being rigorously tested for being in 'genuine need'. Can it be equitable to pay no more to those who demonstrate unfitness for labour than to those quite capable of work, and actually earning? And is it right to penalise the many (housewives, volunteers, activists, students) who qualify for neither tax credits nor benefits? These questions point towards a move in the direction of something like a 'participation income',[66] for which the relevant test is social engagement rather than employment – and the administrative complexities and transaction costs of this point further, eventually to an unconditional basic income for all citizens.[67] This is not the direction in which New Labour policies have started, but it may be the one in which they will eventually, by a circuitous route, reluctantly stumble. Only this principle would allow low-earning workers the same choices about how to combine paid and unpaid work as are enjoyed by mainstream citizens.

This raises another question: to what extent does the concept of community provide an alternative approach to the problems of deprived districts, and a more plausible model of social inclusion? Here again, the new politics of welfare is ambiguous and ambivalent. Its emphasis on 'social and economic regeneration' (in the UK through such institutions as the Social Exclusion Unit, the Single Regeneration Budget and the New Deal for Communities) has hitherto been mainly top down and regulatory, focusing on the problems of areas such as crime, truancy, drugs, homelessness, and improving the housing stock. It has also (through programmes like the Employment Zones) up to now concentrated on creating formal employment, as much as possible in the private sector.[68] In order to promote self-help and the mobilisation of residents, motivated to act collectively to pursue a better quality of life in their districts, a different approach would be required. Instead of enforcing training or employment, a basic income, even at a modest level, would more readily facilitate community and cultural activism in projects which were not economically self-sustaining. And local social services, instead of being tied into the policing of standards for child protection, or rationing resources according to categories of risk, would be required to support and empower residents for participation in such projects. There is some evidence for the viability of this approach,[69] but it would be a major shift from current orthodoxies. It would also allow communitarian and basic income principles to be combined in novel ways.

These dilemmas are particular instances of the central political problem of the new welfare regimes. So far, they have gained electoral support by programmes for 'tough love'[70] – harsh, conditional, enforcement-orientated policies, in the name of taxpayers' requirements, but based on paternalistic interpretations of the long-term best interests of the poor. However, what David Blunkett (in an unconscious reference to Lenin) calls the 'working state' is not sustainable in this form. The bifurcation into communities of choice and communities of fate that results from the logic of exclusive strategic action will require more and more toughness, and less and less love (as the growth in the prison population already attests). Recruiting 'club servants'[71] from abroad to do the dirty work for the members of communities of choice smells strongly of racism, especially when they are granted temporary work permits, and denied all social rights. Panopticon surveillance and enforcement as members of a pauperised underclass is the alternative destination for our most vulnerable citizens, if the new politics of welfare cannot discover more creative and inclusive solutions to these issues.

Notes

1 J. Rawls, *A Theory of Justice* (Oxford, Oxford University Press, 1971).

2 A. MacIntyre, *After Virtue: A Study in Moral Theory* (London, Duckworth, 1981); M. Sandel, *Liberalism and the Limits of Justice* (Cambridge, Cambridge University Press, 1982); M. Walzer, *Spheres of Justice: A Defence of Pluralism and Equality* (Oxford, Blackwell, 1983); C. Taylor, *Sources of Self* (Cambridge, Cambridge University Press, 1989).

3 C. Taylor, 'Cross Purposes: The Liberal-Communitarian Debate', in N. Rosenblum (ed.), *Liberalism and the Modern Life* (Cambridge, MA, Harvard University Press, 1989); W. Kymlicka and W. Norman, 'Return of the Citizen: A Survey of Recent Work on Citizenship Theory', *Ethics*, 104:2 (1994), pp. 352–81.

4 R. Nozick, *Anarchy, State and Utopia* (Oxford, Blackwell, 1974); M. Friedman and R. Friedman, *Free to Choose* (Harmondsworth: Penguin, 1980); F. von Hayek, *The Constitution of Liberty* (Chicago, University of Chicago Press, 1960).

5 W. Willoughby, *Social Justice* (New York, Knopf, 1900); L.T. Hobhouse, *Elements of Social Justice* (London, Allen and Unwin, 1922); A. Vincent and R. Plant, *Philosophy, Politics and Citizenship: The Life and Thought of the British Idealists* (Oxford, Blackwell, 1984).

6 G. Esping-Andersen, *Welfare States in Transition: National Adaptations in Global Economies* (London, Sage, 1996).

7 C. Tiebout, 'A Pure Theory of Local Expenditures', *Journal of Political Economy*, 64 (1956), pp. 416–24.

8 See for instance D.E. Wildasin, *Urban Public Finance* (Chicago, Harcourt Press, 1986); J.M. Buchanan and C.J. Goetz, 'Efficiency Limits of Fiscal Mobility: An Assessment of the Tiebout Model', *Journal of Public Economics*, 1 (1972), pp. 25–58; G.M. Myers, 'Optimality, Free Mobility and the Regional Authority in a Federation', *Journal of Public Economics*, 43 (1990), pp. 107–21.

9 W.E. Oates, *Fiscal Federalism* (New York, Harcourt Brace Jovanovich, 1972); W.E. Oates, 'Searching for Leviathan: An Empirical Study', *American Economic Review*, 75 (1985), pp. 748–57; J.K. Brueckner, 'Property-Value Maximisation and Efficiency', *Joural of Urban Economics*, 14 (1983), pp. 1–15.

10 J.M. Buchanan, 'An Economic Theory of Clubs', *Economica*, 32 (1965), pp. 1–14.

11 J. Cullis and P. Jones, *Public Finance and Public Choice: Analytical Perspectives* (London, McGraw Hill, 1994), pp. 297–300.

12 J. Locke, *Two Treatises of Government* (first published 1698), ed. P Laslett (Cambridge, Cambridge University Press, 1967), especially *First Treatise*, ss. 1–12.

13 F. Foldvary, *Public Goods and Private Communities: The Market Provision of Social Services* (Aldershot, Edward Elgar, 1994).

14 H. Spruyt, *The Nation State and Its Competitors* (Princeton, NJ, Princeton University Press, 1995).

15 C.E. Marske, *Communities of Fate: Readings in the Social Organization of Risk* (Lanham, VA, University Press of America, 1991).

16 L.J. Hume, *Bentham and Bureaucracy* (Cambridge, Cambridge University Press, 1981).

17 Home Office, *Fairer, Faster and Firmer – a Modern Approach to Immigration and Asylum*, Cm 4018 (London, Stationery Office, 1998).

18 B. Roche, 'Migration in a Global Economy', speech to the Institute for Public Policy Research Conference, 8 September 2000.

19 E. Erikson and J. Weigärd, 'The End of Citizenship? New Roles Challenging the Political Order', in C. McKinnon and I. Hampsher-Monk (eds), *The Demands of Citizenship* (London, Continuum, 2000), pp. 274–90.

20 P. 6, 'Can the Obligations in Welfare-to-Work Schemes be Morally Justified?' (Glasgow, Department of Government, University of Strathclyde, 2000).

21 Department of Social Security (DSS), *A New Contract for Welfare*, Cm. 3805 (London, Stationery Office, 1998), p. 31.

22 DSS, *A New Contract for Welfare*, p. 16.

23 DSS, *A New Contract for Welfare*, p. 16.

24 J. Salt, 'Labour-Market Recruitment to the UK', paper given at a Home Office Conference, 'Bridging the Information Gaps: Research in Asylum and Immigration in the UK', National Liberal Club, London, 21 March 2001.

25 R.H. Cox, 'From Safety Nets to Trampolines: Labour-Market Activation in the Netherlands and Denmark', *Governance: An International Journal of Politics and Administration*, 11:4 (1998), pp. 397–414.

26 R.H. Cox, *The Consequences of Welfare Reform: How Conceptions of Social Rights are Changing* (Norman, OK, Department of Political Science, University of Oklahoma, 1999); A. Hemerijck, 'Prospects for Effective Social Citizenship in an Age of Structural Inactivity', in C. Crouch, K. Eder and D. Tambini (eds), *Citizenship, Markets and the State* (Oxford, Oxford University Press, 2000), pp. 134–70.

27 L.M. Mead, *Beyond Entitlement: The Social Obligations of Citizenship* (New York, Free Press, 1986); R. Lister, 'From Equality to Social Inclusion: New Labour and the Welfare State', *Critical Social Policy*, 18:55 (1998), pp. 217–29.

28 A. Giddens, *The Third Way: The Renewal of Social Democracy* (Cambridge, Polity Press, 1998), pp. 102–3.

29 Giddens, *The Third Way*, p. 104.

30 Giddens, *The Third Way*, p. 101.

31 T. Blair, Preface, *A New Contract for Welfare* (CSS), Cm 3805 (London, Stationery Office, 1998), pp. iii–iv.

32 G. Brown, 'Why Labour is Still Loyal to the Poor', *Guardian*, 2 August 1997.

33 F. Hirsch, *The Social Limits to Growth* (London, Routledge and Kegan Paul, 1977).

34 B. Jordan, *A Theory of Poverty and Social Exclusion* (Cambridge, Polity Press, 1996), chs 4 and 5; B. Jordan, *The New Politics of Welfare: Social Justice in a Global Context* (London, Sage, 1998), ch. 4.

35 Jordan, *A Theory of Poverty and Social Exclusion*, ch. 2; J.M. Buchanan, 'An Economic Theory of Clubs', pp. 1–14; D. Mueller, *Public Choice II* (Cambridge, Cambridge University Press, 1989), pp. 153–4; D.A. Starrett, *Foundations of Public Economics* (Cambridge, Cambridge University Press, 1988), pp. 48–52.

36 Jordan, *A Theory of Poverty and Social Exclusion*, ch. 2; Buchanan, 'An Economic Theory of Clubs'.

37 HM Treasury, *Pre-Budget Report* (London, Stationery Office, 2000), s. 4.33.

38 Buchanan, 'The Economic Theory of Clubs'; Mueller, *Public Choice II*, pp. 152–4.

39 E. Evason and R. Woods, 'Poverty, Deregulation of Labour Markets and Benefit Fraud', *Social Policy and Administration*, 29:1 (1995), pp. 40–54; B. Jordan, S. James, H. Kay and M. Redley, *Trapped in Poverty? Labour-Market Decisions in Low-Income Households* (London, Routledge, 1992); K. Rowlingson, C. Whyley, T. Newburn and R. Berthoud, *Social Security Fraud* (London, HMSO, 1997).

40 J. Scott, *Weapons of the Weak: Everyday Forms of Peasant Resistance* (New Haven, CT, Yale University Press, 1985).

41 B. Jordan and A. Travers, 'The Informal Economy – a Case Study in Unrestrained Competition', *Social Policy and Administration*, 32:3 (1998), pp. 292–306.

42 B. Campbell, *Goliath: Britain's Dangerous Places* (London, Methuen, 1993).

43 P. Van Parijs, *Real Freedom for All: What (If Anything) Can Justify Capitalism?* (Oxford, Clarendon Press, 1995), p. 14.

44 A. Etzioni, *The Spirit of Community: Rights, Responsibilities and the Communiarian Agenda* (London, Fontana, 1995), pp. 144–6.

45 Etzioni, *The Spirit of Community*, p. 160.

46 Etzioni, *The Spirit of Community*, p. 264.

47 A. Etzioni, *The Third Way to a Good Society* (London, Demos, 2000), p. 31; see also A. Etzioni, *The New Golden Rule: Community and Morality in a Democratic Society* (London, Profile Books, 1997) and A. Etzioni, *The Limits of Privacy* (New York, Basic Books, 1999).

48 Van Parijs, *Real Freedom for All*, p. 23.

49 Van Parijs, *Real Freedom for All*, p. 4.

50 Van Parijs, *Real Freedom for All*, p. 5.

51 Van Parijs, *Real Freedom for All*, pp. 30–1.

52 Van Parijs, *Real Freedom for All*, p. 31.

53 Van Parijs, *Real Freedom for All*, chs 4 and 5, especially ss. 4.4–4.7.

54 Van Parijs, *Real Freedom for All*, p. 14.

55 B. Jordan, *The New Politics of Welfare*; B. Jordan with C. Jordan, *Social Work and the Third Way: Tough Love as Social Policy* (London, Sage, 2000).

56 T. Malthus, *An Essay in the Principle of Population as It Affects the Improvement of Society* (London, J. Johnson, 1798).

57 S.G. Checkland and E.O.A. Checkland (eds), *The Poor Law Report of 1834* (Harmondsworth, Penguin, 1974); E.P. Thompson, *The Making of the English Working Class* (Harmondsworth, Penguin, 1965).

58 DSS, *A New Contract for Welfare*, pp. 9–10.

59 Roche, 'Migration in a Global Economy', pp. 2–3.

60 B. Jordan, P. Agulnik, D. Burbidge and S. Duffin, *Stumbling Towards Basic Income* (London, Citizens Income Study Centre, 2000), ch. 3; T. Iversen and A. Wren, 'Equality, Employment and Budgetary Restraint: The Trilemma of the Service Economy', *World Politics*, 50 (1998), pp. 507–46.

61 R. Lister, *Citizenship: Feminist Perspectives* (Basingstoke, Macmillan, 1997); R. Voet, *Feminism and Citizenship* (London, Sage, 1998).

62 J. Squires, 'Feminist Visions of Political Citizenship', in C. McKinnon and I. Hampsher-Monk (eds), *The Demands of Citizenship* (London, Continuum, 2000), pp. 35–50.

63 I.M. Young, *Justice and the Politics of Difference* (Princeton, NJ, Princeton University Press, 1990); A. Phillips, *Democracy and Difference* (Cambridge, Polity Press, 1993).

64 Jordan, Agulnik, Burbidge and Duffin, *Stumbling Towards Basic Income*, ch. 3.
65 G. Esping-Andersen, 'The Jobs-Equality Trade-Off', paper presented to the summer school on Welfare States in Transition, European University Institute, Florence, 8 July 1999; Iversen and Wren, 'Equality, Employment and Budgetary Restraint'.
66 A.B. Atkinson, *Public Economics in Action: The Basic Income/Flat Tax Proposal* (Oxford, Oxford University Press, 1995).
67 Jordan, Agulnik, Burbidge and Duffin, *Stumbling Towards Basic Income*.
68 Jordan with Jordan, *Social Work and the Third Way*.
69 M. Leonard, 'Informal Economic Activity: Strategies of Households and Communities', paper presented at 4th ESA Conference, 'Will Europe Work?', Amsterdam, 18–21 August 1999.
70 Jordan with Jordan, *Social Work and the Third Way*.
71 M. Breuer, T. Faist and B. Jordan, 'Collective Action, Migration and Welfare States', *International Sociology*, 10:4 (1995), pp. 369–86.

8
Legitimacy

Alan Cromartie

Introduction

All governments rely, at least in part, on the co-operation of the governed. The power of a simple despotism, exclusively dependent on the terror it evoked, would be restricted to activities that it could supervise in every detail. Even in rather primitive conditions, such a regime would be a feeble thing, so much so one would hesitate to say that it was *governing* its people; in more advanced societies, with complex divisions of labour among experts, it would be certain to collapse in days. Though hated alien conquerors have sometimes governed such societies, they have invariably had to work through an existing cultural apparatus, that is, through personnel and institutions which can secure obedience without the use of bribes or punishments. They have had to find ways of presenting their instructions as being *legitimate*.

A given command has legitimacy to the extent that it secures willing obedience even where it conflicts with the obvious interests of those commanded. The best known modern treatment of the concept is in the later writings of the great sociologist Max Weber (1864–1920). Weber approached legitimacy as a subcategory of 'domination', by which he meant 'the probability that certain specific commands (or all commands) will be obeyed by a given group of persons'. He noted that 'every genuine form of domination implies a minimum of voluntary compliance, that is, an *interest* (based on ulterior motives or genuine acceptance) in obedience'.[1] The probability of obedience thus rests upon the presence of motives to obey (including purely altruistic ones). But no relationship of domination is likely to depend indefinitely on a coincidence of interest:

> An order [that is, system of domination] which is adhered to from motives of pure expediency is generally much less stable than one upheld on a purely customary basis through the fact that the corresponding behaviour has become habitual. The latter is much the most common type of subjective attitude. But even this type of order is in turn much less stable than an order which enjoys the prestige of being considered binding, or, as it may be expressed, of 'legitimacy'.[2]

It is no doubt for this reason that 'domination' never limits itself to 'the appeal to affectual or material or ideal motives'. 'Every such system' also 'endeavours to establish and to cultivate the belief in its legitimacy.'[3]

Weber thus used the word 'legitimate' to characterise one type of domination: the type in which obedience is based in part on the belief that the command is binding. Weberian legitimacy is less an objective attribute of *powers*, entitling some person or persons to be obeyed, than the defining quality of one particular *power-situation*: a relationship in which obedience is partly explained by the attitude of the subordinate to the bare issuing of the instructions. The reason that Weber addressed this situation was that he studied social practices 'insofar as the acting individual attaches a subjective meaning to his behaviour';[4] legitimacy is the subjective meaning attached to the conscious acceptance of a relationship of domination.

Weber has long been famous for classifying legitimate domination into three categories, depending on whether obedience was based on a regard for the qualities of a leader (charismatic), for the sanctity of custom (traditional), or for the legality of a system of rules (bureaucratic). The moral basis of all three is purely arbitrary, but the eventual triumph of the last will be ensured by its efficiency. Though Weber's treatment of this rule-bound future has an oracular obscurity, he clearly felt hostility towards it, in part, no doubt, because bureaucracy is of its nature sterile. Bureaucracy can discipline the bureaucrat himself into acceptance of a professional ethos, but it cannot on its own supply the values by which a rounded human being lives. The modern world, which witnesses the victory of bureaucratic rule, will also see what Weber calls a modern 'polytheism', a moral anarchy of clashing values.[5]

If Weber is broadly correct, legitimacy might be said to fall outside the scope of political theory, if only because it seems to have no content that is susceptible of theorisation. Charismatic and traditional domination are fundamentally non-rational, while it seems that bureaucratic domination is not in a strict sense legitimate; it may persist by virtue of its sheer effectiveness in satisfying our material wants, but it cannot induce a *belief* that its orders are binding. There is, however, a history of trying to explain legitimacy. It is a history that begins when the reflective individual imagines herself as devoid of political ties and sets out to account for their existence. We speak about legitimacy because we can imagine authority as non-legitimate. Capacity to do this derives from a certain conception of our selves, one that excludes the possibility that selves are constituted by their shared activities. Political legitimacy (the subject of this chapter) only becomes a necessary concept when people can imagine human beings as neither governing nor being governed, because their intellectual starting-point is an image of completely separate selves; it consists, one might say, in whatever beliefs may glue selves back to states.

The heart of a legitimating theory is thus the self-conception of the individual. The problem can only arise if there is something in that self-conception detaching his identity from the idea of his obedience; it can only be solved if acceptance of subjection (in whatever form subjection locally takes) can be shown to be consistent with the way that the self is imagined. This suggests two important distinctions. A person who thinks of his state as a part of himself, experiencing his rulers' reverses as his own, has what might be called an 'identity-theory', as does a person who believes he is a natural slave, and therefore incomplete without a master; but to the extent that they construe these common situations as answering needs of pre-existent selves (in no sense *constituted* by subjection), they have 'legitimacy-theories'. These legitimacy-theories are successful if they are logical and *realised*: logical in that whatever characteristics the theories impute to the selves imply a belief that given commands are binding; realised in that the relevant self-conception attains sufficient plausibility to be embraced by actual individuals (a theory might be 'logical' without achieving plausibility to people of a given cultural background).

In fact, of course, the image of the self is likely to have features shaped by the experience of social life; legitimacy becomes possible because a self is pictured that has needs that present practices can satisfy. Our image of the self was shaped by a variety of practices; if legitimate authority seems elusive, it may be that those practices imparted inconsistent expectations.

1

Pre-modern Europeans still took government for granted. They devoted much time to discussing the characteristics of the ideal ruler, but they showed much less interest in justifying rulership in general; the very existence of people who could secure willing obedience was not yet seen as being problematic. Though Greek and Latin writers could imagine the coalescence of communities from isolated individuals, the primary purpose of such narratives was not to explain why governments enjoyed obedience, still less why they could be seen as deserving to do so. The most elaborate attempt to rationalise these assumptions is found in Aristotle's *Politics*. In this first recognisable work of political science, Aristotle of Stagira (384–322 BC) described the behaviour patterns of the inhabitants of city-states (*poleis*), the communities he saw as the natural endpoint of biological developments. He showed less interest in theorising the *supra*-political power by which non-Greeks were generally governed; although he was a Macedonian, who taught Alexander the Great (356–323 BC), he was not interested in his pupil's unnaturally distended polity. Because he was a theorist of small communities, he was able to take it for granted that citizens would have enough in common to make it possible to speak about a 'common good', including the good of mutual interaction by taking it in turns to rule and be ruled. But in any case, this good of interaction was not a need of individuals so much as a fulfilment of their natures; enjoyment of the practices that we call politics was seen as *constituting* human beings.

Thus Aristotle presupposed that somebody should govern; the problem of legitimacy simply did not arise, because co-ordination for a collective good was something that was part of being human. The ultimate source of legitimacy-theories was probably the bias towards individualism that was introduced by Christianity. Because the objective of Christians was salvation (in practice almost invariably conceived of as the avoidance of the pains of hell), political activities were inessential to their self-conception, and it was possible to hold that earthly governments were something contingently willed by Providence. Some Christians, some of the time, especially under the influence of Augustine (354–430), were thus enabled to see government as something extrinsic to humanity. But their type of legitimacy-theory demands for its realisation a homogeneous theistic culture of a kind that is no longer possible. The earliest legitimacy-theories with elements that we could hope to borrow date from the post-Renaissance period.

The first articulation of the problem in something resembling the form it is known today was in the political works of Thomas Hobbes (1588–1679). One explanation of his novel project was that he was facing a novel situation, in which legitimacy was required by the agent that he came to call 'the state'. During the Middle Ages, religious and cultural authority had been to some extent divorced from military and economic power, the former being located, in the main, in the international church. But from the early sixteenth century onwards, the rulers of many communities were forced to decide for themselves if their dominions should accept or repress some version of Protestant doctrine (almost all serious thinkers held that toleration was unthinkable). This meant the early modern polity was exercising a new kind of power: the power to judge the truth of moral teachings. Hobbes was the theorist of an institution that needed to decide between beliefs in order to impose them, through schools and the clergy, on every member of the population.

One reason that legitimacy was more of a problem for Hobbes than his precursors was thus his need to justify new types of government activity. But in any case a dogma about method helped to propel him in the same direction. He wanted to give an account of political life that would deserve the name of civil science, a 'science' being knowledge by means of which 'when we see how any thing comes about, upon what causes, and by what manner; when the like causes come into our power, we see how to make it produce the like effects'.[6] This 'knowledge of consequence' was 'not absolute, but conditional', embodied in statements of the form 'that if This be, That is; if This has been, That has been; if This shall be, That shall be: which is to know conditionally'.[7] To grasp the workings of a commonwealth was thus to grasp how its component parts, its human population, could jointly *cause* the whole phenomenon. Hobbes did not seriously maintain that human beings ever met as isolated equals, but his conception of a civil science dictated 'a need, not indeed to take the commonwealth apart, but to view it as taken apart, i.e. to understand correctly what human nature is like, and in what features it is suitable and in what unsuitable to construct a commonwealth'.[8]

The unsuitable features were more obvious. When seen in isolation, the members of a commonwealth were nothing but material mechanisms, whose 'life' was constituted by an endless succession of appetites and aversions. Contrary to what Aristotle thought, they were not naturally political; indeed their only shared and natural purpose was to continue to have appetites. In the absence of a state's authority, each of them would enjoy a liberty 'to use his own power, as he will himself, for the preservation of his own . . . Life; and consequently, of doing any thing, which in his own Judgement, and Reason, he shall conceive to be the aptest means thereunto'.[9] Under these circumstances, competition for scarce resources, mutual distrust and a competitive instinct known as 'glory' (the wish to do down others) were certain to drive these creatures into conflict, a conflict in which 'there is nothing he can make use of, that may not be a help unto him, in preserving his life against his enemies; it followeth that in such a condition, every man has a Right to everything'.[10] The only known means of escaping this condition was through a covenant (that is, a contractual arrangement in which one party has to trust the other). Only if human beings covenanted to lay down this unfettered liberty could they attain security and comfort, but nobody would act on such a contract unless they thought that it would be enforced upon the other parties. The solution was a covenant erecting a covenant-enforcer, the sovereign state, thus setting up conditions which made it rational for them to trust.

One possible reading of Hobbes holds that a truly sovereign state would be so terrifying that everyone would keep their covenants and follow its instructions. Hobbes certainly often maintained or implied that 'the Passion to be reckoned upon is Fear'.[11] He thought that it could override all other human motives and he explicitly maintained that 'excepting some generous natures, it is the only thing (where there is apparence of profit, or pleasure by breaking the Laws) that makes men keep them'.[12] But he was also well aware that something must be added to physical terror to make a commonwealth sustainable. The sovereign may be frightening, but he cannot be an ever-present threat to somebody not physically restrained. There was a clear distinction in Hobbesian thought between the position of someone who was temporarily at the sovereign's mercy (like someone who is captured in a war) and someone who is permanently subject. Thus captives 'kept in prison or bonds . . . have no obligation at all; but may break their bonds, or the prison; and kill, or carry away captive their Master, justly'.[13] Subjects, by contrast, are *obliged* to be obedient, 'which natural obligation, if men know not, they cannot know the Right of any Law the Sovereign maketh. And for the Punishment, they take it but for an act of Hostility, which, when they think they have strength enough, they will endeavour by acts of Hostility to avoid'.[14]

Thus if a Hobbesian commonwealth is to be feasible, then subjects need to know themselves to have an obligation: they need, in other words, to have legitimacy-beliefs. At times, Hobbes argues that to be obliged quite simply is to have performed a special kind of action, 'there being no Obligation on any man, which ariseth not from some Act of his own'.[15] On this view, only if one knows that one has performed such an act can one be said to know one's obligation.

This doctrine is frequently cited by theorists who hold that legitimacy is based upon consent, but it is worth remembering that Hobbes was easily convinced that someone had consented. As his conception of consent was perfectly consistent with overpowering fear, he presupposed a tacit consent to obey whenever a person with somebody else at his mercy allowed the latter corporal liberty. Thus the authority enjoyed by mothers (unless a subsequent contract intervened) derived from the fact that 'every man is supposed to promise obedience, to him, in whose power it is to save, or to destroy him'.[16]

In practice, then, the act Hobbes called 'consent' was something he imputed to anyone reduced to a state of obedience. A prudently constructed polity would no doubt encourage 'knowledge of obligation' by an insistence on *express* consent, but this type of completed historical act is not the theory's ultimate foundation. Consent is only binding because the institution of consenting has a tendency to favour self-preservation. Though it is true that in a state of war (the condition where we lack a common sovereign) we are inevitably driven to act ferociously, we are nonetheless bound to an inner disposition that favours sociable behaviour. This is evidently a type of obligation which cannot be deemed to arise from an act of our own, unless, that is, we are deemed to have consented to any type of action that we must consistently will, given we also will self-preservation.

The reason Hobbes found it so hard to make himself clear was probably that he could not explain how a self-interested automaton could make a binding promise. Hobbes was no doubt quite right to believe that somebody who is disposed to co-operate with others can be expected, other things being equal, to have a safer, more agreeable life than someone who is not; but it is easy to construct examples that would induce a rational calculator to see advantages in breach of contract. A person with an hour to live, a person whose behaviour could not be scrutinised, or somebody whose breach of faith would place him beyond reach of retribution might all, in Hobbesian terms, have excellent reasons for failing to fulfil their obligations.

Hobbes did show some awareness of objections of this type, and put a vaguely specified example into the mouth of someone called 'the Fool', who 'questioneth, whether Injustice, taking away the fear of God. . .may not sometimes stand with that Reason, which dictateth to every man his own good; and particularly then, when it conduceth to such a benefit, as shall put a man in a condition, to neglect not only the dispraise, and revilings, but also the power of other men'.[17] Hobbes's answer to the Fool's very pertinent question presents interpretative difficulties unlikely to be finally resolved, but the reading that appears to make most sense is that the type of person who reasons like this is likely, in due course, to be found out. The rational self thus chooses *dispositions* (that is to say, habitual virtues or vices) that will in general aid self-preservation.[18] But this involves the unappealing claim that the purely hypothetical decision of someone who can freely choose what type of individual to be ought to affect the conduct of someone with determinate characteristics.

2

Hobbes was the first great thinker to face up to our political predicament. The Hobbesian detachment of a reflective self from the activities that it engaged in involved him in developing a picture of that self as holding beliefs supportive of his state's authority. Unless there is an answer to the Fool, Hobbesian legitimation of the state is plainly unsuccessful. But even if there is a cogent answer, Hobbesian legitimation could not be *realised* in the modern world unless a fully Hobbesian self-conception could somehow attain plausibility. A moment's thought reveals this is unlikely, in part because our picture of the self has several quite unHobbesian characteristics.

The question that Hobbes set himself was how the individuals that his 'science' abstracted from observed activities could be combined so as to form a stable polity. The fundamental basis of his answer was the belief that everybody shares a powerful motive: a common aversion to death that overrides our several and conflicting appetites. Where Aristotle believed in a shared Supreme Good – the good, among other things, of interaction – Hobbes believed in a shared Supreme Evil: violent death. It followed that the main ideological threat to the stability of Hobbesian states was the belief, promoted by the clergy, that there is something worse than violent death: the everlasting torment of the damned.

Our situation is more difficult, because our picture of the self is much more complicated. There are, of course, still social scientists attempting to answer the Fool by pursuing the essentially Hobbesian programme of trying to see political arrangements as products of individual greed and fear (they tend to forget about 'glory'), but most of them present themselves as merely exploring a 'model' of human nature. Their caution is quite understandable, because the basic Hobbesian postulates were much more in tune with Stuart common sense than with more modern assumptions. The Hobbesian conception of the individual as hell- or death-avoiding was an adequate rationalisation of seventeenth-century practice; it was easy to construe the Christian religion as primarily a rational strategy for maximising pleasure (the joys of heaven), and/or avoiding pain (the fires of hell). But rationalisation of *our* accepted moral practices promotes a quite different conception of the individual.

To begin with, we think of the self as a bearer of rights, and in particular of the right to choose *and to express* its own beliefs. Hobbes thought that the state was well advised to interfere as little as possible in the behaviour of individuals, but his assertion of its right to judge precluded the more modern view that there is an intrinsically private sphere, intrusion on which is a violation of individual prerogatives. The origins of this attitude are usually and probably rightly traced to the political theory of John Locke (1632–1704), who founded his ideas upon a duty, given by God, of preserving one's self (and secondarily others), and therefore of protecting all the rights (revealingly known by Locke as 'Property') by which that preservation was assured. There seem to have been two social practices shaping the Lockean self. One was the rationalist Christianity of liberal Protestantism; the other was the experience of a proto-capitalist legal order, assuring to the individual indefinitely transferable property rights. From the perspective of this self, the only purpose that was served by states was the enforcement of his private rights, using coercive powers that they borrowed from pre-political individuals. It was consistent with this view that there was still one sphere of life in which the individual's rights could not be given away or even lent. Where Hobbes allotted to the state the right to determine the details of religion, Locke held that the right to free religious practice was too important to be handed over to the political authorities. Given the risk of hell-fire, this claim was eminently rational, especially when supported by the claim that God rewards sincerity (as opposed to dogmatic correctness).

Though the decline of Christianity has taken away its original foundation, responsibility to a Creator, the secularisation experienced by most societies has actually entrenched the core assumption, for the tendency to abandon dogmatic religion has been in the name of the value of working out one's own morality. Both Christianity's decline and liberalism's survival are no doubt functional with respect to market practices, but both create some rather obvious problems. If Locke's ideas were wholly dominant, it is extremely hard to see how any government could be legitimate and stable, because legitimation based on Lockean self-conceptions encounters two important difficulties. The first is how to deal with the emergence of anti-Lockean moral theories. Locke supported coercive state action to discourage atheism, the theory that threatened the logical basis of Lockean natural law,[19] but secularised Lockeans, with their attachment to sincerity, find it extremely hard to justify the suppression of sincerely held ideas. The freedom Locke defended was freedom to follow one's reason; the freedom prized by many of his successors (including, incidentally, Max Weber) is freedom to make an arbitrary commitment to some particular values. There is, of course, no guarantee that those values will themselves be tolerant; but, in any case, post-Lockean liberalism leads to diversity, and the steady diminution in the stock of shared beliefs is bound to affect the shared belief that state commands are binding.

The second is a problem shared with Hobbes. Like Hobbes, Locke was driven by logic to the view that his abstracted individuals could only be subjected by some action of their own, but the importance he attached to the free exercise of moral judgement meant his criteria for 'consent' were more demanding than his predecessor's. In consequence, his doctrine of tacit consent was even less convincing. Lockean legitimacy would be founded on the memory of an uncoerced decision to put oneself into subjection, but such events are virtually unknown. No major modern state attempts to elicit even the fiction of express consent from native members of its population; at most such states rely on the tacit consent allegedly involved in casting votes.

The self that seems to be implied by modern practices in fact owes more to Rousseau (1712–78); it is a self whose leading characteristic is horror at the notion of being subjected to another's will. Rousseau escaped from the insoluble

problems created by resort to historic consent by tracing the legitimacy of political institutions to the present will of individuals. The crucial move that made
this possible was abandonment of the Hobbesian postulate that natural man
desires to excel. The passion to out-do that Hobbes called glory (and Rousseau
amour-propre) was said to be characteristic of human beings denatured and
corrupted by their society, for natural man is indifferent to his fellows except in
wanting to avoid any dependence on another's will. Rousseau believed that he
could find such selves both in contemporary savages and in the citizens of past
republics, but the ready acceptance of his self-conception suggests that it was
somehow already implicit in eighteenth-century culture; religious introspection
(both sides of the confessional divide), respect for private 'sentiment', and
bourgeois self-assertion were all of them certainly likely to encourage an ideal of
non-dependence. At all events, in Rousseau's theory, love of autonomy replaces
glory in precluding the view that man is innately social and setting the problem
legitimacy must solve.

The essence of Rousseau's solution is quite simple. As Rousseau's selves prize
self-determination above convenience and even safety, legitimacy can never be
realised among people with a healthy self-conception unless a government's
laws can be construed as an expression of a General Will directed to achieving
the shared good of the whole. But there can only be a common good if people
are shaped in such a way that they have goods in common: 'if there were not
some point on which all interests agree, society could not exist'.[20] This was probably why Rousseau attached significance to the institution of the Censorship, a
moral watchdog that enforced correct behaviour in private life, and to the existence of a civil religion whose few and simple doctrines were consistent with,
and reinforced, the values of the state.[21] He went out of his way to acknowledge
an implication: the anti-political nature of Christianity, a religion whose adher-
ents cared too little about conditions in the present life.[22] The same objection
would apply to any way of life that made peremptory demands distracting a person's attention from the collective good. Rousseau's society cannot afford the
presence of values that undermine commitment to the common interest.

3

Most of us have of course imbibed both Locke's and Rousseau's self-conceptions.
We see ourselves both as the bearers of Lockean rights and as averse to government by others. The shared priorities Rousseau guaranteed through civil religion
and pressure upon manners have been assured, in modern times, by the power of
national feeling. Though it is very difficult to say any more about nations than
that they are groups with something important in common that leads them to
aspire to govern themselves, the wish to be a part of such a unit appears to be a
very powerful motive. The urge to create and defend a nation-state has brought
about the kind of sacrifices, up to and including the laying down of life, no Hobbesian self could possibly envisage. Though this phenomenon can appear to rest

upon identity-beliefs (the loyal subject feels his country's triumphs as his own), it can also be construed in a more individualistic spirit. Rulers who come from the same national background find it easier to create within their subjects the impression that they share a common good, in part because they are presumed to share an interest in cultural survival; the rational explanation of the ferocity of nationalism in places like the former Yugoslavia is the entirely plausible assumption that only one culture is likely to survive in a given political unit.

The self that seems to underly much modern political practice is thus a person who attaches value to the persistence of some characteristics she feels that she shares with her neighbours. She may believe this way of being human is better than all others, but she is motivated by the accident that it happens to be hers. Though it is threatened in its turn by the emergence of sub-nationalisms (few nations are so homogeneous that they lack proto-national subdivisions) legitimacy based on this conception has plainly been quite widely realised. The obvious danger with this situation is that promotion of the nation's values is likely to lead to subversion of Lockean ones, whether to do away with competing loyalties or to forestall such loyalties from emerging.

But even if the nation-state had ways of containing this threat without unduly transgressing the rights of its members, it would still be bound to clash, sooner or later, with the international economic order. Modern nations are in practice interdependent in ways that demand the enforcement of quite intangible entitlements. In the foreseeable future, a high proportion of the wealth of the most powerful will take the form of claims on foreign assets and so-called 'intellectual property', that is, of bonds, shares, licences and patents, and other entities whose very existence is constituted by a legal system. Even if we suppose, implausibly, that everybody has an interest in the existence of this legal system, it is bound to be experienced by some people (and some peoples), some of the time, as standing between them and self-determination.

This chapter has been arguing that a legitimating theory has to be based upon a self-conception that people actually find acceptable. Precisely this thought can be found in the most celebrated work of later twentieth-century liberal theory. John Rawls's *A Theory of Justice* (1971) maintained that just arrangements were those that would be chosen by rational selves behind a 'veil of ignorance' concealing, amongst other things, their talents, social status and 'conception of the good'.[23] This remarkably ignorant self would still, however, be a 'moral person', that is, someone 'with a fundamental preference for conditions that enable him to frame a mode of life that expresses his nature as a free and rational being as fully as circumstances permit'.[24] Rawls thought this self-conception has actually been realised in our culture: 'The hypothetical nature of the original position invites the question: why should we take any interest in it, moral or otherwise? Recall the answer: the conditions embodied in the description of this situation are ones that we do in fact accept.'[25]

The question is obviously right, but it invites a gloomier response. The postulated Rawlsian self, abstracted from its actual characteristics, seems as irrelevant to us as the virtue-choosing self to Hobbes's Fool. Rawls's more recent work has explained that 'free and rational' ought to be understood as 'reasonable', as 'ready to propose principles and standards as fair terms of co-operation and to abide by them willingly, given the assurance that others will likewise do so'.[26] Borrowing from T.M. Scanlon, Rawls claims that we are given by our culture 'a basic desire to be able to justify our actions to others on grounds they could not reasonably reject'.[27] This Rawlsian self-justifying self can no doubt be abstracted from some current practices (on a somewhat idealised view of the character of university life, it might be found, for instance, in the activities of academics). It is a cousin of the self implicitly imagined by Jürgen Habermas, with his principle that 'just those action norms are valid which all possibly affected persons could agree as participants in rational discourses'.[28] But nobody spends all their time as a rationally discursive individual, and there is no obvious reason why rational discourse should be seen as more essential to the self than, say, sex, sport, jokes, poetry or religion.

Even a sketchy survey of the history of legitimacy-beliefs raises a troubling possibility. Our present intuitions about a separate self owe something to Hobbesian 'science', something to secularised Lockeanism, and something to Rousseau's hatred of dependence. Because there is no answer to the Fool, no Hobbesian self-conception can really support legitimate arrangements. But the more elaborate selves we can imagine are also fundamentally unsuited to the legitimation of our actual practices. The privileges attributed to the post-Lockean self will offer it the space to make non-Lockean commitments, while Rousseau's self-governing selves will be affronted by dependence on an international order. What actually sustains our present arrangements may be no more than habit, combined with faith in their effectiveness, effectiveness being narrowly defined in terms of the delivery of economic growth. We find ourselves, in fact, in Weber's world. If and when our economic growth should falter, the outlook will be bleak.

Notes

1 M. Weber, *Economy and Society*, eds G. Roth and C. Wittich (New York, Bedminster Press, 1968), 3 vols., vol. I, p. 212.

2 Weber, *Economy and Society*, vol. I, p. 31.

3 Weber, *Economy and Society*, vol. I, p. 213.

4 Weber, *Economy and Society*, vol. I, p. 4.

5 From M. Weber, *Max Weber: Essays in Sociology*, eds H. Gerth and C. Wright Mills (London, Routledge, 1991), pp. 147–9.

6 T. Hobbes, *Leviathan*, ed. R.Tuck (Cambridge, Cambridge University Press, 1991), pp. 35–6.

7 Hobbes, *Leviathan*, p. 47.

8 T. Hobbes, *On the Citizen*, eds R. Tuck and M. Silverthorne (Cambridge, Cambridge University Press, 1998), p. 10.

9 Hobbes, *Leviathan*, p. 91.

10 Hobbes, *Leviathan*, p. 91.

11 Hobbes, *Leviathan*, p. 99.

12 Hobbes, *Leviathan*, p. 206.

13 Hobbes, *Leviathan*, p. 141.

14 Hobbes, *Leviathan*, p. 232.

15 Hobbes, *Leviathan*, p. 150.

16 Hobbes, *Leviathan*, p. 140.

17 Hobbes, *Leviathan*, p. 101.

18 D. Boonin-Vail, *Thomas Hobbes and the Science of Moral Virtue* (Cambridge, Cambridge University Press, 1994), pp. 147–53.

19 J. Locke, *A Letter Concerning Toleration in Focus*, eds J. Horton and S. Mendus (London, Routledge, 1991), p. 47.

20 J.-J. Rousseau, *The Social Contract and Other Later Political Writings*, tr. V. Gourevitch (Cambridge, Cambridge University Press, 1998), p. 57.

21 Rousseau, *Social Contract*, pp. 141–2, 150–1.

22 Rousseau *Social Contract*, pp. 147–9.

23 J. Rawls, *A Theory of Justice* (Oxford, Oxford University Press, 1972), p. 137.

24 Rawls, *Theory of Justice*, p. 561.

25 Rawls, *Theory of Justice*, pp. 140–1, 587.

26 J. Rawls, *Political Liberalism* (New York, Columbia University Press, 1993), p. 49.

27 Rawls, *Political Liberalism*, p. 49, n. 2. Scanlon's current position (which is different) is set out in T. Scanlon, *What We Owe to Each Other* (Cambridge, MA, Belknap Press, 1998).

28 J. Habermas, *Between Facts and Norms: Contributions to a Discourse Theory of Law and Democracy*, tr. W. Rehg (Cambridge, Polity Press, 1996), p. 107.

9
Democracy

David Owen

Introduction

The concept of democracy is central to our contemporary political vocabularies, yet agreement on how to conceptualise democracy is far from widespread.[1] As Adam Przeworski has recently remarked: 'Perusing innumerable definitions, one discovers that democracy has become an altar on which everyone hangs his or her favorite *ex voto*.'[2] Certainly we can say that democracy is a form of government that appeals to an idea of popular sovereignty and, hence, an answer to the question 'who rules?' – but to flesh out this answer will very quickly mire us in controversy. This point is of more than merely academic interest for two reasons. First, how we understand the concept of democracy guides our practical reflections on how to design or reform democratic institutions, it generates criteria governing what we can reasonably expect from democratic government and it animates our debates concerning political legitimacy. Second, in so far as reasonable disagreement is an abiding circumstance of politics and democratic rule is a condition of political legitimacy, it follows that disagreement concerning the nature of democratic rule, and hence of the criteria of political legitimacy, is itself liable to be a persistent feature of democratic politics. For this reason, this chapter will begin by considering a recent minimalist view of democracy, before going on to consider two important contemporary models of democracy: the interest-aggregating model and the deliberative model. It will then briefly consider a supplement to each of these models in the form of 'contestatory' democratic mechanisms. The chapter will conclude by indicating what is arguably the main contemporary challenge to democratic theory and practice in the era of globalisation.

1 A minimal view of democracy

Perhaps the best known minimal view of democracy is that advanced by Schumpeter as 'a system in which rulers are selected by competitive elections',[3] where such elections are held on a regular basis and under conditions of universal suffrage. The main question that arises here is this: why should we value democracy understood in this minimalist way?

Przeworski has argued that we do have good reasons to value democracy on a minimal understanding of it; even if it is the case, as he also argues, 'that choosing rulers by election does not assure either rationality [of decision-making], or representation [of the interests or will of the people], or equality [of citizens]'.[4] He advances this argument on two main grounds: first, 'the mere possibility of being able to change governments can avoid violence' and, second, 'being able to do it by voting has consequences of its own'.[5]

With respect to the first point, Przeworski puts his argument thus:

> assume that governments are selected by a toss of a, not necessarily fair, coin . . . the very prospect that governments would alternate may induce the conflicting political forces to comply with the rules rather than engage in violence, for the following reason. Although the losers would be better off in the short run rebelling rather than accepting the outcome of the current round, if they have a sufficient chance to win and a sufficiently large payoff in the future rounds they are better off continuing to comply with the verdict for the coin toss rather than fighting for power. Similarly, while the winners would be better off in the short run not tossing the coin again, they may be better off in the long run peaceably leaving office rather than provoking violence to their usurpation of power.[6]

Notice that this argument suggests that the chances of maintaining democratic rule are increased in having at least two relatively matched political parties and where political loyalty is primarily to political parties rather than individuals. In the absence of these conditions, as the current state of affairs in Zimbabwe illustrates, democratic rule may become very fragile.

Przeworski's second point turns on the fact that we do not actually toss coins but vote:

> Voting is an imposition of a will over a will. When a decision is reached by voting, some people must submit to a decision different from theirs or to a decision contrary to their interests . . . Voting generates winners and losers, and it authorises the winners to impose their will, even if within constraints, on the losers. This is what 'ruling' is.[7]

This fact has consequences not because voting imposes an obligation to respect the results of voting (although it may, Przeworski is more sceptical of this claim that I am) but because 'voting does reveal information about passions, values and interests':

> If elections are a peaceful substitute for rebellion, it is because they inform everyone who would mutiny and against what. They inform the losers – 'Here is the distribution of force: if you disobey the instructions conveyed by the results of the election, I will be more likely to beat you than you will be able to beat me in a violent confrontation' – and the winners – 'If you do not hold elections again or if you grab too much, I will be able to put up a forbidding resistance.'[8]

In other words, voting not only provides a mechanism, like coin-tossing, that avoids violence but also provides current rulers and possible future rulers with information concerning the political constitution of those subject to their rule, information which (given their interest in re-election and election, respectively) is likely to inform the character of their rule.

These are, I think, compelling arguments for the value of democracy even on a minimal view. But that we should value democracy on these grounds does not imply that we cannot reasonably and plausibly expect more – at least from relatively mature and relatively wealthy democracies – than simply the avoidance of internal violence and the provision of informational constraints on rational rulers. What more can and should we expect? The reflections offered in this chapter will begin from the delineation of a formal concept of democracy as: *a mode of government in which the members of the unit of rule are equal consociates and have collectively an* effective *capacity to govern, either directly or via intermediaries, matters of common interest (or concerning the common good)* qua *membership of this unit of rule.*

This formal concept highlights two features which are typically taken to be basic to any substantive account of democracy: the political equality of citizens and the idea of collective self-rule. Hence on any more than minimal view of democracy, it is suggested, we can and should expect that democratic institutions will, at least to a significant extent, be shaped by commitments to ensuring the political equality of citizens (in terms of, for example, public and private rights) and to facilitating 'collective self-rule', where this phrase implies not simply a right to the periodic selection of one's rulers by way of competitive elections but also that 'important decisions on questions of law and policy depend . . . upon public opinion formally expressed by citizens'.[9] How we understand these commitments (and the obligations that they impose), however, will hang to a large extent on the way in which we conceptualise democracy. For this reason, the next two sections of this chapter examine two different models – or, more strictly, regulative ideals – of democracy, tracing the distinct ways in which these commitments are cashed out.

2 The interest-aggregating model

This first model begins with the intuitively simple and appealing thought that the basic substance of political reflection and action is *interests*, where these interests are expressed by political actors as preferences. This basic thought orients the justification and conceptualisation of democracy as a mode of political government. The argument for democracy on this understanding runs as follows:

> If the good or interests of everyone should be weighed equally, and if each adult person is in general the best judge of his or her good or interests, then *every adult member* of an association is sufficiently well qualified, taken all around, to participate in making collectively binding decisions that affect his or her good or interests, that is, to be a *full citizen* of the demos. More specifically, when binding decisions

are made, the claims of each citizen as to the laws, rules, policies, etc. to be adopted must be counted as equal and equally valid. Moreover, no adult members are so definitively better qualified than the others that they should be entrusted with making binding collective decisions. More specifically, when binding decisions are made, no citizen's claims as to the laws, rules, and policies to be adopted are to be counted as superior to the claims of any other citizen.[10]

To argue against democracy on this view requires that one reject either or both of the conditional statements at the beginning of Dahl's remarks. Hence, the anti-democrat must argue that the interests of everyone should not be weighed equally and/or that each adult person is not in general the best judge of his or her interests. Although historically both of these anti-democratic arguments have been made, it is not clear that they can easily be sustained.

Given this interest-oriented argument for democracy, what ideal standards are appropriate to a democracy? Dahl suggests the following five ideal standards as the core normative commitments of democracy:

1 Effective participation
2 Equality in voting
3 Gaining enlightened understanding
4 Exercising final control over the agenda
5 Inclusion of adults.[11]

Why these criteria? Dahl's response is that, given the assumption that democracy is to be understood in terms of interests, 'each is necessary if the members . . . are to be politically equal in determining the policies of the association'.[12] This establishes (1), since to deny any citizen the opportunity to express their preferences, place questions on the agenda or give reasons for endorsing or rejecting a given proposal is to mute their political voice; it justifies (2), since to weigh votes unequally is to weigh interests unequally; it implies (4), since otherwise the agenda may not represent the full range of interests of the citizens; and it establishes (5), since otherwise the interests of some competent persons are not counted. But what of (3)? Dahl's point here is that citizens must have an adequate and equal opportunity *'for discovering and validating (within the time permitted by the need for a decision) the choice on the matter to be decided that would best serve the citizen's interests',*[13] since otherwise some citizens may be disadvantaged relative to others in terms of being able to accurately determine the choice which best expresses their fundamental interests with respect to a given decision. Essentially the democratic idea expressed here involves two elements. First, that what count as matters of collective interest (that is, matters on which political decisions may be appropriate) should be determined by equal citizens as a collectivity within the constraints imposed by the conditions of democratic rule. Second, that what is held to be in the collective interest (that is, what is the best course of action for the polity to adopt) in relation to a given issue should be decided by equal citizens collectively in accordance with the principles of democratic rule. This is why Dahl stresses the importance of both the collective ability of citizens as political equals to set the agenda and to decide what to do. Any form of government that fails to meet both of these conditions subjects citizens, in one way or another, to the rule of guardians.

But how are decisions concerning what is in the collective interest to be determined? The aim of democracy, as David Miller noted, 'is to aggregate individual preferences into a collective choice in as fair and efficient a way as possible'.[14] Now in so far as these collective choices take the form of a single-issue choice between option A and option B, such aggregation is straightforward and, for issues which are not constitutionally basic, it seems reasonable to adopt the principle of majority rule, that is, that the option with the majority of votes wins.[15] But what of collective choices where there are more than two options and no option receives an absolute majority of the votes cast? Here determining the collective interest may be harder than it immediately appears to be.

Consider that there are numerous ways in which an aggregation of these votes might be accomplished. On the one hand, there are majoritarian decision-making rules such as the plurality rule (whichever option gets the most votes wins) and the Condorcet rule (the winning outcome is the option which defeats each of the others in a vote on every pair of alternatives). The problem here is that the plurality rule implies that a choice is simply that of the largest minority, while the Condorcet rule is incomplete in that for a given distribution of votes there may not be a Condorcet winner. On the other hand, there are positional decision-making rules such as the Borda count (the winning outcome is determined by scoring each option according to its place in a voter's ranking, thus the top option gets n points, the second $n-1$ points, etc., and then aggregating the point for each option across all votes cast). The problem here is that 'it may make the decision among quite popular options depend on the way that some voters rank way-out or eccentric options if these are on the ballot paper'[16] and, for just the same reasons, this decision rule is highly vulnerable to strategic voting. Things get worse! As Arrow has demonstrated in his famous Impossibility Theorem, given certain reasonable conditions which we might wish a decision rule to satisfy,[17] 'if there are more than two alternatives, any method for making social decisions that ensures transitivity in the decisions must be necessarily either dictated by one person or imposed against the preferences of every individual'.[18] The implication drawn from this and related social choice theorems is that no rule for collective decisions can be discovered that does not produce arbitrary or meaningless outcomes and hence both (a) there is no decision rule for aggregating preferences which is clearly fair and rational and hence superior to other possible rules and (b) different rules may produce different outcomes. In this context, Riker has argued that it makes no sense to speak of discovering the 'popular will' at all.[19]

This is clearly *in principle* a very serious challenge to this model of democracy and it is one that might encourage us to give up trying to make sense of the notion of majority rule. We might, then, instead adopt a principle of unanimity in which each citizen has a right of veto over laws, policies, etc.[20] The main objection to this proposal by Buchanan and Tullock is that it is unfeasible, making government (to all intents and purposes) impossible.[21] This conclusion is a little quick since, under conditions in which each of us knows that any of us can veto a given proposal, it seems likely that we will rapidly develop a political culture of bargaining, compromise and trade-offs such as characterises existing political contexts in which decisions are subject to this rule (for example, treaty negotiations). Still although the conclusion drawn by Dahl is hasty, it is the right one – under contemporary conditions, it makes little sense to propose that a community's capacity to govern itself be subject to the dogmatic convictions of every member. However, since unanimity is the only way of avoiding the problems concerning majority rule raised by social choice theory, we are thrown once more back on to the task of making sense of this notion. One way to avoid this problem would be to adapt the unanimity principle so that what requires unanimity is not a proposal but a choice between two proposals – and then decide between these proposals on the basis of a majority vote. This would avoid the most obvious difficulty with the unanimity principle while ensuring that all decisions can be unproblematic expressions of majority rule. However, although such an adapted unanimity principle would avoid the problems raised by social choice theory, it is difficult to see how such a demanding principle would be practicable.

But does the arbitrariness of decision rules really matter that much? Recall that the problem is this:

> The problem of arbitrariness arises because it is not clear which of the many possible rules best matches our intuitive sense of 'finding the option which the voters most prefer', or to put the point another way, for any given rule it is possible to give examples where using the rule produces an outcome that seems repugnant to our sense of what a democratic decision should be.[22]

It was for this reason that Riker insisted that the notion of 'popular will' is just an empty phrase. But to reach this conclusion Riker would need to assume that the fact that different decision rules produce different results or expressions of the 'popular will' vitiates the notion of the 'popular will' and this does not follow: the popular will (or collective interest) is just whatever is the result of the decision rule that we take to be *authoritative* for a given decision, that other rules may produce other results is neither here nor there. The real question is how, knowing that different rules may produce different results, we decide which rule to employ for a given decision. Now it might seem that this simply pushes the whole problem back one stage but it does not. From a democratic point of view, what matters is not that a given decision rule may produce results which conflict with our intuitions concerning what a democratic decision would be but that the democratic community has determined what the authoritative rule is for a given class of decisions – and this is the point at which the principle of unanimity has a role to play. In other words, what matters democratically is not that the rule may produce counter-intuitive outcomes but that the choice of the rule is not arbitrary – and the only way to secure this is to adopt the principle of unanimity. It is, in other words, to treat the choice of decision rule (or rules, where different rules may be used for different decisions) as if it were analogous to a treaty – or contract! – in which all parties are required to agree. Indeed, this is, I think, why Rousseau insisted that the contract to form a political community must be unanimous. (Moreover, if the members of a community are particularly troubled by the thought of strategic voting, they might choose to introduce a meta-rule to the effect that the decision rule will be chosen randomly once the votes are cast. This would have the advantage of blocking attempts at the strategic manipulation of the outcome.) But does not this proposal suffer from the same disadvantage as the proposal of unanimity as a decision rule? No. The problem there was that where unanimity is used as a decision rule for specific issues, any member who had particularly strong or dogmatic convictions on that issue could veto any proposal that did not conform with their convictions. But in this case unanimity is being used as a decision rule for deciding between decision rules and not for deciding between proposals on concrete topics – and this means that no member of the community will be in a position to know (in more than very general terms) whether or not the choice of decision rule x for treating decisions of type y is likely to work out in ways that tend to favour them and hence members will have no interest-based motive to veto the proposal of particular decision-rules. (Note that if this turned out to be false, it would provide a general incentive for adopting the randomising meta-rule suggested above.) In this respect, it seems to me that we can talk intelligibly of the popular will or collective interest, and hence that the apparent threat posed by social choice theory to this model of democracy is dissolved.

To conclude this section, let us return to the question of what more we might expect from democracy in terms of cashing out the principles of political equality and ensuring an effective capacity for collective self-rule. In terms of this interest-aggregation model, it is clear that what we can and should expect is a commitment to realizing as fully as practicable the five ideal standards which Dahl sketches and thus, most importantly, to measures which seek to ensure our equal freedom to form and identify our own interests, our equal freedom to express these interests at all stages of the democratic process from agenda-setting to final decision-making and the equal weighting of our interests in determining our collective decision. Our democratic institutions are to be evaluated in terms of their design and performance against their satisfaction of, and commitment to, such measures.

3 The deliberative model

Whereas the first model takes interests as the basic currency of politics, the second model takes public reasons as occupying this position. Joshua Cohen has helpfully summarized the distinction thus:

According to an *aggregative* conception of democracy . . . decisions are collective
just in case they arise from arrangements of binding collective choice that give *equal
consideration to . . . the interests of each person* bound by the decisions. According to
a *deliberative* conception, a decision is collective just in case it emerges from arrangements of binding collective choice that establish conditions of *free public reasoning
among equals who are governed by the decisions.* In the deliberative conception, then,
citizens treat one another not by giving equal consideration to interests . . . but by
offering them justifications for the exercise of collective power framed in terms of
considerations that can, roughly speaking, be acknowledged by all as reasons.[23]

The deliberative argument for democracy, thus, emerges from a claim about the
political equality of citizens as grounded on their equal moral status as
autonomous individuals capable of giving and exchanging reasons – and,
hence, on what Rainer Forst has called their basic moral right of justification,
that is, the basic right to have exercises of collective power over their free activity as citizens justified by reasons that are acceptable to them as citizens.[24]

Given this argument for democracy, what ideal standards does it invoke? On
Cohen's account, these standards can be given by presenting 'an idealized procedure of political deliberation, constructed to capture the notions of free,
equal and reason that figure in the deliberative ideal'.[25] We can summarise this
ideal procedure thus:

1 All citizens acknowledge the freedom of each citizen to participate.
2 Citizens are formally equal in that each has the same rights to propose issues
   and solutions, to offer reasons for or against proposals, and to have an equal
   voice in deciding the outcome.
3 Citizens are substantively equal in that each has an equal opportunity to
   exercise their rights of participation.
4 Citizens are reasonable 'in that they aim to defend and criticize institutions and
   programs in terms of considerations that others, as free and equal, have reason to accept, given the fact of reasonable pluralism and on the assumption
   that those others are themselves concerned to provide suitable justifications'.[26]

The standards invoked by this idealised procedure are interestingly analogous
to those proposed by Dahl in that this procedure ensures the opportunity for
effective participation (proposing issues, solutions and offering reasons), equality of voting (each has an equal say and each counts as one in a vote), gaining
enlightened understanding (where this now implies the opportunity to consider and determine, within the time available, the reasons that one considers
best concerning the issue at hand), exercising final control over the agenda
(equal rights to propose issues) and inclusion of adults (all persons with the
deliberative capacities). In addition, this model also invokes the standard of
reasonableness, namely, that citizens acknowledge the fact of reasonable
pluralism and seek to offer reasons that other reasonable citizens could not reasonably reject.[27] In this respect, the deliberative model is more demanding than
the interest-aggregation model since it requires that citizens exercise a form of

democratic self-restraint, namely that they reflect as citizens and not in terms of their private interests.

At this stage, we can turn to the issue of what it means to talk of 'collective self-rule' in this context. Ideally, of course, collective self-rule here refers to the generation of a consensus such that for any given law or policy, it can be justified to *all* citizens in terms that they could not reasonably reject. (This does not require that the justification is the same for all citizens; an overlapping consensus will do as well as a common consensus.) However, since it is unlikely that such a consensus will emerge on most, if not all, issues, it is clear that most decision-making will require the use of some decision-rule in this same way as required for the interest-aggregration model.[28] The deliberative model is, however, arguably better placed with respect to the issues raised by the need to select a decision-rule. Thus David Miller has argued that the interest-aggregation model is exposed to social choice dilemmas in part because it posits choosing a decision rule independently of consideration of the content of the citizens views, whereas because the deliberative model sees the content of citizens' judgements concerning the collective interest as emerging in the course of reasonable deliberation, it is less vulnerable to these problems in three ways.[29] First, we may plausibly expect that the deliberative process may produce voters' rank orderings that are 'single-peaked', that is, 'the alternatives can be arranged on a continuum such that if, say, a voter ranks the alternative on the left highest, he does not rank the alternative on the left above that in the centre'.[30] This matters because in cases where such single-peaking occurs, there is always a Condorcet winner. We can expect this because in many cases the policy options represent a choice between two values and voters' ranking reflect their weighing of these values. Second, where such single-peaking does not occur, it is likely to be the result of more than one dimension of disagreement emerging in the deliberative process – but precisely because the dimensions of disagreement become apparent through deliberation, it may be possible to disaggregate the original choice scenario into components such that for each component there is single-peaking. Third, if we consider majoritarian (for example, Condorcet) and positional (e.g., Borda count) types of decision-rule, we can note that whereas the former aim to satisfy as many people as possible, the latter aims to satisfy everyone collectively as much as possible and, consequently, which of these aims is best may hang on the nature of the issue over which we are seeking to come to a decision. Miller's point is that deliberative democracy will be well placed to choose decision-rules that are appropriate to the issue at hand since the nature of this issue will be revealed in deliberation, whereas the interest-aggregating model of democracy will not be so well placed. Whether or not it is actually the case that the deliberative model is better placed, however, depends on whether or not citizens do in fact exhibit the commitment to reasonableness that this model calls for, and that, in turn, hangs to a significant extent on whether the claim that involvement in deliberation with free and equal others has transformative effects on individual citizens, that is, cultivates a disposition to reasonableness.

In considering the question of what more we might expect from democracy in terms of cashing out the principles of political equality and ensuring an effective capacity for collective self-rule, we can note that the deliberative model involves a commitment to realising as fully as practicable a framework of social and institutional arrangements that 'facilitate free reasoning among equal citizens . . . while ensuring that citizens are treated as free and equal in that discussion; and tie the authorization to exercise public power – and the exercise itself – to such public reasoning'.[31] It is against such criteria that our democratic polity is to be judged.

4 Contestatory democracy

Given the above account of the two models of democracy, we might still reasonably be concerned by the potential problem posed by the tyranny of the majority. While both models provide effective arguments for liberal freedoms such as freedom of speech and freedom of association as intrinsic to democratic rule, it remains plausible that, under non-ideal conditions, the interests or reasons expressed by minority groups may be ignored or, at least, not granted equal status within the decision-making process. In the practical context of democratic rule by way of representative government, addressing this problem 'would require not just that the majority are heard in determining what common, perceived interests ought to be pursued by government, but also that the relevant minorities get a hearing, 'So the question is whether there is any way of subjecting government to a mode of distributive or minority control in order to balance the electorally established mode of collective or majority control.'[32]

Pettit's suggestion is to introduce contestatory mechanisms. These are mechanisms through which a minority group who hold that the decision reached has not adequately acknowledged their political voice can contest the decision through 'a procedure that would enable people, not to veto public decisions on the basis of their avowable, perceived interests, but to call them into question on such a basis and trigger a review; in particular, to trigger a review in a forum that they and others can all endorse as an impartial court of appeal'.[33]

This supplement to both the major models is important not least because it contributes to maintaining an effective sense of political belonging among minority groups. After all, as Pettit notes:

> There is an enormous gulf between being subject to a will that may interfere in your affairs without taking your perceived interests into account and being subject to a process such that, while it takes your interests and those of others equally into account, it may deliver a result – for reasons you can understand – that favours others more than you.[34]

Consequently, under non-ideal conditions, a concern with promoting democratic stability in the sense of a strong identification of citizens with their democratic institutions entails that we have good reasons to adopt a contestatory supplement to our basic democratic fora and that this is the case whether our democratic understanding is primarily informed by either of the two main models considered.

5 Globalisation and democracy

In this final section, I want to mention a significant contemporary issue for democratic theory, namely, the problem of the embeddedness of democratic polities within networks of transnational governance.

It is increasingly becoming a commonplace that democratic polities in the form of the sovereign nation-state are situated within, and subject to, forms of regional and/or global governance by way *either* of regional organisations such as the European Union (EU) and the North Atlantic Free Trade Area (NAFTA) (which may or may not be polities themselves: the EU is a polity but NAFTA is not) or the multilateral institutions of global governance such as the World Trade Organisation (WTO), the International Monetary Fund (IMF) and the World Bank. In this context, recall our basic formal definition of democracy as *a mode of government in which the members of the unit of rule are equal consociates and have collectively an* effective *capacity to govern, either directly or via intermediaries, matters of common interest (or concerning the common good)* qua *membership of this unit of rule.* Up to this point we have been considering the issue of citizens possessing '*an* effective *capacity to govern*' in terms of the internal arrangements and conditions of a polity, but it is equally clear that such an effective capacity can be undermined by virtue of being subject to external forms of governance such that, for example, policies concerning the subsidisation of manufacturing industry within the polity are politically disconnected from public opinion on this topic and subject to the authority of the WTO. The dilemma, therefore, is that a polity which has the *form* of a democratic polity may only exhibit the appearance of democratic rule rather than the reality of such rule – or, more strictly, may only exhibit the reality of such rule in externally limited and con-strained contexts. In this real world contemporary context, maintaining the claim that a polity is democratic requires *either* a highly implausible and imprac-ticable reassertion of its autonomy *or* a democratisation of the forms of transna-tional governance to which it is subject. In this respect, as David Held has powerfully argued, a concern with democratic rule cannot be restricted to the level of the sovereign state but must track the levels of governance to which we, as peoples, are subject.[35] This raises a plethora of theoretical and practical issues for democracy but the challenges posed by these difficulties need to be met if we are to maintain our practical identities as democratic citizens.

Conclusion

This chapter began with reference to a minimalist view of democracy and it did so because reflecting on this view should remind us of a point which needs to be borne in mind when considering the concept of democracy. This is that the more we demand from democracy, the more we are likely to be disappointed by our democratic institutions and, in our disappointment, to lose sight of the very real benefits which democracy delivers even on a minimalist view. With this warning in mind, however, it has been argued that we can, at least in some circumstances, expect more from democracy than the minimalist view admits and I have tried to sketch what more we might reasonably expect by reference to the two major contemporary models – or regulative ideals – of democracy as well as suggesting that contestatory mechanisms can play an important supplementary role with respect to these models. Finally, the chapter has indicated the central issue for the future of democratic theory and practice, namely, our subjection to forms of transnational governance over which, at present, we can exercise little or no effective democratic control.

Notes

1 The best recent studies of democracy are: from a political theory standpoint, A. Weale, *Democracy* (London, Macmillan, 1999); from a philosophical standpoint, R. Harrison, *Democracy* (London, Routledge, 1993); and from a historical point of view, J. Dunn (ed.), *Democracy: The Unfinished Journey* (Oxford, Oxford University Press, 1992). For an overview of models of democracy, see D. Held, *Models of Democracy* (Cambridge, Polity Press, 1996, 2nd edn).

2 A. Przeworski, 'Minimalist Conception of Democracy: A Defense', in I. Shapiro and C. Hacker-Cordon (eds), *Democracy's Value* (Cambridge, Cambridge University Press, 1999), p. 24.

3 Przeworski, 'Minimalist Conception of Democracy', p. 23.

4 Przeworski, 'Minimalist Conception of Democracy', p. 43, my insertions.

5 Przeworski, 'Minimalist Conception of Democracy', p. 45.

6 Przeworski, 'Minimalist Conception of Democracy', p. 46.

7 Przeworski, 'Minimalist Conception of Democracy', p. 47.

8 Przeworski, 'Minimalist Conception of Democracy', p. 49.

9 Weale, *Democracy*, p. 14.

10 R. Dahl, *Democracy and its Critics* (New Haven, CT, Yale University Press, 1989), p. 105.

11 R. Dahl, *On Democracy* (New Haven, CT, Yale University Press, 1988), p. 38; see also Dahl, *Democracy and its Critics*, pp. 106–31.

12 Dahl, *On Democracy*, p. 38.

13 Dahl, *Democracy and its Critics*, p. 112 (original emphasis).

14 D. Miller, 'Deliberative Democracy and Social Choice', *Political Studies*, 40 (1992), p. 55.

15 For four justifications of majority rule, see Dahl, *Democracy and its Critics*, pp. 138–44.

16 Miller, 'Deliberative Democracy and Social Choice', p. 58.

17 These conditions are transitivity (that is, that the final choice is independent of the order in which the alternatives come up for decision), universal domain, respect for the Pareto principle, the independence of irrelevant alternatives and non-dictatorship. See Kenneth Arrow, *Social Choice and Individual Values* (New Haven, CT, Yale University Press, 1963, 2nd edn).

18 R. Dahl, *A Preface to Democratic Theory* (Chicago, University of Chicago Press, 1956), pp. 42–3, cited in Weale, *Democracy*, p. 140.

19 W. Riker, *Liberalism against Populism* (San Francisco, CA, Freeman and Co., 1982).

20 J. Buchanan and G. Tullock, *The Calculus of Consent* (Ann Arbor, MI, University of Michigan Press, 1962).

21 Dahl, *Democracy and its Critics*, pp. 198–9.

22 Miller, 'Deliberative Democracy and Social Choice', p. 58.

23 J. Cohen, 'Democracy and Liberty', in J. Elster (ed.), *Deliberative Democracy* (Cambridge, Cambridge University Press, 1998), p. 186 (original emphases).

24 R. Forst, *Contexts of Justice* (Berkeley, CA, University of California Press, 2002).

25 Cohen, 'Democracy and Liberty', p. 193.

26 Cohen, 'Democracy and Liberty', pp. 193–4.

27 See T. Scanlon 'Contractualism and Utilitarianism', in B. Williams and A. Sen (eds), *Utilitarianism and Beyond* (Cambridge, Cambridge University Press, 1982).

28 It has been suggested by D. Miller that the deliberative model is better placed than the interest-aggregation model to deal with the problems raised by social choice theory. See the discussion in the next section.

29 Miller, 'Deliberative Democracy and Social Choice', pp. 62–6.

30 Miller, 'Deliberative Democracy and Social Choice', p. 63.

31 Cohen, 'Democracy and Liberty', p. 186.

32 P. Pettit, 'Contestatory Democracy', in I. Shapiro and C. Hacker-Cordon (eds), *Democracy's Value* (Cambridge, Cambridge University Press, 1999), p. 178.

33 Pettit, 'Contestatory Democracy', p. 179.

34 Pettit, 'Contestatory Democracy', p. 179.

35 D. Held, *Democracy and the Global Order* (Cambridge, Polity Press, 1995).

10
The rule of law

Richard Bellamy

Introduction

Many political theorists view the rule of law with suspicion. On the one hand, it can appear mere political rhetoric. For example, politicians habitually invoke the doctrine to suggest that any failure to comply with decisions made within the current political system leads to anarchy and the end of law. Opponents must play by the rules of the game and, when they lose, obey the winners. So employed, it operates as a self-serving ideological device whereby governments assert the legitimacy of all their actions. As Judith Shklar has remarked, it seems unnecessary to waste intellectual effort 'on this bit of ruling-class chatter'.[1] On the other hand, certain critics of this rhetorical position identify the rule of law with some notion of good or just law. In this case, however, the doctrine risks becoming indistinguishable from a comprehensive political philosophy and better designated as such. No distinctive role appears to be allotted to law or legality per se.

To escape vacuity, therefore, a theory of the rule of law must avoid collapsing into either of these two interpretations. A standard approach associates the rule of law with those properties of legality and due process that allow people who disagree about the just society to peacefully coexist and, where necessary, to work through their differences. However, this thesis immediately confronts the original dilemma. If the rule of law merely requires that formal procedures exist and are followed, it will amount to little more than an endorsement of the prevailing formalities. All regimes may need a degree of procedural and legal formality to hold together, thereby setting certain limits to what even the worst tyrant can do if he wants his state to function with any efficiency and avoid collapse, but these limitations need not be terribly demanding. Yet strengthening them could lead to the doctrine incorporating contentious substantive notions and thereby losing its distinctiveness vis-à-vis comprehensive theories of the just and good polity.

Section 1 argues that some of these problems can be avoided if we see the main task of the rule of law as the prevention of arbitrary rule. Two broad approaches are identified. The first centres on the very nature of rules and the constraints that arise from following them. The second focuses on political checks and balances for constraining power. Though related, both historically and substantively, I shall argue the second offers the chief defence. Sections 2 and 3 defend this argument by analysing respectively an example of each approach.

1 The idea and value of the rule of law

The core idea of the rule of law can be grasped via the classic contrast with the 'rule of persons'. The objection to the latter resides in the fear that unfettered personal rule, be it by a single individual, such as a monarch, a group, such as a democratic majority, or a corporate agent, such as a bureaucratic body, places the ruled under the arbitrary sway of their rulers. In other words, such rulers have the capacity to intentionally coerce, obstruct, manipulate or otherwise interfere with the ruled, without consulting the views or interests of those affected. By forcing rulers to follow certain forms and procedures, law constrains such arbitrary power – though theorists differ as to the effectiveness and normative implications of different sorts of constraint. Naturally, the capacity for arbitrary interference is never absolute. No agent can always choose when, where, how and with whom to interfere, or to what degree. Nor can arbitrary interference ever be eliminated entirely. Paradoxically, the rule of law always depends on the rule of persons to make and uphold it. Even if their rule is carefully controlled, no political system can avoid giving either executives or minor officials a degree of personal discretion which could be abused. The aim must be to limit such opportunities as far as possible without producing inflexibilities in decision-making that lead to inefficiencies and a lack of responsiveness that are themselves sources of injustice.

Three related concerns are involved in the fear of arbitrariness. First, there is the danger that rulers will simply govern wilfully and capriciously. As a result, there will be no consistency or coherence to policy, so that people will not know where they stand. An act that appeared unexceptional before could suddenly and for no apparent reason attract a severe penalty simply because the ruler has taken a dislike to it or become unusually attentive. Second, people will feel dominated by their rulers. They will be permanently in awe of their power, attempting to second guess their next move either to escape their wrath or win their favour. Finally, arbitrariness can produce oppression when people's legitimate expectations and needs are overridden or ignored for the sake of another's self-interested ends. Though linked, one kind of arbitrariness can exist without necessarily involving the others. For example, an enlightened despot may not act capriciously or oppress people's interests, but by virtue of his comparatively unchecked power will still exert domination over them. All three kinds reduce the ruled to slaves of their ruler by removing their capacity to act autonomously. In each case, individuals lose the capacity to plan ahead on their own account, without the anxiety of being subject to unpredictable and possibly malicious interferences by either the public authorities and their supporters or the inadvertent actions of others.

This feature of arbitrary rule provides the key to the purpose and value of the rule of law. If domination is the condition to be avoided, then the task of the rule of law must be to guarantee people's status as free and equal citizens. All non-trivial accounts of the rule of law conceive equality and freedom as intimately related. It is because there is no ascribed status justifying seeing some as the natural servants of others, that individuals should be treated as moral equals, able to act as responsible and autonomous agents free from the domination of others. However, different versions of the rule of law cash out this linkage between equality and autonomy in different ways. One version, surveyed in section 2, argues that the key lies in the law having a certain form: namely in being general, public, clear, prospective, stable and applying equally to all. As a result, none are above the law and it is hard to manipulate for self-serving and partial purposes. Another version, examined in section 3, suggests the crucial factor is the process of law-making: equality in the making of the law must be such that legislators show equal concern and respect to different points of view by 'hearing the other side'.

Despite their differences, these two versions of the rule of law do not necessarily pull in opposite directions . First, both try to tread the line between offering a purely formal or procedural and an overly substantive account of law. The first version tries to pack these substantive features into the form taken by the law, the second into the process of legislation. The aim in each case is to ensure not only a reduction of uncertainty by limiting the ability of rulers or others to act totally wilfully, but also to ensure the law embodies non-arbitrary or dominating ends by virtue of treating those subject to it as moral equals.

Second, the two versions are not logically incompatible. Certain theorists have argued that only laws having the form advocated in the first version could be agreed to by the law-making process recommended by the second. Whether such a process actually has to be employed then becomes a largely prudential matter. Thus, some analysts have argued that it offers the most realistic safeguard for ensuring rules have the desired form, whereas others believe it is too difficult to institutionalise in practice, so that laws must simply be drafted 'as if' they had emerged from it. However, I shall argue that this fit is not quite so neat, and that departures from rule formality are often necessary in ways that are only likely to be satisfactory if checked by a particular process. That process, though, does have certain formal rule of law features.

Third, both versions engage with different aspects of what could be termed 'the Hobbesian challenge'. Stated crudely, Hobbes argued that in circumstances of conflicting interests and deep disagreements about values and judgements, laws would only be equitably and coherently drafted and applied by all individuals being equally in awe of a sovereign who was outside the law and whose power was indivisible. All law has to be interpreted and these interpretations are necessarily controversial. As a result, political stability cannot result from the rule of laws per se but only from having an unquestioned authority vested with the power to formulate, interpret and apply the laws. To suggest that any agent or agency is subject to the law is simply to place another interpreter of the law above them, while to divide sovereign power is to create a divisive conflict between interpreters.[2] By contrast, both versions of the rule of law seek to place all persons within the law and to divide law-making power, although the ways they do so differ.

Fourth, the theories of the rule of law discussed here differ from certain notions of the *Rechtsstaat* with which the doctrine is sometimes conflated. These last centre on upholding a certain list of rights reflecting a particular conception of justice, rather than simply preventing the arbitrary use of political power by virtue of law or law-making having a given form. Joseph Raz cites as an instance of this approach the International Congress of Jurist's equation of the rule of law with the creation and maintenance of 'the conditions which will uphold the dignity of man as an individual' – a requirement that includes 'not only recognition of his civil and political rights but also the establishment of the social, economic, educational and cultural traditions which are essential to the full development of his personality'.[3] This view simply takes on too much. Its not just that people may hold differing visions of the good life. Even within a particular vision, a distinctive role exists for law and the legal and political system as mechanisms for facilitating social interaction and protecting against abuses of power: for example, by managing discussions over how best to achieve agreed goals and ensuring the appropriate administration of the distribution of goods on which 'human dignity' allegedly depends. As Catriona McKinnon argues in her chapter, contemporary rights theorists seek to avoid turning them into a wish list of all good things. Thus, more sophisticated versions of this approach to the rule of law aim simply at delineating a narrowly 'political' conception of justice.[4] As we shall see, the two accounts discussed here differ also from these versions. Naturally, both accept that legal rules and political arrangements give rise to rights, but neither takes them as their starting point. Limits of space prevent giving chapter and verse of their critique of rights-based theories. Instead, I shall focus on the coherence of their positive claims to offer an alternative to theories centred on a set of constitutional rights that define and limit the political sphere.

2 Hayek and the rule-like nature of law

Among contemporary political theorists, the rule of law has been closely associated with the work of F. von Hayek, who gave it a pivotal role in his constitutional theory. Hayek's account developed out of a critique of economic planning.[5] He believed interventionist economic policies and totalitarian politics were intimately connected: the one entailed an incremental increase in arbitrary interferences with individual liberty that ultimately led to the other. To understand Hayek's view of the rule of law, therefore, we must turn to his contrast between planned and market economies and see why he identified the former with a legal-positivist view of law as 'command' and the latter with a formal conception of law as the 'rules of the game'.

Briefly, Hayek maintained that economic planning required God-like powers. Planners would have to be omniscient, knowing on the one hand what consumers actually wanted and what they might want if it was available, and on the other how producers might best utilise existing resources not just to meet existing demand but to create demand. They would then have to use this information to fix prices. The problem in each case is that producers and consumers not only engage in conceptual innovations but also respond to unpredictable events of various kinds, such as changes in the supply of natural resources resulting from unexpected disasters such as droughts. These innovations, events and the responses they elicit are impossible to second-guess yet are constantly altering the character of supply and demand. Since attempts to predict the future are futile, planners end up arbitrarily imposing their views on others and vainly trying to prevent any unplanned innovations or choices that might upset their calculations. Even so, they lack the omnipotence required to precisely coordinate everyone's activities to the plan. The result is a hopelessly inefficient economy and an increasingly authoritarian state.

Hayek contended this foolhardy enterprise was encouraged by the misguided belief in social justice and the doctrine of popular sovereignty. He interpreted social justice as the conviction that an ideal distribution of goods existed, whereby each individual's needs and deserts could be determined by certain rational criteria and the economy so planned that they were precisely met. As we saw, he thought this state of affairs was impossible to achieve and entailed severe restrictions on individual freedom. Democracy fostered and legitimated the pursuit of this ideal. First, politicians would always be tempted to woo voters by offering to promote their sectional interests, while these demands could be rendered generally acceptable by being presented as claims for social justice. Second, popular sovereignty transferred the despotic authority of monarchs to legislatures, with law whatever the duly elected government decreed. It thereby became legitimate for governments to issue legally binding directives aimed at pursuing certain policy goals.

Hayek maintained the democratic pursuit of social justice was gradually moving western states along 'the road to serfdom'. To question the legitimacy as well as the economic advisability of such actions, he had to attack the conception of law on which they rested. In sum, he wished to claim that planning and the pursuit of social justice infringed the 'rule of law'. Hayek accepted that most bureaucratic organisations, including the state apparatus, often operated on the basis of commands issued by an executive. That was because they had clear organisational goals. But the wider society had no common purposes of this kind, just the very diverse and evolving ends of the individuals who composed it. To make laws that could realise the ends of each individual would require the same sort of God-like powers needed to plan the economy and involve similar restrictions on individual liberty. The true role of law was to provide stable conditions in which individuals could choose for themselves which ends to pursue without being arbitrarily interfered with by governments and other individuals or arbitrarily interfering with others themselves. As he put it, the law should operate like a Highway Code: it provides those rules of the road needed for people to drive about with a reduced risk of accidents, not a set of orders directing people where to go, when and how.[6]

Thus, Hayek thought the 'rule of law' involved precisely those features I identified at the start of this chapter: namely, it must offer a framework for human interaction which neither regards law as whatever legislation has been duly enacted nor attempts to promote a particular vision of the good society. It was impossible to construct an ideal legal code aimed at achieving certain ends. Rather, rules arose spontaneously through individuals trying to adapt to each other and their environment. Rational appraisal involved weeding out poor conventions through trial and error, not assessing their fit within a supposed rational system of law. To continue the Highway Code analogy, it is custom rather than a priori reasoning that determines whether one drives on the right or left, and experiment that tends to fix the most appropriate speed limits. However, laws had to have certain formal features to avoid becoming instruments of arbitrary power. They had to be universalisable, expressed in general terms and apply equally to all (while taking into account relevant differences), be prospective (only invoking retroactivity as a curative measure), public (albeit often through publicly funded experts), clear (avoiding vague terminology open to wide discretionary interpretation) and relatively stable (but not so as to ossify). Taken together, he believed these criteria would prevent ad hoc, discretionary decision-making that was aimed at either benefiting or harming certain individuals or groups of persons. His claim was that their very generality and abstractness meant that it was impossible to know how they might effect particular people. As a result, law-makers had an incentive to ensure legal rules and procedures were as fair as possible and enacted solely for purposes requiring collective agreements that were in the public interest. Hayek thought only laws that protected the individual's negative liberty were compatible with these constraints because laws serving any other purpose would need to refer to particular persons, places or objects and treat some differently to others.

Although these rules give rise to rights, some of which – notably the standard civil rights – he thought so important as to possibly warrant being given special protection within a constitution, his argument was not right based. Consequently, though Hayek saw judicial independence and review as vital for ensuring the integrity of the law and preventing its arbitrary use or abuse by the authorities, he was against the idea of an activist judiciary promoting certain policies and obliging new laws to be passed through the creative interpretation of constitutional rights. In other words, he favoured formal over substantive judicial review. Otherwise, he feared the courts would lapse into acting like a Hobbesian sovereign, issuing commands rather than merely ensuring conformity to the law. All the same, Hayek maintained constitutional checks on the legislature were necessary, since the chief cause of the expansion of command-like law had been popular sovereignty. He suggested that as well as separating the judicial, legislative and executive functions, as in the American system, one should also separate the legislation needed to run the public administration from law-making for the wider society and proposed the latter be assigned to a representative body that was free from some of the perverse electoral pressures that afflicted modern parliaments. The details of this ingenious scheme cannot be gone into here.[7] Instead, I shall concentrate on the coherence of his attempt to distinguish formal, general rules from particular commands, and the contribution this distinction makes to controlling arbitrary power.

Rules can reduce certain kinds of ad hoc and discretionary decision-making in ways that remove some sources of uncertainty, insecurity and inefficiency. For example, the rule that one cannot be imprisoned for a crime that has not been previously declared an offence in law and before the proper procedures for conviction have been followed, constrain the arbitrary power of a government to gaol people it dislikes or finds troublesome. However, properly passed and applied laws may still be harsh and unjust, even if they are not completely capricious. True, the consistent application of unjust laws means that one can often learn how to get around or avoid them. But consistency also prevents sympathetic judges and officials quietly bending the rules to avoid injustices. Similarly, rules can economise on the time and effort needed for case-by-case decision-making, and will often guard against carelessness, a lack of thoroughness or prejudice on the part of officials. Likewise, rules increase visibility and accountability. If citizens know the rules, they can ensure officials play by them. Rules can also embolden officials to make hard decisions because they are simply applying the rule rather than making a personal judgement. Indeed, agreement on a fair procedural rule, such as majority vote or first come first served, can often help us reach a decision in areas where there is considerable substantive disagreement. In part, that's because the impersonality of rules involves a rough and ready form of equality and fairness. Like the traditional image of justice, rules are 'blind' with regard to their effects. Still, these same qualities also create difficulties. Rule-bound decisions can become mechanical and unsuitable. Officials who stick to the letter of the law rather than its spirit often appear obtusely or maliciously oppressive, with an inflated view of their own importance. The very blindness of rules to difference can render them inappropriate and inefficient or even discriminatory. For example, small businesses often complain about being subjected to the same regulations as large ones, and feminists have criticised equal opportunities law for including a covert 'male comparator test' that overlooks relevant differences such as pregnancy or the structural factors that have relegated women to low-paid, casual employment. In such circumstances, transparency may be lost either by people surreptitiously evading or bending certain rules, or by their devoting considerable effort to playing them in ways that exchange form for substance.

In sum, rules guard against certain kinds of arbitrariness but embody other kinds. Clearly, one could not imagine a legal *system* existing without some general rules setting up judicial institutions and authorising particular agents and agencies to adjudicate on certain matters according to a given set of procedures. To be followable, laws will also need to possess various formal qualities without which people would be unable to modify their behaviour so as to conform to them in consistent ways that others could reasonably rely on. In other words, law to be law in any meaningful sense must have certain characteristics to a given degree, much as a ball would not be a ball without a measure of roundness and volume. But just as notions of 'ballness' do not tell you per se whether it is a cricket or a rugby ball, so notions of 'lawness' or 'legality' do not say anything about the purpose or content particular laws might have.

Law as such does eliminate many forms of arbitrary rule in ways that entail equity and promote autonomy. Clarity, prospectiveness and regularity in the law and the rules governing the processes that regulate it reduces the dangers of social relationships and interactions being disrupted by unpredictable changes in people's behaviour. Formal rules provide a degree of stability and certainty essential for fixing goals and working to achieve them. For example, traffic laws give me a certain security when navigating the roads in my car, giving me a reasonable expectation that people will stop at red lights and so on. And these laws would not work unless they applied equally to all and could not be changed except by procedures designed to ensure everyone knew and could abide by the reformed code. However, law can meet these formal criteria and still embody dominating ends, including the institution of slavery.

Meanwhile, eliminating all discretion in applying the law or denying it any purposeful content, as Hayek proposed, appear neither possible nor desirable. Thus, traffic regulations have elements of generality to secure fairness and the benefits of co-operation but are also determined in part by notions of expediency and various substantive purposes (for example, decisions about speed limits and their enforcement, which usually allow for a number of exceptions for emergency services, say). Hayek is no doubt right to observe that legislators rarely set out to frame laws in formal terms per se. But that is because it would be nonsensical to do so. They devise laws with certain ends in mind and then give them a certain form in order to obtain the law-like characteristics which enable these purposes to be achieved. Yet these purposes need not be that benign and Hayek's formal criteria fail to ensure that they will be.

These difficulties become apparent if we turn to Hayek's two main claims with regard to the 'rule of law' – that they will operate against redistribution and economic planning while protecting liberty. Hayek's problem is that there are no particular purposes that cannot be framed within some general description that applies to them alone or be derived from some suitably designed general rule. 'All persons earning above £100,000 pay supertax' is a general, equal rule. Likewise, stable prices and plans announced well in advance may also be consistent with a purely formal view of the rule of law. The point in such cases is whether these policies are socially or economically sound. Far from being incompatible with the pursuit of social purposes, rules help promote them by moving officials and citizens consistently towards that objective without the need for continuous commands. If, as Hayek rightly insists, it would be impossible to direct centrally all the activities of a complex society, it appears equally problematic to employ solely abstract procedural norms possessing no reference to particular persons or sensitivity to local conditions. For example, Hayek suggests that 'measures designed to control the access to different trades and occupations, the terms of sale, and the amounts to be produced and sold' all 'involve arbitrary discrimination against persons' and so offend the rule of law as he conceives it.[8] Yet he immediately backtracks, admitting it is sensible to ensure doctors are suitably qualified before being allowed to practise, pilots pass eye tests, and even that sellers of firearms and poisons should be 'persons satisfying certain intellectual and moral qualities'. In fact, most government regulations – including much social legislation – arise not as part of a rational plan but as responses to particular problems, being progressively modified through the trial and error mechanism Hayek approves.

These problems prove even more acute in the case of liberty. Hayek's central contention is that 'when we obey laws, in the sense of general abstract rules laid down irrespective of their application to us, we are not subject to another's will and are therefore free'.[9] At times, he appears to suggest that so long as everyone is similarly affected by a rule, it is not aimed at anyone personally, and infraction is avoidable, then no coercion is involved. Law-givers do not know the particular cases where their rules will be applied and the judge is simply applying that law. Consequently, law is like a natural obstacle. But this too leads to absurdities. As Hamowy has observed,[10] by these criteria a gangster-ridden neighbourhood – being like a plague-infested swamp, neither aimed at me personally nor unavoidable – represents no limit on my freedom. This is a serious problem given that his purely formal criteria not only offer no guidance as to which rules should apply to what sorts of activity, but also are consistent with all kinds of hidden or overt biases that can discriminate against particular groups. Hayek partially acknowledged this difficulty in accepting that it can be misguided to apply the same rules to everyone in all circumstances. Law frequently discriminates on grounds of age or sex, for example. The key is to discover when such discrimination is reasonable or not. His response to this problem is extremely suggestive: 'Such distinctions will not be arbitrary', he wrote, 'will not subject one group to the will of others, *if they are equally recognised as justified by those inside and those outside the group*'.[11] However, the appeal here is to the test of the rule of law being less its formal qualities than its capacity to evince reciprocity and, hence, obtain mutual assent from citizens. Equality before the law involves the content of legal rules taking everyone into account and giving equal weight to different points of view. Put another way, Hayek appears to be suggesting that law must reflect the general rather than any particular will. The republican tradition, explored next, agrees, but argues achieving this result depends on the form of the legislative process more than of the law.

3 Republicanism and the process of legislation

That a political system should constitute 'an empire of laws and not of men'[12] was a key tenet of the republican tradition, at least in the neo-Roman variant of Cicero, Machiavelli and Harrington recently identified by Quentin Skinner and Philip Pettit.[13] However, republicans grasped the nettle posed by the paradox that only 'men' could bring about this condition and linked the rule of law to democratic self-rule. Freedom from arbitrary rulers, who need not consult the concerns of the ruled, only arises when the people make their collective rules for themselves. To quote Harrington again, it is only when all are equal in the making of the laws that they will be 'framed by every private man unto no other end (or they may thank themselves) than to protect the liberty of every man'.[14] Thus, the political system must allow the people, usually through their representatives, to ensure the laws show them equal concern and respect. Legislators must be obliged 'to hear the other side', displaying reciprocity and an effort at mutual understanding to reach agreement on their collective interests and the various respects in which people merit equal or unequal treatment.

Republicans trace arbitrariness and domination to asymmetries of power. Given that any polity contains groups with conflicting interests and values, power must be so divided that groups may check others – thereby forcing all laws to be collectively negotiated and rendered mutually acceptable. The political constitution must reflect the social complexion of the polity, balancing the various groups in ways that prevent any one dominating another. Standard devices have included bicameral legislatures operating different systems of representation and various forms of federalism. It is the 'mixed' form of popular government and the processes of negotiation it fosters rather than the form of law itself that guards against the arbitrary use of power.

As we saw, Hayek voiced the standard liberal fear that popular sovereignty merely transfers the potentially tyrannous powers of the Hobbesian sovereign to electoral majorities. The equitable dispersal of power is designed to guard against this possibility. On the republican view, all individuals must be free to contest both the rules regulating social interaction and those governing how these rules are determined. The purpose of such contestation is to ensure the law serves only the public good – the *res publica* – rather than the factional interests of particular persons. The public good does not comprise only those goods that de facto would be in every individual's rational interest to have provided publicly. In this case, those well provided for could always object to contributing towards a similar provision for others. Even standard public goods might not pass such a lowest common denominator test. In fact, such objections involve a factionally motivated block on the pursuit of the public good. Rather, the test is whether the law and the purposes it promotes are publicly justifiable. In accordance with the injunction that legislators should 'hear the other side', such public justification entails the giving of reasons that are shareable by others. Thus, common rules should not only treat all individuals as moral equals capable of autonomous action, but also be attentive to the variety of circumstances in which they find themselves and the diverse forms of practical reasoning they adopt. To meet these criteria, legislators will have to drop purely self-interested and self-referential reasoning and look for forms of argument that other individuals constrained by a similar requirement for public justification could accept.[15] In other words, there will be an assumption that in evaluating laws we start by taking into account the effects of their general performance for securing the various generic goods that one could expect individuals to value in the different situations they find themselves. This assumption implies neither that all are similarly situated nor that they value the same goods. On the contrary, it would exclude any such arguments that failed to heed the plight or concerns of others and could not be plausibly shared. For example, self-serving arguments by the prosperous that there could never be grounds for mutual aid would be unlikely to pass this test. But it does require that arguments be made in terms all could relate to. That requirement is consistent with groups or individuals pointing out either how their peculiar circumstances create special demands which would be felt by others in their place, or asking for special recognition for their particular ideals by relating them to the views or claims of others and justifications based on equal concern and respect.

As a result of these constraints, arguments will tend to have many of the formal features of abstractness, generality and equality that Hayek associates with the rule of law. However, they will operate in a less mechanical manner, allowing the substance of the law to develop as people grow more appreciative of each other's diverse and evolving experiences and concerns. Arguably this logic has operated to produce a number of the policies Hayek finds objectionable as well as those he does not. Thus, much welfare legislation has arisen from acceptance of equality of opportunity as a fair general principle, on the one hand, and an enhanced sensitivity to the disadvantages encountered by people finding themselves in certain social circumstances, on the other. Likewise, if more contentiously, multicultural arguments for group rights have often been based on the claim that members of minority cultures are disadvantaged in parallel ways. In these and similar cases, criticism of the existing law has frequently been tied to a critique of the prevailing process for deciding it, with the demand for equality in the latter preceding improved equal recognition in the former. Indeed, it may often be harder to get agreement on a fair resolution of a substantive issue than a fair procedure for resolving it. However, proposed modifications to the process must also be publicly justifiable. Standardly, such proposals are for the extension of democratic decision-making to spheres where arbitrary rule still prevails because it is not subject to public contestation, such as private corporations, or for new styles of decision-making that allow significant differences of experience to be taken into account, as in demands for various forms of devolution or the enfranchisement of excluded groups. But these proposals need not turn on specific cases per se. Usually they appeal to reasons that similarly situated others could share and, so, might be applied generally.

Obviously, all rules and political systems give rise to rights. But this argument is not rights based. For rights and their application to particular cases must themselves be specified through the process of public justification. Moreover, rights, like the rules or procedures from which they flow, must be open to contestation. Nevertheless, it might be thought advisable to give certain rights special constitutional protection as a prudential measure. However, this would be consistent with having democratic procedures for reviewing them – albeit ones that require a higher than usual threshold of agreement from various constituencies for any change to pass. Meanwhile, in protecting such entrenched rights, constitutional courts will also be obliged to base their interpretations of their scope and bearing in particular cases on publicly justifiable reasons. Indeed, a standard rationale for handing rights over to the courts is that the absence of electoral pressures renders them more immune to self-interested bargaining than legislatures. Yet the typically limited social range and experience of their membership can also make them unaware or unresponsive to certain demands, while a focus on particular cases can lead them to overlook knock on effects in other areas of policy-making. My aim is not to settle this debate over the advisability of judicially protected bills of rights here, merely to indicate that arguments for them have a procedural and democratic foundation in terms of their responsiveness to public justification and hence are amenable to criticism on those grounds. In any case, we saw that all laws will need to have certain formal characteristics to be followable and that having independent courts that ensure they are consistently and equitably applied provides an important break on arbitrary rule. As such, the judiciary plays a crucial role within a republican system.

Conclusion

The rule of law offers an indispensable defence against arbitrary rule. Formalities with regard to legal processes and the law itself both secure certain benefits in this regard, but are not decisive. The crucial elements are that law is not only public in the sense of being followable, which Hayek's formal criteria help ensure, but also publicly justifiable, which republicans insist is the task of a properly designed democratic system. Within this framework it then becomes possible for people to debate the nature of the good society while devising both the general laws required to further their collective interests and those particular ones needed to respect their differences.

Notes

1 Judith Shklar, 'Political Theory and the Rule of Law', in A.C. Hutchinson and P. Monahan (eds), *The Rule of Law: Ideal or Ideology* (Toronto, Carswell, 1987), p. 1.

2 T. Hobbes, *Leviathan* (Cambridge, Cambridge University Press, 1991), pp. 143, 169.
3 J. Raz, *The Authority of Law* (Oxford, Clarendon Press, 1979), pp. 210–11.
4 For example, J. Rawls, *Political Liberalism* (New York, Columbia University Press, 1993).
5 F. von Hayek, *The Road to Serfdom* (London, Routledge, 1944), ch. 6.
6 Hayek, *Road to Serfdom*, pp. 55–6.
7 See F. von Hayek, *The Political Order of a Free People* (London, Routledge, 1979).
8 F. von Hayek, *The Constitution of Liberty* (London, Routledge and Kegan Paul, 1960), pp. 227–8.
9 Hayek, *Constitution of Liberty*, pp. 153–4.
10 R. Hamowy, 'Law and the Liberal Society', *Journal of Libertarian Studies*, 2 (1987), pp. 287–97.
11 Hayek, *Constitution of Liberty*, p. 154, emphasis added.
12 J. Harrington, *The Commonwealth of Oceana* (Cambridge, Cambridge University Press, 1992), p. 81.
13 Q. Skinner, *Liberty before Liberalism* (Cambridge, Cambridge University Press, 1998), pp. 44–5; P. Pettit, *Republicanism: A Theory of Freedom and Government* (Oxford, Oxford University Press, 1999, 2nd edn), pp. 172–3.
14 Harrington, *The Commonwealth of Oceana*, p. 20.
15 As David Owen notes in his chapter, this is a standard requirement of deliberative theories of democracy, which tend to adopt a similar account of public reason to that employed by modern contractarian theorists of justice such as John Rawls (for example, *Political Liberalism*, lecture 6) and Thomas Scanlon, *What We Owe to Each Other* (Cambridge MA, Belknap Press, 1998). What follows is a slightly weaker (and hence more realistic) version of such theories.

11
Public and private

Judith Squires

Introduction[1]

The public–private distinction is one of the 'grand dichotomies' of western thought.[2] The dichotomy has a complex history, which has generated numerous formulations of the opposition between public and private, most of which still inform contemporary understandings of the terms. In this context, subjecting the public–private dichotomy to critique, as many feminists have done, will inevitably also be a complex project. In this chapter I shall survey contemporary understandings of the public–private distinction and feminist critiques of these. I shall then consider recent feminist moves to go beyond critique, which entail attempts to de-gender the dichotomy, to reconceive the public and the private spheres, and to deconstruct the dichotomy itself. Together these attempts to reconceive the public and the private indicate that it is helpful to retain and rework the concepts, but that they are better understood as different modes of interaction rather than as separate spheres.

1 Differing definitions of public and private

There is no single public–private distinction. Political theorists tend to acknowledge two broad traditions for distinguishing between the public and the private – the classical and the liberal. While both the classical and the liberal traditions share a common emphasis on the importance of a public–private distinction, the nature of the distinction is profoundly different in each.

The public–private distinction is usually cast within liberal discourses as a distinction between market and state. It is standardly interpreted as a governmental, non-governmental distinction among neo-classical economists, whose primary concern is to demarcate the sphere of the 'public' authority of the state from the sphere of voluntary relations between 'private' individuals in the market. By contrast, the distinction is cast within the classical traditions as an opposition between *oikos* – the domestic sphere of production and reproduction inhabited by women and slaves, and *polis* – where the public is also equated with the political, though not the politics of an administrative state (as in the liberal distinction), but the politics of discussions, deliberation, collective decision-making and action in concert.[3] Although liberal discourses have frequently claimed to supplant the classical distinction, they have in practice incorporated many of its elements. As a result, much of the ambiguity surrounding the public–private distinction derives from the fact that two different traditions of political thought are at work in the public–private distinction.

The complexity does not stop there, however, for liberal discourses also frequently invoke a romantic tradition as well. Will Kymlicka suggests that there are two different conceptions of the public–private distinction at work within liberalism: the state–civil society distinction and the social–personal distinction. In the first, civil society is private in the sense that it is not governed by the public power of the state. In the second, which arises later than the first and in some ways may be viewed as a response to it, the personal is private in that it represents a sphere of intimacy to which one might retreat in face of the pressures to conform within society. These two combined create a tripartite, rather than a dual, division of social relations: the state, civil society and the personal.[4] It is clear that the state is always cast as public. It is equally clear that the personal (when considered within political theory) is cast as private. Confusingly, civil society is cast as private when opposed to the state, and public when opposed to the personal.

In an attempt to highlight the ambiguity concerning the place of the domestic in relation to contemporary understandings of the private, feminist theorists have demanded the explicit recognition of yet another public–private distinction. Neither of the liberal distinctions explicitly invokes the family (which cannot be assumed to be synonymous with the personal sphere of intimacy). By contrast, a third form of the public–private distinction opposes the public, comprising both the state and civil society, with the private, defined institutionally as the relations and activities of domestic life. The intriguing and politically significant issue, which feminist theory draws attention to, is the fact that contemporary liberal theory nowhere explicitly theorises the relation between this third articulation of the public–private dichotomy and either of the other two. For some feminist theorists this neglect renders the entire liberal project suspect. Had the family been viewed as a part of civil society, liberal theorists would surely have been compelled to oppose its hierarchical form and argue for its organisation on the basis of equality and consent as they did with all other forms of civil co-operation.

In response, feminists have tended to label the domestic as private and all else – civil society, government, political deliberation, sociability – as public. The public becomes simply a residual category.[5] This is not quite a return to the public–private dichotomy of the classical tradition. For while the private did equate, in the work of Aristotle for example, with the household (or *oikos*), the public was equated specifically with the *polis* – a sphere for the practice of citizenship. In the feminist articulation of the divide the account of the private is similar, and fundamentally at odds with accounts of the private within the liberal tradition, but the account of the public is much less theorised and much more eclectic. It frequently entails not only the notion of the polis, but also civil society, and the state. Dichotomous thinking is reproduced within many feminist critiques of the public–private dichotomy, which offer yet another articulation of the nature of the oppositional identities under consideration when we speak of public and private. In this way, some feminist critiques of the public–private dichotomy appear to have gelled into simply another articulation of the dichotomy, to add to the others already in play.

Critiques of *the* public–private distinction must be unravelled then to disaggregate the various strands within these dichotomous discourses. In many respects feminist theorists have been particularly attuned to the operation of this ambiguity: they have focused attention on the incompatibility of the two notions of the private commonly adopted. The liberal tradition depicts a private sphere of voluntary relations between free and equal individuals. The classical tradition offers a private sphere of natural inequality between master and slave, parent and child, husband and wife. Numerous feminist texts have shown how the application of a liberal conception of the private to the domestic sphere has worked to shield the abuse and domination that occurs within it, while the classical conception has worked to justify and perpetuate it. In practice, the ambiguity between these two conceptions of the private has worked to the benefit of patriarchal norms, not women. It is for this reason that many feminists have taken the operation of the public–private dichotomy to be essential to understanding women's oppression.

2 Feminist critiques of the public–private distinction

The feminist literature on the public–private distinction has focused primarily on critiquing the liberal formulation of the public–private distinction. These critiques fall into three broad strands, of which the first criticises the premises of liberalism as being androcentric, the second criticises the extent to which elements of the classical tradition are imported into the liberal model of social contract theory and the third criticises the actual patriarchal practices of 'liberal' regimes. While the first of these feminist critiques directly rejects the liberal conception of the public–private distinction, the second suggests that liberalism has been compromised in its theoretical formulation by the importation of classical or patriarchal norms, and the third suggests that, although the public–private distinction proposed by liberalism may in theory be gender-neutral, liberal regimes have in practice worked against the interests of women.

The first critique focuses on the question of subjectivity, claiming the liberal discourse of individual autonomy to be prescriptive rather than descriptive; structuring, rather than simply reflecting, social relations. The liberal theory of the self, as a rational individual engaged in abstract moral reasoning with strong ego boundaries, is not a neutral description of human nature; rather it is part of a discourse that constructs individuals in this image.[6] Recognition of this fact leads to two further insights. The first is that very particular social structures and institutions are needed to shape individuals into this mould; the second is that this conception of subjectivity may not apply equally to everyone. The first insight leads to a concern with the processes of reproduction, nurturance and socialisation – those material processes which construct people as autonomous individuals.[7] These are processes which have conventionally been located within the family and so hidden by the liberal construction of the public–private distinction as a state–civil society distinction. The second insight leads to an exploration of the extent to which women have been understood as subordinate, dependent and emotional, and so excluded from the category of 'individuals' within liberal theorising.[8] The discourse that privileges autonomous reasoning as distinctly human has generally assumed women to be incapable of such rationality, and so not properly deserving of the rights granted to individuals by the liberal state. These two issues are linked in women's status as primary carers. Neither the process of caring and nurturing nor the status of carers and nurturers are theorised in liberal theory. The concern of feminist theorists is that, as a result of this omission, not only have women been denied the rights and privileges granted to the 'rational individuals' of liberal societies, but also that a crucial aspect of life, associated with the caring performed by women, has been glossed over. This insight has implications not only for the role of caring as a practice, but also for its role as a perspective. The significance of caring, as both practice and perspective has generated a large feminist literature on the 'ethic of care'.[9]

This critique of the public–private distinction is complemented by a second, which focuses on contract. Here the object of concern is not the rational liberal individual, but liberalism's origins in social contract theory. This contract-based critique places the subjectivity-based critique in historical context. The focus here is the particular social and political forces that created the situation in which women were confined to a private, domestic, care-taking role while men were presumed to be able to move freely between the private (domestic) and the public (civil society and state) spheres. The most influential theorist here is Carole Pateman. She claims that the social contract that generates liberal politics and establishes the political freedom of individuals simultaneously entails the sexual subordination of women in marriage.[10] The social contract that is required to create both civil society and the state requires a sexual contract to accommodate the patriarchalism that pre-dates liberalism. The liberal social contact therefore represents the reorganisation, but not the abolition, of patriarchy. Patriarchy was relocated into the private domain and reformulated as complementary to civil society. Moreover, gender is given a highly specific and structuring role within liberal theory at the same time as liberal theory presents itself as gender-neutral. As Pateman influentially suggested: 'Precisely because liberalism conceptualises civil society in abstraction from ascriptive domestic life, the latter remains "forgotten" in theoretical terms. The separation between private and public is thus re-established as a division within civil society itself, within the world of men.'[11]

These first two critiques suggest that a holistic rejection of the liberal model of the public–private distinction is needed. It is not just contingent bias in the application of the liberal model that is at fault; the very model is constituted by its exclusion of the dependent, emotional and caring relations that are taken to characterise family relations, and those who are primarily defined by their relation to these – women. By contrast, the third critique of the public–private distinction that emerges within feminist theory is basically supportive of liberalism, seeking only to rid it of patriarchal distortions.

This third critique of the public–private dichotomy, articulated most clearly by Susan Moller Okin, focuses on the historical practice of liberal regimes. It might best be characterised as a weak or limited form of the second, rather than an alternative to it. The charge here is that, notwithstanding the abstract commitment to the importance of a prohibition on state intervention in the private sphere, liberal states have in practice regulated and controlled the family.[12] Not only has this practice been contrary to the fundamental principle of liberalism, it has been adopted in pursuit of a profoundly illiberal end: the perpetuation of patriarchy. While the state adopted this directly non-neutral relation to personal and domestic life, it also upheld practices within the marketplace, which presumed that those engaged in waged-work could rely on the support and care of someone at home. To add to the insult, from the perspective of women, the principle of non-intervention in the private sphere has been used by the state to justify inaction regarding cases of child abuse, marital rape and domestic violence. As Zillah Eisenstein has pointed out: 'The state is said to be public (by definition) and therefore divorced from the private realm, which is the area of women's lives. The state can appear through its own ideology, to be unrelated to the family as the private sphere, when in actuality this sphere is both defined and regulated *in relation* to the state realm.'[13] In short, liberal states have actually enforced patriarchal power relations within the family, while formally denying their responsibility to intervene in familial disputes on the grounds that it is essential to limit state intervention in civil society and personal relations. This tension, arising from the very formulation of liberalism itself, is the inevitable conclusion of the ambivalent role of the family in relation to the private sphere. It emerges as a result of the way in which liberal discourses concerning the public–private distinction inconsistently incorporate classical and patriarchal discourses into their own.[14]

All three critiques have effectively highlighted the tension running through contemporary conceptions of the public–private distinction, a tension that grows out of the simultaneous appeal to the classic notion of the private as a sphere of repetitive, domestic drudgery, and the liberal notion of the private as a sphere of unconstrained individual liberty. The critical contribution of the feminist engagement with this dichotomy is to focus on the extent to which women have been made to carry the burden of this tension. While men were encouraged to view the domestic as a sphere of personal privacy (a particular combination of the two liberal distinctions – state–civil society and social–personal), women have frequently experienced it as a sphere of constraint and oppression (a manifestation of a classical, or patriarchal, distinction). The two sexes were apparently living different manifestations of the dichotomy simultaneously. Yet, importantly, both were subsumed within a liberalism that played with the ambiguity to its own benefit. Liberalism, Diana Coole notes 'tends to hold a schizoid attitude toward the private realm as civil society and domestic sphere, modern and traditional, masculine and feminine, individualist and familial, contractual and natural ... Although its inconsistencies are theoretically unsatisfying, in the economy of gender power, they permit an entirely functional flexibility'.[15]

Taken together, these three feminist critiques of the public–private distinction draw attention to the way in which the liberal notion still incorporates an earlier classic notion of the public–private distinction as a division between the political sphere and a pre-political natural sphere of the home. They differ in that the second feminist critique (advocated by Pateman) views this incorporation as defining of liberalism itself, while the third feminist critique (advocated by Okin) views the incorporation as inconsistent with liberalism. They concur though in the assessment that, to the extent that women are part of this home world they become, like slaves, the unacknowledged preconditions of the male public world of autonomous individuals.

Notwithstanding their differences, feminist approaches to the public–private dichotomy have collectively made three related points. First, most mainstream political theorists have ignored the domestic sphere; second, the public–private distinction is deeply gendered, operating as a discourse that legitimates the assignment of men and women to different spheres of life (which has been particularly oppressive for women, who have conventionally been assigned to a domestic sphere that – as the first point suggests – has been marginalised within political discourses); third, by classifying the family as private, the public–private distinction has frequently worked to shield abuse and domination within familial relations, placing them beyond political scrutiny or legal intervention.[16]

Given these critiques, the challenge is to understand how some views of the public–private distinction have oppressed women and to reconstruct, if possible, another understanding of the distinction which does not.

3 Re-theorising public and private

In this context, feminist theorists have turned towards the project of reconceptualising the public and private in new, less gendered ways. There is evidence that the feminist literature on the public–private distinction takes one beyond critique to prescription. Indeed some have suggested that a single alternative feminist model of the public–private distinction has emerged. A recent typology of public–private distinctions proposes four major ways in which the public–private distinction is currently used: the liberal-economistic approach, which focuses on a distinction between state administration and the market economy; the republican-virtue approach, which sees the public realm in terms of political community, distinct from both the market and the administrative state; the anthropological approach, which focuses on the public realm as a sphere of fluid and polymorphous sociability; and the feminist approach, which conceives of the distinction as one between the family and the larger economic and political order.[17] Within this typology feminist critiques become a feminist approach, offering its own normative endorsement of the distinction between public and private.

Yet one need not endorse this 'feminist approach' in order to find one or all of the critiques valuable. One can point out the extent to which the public–private distinction has been drawn upon to justify inaction in 'private' affairs such as marital rape and domestic violence, without suggesting that this discourse has any significance in theorising what constitutes a just distribution of benefits and burdens in the social world today. Indeed, a closer inspection of the feminist attempts to re-theorise the public–private distinction reveals three distinct strategies rather than a single model. These are first, the de-gendering of the values associated with the public and the private; second, the reconceptualisation of either the public or the private, or both; and third, the deconstruction of the dichotomy itself.[18]

In contrast to the early feminist slogan that 'the personal is political', theorists advocating both the first and second strategies surveyed here are unified in their endorsement of the importance of maintaining some form of distinction between the public and the private. Okin, for instance suggests that 'there are some reasonable distinctions to be made between the public and domestic spheres' and Pateman acknowledges that 'the personal is the political' is merely a slogan, which should not obscure the fact that different criteria ought to order our interactions as citizens and as 'friends and lovers'.[19] These strategies attempt 'to break down the rigid demarcation between public and private without obliterating the distinction between these two domains'.[20] Accepting the normative desirability of a public–private distinction, theorists worked to first disentangle gender discourses from the dichotomy, then to reconsider the nature of the two entities, public and private, that might best constitute the de-gendered dichotomy. Much of this thinking is implicitly informed by a desire to reclaim the second liberal-romantic conception of the private as a sphere of intimacy, in the face of the dominance of an ambiguous alliance between the conceptions of the private sphere as a sphere of domestic oppression (and with the classical conception) or of civil contract (as with the first liberal conception). By contrast, the third attempt to rethink the public and private would deconstruct the continued pertinence of the distinction itself.

The first attempt to rethink the public and private focuses on the importance of de-gendering the separate spheres. This approach focuses on the second of the general claims made within the feminist critiques of the distinction, namely, that the public–private distinction is deeply gendered, operating as a discourse that legitimates the assignment of men and women to different spheres of life. An important strategy for undermining the gendered nature of the distinction

has involved challenging the idea that women have actually always been confined to the 'private' realm. To accept this claim (even if only to criticise the negative effect that it has had on women), is to perpetuate a patriarchal discourse
rather than destabilise it. The reality has always been more complex than this.
Working-class women, for example, have rarely been afforded the luxury of
remaining entirely within the home.[21]

In addition to producing alternative historical narratives which explore the
complexity of male and female relations to the public and private spheres
(thereby destabilising the binary narratives that help perpetuate women's confinement to the private), many feminists have urged reforms that would facilitate women's actual increased participation in the public sphere. The ambition
here is to allow women access to the participatory political sphere of positive
freedom and public recognition along with men. Betty Friedan, for example,
saw women's confinement to the private sphere as the source of 'the problem'
and encouraged their entry into the public sphere of professional employment
and political engagement as the source of their liberation. In so doing, she
accepted and reinforced prevailing understandings of the private as natural
drudgery and the public as the site of human achievement. Friedan accepted
the notion of the private sphere as oppressive, and suggested that women
escape its confines as men have done rather than advocating men participate
in it more.[22]

By contrast, the second attempt to rethink the public and private focuses on
the construction of the spheres themselves, not just the gender of their occu-
pants. As part of this broad project feminist theorists have proposed revised
conceptualisations of both the private and the public spheres. Susan Moller
Okin focuses on the failure of liberal states to extend the principles of justice
to the private sphere as the problem, and locates the resolution in an extension
of liberal rights to domestic and familial relations. She advocates granting
women the rights of negative liberty within the private sphere already claimed
by men. Her suggestion is that the liberal notion proper of privacy, as represented by John Stuart Mill's view of the sphere where you can think freely and
not be interfered with, has value if agents are in a position to be able to use that
privacy constructively. Nonetheless, she accepts a threefold definition of the
private sphere as a place for intimate relations with others, a space where one
can temporarily shed one's public roles and as a means of securing the time
alone to develop one's creativity.[23] In order to realise this ideal she proposes an
extension of the principles of liberal justice, already applied to the realm of
civil society, to the domestic realm. One could then reclaim and de-gender the
liberal conception of privacy, ridding it of its contingent incorporation of non-
liberal traditions.[24]

Similarly Jean Bethke Elshtain depicts the private sphere as a potential sphere
of intimate human relations protected from the influence of the political[25] and
Iris Marion Young proposes a definition of the private as, 'that aspect of his or
her life and activity that any person has the right to exclude from others'.[26]

There is, in these texts, a shared commitment to maintaining a private sphere which is equally realisable for both men and women and a clear acknowledgement that any such sphere will be socially constituted and historically contingent. These writings attempt to reclaim the concept of privacy, endorsing its normative value while distancing it from a geographical location within the domestic sphere. However, various issues remain unresolved in these revisionings. For example, it is unclear whether one can maintain an idea of private affairs which is socially and politically decided without that idea also being 'institutional' in some sense. Moreover, this recovered notion of privacy may be dissociated from the family and the domestic and may not be overtly spatial, but it could well continue to be restrictive in the sense that what one has a 'right to exclude from others' will be decided by the community, or the powerful groupings within it.

In addition to these attempts to map out new, de-gendered conceptions of the private, various new articulations of the public have also recently emerged. Whereas the reconceived models of the private sphere tend to appeal to a liberal tradition, many of the reconceived models of the public sphere have been influenced by Jürgen Habermas's work. His major contribution was to isolate the public sphere as a structure within civil society in which he locates 'the political', which is distinguished from both the narrow conception of politics as the state and a wider notion of the political as power relations.[27] This conception of a public sphere is characterised by the institutionalisation of the ideal of equality, the existence of rational communication and deliberation on issues of general significance. Many feminist theorists have criticised this model for being overly universalistic and so suppressing concrete difference, which has the effect of marginalising women from the public.[28] Yet several aim to revise and 'feminise' this vision of the public sphere rather than reject it.[29] Iris Young, for example, proposes a more heterogeneous public, open to 'bodily and affective particularity'.[30] Her suggestion is that the public should be open and accessible, which will require the rejection of the tradition of Enlightenment republicanism that, in aspiring to the 'common good', inevitably submerges particularity. If public spaces are to be inclusive, Young maintains, they must promote the positive recognition of differences of perspective, experience and affiliation. The distinction between public and private is maintained, but its association with distinct institutions or human attributes is firmly rejected.[31]

This second type of attempt to rethink the public–private distinction covers a wide range of theoretical perspectives (liberal, republican and postmodern). What binds these together as a group is the determination to retain a distinction between, newly reworked, conceptions of public and private. This commitment stands in contrast to an earlier feminist tendency to adopt an over-inclusive notion of the public as all that is non-domestic, including civil society, the market economy and the political realm. It also contrasts with a more recent tendency to reject the public–private distinction altogether – which characterises the third perspective to be considered.

The third strategy draws on a general deconstructive challenge to dichotomous thinking. Such thinking entails an accepted opposition between two identities, which are hierarchically ordered, where this pair is held to define the
whole.[32] In other words, it generates two polarised terms, one of which is
defined by its not being the other, such that the secondary status of the subordinate term is a condition for the possibility of the dominant one. These two
terms are assumed to constitute a whole, not simply parts of an open-ended
plurality. The deconstruction of dichotomies, revealing the ways in which each
side of a binary division implies and reflects the other, is one of the central
methodological devices of an increasingly prevalent theoretical approach, now
highly influential within feminist theory.[33]

Those who adopt this third approach to the public–private distinction highlight the extent to which previous critiques have reinforced the notion that
there actually is *a* dichotomy at work. When Pateman famously asserted that
the public–private dichotomy is 'ultimately, what the feminist movement is
about',[34] she may have actually entrenched the apparent dichotomy between
public and private by accepting its status as a binary divide. More recently, theorists have begun to question this assumption.

Joan Scott, for example, suggests that: 'It makes no sense for the feminist
movement to let its arguments be forced into pre-existing categories and its
political disputes to be characterised by a dichotomy we did not invent.'[35] And
Coole argues that 'a dichotomous cartography looks both anachronistic and
complicit'.[36] Public and private are consistently presented through a series of
spatial metaphors, each space defined by not being its other. Moreover, 'such
spaces are normatively interpreted ... on the basis of certain metaphysical
judgements about what it means to excel as a human subject'.[37] Although the
metaphor is a spatial one, there is a disciplinary project embedded within it: 'the
location and permeability of this boundary, as well as the association of the
spaces it divides with particular groups or qualities, is not about geography, but
power'.[38] Both activities and populations are spatially distributed, disciplined by
the normative hierarchy of spaces.

Following the achievement of women's right to vote and stand for election,
the rise of 'girl power' and the feminisation of the workforce, Coole suggests, it
is simply not clear that women are any longer primarily confined to, or associated with, the private sphere. Moreover, in the context of diversity politics it is
increasingly problematic to assume that 'women' as a coherent category have
any single and stable relation to spheres of life: 'Not only are women themselves
seen to be differentially distributed across a series of spaces, due to their complex identities, but it becomes increasingly difficult to maintain that gender is
the privileged index of spatial politics.'[39] In the context of the increasing mobility and visibility of populations following new technological developments, it is
perhaps no longer remotely realistic to maintain a commitment to privacy as a
spatially guaranteed phenomenon. As Peter Steinberger recognises, feminist
writers 'have demonstrated, beyond any doubt, that the idea of a separate and

distinct sphere of privacy is indeed an ideological distortion, incompatible with our moral institutions and inconsistent with the realities of a complex, highly differentiated society'.[40]

This third approach is committed, like the first, to deconstructing the apparently natural correlation between women and the private sphere, men and the public sphere. It is also committed, like the second, to deconstructing the current dominant binary dualism between public and private. But, unlike the other two, this third approach would deconstruct the pertinence of the dichotomy itself, suggesting that not only patriarchal, but also feminist articulations of the dichotomy are both anachronistic and disciplinary.

Despite the diversity among the proposals to reconstruct the meaning and significance of the public and private, the second group of theorists nonetheless maintain a dichotomous framework and a language of binary spheres. The danger, as Coole points out, is that, 'because feminism is so closely identified with the language of public and private ... we might carry on using it in a situation where it is no longer empirically relevant or politically useful'.[41]

Conclusion

Feminist engagement with the public–private dichotomy has resulted in innumerable positive contributions to political theory and practice. On the theoretical level, the most significant contribution has been the uncovering of the place of the domestic within mainstream political theory. Inverting the standpoint of the observer, feminist theorists looked out from the domestic sphere and asserted that the liberal insistence on labelling civil society as private had the effect of hiding the very existence of the domestic.

Most of the feminist writing on public and private has worked to undermine the stability of the dichotomy in that it has uncovered the historical contingency of any distinction between the public and the private, and has drawn attention to the ambiguities arising from the co-existence of several distinct articulations of the distinction within contemporary discourses. However, it is possible that this writing has become complicit in the perpetuation of the dichotomous thinking that surrounds debates about public and private.

Phillips suggests that the public–private dichotomy 'was early identified as the crucial underpinning to patriarchal political thought'.[42] This has been the received wisdom about the public–private dichotomy within feminist theory for a number of years. But this new orthodoxy stands in need of disturbance. We should question 'whether it still makes sense ... for feminists to privilege this particular spatial division' if 'this particular map of gendered space is becoming anachronistic due to changing topography'.[43] Were more attention to be paid to the differences between individual autonomy and small-group intimacy, between state administration, market economy, political community and urban sociability, the pertinence of a binary image of spheres would lessen and new explorations in plural spheres might emerge.[44] Dispensing with the language of dichotomous spheres would allow for either a fuller exploration of the notion of multiple separate spheres, or the rejection of spatial metaphors altogether allowing for a greater focus on the meaning of privacy and publicness, disentangled from the prejudices of geographic tradition.

Notes

1 I would like to thank Andy Mason, Richard Bellamy, Chris Armstrong and Johanna Kantola for their helpful comments on an earlier draft of this chapter.
2 N. Bobbio, 'The Great Dichotomy: Public/Private', in N. Bobbio, *Democracy and Dictatorship*, tr. P. Kennealy (Minneapolis, MN, University of Minnesota Press, 1989).
3 See H. Arendt, *The Human Condition* (Chicago, University of Chicago Press, 1958).
4 W. Kymlicka, *Contemporary Political Philosophy* (Oxford, Oxford University Press, 2001, 2nd edn), pp. 388–98.
5 J. Weintraub, 'The Theory and Politics of the Public/Private Distinction', in J. Weintraub and K. Kumar (eds), *Public and Private in Thought and Practice: Perspectives on a Grand Dichotomy* (Chicago, University of Chicago Press, 1997), p. 28.
6 Catharine MacKinnon adopts one of the most directly hostile stances in relation to the public/private distinction itself, arguing that the idea of a private realm is 'a means of subordinating women's collective needs to the imperatives of male supremacy': C. MacKinnon, *Toward a Feminist Theory of the State* (Cambridge, MA, Harvard University Press, 1989), p. 188.
7 N. Chodorow, *The Reproduction of Mothering: Psychoanalysis and the Sociology of Gender* (Berkeley, CA, University of California Press, 1978); M. O'Brien, *The Politics of Reproduction* (London, Routledge and Kegan Paul, 1983).
8 K. Green, *The Woman of Reason. Feminism, Humanism and Political Thought* (Cambridge, Polity Press, 1995); A. Jaggar, 'Love and Knowledge: Emotion in Feminist Epistemology', in S. Kemp and J. Squires (eds), *Feminisms* (Oxford, Oxford University Press, 1997), pp. 188–93; G. Lloyd, *The Man of Reason: 'Male' and 'Female' in Western Philosophy* (London, Methuen, 1984).
9 D. Bubeck, *Care, Gender and Justice* (Oxford, Clarendon Press, 1995); J.B. Elshtain, *Public Man, Private Woman: Women in Social and Political Thought* (Oxford, Martin Robertson, 1981); C. Gilligan, *In a Different Voice: Psychological Theory and Women's Development* (Cambridge, MA, Harvard University Press, 1982); S. Ruddick, *Maternal Thinking: Towards a Politics of Peace* (Boston, MA, Beacon Press, 1989); J. Tronto, *Moral Boundaries: The Political Argument for an Ethic of Care* (New York, Routledge, 1993).
10 C. Pateman and T. Brennan, 'Mere Auxiliaries to the Commonwealth: Women and the Origins of Liberalism', *Political Studies*, 27 (1979), pp. 183–200; C. Pateman, 'Feminist Critiques of the Public/Private Dichotomy', in S. Benn and G. Gaus (eds), *Public and Private in Social Life* (London, Croom Helm, 1983), pp. 281–303; C. Pateman, *The Sexual Contract* (Cambridge, Polity Press, 1988).
11 C. Pateman, *The Sexual Contract*, pp. 121–2.
12 S.M. Okin, *Gender, Justice and the Family* (New York, Basic Books, 1989); S.M. Okin, 'Gender, the Public and the Private', in A. Phillips (ed.), *Feminism and Politics* (Oxford, Oxford University Press, 1998), pp. 116–41.
13 Z. Eisenstein, *The Radical Future of Liberal Feminism* (New York, Longman 1981), p. 26.

14 Advocates of the second critique, such as Pateman, by and large accept the third critique as well. Whereas Pateman would want to see this as a symptom of a wider interconnection, discussed in the second critique (about social contract theory), Okin characterises this third critique as the totality of the problem.

15 D. Coole, 'Cartographic Convulsions: Public and Private Reconsidered', *Political Theory*, 28:3 (2000), p. 343.

16 Weintraub, 'The Theory and Politics of the Public/Private Distinction', p. 29.

17 Weintraub, 'The Theory and Politics of the Public/Private Distinction', p. 7.

18 Ruth Lister, *Citizenship: Feminist Perspectives* (Basingstoke, Macmillan, 1997) pp. 120–1.

19 Okin, *Gender, Justice and the Family*, p. x and C. Pateman, *The Disorder of Women* (Stanford, CA, Stanford University Press, 1989); pp. 112–13. See also J.B. Elshtain, *Public Man, Private Woman* and I.M. Young, *Justice and the Politics of Difference* (Princeton, NJ, Princeton University Press, 1990).

20 M.L. Shanley and U. Narayan, *Reconstructing Political Theory* (Cambridge, Polity Press, 1997), p. xiv.

21 D. Helly and S. Reverby (eds), *Gendered Domains: Rethinking Public and Private in Women's History* (Ithaca, NY, Cornell University Press, 1997).

22 B. Friedan, *The Feminine Mystique* (Harmondsworth, Penguin, 1963).

23 Okin 'Gender, the Public and the Private', p. 136.

24 Okin, *Gender, Justice and the Family*.

25 Elshtain, *Public Man, Private Woman*.

26 Young, *Justice and the Politics of Difference*, p. 119.

27 J. Habermas, *The Structural Transformation of the Public Sphere*, tr. T. Burger (Cambridge, MA, MIT Press, 1989).

28 S. Benhabib, *Situating the Self: Gender, Community and Postmodernism in Contemporary Ethics* (Cambridge, Polity Press, 1992); N. Fraser, 'Rethinking the Public Sphere: A Contribution to the Critique of Actually Existing Democracy', in C. Calhoun (ed.), *Habermas and the Public Sphere* (Cambridge, MA, MIT Press, 1992); A. Yeatman, *Postmodern Revisionings of the Political* (New York, Routledge, 1994).

29 Benhabib, *Situating the Self*; Fraser 'Rethinking the Public Sphere'; J. Landes, 'The Public and the Private Sphere: A Feminist Reconsideration', in J. Landes (ed.), *Feminism, the Public and the Private* (Oxford, Oxford University Press, 1998), pp. 135–63.

30 I.M. Young, 'Impartiality and the Civic Public', in J. Landes (ed.), *Feminism, the Public and the Private* (Oxford, Oxford University Press, 1998), p. 443.

31 Young, *Justice and the Politics of Difference*, pp. 166–71.

32 See R. Prokhovnik, *Rational Woman: A Feminist Critique of Dichotomy* (London and New York, Routledge, 1999), pp. 23–31.

33 See M. Barrett and A. Phillips (eds), *Destablising Theory* (Cambridge, Polity Press, 1992). p. 8.

34 Pateman, 'Feminist Critiques of the Public/Private Dichotomy', p. 281.

35 J. Scott, 'Deconstructing Equality-Versus-Difference: Or, the Uses of Poststructuralist Theory for Feminism', in D.T. Meyers (ed.), *Feminist Social Thought: A Reader* (New York and London, Routledge, 1997), p. 765.

36 Coole, 'Cartographic Convulsions', p. 350.

37 Coole, 'Cartographic Convulsions', p. 338.

38 Coole, 'Cartographic Convulsions', p. 339.

39 Coole, 'Cartographic Convulsions', p. 350.

40 P. Steinberger, 'Public and Private', *Political Studies*, 42 (1999), p. 312.

41 Coole, 'Cartographic Convulsions', p. 346.

42 A. Phillips, 'Universal Pretensions in Political Thought', in A. Phillips and M. Barrett (eds), *Destablizing Theory* (Cambridge, Polity Press, 1992), p. 17.

43 Coole, 'Cartographic Convulsions', p. 338.

44 Michael Walzer has of course offered one articulation of a theory of separate spheres: see M. Walzer, *Spheres of Justice: A Defence of Pluralism and Equality* (Oxford, Blackwell, 1983). This model has been largely ignored within feminist writings however: see C. Armstrong 'Philosophical Interpretation in the Work of Michael Walzer', *Politics*, 20:2, May (2000).

12

Community: individuals acting together

Keith Graham

Introduction

The background (though most emphatically not the topic) of this discussion is the liberal/communitarian debate. Many believe that debate has now run its course, but it has left an indelible mark on the way that perennial questions about the relations between individual and community are framed. In this chapter I attempt to articulate the idea of one kind of community, pertinent to social and political questions, which is present in many areas of actual human life. In section 1 I discuss the general idea of community, then offer and explore a specific conception of community as collective agency. In section 2 I suggest that membership of a collective agency raises, but does not of itself settle, important questions about loyalty, allegiance and dissociation. In section 3 I suggest that the existence of collective agencies casts doubt on the adequacy of the doctrine of the distinctness of persons.

1 Community and collective agency

The concept of community is a protean one. At its broadest it applies simply to a number of individuals who share something in common. But what they share in common, and indeed how the idea of sharing is to be understood, are matters for further elaboration. For example, they may constitute a community by virtue of *sharing the same physical location*: in that sense, the squire and the peasant may belong to the same community though in other important respects they stand in relations of separation and even opposition. By contrast, people talk of the gay community or a linguistic community, where the individuals who compose that community may be spatially separated and unknown to one another. Presumably, what underlies the idea of community in the non-spatial sense is some notion of common or *shared interests*. That in its turn would have to be distinguished from a community involving not merely shared interests but, as it is often put, *shared meanings and understandings*. Charles Taylor suggests:

Common meanings are the basis of community. Inter-subjective meaning gives people a common language to talk about social reality and a common understanding of certain norms, but only with common meanings does this common reference world contain significant common actions, celebrations and feelings. These are objects in the world that everybody shares. This is what makes community.[1]

The idea of community can also vary depending on whether we think of the individual as belonging to one *overarching* community or to a *series* of communities. It has been a matter of contention whether communitarianism insinuates the idea that there is just *one* relevant community in which an individual is located.[2] I do not attempt to settle that question. Some communitarians certainly acknowledge the fact of multiple and conflicting communities (as they must). Sandel, for example, says 'There is no such thing as "*the* society as a whole" . . . Each of us moves in an indefinite number of communities'.[3] But it is another matter whether that explicit acknowledgement is accompanied, either in Sandel's or in others' case, by the acknowledged fact's playing an appropriately prominent role in subsequent thinking.[4]

Once the existence of multiple communities is acknowledged, questions arise about the priority among them. Amitai Etzioni has argued for layered loyalties 'divided between commitment to one's immediate community and to the more encompassing community, and according priority to the overarching one on key select matters'.[5] But it may be less than clear which community counts as the overarching one. Neera Badhwar says that she 'will follow communitarian practice in using "society", "nation", "state", and "political community" interchangeably'.[6] In a discussion of state authority which is pertinent for considerations of community, Joseph Raz says 'Throughout the discussion I refer interchangeably to the state, which is the political organization of a society, its government, the agent through which it acts, and the law, the vehicle through which much of its power is exercised'.[7] But since these different terms refer to distinct institutions, that raises problems about priority. What if a government has acted illegally, for example? What if the actions of the state are inimical to the interests of the nation? What if the state represents some sectional interest rather than the interests of the whole society? In these circumstances it will be a matter of deep contention what is required for according priority to the overarching community, because it will be contentious which community *is* the overarching one.

'Community', then, can be used for a variety of different purposes, to pick out different phenomena in our life as social creatures: shared location, shared interests, shared meanings and understandings, and so on.[8] In the midst of these varying conceptions of community, there is no point in being essentialist or prescriptive: in what follows I attempt to isolate and characterise one form of community which is highly salient in the social and political lives of individuals, and to indicate what follows from its existence for some of the issues which were at stake in the liberal/communitarian debate. The form of community in question is a *collective agency*: what its members share in common is participation in collective action.

Sometimes the actions of individual human beings are best seen as part of some collective action. For example, I may join a number of other people in collectively pushing a broken-down car. The most appropriate and informative description of what I am doing will make reference to the fact that I am acting with others in this way. In this kind of case, there is little conceptual distance between individual and collective action. Each of us individually is attempting to do that very same thing which all of us collectively succeed in doing. Often, moreover, the collection of people involved will be an ad hoc one which dissolves after the task in hand has been achieved. But it is a significant contingent fact about the world we inhabit that there are collective agencies of a more persistent and distinctive character.

Consider two examples of more persistent and distinctive collective agencies (rather special examples, as it will turn out). I may be not merely kicking a ball around a field but playing in a football team. Or I may be not just playing a clarinet but participating in an orchestral performance. Collective agencies like football teams and orchestras typically exist over a period of time and engage in a whole series of related actions – in other words, they persist in a way that, typically, a collection of car-pushers does not. Connected to that persistence is the further fact that the collective agency can survive a change in its constituent membership. Particular individuals come and go but the team or the orchestra goes on. Moreover, these collective agencies are distinctive in that what they do is distinct from what their individual constituents do: it is only the collective agent, the team, which wins a match and is awarded points for doing so; it is only the orchestra which produces an orchestral performance. (Indeed, one reason why these examples are special is that these collective agencies do things which it would be conceptually *impossible* for individuals to do.)

I shall refer to collective agencies which exhibit these properties of persistence and distinctiveness as CAs.[9] They have an ineliminable presence in our social world, in that we cannot say all that we need to say about that world without referring to them. We may insist that a team's or an orchestra's playing is just a matter of a number of individuals acting in various ways, and in a sense this is true. But it is a matter of their doing things *as members of that entity*, and something important is left out of any description of their activities which does not make that clear. There is, then, a certain kind of irreducibility and priority here: our best descriptions of the social world will contain irreducibly collective terms, and there will be a portion of individuals' behaviour where an adequate description will require prior reference to the collective agency in which they are acting. Whether any kind of *ontological* or *moral* priority attach to CAs are further questions.[10] Our social world contains many instances of CAs as described here. Committees, neighbour associations, trade unions, churches, electorates, governments, classes, business corporations, for example, all exhibit the characteristics of persistence and distinctiveness of action. They do things which individuals do not, they possess resources which individuals do not, and their existence is recognised in law.

Collective agencies, communities of individuals sharing collective action, will often be co-extensive with communities of individuals sharing some of the different characteristics mentioned earlier, such as shared location, shared interests, shared meanings and understandings. But for any given CA it will be an open question whether it possesses all or any of these other characteristics. Thus, a CA may consist of individuals located in the same place or it may not: a team does, but a trade union does not. Similarly, a CA may consist of individuals sharing a common interest or it may not: The National Association for the Advancement of Colored People does, but a court does not.[11] Most importantly, and least easily seen, a CA may consist of shared meanings and understandings in the way described earlier *or it may not.*

The point is not easily seen because shared meanings and understandings are certainly necessary for the collective actions of *some* CAs, such as teams and orchestras, to take place at all. A team's winning is an 'institutional fact'. There are rules which specify what counts as winning, and without those rules winning is not possible at all. The fact that Team X won, unlike the fact that the sun is 93 million miles from the earth, depends on a complicated set of attitudes taken up by the agents involved.[12] (That is a further respect in which the cases of teams and orchestras are special.) But not all collective agency will have this character: there is also a phenomenon which might be called *hidden* collective agency.

This may also be introduced by example. A number of individuals may form a clique. (Perhaps they all went to the same school or belong to the same leisure interest club.) They interact in ways which have an excluding effect on others: they make allusions which they, but not others, immediately recognise; they anticipate each other's reactions as others cannot; they share a history and a set of attitudes which others do not. The consequence is that non-members of the clique cannot engage in social exchange in the same way, and feel a general sense of exclusion. Now this phenomenon exhibits the following features of the original examples of collective agency: the entity is a continuing one rather than an ad hoc one lasting only briefly; we may assume that it can persist while some (or over a period perhaps even all) of its constituents change; and it does something distinctive which its individual members do not. (Indeed, perhaps the individuals even *cannot* do the same, since no individual could have a general excluding effect in this way.) But the phenomenon precisely does not exhibit the feature that its activities come into being as a result of the attitude which its constituents have towards what they are doing. On the contrary, they may simply be unaware of what they are doing collectively, though each is perfectly aware of what they are doing individually.[13] Even here the point may easily be missed, since shared understandings abound in cliques. However, what is not necessarily present is a shared understanding among its members *that they constitute a clique!* The example itself may be of no great moment, but its structural features are reproduced in more important contexts. For example, an indigenous population may unwittingly act towards strangers in its midst as members of a clique do, but with results which are politically much more serious.

The notion of a hidden CA actually covers several different possibilities. We may be unaware that a CA exists at all, or unaware of its exact nature; we may be unaware that it has acted on some particular occasion or unaware of the actual significance of what it has done. And 'we' here may be either the constituents of the collective agency or observers. In any event, a CA does not necessarily involve shared meanings and understandings in the way intended in some conceptions of community. Though it is necessary for a number of individuals to act together for a CA to be in operation, they may *or may not* have any shared conception of what they are collectively doing (because individually they may not have *any conception at all* of what they are collectively doing).

Notice that a CA is not necessarily an overall community. True, a whole village or a whole culture may act in some way significantly different from its constituents taken severally, so that we wish to characterise it as a CA; but at the same time there will many CAs which are very local and partial communities. This has consequences for the issues discussed in section 2.

2 Community, identification and dissociation

One of the central matters of contention in the liberal/communitarian debate was whether 'the self is prior to the ends which are affirmed by it'.[14] The negative communitarian answer held that the self is an embedded self: it approaches the selection of ends with a particular social identity which predetermines its mode of selecting them, so that, for example, a shared communal end is 'not a relationship [people] choose (as in a voluntary association) but an attachment they discover'[15] and 'agency consists less in summoning the will than in seeking self-understanding'.[16]

Now any tolerably adequate description of me as an individual will include reference to various social roles which I inhabit – teacher, parent, voter, and so on – and these descriptions will therefore constitute part of my identity. It is then tempting to infer that 'what is good for me has to be the good for one who inhabits these roles'.[17] Or, as Ross Poole has recently expressed it: 'An identity defines a perspective on the world and our place in it . . . It calls upon us – or those who have the appropriate identity – to act in one way rather than another.'[18] But the inference is too hasty. There is an important distinction to be observed between *identity* and *identification*. As a creature capable of self-consciousness, deliberation and action, it is always open to me to reflect on my identity, to consider whether I wish to continue in the roles I occupy, and (sometimes) to act to divest myself of one or more of them. I can, in other words, choose to *identify with* or *dissociate from* a given role. So, for example, if I am a victim of racial or domestic violence, what is good for me is to cease having those descriptions applicable to me. Arguably, something similar is true if I am a member of the Ku Klux Klan. In that way, what is good for me may not be what is good for the inhabitant of a given role. On the contrary, what is good for me is to divest myself of the role. Of course, divesting oneself of a role is not always an option. I cannot cease being someone's parent or offspring (though even there I may choose not to act in ways associated with the role) and perhaps in practice I cannot cease being a citizen of the state I live in, for example.

Similarly, dissociation specifically from a CA[19] is not always an option. Here, as in the case of individual action, there are the possibilities of compulsive or coerced action, where some of the normal features of control and decision are lacking. (I may act in an army as a conscript, for example). But membership of a CA is peculiarly susceptible to the possibility of dissociation, for reflection on such membership is, precisely, reflection on what one is participating in *doing*; and, anxieties about determinism aside, what one does is a matter where choices and decision are in principle involved. Moreover, even in cases of coercion a shadow of the options of identification and dissociation persists, in the form of the attitude with which someone participates. If I have been coerced, for example, into taking part in some collective practices which humiliate others, I can still do so reluctantly, affirming to myself that this is something I do not wish to be doing, rather than willingly and with relish.

The need for choice and decision and the possibility of dissociation, rather than solely discovery, are all the more apparent given that CAs are typically partial rather than overall communities. Collective agencies engage in courses of action which sometimes conflict. There may be deep-rooted conflicts between classes or nations or ethnic groups, there may be more tractable conflicts between neighbourhood associations and residents of a particular street. And then sometimes an individual finds that they belong to a number of different CAs which are locked in conflict. You are, say, a parent, an employee, a manager, a member of the board of school governors; and the CAs associated with these descriptions are pulling in different directions. The conflicts *between* CAs are then reproduced *within* an individual, who will experience the pull of acting in different directions and will have to make decisions about priorities.

It is not clear to me how wise it is to take a stand on the blanket question whether or not the self is prior to its ends. What can be said with more confidence, however, is that the self is importantly distinct from its ends in the context of particular CAs. Where an individual is participating in collective action with others, a space must always be left for critical reflection, options of identification with or dissociation from the CA and (where this is a live possibility) even actual detachment from a CA. None of this will be settled by mere membership of a CA. But then since CAs are sometimes co-extensive with communities defined in other ways, exactly the same options must remain open in those contexts. To that extent, an individual's embeddedness fails to settle questions of ends without the addition of critical reflection. (Whether the critical reflection proceeds by reference to abstract principles or to the values of some *other* community to which someone belongs will be a further question.)

3 Community and the distinctness of persons

A perennial concern in relations between individual and community is the question whether the one type of entity has priority over the other (though it is an important philosophical error to suppose that there is only one kind of priority and that therefore priority must always attach entirely either to the one or to the other). Here, too, current thinking has been influenced by the liberal/communitarian debate, in particular by the appeal to the distinctness of persons frequently made by liberals. Rawls, for example, has argued that 'the plurality of distinct persons with separate systems of ends is an essential feature of human societies.'[20] What we cannot then do, according to Rawls, is use the same kind of reasoning when arriving at social decisions as that used by one individual with one set of ends: the 'reasoning which balances the gains and losses of different persons as if they were one person is excluded'.[21]

Nozick makes a similar point. Individually, we sometimes choose to undergo some pain or sacrifice for a greater benefit or to avoid a greater harm: in other words, we accept some cost for the sake of the greater overall good. Why should we not also argue that some people must bear some costs so that others may gain, for the sake of the greater overall social good? Nozick's reply is that

> there is no *social entity* with a good that undergoes some sacrifice for its own good. There are only individual people, different individual people, with their own individual lives. Using one of these people for the benefit of others, uses him and benefits the others. Nothing more. What happens is that something is done to him for the sake of others. Talk of an overall social good covers this up. (Intentionally?) To use a person in this way does not sufficiently respect and take account of the fact that he is a separate person, that his is the only life he has. *He* does not get some overbalancing good from his sacrifice, and no one is entitled to force this upon him.[22]

According to the doctrine, it is particularly important to bundle together the desires of a single individual. By contrast, no special importance attaches to a bundle which represents the desires of different individuals for the same end. That explains why the doctrine is invoked to criticise classical utilitarianism, which is taken to allot special importance to the latter kind of bundle, in the interest of maximising overall desire-satisfaction, regardless of whose desires they happen to be.

There is both an implausibility and an incompleteness in the doctrine of the distinctness of persons.[23] The implausibility arises from neglecting the complexity of individuals' desires. They can reflect on them, accord some higher priority than others, and also acquire meta-desires (as when I desire to smoke but desire not to desire to smoke, or desire that people's desires should be less conventional). Consequently, individuals themselves may attach importance to the fact that a given end is desired by a number of other people, and they may themselves attach more importance to some desire jointly held by a number of people than to the bundle of their own individual desires. Thus, I might desire a cessation of some incidence of racial oppression, regard this desire as having much higher priority than any other desires I have, recognise that it is a desire held by others, and believe that it is important that there is a high level of desire for this cessation. This combination of beliefs and desires among a number of individuals can itself generate a sense of community – in terms of shared desires – across individuals: we identify with one another as desirers of the same end. Where individuals themselves sum desires across individuals in this way, rather than only seeing them as desires which each of them has individually, it is not clear that we can be so confident that no importance should be attached to such a process of summation across individuals.

Consider an objection. It might be said that in the case in hand the desire is for a state of the world, cessation of racial oppression, rather than for a state of an individual. But, it might be objected, it is only the latter kind of desire which the doctrine is meant to cover. This objection is weak, because all the essentials of the claim could be re-run with individuals' desire for states of themselves. The earlier example of the National Association for the Advancement of Colored People would illustrate the point. It may matter to me what happens to me as a coloured person, and it may therefore matter to me what happens to people who are like me in that respect. And that may matter more to me than any other questions about my own well-being. Moreover, since many desires *are* for general states of the world rather than for the individual, it would be a considerable restriction on the scope of the doctrine if it were thought not to be applicable to such general desires. For example, suppose I desire to own a watch. The realisation of the desired state of affairs would involve others (those who make, sell and transport watches). Although the desiring is a state of an individual, the realisation of what is desired would involve other individuals, and it is not clear why the latter fact should be thought any less important than the place of residence of the desire, as it were.[24]

The incompleteness of the doctrine of the distinctness of persons lies in its failure to allow for the existence of necessarily collective ends, such as winning a team game, performing a symphony or electing a government. It is not at all surprising that we encounter *collective* desires for such ends, since it is only collectivities of individuals which can actually bring them about. And where CAs have their own characteristic good, such as winning a game, performing a symphony, furthering the interests of the nation or the culture, they or their constituents can indeed undergo sacrifices for the good of that entity: the team sells some of its collective assets, or a member foregoes their wages, in order to buy a player whose presence will enhance the team's results. Hence, *pace* Nozick, it is not true that there is no social entity which can undergo a sacrifice for its own good.[25]

At this point a kind of premature moral panic may occur. It may be felt that, once we reject the distinctness of persons and allow a place for the possibility of a collectivity or an individual being sacrificed for the collective good, we are on the slippery slope to allowing the eclipse of individuals and the incursion of totalitarian collectivism. Such a thought clearly exercises Nozick. The panic is premature for two reasons. First, we are at this stage exploring the appropriate characterisation of the world we live in which will allow us then to draw defensible moral conclusions. To say that the local football team and the Ku Klux Klan each has a characteristic good is not to say that *either* good should be promoted: that is a further question. If the distinctness of persons erroneously characterises that world, it has to be rejected, and a more suitable characterisation found which will support any set of moral convictions we wish to retain. Second, even if all the claims in section 1 about the irreducibility of CAs are correct, we need to bear in mind that CAs are themselves composed of individuals and nothing else. In the context of a CA individuals have not been eclipsed, but we have to take seriously the idea that in this context they are indissolubly linked. There are, that is, circumstances where *we* collectively desire something, and that fact is not further dissolvable into circumstances where *I* do and *you* do and *she* and *he* do. We want to win and we can only want that *as a team*.

The existence of CAs, therefore, can be invoked in challenging liberal claims that there are only distinct individuals and that desires cannot be summed in any way except as belonging to individuals, just as, in the previous section, it provided the context for challenging the claim implicit in some communitarian thinking that socially embedded people discover rather than selecting their ends.[26]

Conclusion

In one way the nature of the contemporary world is congenial to a stress on the idea of community, and in another way not. On the one hand, globalisation is a cliché and the interconnections between large numbers of people on a worldwide scale are ever more apparent. The idea of human beings as isolated units seems in that respect less defensible than ever and the expression 'global village' more appropriate than ever. On the other hand, the contemporary world signally lacks a feature possessed by at least some literal villages at some times and places, namely that of providing an all-embracing community in which an individual's life gained its significance from their place in a closed social network. In that connection, it has been a familiar criticism of communitarian theory that it might have been appropriate for well integrated societies, where there was a workable notion of an all-embracing community, but that this presupposes a world which no longer exists (or perhaps never was). As I have indicated in this chapter, there are many conceptions of community more circumscribed than this all-embracing one. The conception I have concentrated on, where what people share in common is participation in collective action, has many instances in actual life, including some (such as multinational corporations) which are peculiar to modern conditions.

We need a fuller account of individuals' relations to communities of this kind than I have been able to provide here, an account of the forms which identification with them can take and the circumstances in which dissociation is justified, as well as an account of how the actions of collectivities are to be compared and contrasted with the actions of individuals. One aspect of these further matters, alluded to earlier, seems to me particularly important. Just as an individual is not necessarily in the best position to understand the existence or the nature of all of their own actions without further reflection, so collectivities of individuals may be unaware of the existence or the nature of their collective actions. People can co-ordinate their actions in subtle and complex ways and collectively produce results of which they are quite unaware. In that respect, there may be more communities around than are dreamt of in our political philosophy.

Notes

1 C. Taylor, *Philosophy and the Human Sciences* (Cambridge, Cambridge University Press, 1985), p. 39; cf. ibid., p. 96.

2 Thus, Stephen Mulhall and Adam Swift claim, for example, that the liberal/communitarian debate concerns 'the importance of the individual's right to choose her own way of life and to express herself freely, even where this conflicts with the values and commitments of *the* community or society of which she is a member' (S. Mulhall and A. Swift, *Liberals and Communitarians* (Oxford, Blackwell 1992), pp. xi–xii; italics added). Chandran Kukathas objects that the communitarian view 'neglects the fact that, even if individuals are constituted by the communities to which they belong, they are invariably members of different communities which contribute to the shaping of their lives in different ways and to different degrees' (C. Kukathas, 'Liberalism, Communitarianism and Political Community', *Social Philosophy and Policy*, 13 (1996), p. 91). Christopher McMahon claims that communitarianism 'is associated with the view that a good society is one that is organized around the promotion of a single, shared conception of the good' and he objects: 'Different members of a given society will have different selves constituted by different commitments' (C. McMahon, *Authority and Democracy* (Princeton, NJ, Princeton University Press, 1994) pp. 78–9). In contrast, Neera Badhwar seeks to show that communitarians allot a primary place to the specifically political community and to trace the implications of this for partial communities such as family or friends (N. Badhwar, 'Moral agency, commitment and impartiality', *Social Philosophy and Policy*, 13 (1996), p. 2).

3 M. Sandel, *Liberalism and the Limits of Justice* (Cambridge, Cambridge University Press, 1982), p. 146; original italics.

4 For further discussion of Sandel's position, see D. Bell, *Communitarianism and its Critics* (Oxford, Clarendon Press, 1993), pp. 91, 114, n. 8.

5 A. Etzioni, *The New Golden Rule: Community and Morality in a Democratic Society* (London, Profile Books, 1997), p. 203.

6 Badhwar, 'Moral Agency, Commitment and Impartiality', p. 4, n. 6.

7 J. Raz, *The Morality of Freedom* (Oxford, Oxford University Press, 1986), p. 70.

8 For an exhaustive account of the varying conceptions of community, see E. Frazer, *The Problems of Communitarian Politics* (Oxford, Oxford University Press, 1999), ch. 2.

9 For a more systematic characterisation of collective agency, see K. Graham, 'Collective Responsibility', in T. van den Beld (ed.), *Moral Responsibility and Ontology* (Dordrecht, Kluwer, 2000), pp. 51–3.

10 For discussion of those further questions, see K. Graham, *Practical Reasoning in a Social World: How We Act Together* (Cambridge, Cambridge University Press,

2002), McMahon, *Authority and Democracy*, and M. Gilbert, *Living Together: Rationality, Sociality and Obligation* (New York, Rowman and Littlefield, 1996).

11 Or it does only in some strained sense, such as that the individuals composing a court have an interest in making it work efficiently. But even this can be doubted in view of the arguments advanced in section 3.

12 See, for example, J.R. Searle, *The Construction of Social Reality* (Harmondsworth, Penguin, 1995), pp. 26–8, 87–8, 122.

13 And they may not be unaware. There are witting as well as unwitting cliques. Cf. Graham, *Practical Reasoning in a Social World*, ch. 3, s. 2.

14 J. Rawls, *A Theory of Justice* (Oxford, Oxford University Press, 1971), p. 560.

15 Sandel, *Liberalism and the Limits of Justice*, p. 150.

16 Sandel, *Liberalism and the Limits of Justice*, p. 152.

17 A. MacIntyre, *After Virtue: A Study in Moral Theory* (London, Duckworth, 1981), pp. 204–5.

18 R. Poole, 'Liberalism, Nationalism and Identity', in B. Brecher, J. Halliday and K. Kolinská (eds), *Nationalism and Racism in the Liberal Order* (Aldershot, Ashgate, 1998), p. 52.

19 As opposed to dissociation from some social role, which may or may not reflect membership of a CA.

20 Rawls, *Theory of Justice*, p. 29.

21 Rawls, *Theory of Justice*, p. 28.

22 R. Nozick, *Anarchy, State, and Utopia* (New York, Basic Books, 1974), pp. 32–3; original italics.

23 There is also ambiguity. For discussion of the ambiguities, see D. Brink, 'The Separateness of Persons, Distributive Norms and Moral Theory', in R. Frey and C. Morris (eds), *Value, Welfare and Morality* (Cambridge, Cambridge University Press, 1993), pp. 252–89, D. Brink, 'Rational Egoism and the Separateness of Persons', in J. Dancy (ed.), *Reading Parfit* (Oxford, Blackwell, 1997), pp. 96–134, K. Graham, 'Being Some Body', in B. Brecher, J. Halliday and K. Kolinská (eds), *Nationalism and Racism in the Liberal Order* (Aldershot, Ashgate, 1998), pp. 182–8, Raz, *Morality of Freedom*, pp. 271–87.

24 Matters are even more serious for the doctrine if desires for a state of oneself are always in effect desires for a general state of the world. For an argument that they are, see K. Graham, 'Are All Preferences Nosy?', *Res Publica*, 6 (2000), pp. 133–54.

25 When Nozick says that there is no social entity, he may mean that there is no *overall* social entity, of the kind postulated when 'community' is used in the overarching sense described in section 2. That claim may or may not be true, so far as community in the CA sense is concerned, but will in any case not suffice for escaping the objection to the doctrine based on an appeal to the existence of CAs. If there is a multiplicity of CAs with the characteristics described, it will not be true that there are only individual people or that oly they can undergo sacrifices for their own good. See my further comments on all-embracing community in the conclusion.

26 Note that the arguments of this section do nothing to reinstate utilitarianism in the face of the criticism that it fails to take seriously the distinctness of persons. In so far as utilitarianism itself merely sums individual desires on a different basis, it too fails to take seriously the possibility of non-individual goods.

13
Multiculturalism

Jonathan Seglow

Introduction[1]

Multiculturalism can be acknowledged, championed, challenged or rejected, but it cannot be ignored because it describes a central feature of the world in which we live. Oddly, however, for many years it was ignored, despite decades of struggle by black Americans for full political inclusion, the confederalism adopted by several European states to accommodate linguistic and religious diversity and the multicultural policies adopted by Australia and Canada in the 1970s, to name just three examples. In the 1980s communitarian writers embraced the culture-friendly virtues of solidarity, togetherness and belonging, but ironically, while community was prized as homely and familiar, it was never spelt out which communities – cultural or otherwise – were being invoked. Only in the early 1990s did the liberal-communitarian controversy begin to transform itself into a more particular debate about how to accommodate cultural and ethnic claims within a broadly liberal political theory. Here Will Kymlicka's *Liberalism, Community and Culture* led the way.[2] By now, it is increasingly recognised that liberal constitutions are shot through with partisan ethnocultural norms.[3]

This is the first claim I want to make then. Multiculturalism cannot be avoided. Whether endorsed as a policy (cultural diversity is good), it cannot be circumvented as a social fact, not so long as we are thinking about theories for the world in which we live and not a cultureless planet far away. Theories of justice, democracy and human rights are necessarily abstract since they have a more or less extensive reach and describe a reality not yet arrived. Abstraction is no bad thing. But when you argue that democracy fosters community, that social justice includes equal opportunity, or that there is a right to free speech but not against hate speech you move from the abstract to the ideal since, as a matter of fact, a community will need to take some stand on immigration, on ethnic patterning in work and education, and on offence to marginalised groups. Saying nothing has no less import than saying something when, like encountering a difficult aunt at Christmas, social circumstances demand a response. It is not necessarily wrong to suppose that cultural membership is irrelevant (at least in certain cases). But the point is that *that* position will need to be argued for no less than its opposite: there is no culturally neutral baseline.

In sum, then, we must recognise that our multicultural reality is pertinent for politics as soon as we start theorising about it. It is not something which, as some writers imply, we can accommodate in larger theories of democracy, freedom and social justice that are first formulated in a culture-blind way. Multiculturalism is a problem for these theories only because of assumptions and premises that made it so. Approaching multiculturalism with honesty and integrity means accepting that it is not a decorative but a permanent feature of our public social world.

In this chapter I want to explore what it means to move multiculturalism from the outskirts to the centre of our political thinking. Section 1 surveys the range of multicultural rights, while section 2 examines an important recent attempt to theorise them, Will Kymlicka's *Multicultural Citizenship*.[4] Section 3 explores attempts to go beyong Kymlicka's largely liberal approach with a more radical 'politics of recognition', which says that we recognise cultures on their own terms. Here I make a number of positive claims about what recognising multiculturalism should involve; with the conclusion drawing these points together.

1 Multicultural rights

The first stage in this exploration is a careful consideration of the kinds of demands made by minority cultures. Here I shall mention three kinds. First, there are rights to do with government. They include the special representation rights such as the guaranteed seats for Maori representatives in the New Zealand Parliament, and the race-conscious drawing of district lines to boost black representation in the USA. It also includes devolved power of the kind fought for by Aboriginal peoples in Canada and Australia, the Scots, Welsh and Irish national minorities in the UK or the two million Hungarians spread across Romania, Slovakia and Serbia. At the limit, self-government means the right to national self-determination, whether secession from one state aims at unity with another (as republicans in Northern Ireland want) or a wholly new entity (as happened when Norway split from Sweden).

The second family of multicultural rights seeks to accommodate a variety of distinct cultural practices within larger states. Sometimes these seek to release ethno-cultural groups from a burden that state laws would otherwise impose, such as the efforts made by some Amish parents to withdraw their children from state education at fourteen, the exemption from wearing hard hats on building sites sought by Sikh men, or exemptions on animal slaughter legislation sought by Muslims and Jews. In other cases cultural rights seek to give special assistance to a disadvantaged minority such as affirmative action programmes to increase minority representation in colleges in the USA, or its Bi-Lingual Education Act (1978) designed to help enable parallel instruction in non-English languages for children who spoke them at home. In some cases rights of exemption or assistance overlap with the first category of government rights, such as Aboriginal people's demand that an indigenous legal tradition take precedence over a state's legal code.

The third family is most difficult to define. It does not involve rules or rights but the more amorphous issue of collective esteem, a group's attitude towards itself. This becomes a matter for public policy when the symbolism of flags, currencies, names, public holidays, national anthems, public funds for cultural activities and the content of school curricula bear on a minority's fragile presence in the public political culture. Inevitably affecting how the mainstream regards it, the gaze of recognition affects how members perceive themselves, and in turn their attitude towards the wider society of which they are a part. Prince Charles's recent declaration that as king he would be called defender of faith, not *the* Christian faith, acknowledged the importance of symbolic recognition for minority religions which many in the mainstream would be hard pressed to conceive. Romania's large Hungarian minority demanded an explicit acknowledgment of their existence in the light of the clause in the Romanian constitution that declared it to be 'a unitary state of the Roumanian people'.[5] Defending the controversial decision to ban Muslim girls from wearing headscarves in French schools, the former Education minister later declared that it was 'impossible to accept' signs whose very purpose was to 'separate certain pupils from the communal life of the school'.[6] Some multicultural rights such as the exemptions from common laws and limited self-government cause very little pain to the majority. Political issues of recognition are not like this. They are hard to resolve because they call into question not just a minority identity but the majority's too, and a problem caused by others is always a resented gift.

The rights and issues I have identified – self-government, exemptions and privileges, and recognition – overlap in various and complex ways. Bilingual schooling, for example, is both a collective right and a policy of recognition. Indeed all the second family of multicultural rights involve recognition of some sort where a minority wants to participate in the culture, rather than (as with the Amish) take their leave of it.[7] Demands and challenges are made with the overriding need for cultural survival; multiculturalism is a battle fought on several fronts.

2 Kymlicka's *Multicultural Citizenship*

As an example of how these multicultural claims are theorised, let us consider Will Kymlicka's *Multicultural Citizenship*. Kymlicka wants to defend cultural protection along liberal lines. He is exercised, therefore, by whether groups can bear rights, by the need for toleration, and by the problem of sustaining a common civic identity. The result is that he comes to view cultures in a very particular way. Influenced by Inuit communities in the Canadian Northwest Territories, Kymlicka regards a culture as a civilisation, self-sufficient and with its own social institutions.[8]

Three further moves assist the conscription of cultures to the liberal side. The first move consists in saying that cultures are (a) valuable and (b) distinct, but that (c) they do not consist of shared values.[9] (a) Since cultures are valuable, at least for their members, there is a loss involved if they begin to erode. This gives the basic rationale for a theory of cultural justice. (b) Since each culture is different from its neighbours, this loss is not just a general complaint about increasing cultural homogeneity, but a particular worry about the loss of a particular culture. Finally (c) cultures are not tightly knit clusters of shared values, and hence do (despite liberal worries) allow for freedom and autonomy. These three claims can each be questioned. Questioning (a), we can say that lots of valuable cultures have degraded or died, not just cultures of ethnic descent which are Kymlicka's prime interest. Mining communities in South Wales also provided their members with strong identities and a sense of belonging, and have also declined.[10] Do they too merit cultural rights? Examining (b), many ethnic groups need not have distinct cultural attributes. As Appiah has commented on the situation of blacks in the USA, '[c]ulture is not the problem and it is not the solution'.[11] The problem is racism. Claim (c) is correct: cultures do not consist of shared values. They consist of people. If people in the same group share some values, they need not share them all. By implication, not every value is valued by each person in the group. The truth is more interesting and complicated than that. Moreover, while (a) combines easily with (b), the picture they conjure up together, of self-contained cultures each unique, sits a little oddly with (c) the non-shared values claim. In addition (a) and (b) together open the way for a fruitless search for cultural *thingness* that I shall later take issue with.

Kymlicka's second move is to distinguish between culture contexts, as media that provide meaning, orientation, identity and belonging, and cultural options, particular elements within that context.[12] This distinction allows Kymlicka to advance two divergent arguments. Conceiving cultures as contexts means they can fulfil their purpose of over-arching individual choices. Cultures are a necessary frame to human action; hence there is a loss if one's cultural context begins to erode. This is the justice argument, and it says that each person has the right to a secure cultural context, not just any context but her own. The freedom argument says that people are autonomous choosers, and what they choose between are different cultural options. Unitary optionless contexts, like seamless webs of shared values, would leave cultural members without liberal choices. But contextless constellations of free-floating options, would suggest there is no special loss if a culture declines – contrary to (a) and (b) above.[13] One always loses something, not nothing; contexts provide that thing. Once again, this encourages the search for the identity of the context. Not language (because languages are not unique to cultures), not history (what has had the history?), not, as Kymlicka insists, shared values, it is never finally spelt out what a culture actually is, and hence not clear what is lost.

Finally, Kymlicka's third move distinguishes between national minorities and ethnic groups.[14] The former are incipient nations who found themselves incorporated into a larger multinational state. Examples include the Aboriginal peoples in Canada and Australia, Maori in New Zealand and the various national groups that make up multinational states like Switzerland and Belgium. Ethnic groups, by contrast, are largely the result of immigration. This includes all the very different groups of migrants found in Canada, Australia and the USA (the three countries with the very highest rates of immigration), as well as Turks in Germany and Commonwealth immigrants in the UK, for example. The point of this distinction is to justify his hierarchy of cultural rights: while national minorities merit rights to special representation and devolved self-government, ethnic groups deserve only rights to help them assimilate on terms that are fair. Supporting this division are Rawls's and Dworkin's theories of social justice which say that we should compensate people for the circumstances they involuntarily find themselves in, while respecting their voluntarily made choices. National minorities merit more rights than ethnic groups because they generally find themselves in a situation not of their own choosing. However, some ethnic groups did not choose to migrate – black Americans are the best example. Even where they did, the choice was only made by the first generation not subsequent ones. The latter often find they have most in common with the country of their birth, however strange it was to their parents who first arrived. Reversing matters, some national minorities do not want self-government, but instead choose to assimilate into the larger culture. Even where self-government is demanded, its purpose need not be to maintain and transmit a unique cultural identity.

To be fair to Kymlicka, he does appreciate the difficulties involved in bringing cultures into the ambit of normative analysis and he explicitly says that cultural claims must be assessed on a case by case basis. He further distinguishes between justifying a theory of minority rights and imposing it in practice.[15] (As J.L. Austin once said, 'There's the bit where you say it and the bit where you take it back'.)[16]

3 The politics of recognition

The difficulty of legislating when a culture qualifies for minority rights is not unique to Kymlicka. Charles Taylor wants to recognise cultures that have fairly large numbers of members, have survived for some time and articulate a language of moral evaluations. Influenced by his native Quebec, he seems to see the essence of culture as possession of a shared language.[17] Parekh maintains that a culture has a claim to rights if it is vital to the fundamental interests of its members and contributes to the wider society.[18] David Miller claims a national community is constituted by shared beliefs, a historical narrative and territorial home, is active in character and has its own public culture. National communities that pass these five tests have a prima facie right to self-determination.[19]

Parekh, Miller and Taylor, and beyond them Young, Tully and Tamir, together go a little further than Kymlicka in their defence of cultural rights.[20] For

Kymlicka, the main value of cultural membership and cultural diversity is to sustain those options within which autonomous persons can exercise choice. Independent of autonomy, there are limits as to how far cultural diversity is morally or aesthetically valuable.[21] For these other writers, the value of cultures, nations and ethnic groups is not primarily routed through their contribution to autonomy. The perspective begins to shift towards their collective value as such. In Taylor's hands, this value supports what has come to be called a 'politics of recognition'.

Charles Taylor's elegant essay 'The Politics of Recognition' has given the politics of recognition a rich philosophical background.[22] Arguing for a model of liberalism that can include important collective goals, Taylor distinguishes between the crucial liberties central to any liberal society and the less critical rights and opportunities that may on occasion be over-ridden. The pro-French policies of Quebec are such a collective good. The goal here is not just to sustain but actively to create a community of French speakers into the indefinite future. Two strands make up this argument. In the early sections of the essay, Taylor defends the notion that individuals require, not just respect, but others' recognition: they need to be the object of others' positive attitudes. Through a matrix where affirmation is given and received, individuals acquire a positive relation to themselves.[23] Recognition, therefore, is not an optional extra, but a vital human need.[24] Second, Taylor distinguishes between two modes of being in late modernity, autonomy and authenticity. While autonomy is the seed bed in which the modern rational, disengaged self has grown, authenticity invokes the alternative Romantic tradition of spontaneity, uniqueness and difference. 'There is a certain way of life that is my way; I am called upon to live my life in this way and not in imitation of anyone else's life'.[25] These two traditions are not opposite, but divergent: both free the individual from obligation to a larger order, but only authenticity invests the self with a unique life-project which she has a duty to fulfil. Taylor, however, interprets authenticity not just in an individual but a collective sense: cultures too have their own unique authentic essences.[26] When this is added to the first strand we arrive at the view that cultures need recognition in their authentic particularity. Quebec is one case, but there are others besides.

We have already encountered one key assumption underlying the politics of recognition. In commenting on Kymlicka, I recorded claim (b), that each culture has its own cultural attributes. Individuals are unique – Taylor's individual authenticity – but not cultures, or at least not every culture, not American blacks for example. Still, as we shall see, whether a group does or does not have a distinct identity is a political and not an empirical question. In any case, let us turn to the main demand of this kind of politics, the public affirmation of cultural difference.

Barry believes that public recognition is impossibly demanding and logically incoherent. The equal treatment that liberalism demands of us is relatively easy to fulfil. Whatever our real views on the merits of others' ways of life, we can treat them with civility, courtesy and respect. Recognition, however, politicises those private judgements that could otherwise remain concealed behind the formal practice of equal treatment. Hence '[t]he notion that everybody should be entitled to an equal ration of "recognition" cannot be accepted by those who attach any value to individual liberty'.[27] In any case, recognition is incoherent. It is not just that an across the board affirmation of each culture's value is a meaningless activity. (It devalues the idea of value). The problem is also that to believe in the worth of one's own culture must include a belief in the values and virtues it embodies. Faced with the demand to affirm the value of a culture that espouses contrary values to our own, we are put in an impossible situation. The Southern Baptist who believes homosexuality is a sin (this is Barry's example) cannot, consistent with retaining her Baptist beliefs, also affirm the value of a homosexual lifestyle.[28] You cannot believe in something while sincerely advocating its opposite.

These criticisms are somewhat overstated. Taylor's account of recognition seems to hover between endorsing the values a culture subscribes to, and affirming a culture's specific identity, which need not require endorsing all its values. The latter interpretation has less of a problem with Barry's argument. It is also the view of the other main proponent of a politics of recognition, Iris Marion Young, for whom justice towards groups, before anything else, involves acknowledging what is different about each group.[29] Still, besides this specificity-claim, there remains a good deal of plausibility to Barry's strictures against recognition.

Against Barry's first point, however, the public expression of private attitudes is not unusual but routine. The shopkeeper whose veil of politeness to his Asian customers hides a deeper racism will let the mask slip with his friends in the pub. Since the communities we inhabit are diverse and several, a member of a liberal society might encounter those who value and affirm the culture which his other acquaintances ridicule and despise. This at least brings the possibility for a re-evaluation of attitudes, if not engineered by the state, then encouraged and fostered by it. Second, while the demand to affirm the worth of a culture represents an invasion of freedom, Barry implies that the burden of belonging to a disparaged one does not. This, however, rests on a particular notion of what freedom involves. It rests on the notion that freedom consists solely in doing what one wants, with no attention to the social relations – including those of servility, submission and domination – within which our wants are formed and acted on. Recent work on freedom has viewed the absence of these social circumstances as central to an elaboration of the concept.[30] For republicans, freedom is non-domination. Even if this view is rejected, we could still maintain that a subject, disparaged and degraded by her peers, is hardly likely to make use of whatever legal freedom she enjoys. This is the point of insisting that recognition is a vital human need.

In order to reply to Barry's second argument, and hence clear the way for a partial vindication of a politics of recognition, we shall need to tackle some difficult issues of culture and value. I earlier took issue with Kymlicka for encouraging us to think of culture as a thing, a tendency encouraged by his assumptions that cultures were valuable and unique. An alternative liberal view sees culture as secondary quality, apt to fade away under the Enlightenment torch. Both these perspectives depart from the dominant view of cultural anthropology, which regards culture as a process, a manifestation, in diverse material and symbolic circumstances, of the universal human capacity to manufacture frames of social action.[31] Men and women make culture, but they do not do so just as they please, but in circumstances directly encountered and transmitted from the past. Baumann's analysis theorises culture as 'dual discursive construction'.[32] Cultural agents, in their day-to-day interactions, shape and change their culture as they act to reproduce it. At the same time, cultural elites, outsiders and the media tend to reify culture, they accentuate its thingness for a particular purpose: if you want to attack or defend something, it must be, just that, a thing. Better still, it should be a unique thing. During the Rushdie affair, for example, both Muslim leaders and their opponents had powerful reasons for maintaining that there was a fixed and characteristic Muslim community in the UK.[33] 'Yet in the end, all the comforts of having a culture rely upon remaking that culture, and the dominant discourse of culture as an unchangeable heritage is only a conservative-sounding subcomponent of the processual truth.'[34]

If this view of cultures is correct then they cannot include, among other components, subscription to a relatively static core of principles and values, as Barry maintains. For as cultural agents remake their worlds and endow them with cultural meaning, they revise the contexts within which apparently immutable values are defended and maintained. Abstract principles receive their meaning from a particular context. Hence '[t]o repeat the same statement in new circumstances is to make a new statement'.[35] Cultures are not clubs whose members must affirm a set charter of principles. Values, like rules, receive their meaning in the everyday production of social life. (Both theorists and practitioners have a motive for absolutising normative principles, theorists for intellectual robustness, practitioners for practical power.) There is, therefore, no simple conflict between cultural values. Recognised in one context, they can be criticised in another. In fact this is almost inevitable, given the different communities liberal citizens usually inhabit. It also means that a culture does not lose its identity when members revise their attitude towards the values of others. Such revising is only a more self-conscious version of the cultural creation that is ongoing anyway, and this should give us grounds for hope.

The first claim I made in the introduction to this chapter was that multiculturalism was unavoidable and that the circumstances of a liberal politics cannot but be culturally charged. A second claim, emerging from the discussion above, is that we understand culture in processual not reified terms. This implies, among other things, that theory is accompanied by a fine-grained empirical analysis of cultural identity and cultural change. I now want to make two further claims – a third concerning recognition and a fourth to do with freedom.

Returning to the politics of recognition, we find a vision that has become somewhat complicated. Cultural communities and legal norms exist in dynamic relation to each other. Contrary to what Charles Taylor assumes, there are no authentic cultural essences awaiting legal recognition. If there is money for members of a culture we can be sure that its membership will increase, a phenomenon familiar with Native Americans in the USA.. On what grounds, then, should the liberal state recognise cultures?

It is indeed impossible to demand that we go around valuing other cultures, and illiberal to ask that we act as though we did. There is, however, an important asymmetry between how Barry treats recognition and how he theorises respect. In his other work, he argues that we show others respect by seeking to justify to them the norms we wish our common polity to adopt.[36] But when he turns to recognition, Barry assumes it can be claimed by disparaged cultures as a right. He seems to imagine there would be an organ of the state charged with the task of bolstering attitudes towards marginalised cultures. But recognition, too, can be assimilated to the notion of public justification he elsewhere defends. On this view, when and whether we recognise a culture is itself a matter for democratic decision. This has two aspects. First, the majority needs to recognise that the public culture they share with minorities is not a neutral arena for settling claims but is inevitably culturally punctuated. There is no culture-free baseline that will secure the autonomy of equal respect. Moreover, the cultural perspectives which minorities inhabit are relevant to determining what the substantive values of our shared public culture should be. Not beyond culture, our shared public life is the collective cultural creation of us all. Building on this first point, the second argument says that each group should have a fair opportunity to participate in public deliberation on what our public culture should be. Fair opportunity involves measures promoting the inclusivity of political institutions, fighting institutional racism and removing segregation in residence and employment. These measures are delivered, not just for their own sake, but in order that the perspective on the world that minority cultures occupy can more easily be entered into democratic debate about what values our public culture should promote. Such promotion does involve recognition, but it cannot be claimed by any group as a right. Take the recent debate in the UK about faith schools. One solution (and one interpretation of equal respect) is to have no religious segregation in education at all – and hence no faith schools. Another solution is to allow faith schools on the grounds that it publicly affirms and acknowledges the distinctive value and contribution of Muslim, Jewish and other communities.[37] The view of recognition I have been arguing for takes a third perspective. Faith schools affect the self-perceptions not just of the groups that have them, but those who do not, and they call into question the values of the common public culture that all of us share. Whether there are faith schools or not is for us as citizens to decide. We should not grant them as part of an automatic right to recognition because we do not take a minority culture's claims about itself at face value (no more than we should take our own). But neither should we reject them out of hand as part of a culture-free notion of equal respect.

Recognition, if it is to have any value, can only ever be voluntarily conferred. Once we appreciate that some set of values are always and inevitably publicly sponsored, we can better enter a debate about which ones they should be. By trying to give all groups a fair opportunity to participate in democratic debate, the state can help create the conditions where recognition is granted by citizens on grounds they agree. Positive recognition is not a right, but a creation of multiculturalism's everyday practitioners. That is my third claim.

My final claim concerns freedom. As we have seen, recognition already suggests a conceptual connection between freedom and the social circumstances in which some are disparaged and demeaned, but there is a bit more we can say. Kymlicka's theory, I believe, contains the resources for a reconceptualisation of freedom more attuned to cultural membership. For Kymlicka, freedom exists in the medium of a cultural context. It consists in exploring the possibilities provided by that context. On this view, then, freedom requires not just an agent who is uncoerced and whose will is his or her own, but also a viable cultural structure which provides the options in and through which freedom is exercised. Raz similarly writes that '[f]reedom depends on options' which invoke a culture of 'shared meanings and common practices'.[38] Imagine a situation in which nothing prevents a person from acting as he or she wishes but in which there are no options, cultural or otherwise, for him or her to take advantage of. A supermarket liberalism of shopping malls, cosmetic surgery and the Internet delivers freedom of a kind, but it does not deliver meaningful opportunities. Where these are present we have 'opportunity-freedom'. The core of the idea is that freedom takes place in a social context constituted by rules which make our actions intelligible and meaningful.

Opportunity-freedom has no specifically ethnic colouring but it can be usefully linked to the idea of culture as process that I raised earlier. Raz appreciates that cultures change, thereby changing the options available, but Kymlicka's theory is more problematic. Although he accepts the fact of cultural change, his promotion of a cultural context (necessary for cultures to have a case in justice) pushes him towards the view that cultures are a thing. In any case, neither writer explores how cultural options, ethnic or otherwise, are created by us. Social not just cultural life is a process. Social action can be directed in ways that make the public culture richer and more meaningful, or that degrade and destroy the opportunities for freedom it provides. The best polity is not one where each person is free from the will of others. It is one where democratic communities assume responsibility for the social opportunities available to all, and no person is demeaned in that process. It is one where we actively try to create the conditions where what is culturally valuable can be publicly affirmed and esteemed. Multiculturalism involves an acknowledgement of the full particularity of what at first appears alien and strange. No person is in command of the particulars that go to build his or her own identity, but together we can collectively take some control of them. Decoupled from an obsession with ethnic descent, multiculturalism supports a politics in which men and women come together to take control of the production of their public social world.

Conclusion: a republican multiculturalism

I have argued in this chapter that (1) multiculturalism must be central not peripheral to any adequate theory of principles to inform the liberal polity; (2) that culture is a process not a thing, and that a culture's favoured values must be understood in terms of those processes; (3) that recognition involves democratic deliberation not automatic affirmation; and finally (4) that freedom as opportunity helps resolve the tension between freedom and cultural membership. Let me end with a sketch that ties these claims together.

I referred earlier to republican writers for whom freedom is the absence of domination. On this view, freedom and democracy are tightly linked because the free agent is one who plays his or her part in determining his or her community's laws and norms.[39] Interference as such does not limit freedom; only arbitrary interference that assails you from without. Thus whether a person is free or unfree can only be discovered by examining whether he or she had a say in deciding what he or she can do. The free community is one where citizens of equal standing deliberate on the possibilities open to them all. In my view, this is a fruitful paradigm for theorising multiculturalism. Liberal writers, however sympathetic to multiculturalism, will always view multicultural rights and measures with some suspicion since they so often reduce the freedom of individuals to live as they wish, neither interfered with by others, nor interfering with them in turn. But, by transcending the thought that others' interference must reduce our freedom, there is less objection to the democratic view where citizens of different cultures come together to deliberate on the rights and recognitions that different groups should enjoy. The public culture they create, open, plural and always subject to revision, is both a space for freedom and a medium of value. An important lesson for liberalism (and for life) is that what a person finds valuable need not hinge on what he or she chooses to pursue.[40] There are other sources of value that, not chosen, we later come to appreciate. If this is true, then multiculturalism might even increase our freedom, not reduce it.

Notes

1 I would like to thank Richard Bellamy, Andy Mason, Gerd Baumann and Judith Squires for helpful comments on an earlier draft of this chapter.
2 W. Kymlicka, *Liberalism, Community and Culture* (Oxford, Oxford University Press, 1989).
3 W. Kymlicka, *Contemporary Political Philosophy* (Oxford, Oxford University Press, 2001, 2nd edn), pp. 343–7.

4 W. Kymlicka, *Multicultural Citizenship: A Liberal Theory of Minority Rights* (Oxford, Oxford University Press, 1995).

5 E. Kiss, 'Democracy and the Politics of Recognition', in I. Shapiro and C. Hacker-Cordón, *Democracy's Edges* (Cambridge, Cambridge University Press, 1999), p. 205.

6 Cited in G. Baumann, *The Multicultural Riddle* (London, Routledge, 1999), p. 50.

7 Conversely, however, recognition need not involve rights.

8 Kymlicka, *Multicultural Citizenship*, p. 76.

9 Kymlicka, *Multicultural Citizenship*, pp. 89–90 (claim a); pp. 101–3 (claim b); pp. 91–3 (claim c).

10 Cf. B. Walker, 'Plural Cultures, Contested Territories: A critique of Kymlicka', *Canadian Journal of Political Science*, 30 (1997), pp. 211–34, 216–25.

11 K.A. Appiah, 'Multicultural Misunderstanding', *New York Review of Books*, 44, 9 October (1997), p. 36; B. Barry, *Culture and Equality: An Egalitarian Critique of Multiculturalism* (Cambridge, Polity Press, 2001), pp. 306–10.

12 Kymlicka, *Multicultural Citizenship*, pp. 82–4.

13 J. Tomasi, 'Kymlicka, Liberalism and Respect for Cultural Minorities', *Ethics*, 105 (1995), pp. 580–603; cf. J. Seglow, 'Universals and Particulars: The Case of Liberal Cultural Nationalism', *Political Studies*, 46 (1998), pp. 963–77, 968–9.

14 Kymlicka, *Multicultural Citizenship*, pp. 11–26.

15 Kymlicka, *Multicultural Citizenship*, pp. 164–70.

16 J.L. Austin, *Sense and Sensibilia* (Oxford, Oxford University Press, 1962), p. 2.

17 C. Taylor, 'The Politics of Recognition', in A. Gutmann (ed.), *Multiculturalism: Examining 'The Politics of Recognition'* (Princeton, NJ, Princeton University Pres, 1994, 2nd edn).

18 B. Parekh, *Rethinking Multiculturalism* (London, Macmillan, 2000), pp. 217–18.

19 D. Miller, *On Nationality* (Oxford, Oxford University Press, 1995), pp. 22–7, 81–118.

20 I.M. Young, *Justice and the Politics of Difference* (Princeton, NJ, Princeton University Press, 1990); J. Tully, *Strange Multiplicity: Constitutionalism in an Age of Diversity* (Cambridge, Cambridge University Press, 1995); Y. Tamir, *Liberal Nationalism* (Princeton, NJ, Princeton University Press, 1993).

21 Kymlicka, *Multicultural Citizenship*, pp. 121–3.

22 Taylor, 'The Politics of Recognition'.

23 A. Honneth, *The Struggle for Recognition: The Moral Grammar of Social Conflict* (Cambridge, Polity Press, 1995); cf. J. Seglow, 'Liberalism and the Politics of Recognition', in M. Evans (ed.), *The Edinburgh Companion to Contemporary Liberalism* (Edinburgh, Edinburgh University Press, 2001).

24 Taylor, 'The Politics of Recognition', pp. 32–7.

25 Taylor, 'The Politics of Recognition', p. 30

26 Taylor, 'The Politics of Recognition', p. 31.

27 Barry, *Culture and Equality*, p. 269.

28 Barry, *Culture and Equality*, pp. 270–1.

29 Young, *Justice and the Politics of Difference*.

30 P. Pettit, *Republicanism: A Theory of Freedom and Government* (Oxford, Oxford University Press, 1997).

31 T. Turner, 'Anthropology and Multiculturalism: What Is Anthropology that Multiculturalism Should Be Mindful of It?', *Cultural Anthropology*, 8 (1993), pp. 411–29.

32 Baumann, *The Multicultural Riddle*.

33 M. Ignatieff, 'Why "Community" Is a Dishonest Word', *Observer*, 3 May 1992, p. 17
    (cited in Baumann, *The Multicultural Riddle*, p. 72).
34 Baumann, *The Multicultural Riddle*, p. 95.
35 Baumann, *The Multicultural Riddle*, p. 69.
36 B. Barry, *Justice as Impartiality* (Oxford, Oxford University Press, 1995), ch. 7.
37 Cf. Parekh, *Rethinking Multiculturalism*, pp. 331–4.
38 J. Raz, 'Multiculturalism: A Liberal Perspective', *Dissent*, Winter (1994), p. 70. Cf.
    J. Raz, *Ethics in the Public Domain* (Oxford, Oxford University Press, 1994), ch. 7.
39 Pettit, *Republicanism*, pt 1.
40 C. Larmore, 'The Idea of a Life Plan', in E.F. Paul et. al. (eds), *Human Flourishing*
    (Cambridge, Cambridge University Press, 1999).

14

Gender

Terrell Carver

Introduction

Like all concepts in political theory, gender has a history. Unlike most of these concepts, though, the history of gender is comparatively short. The term itself originated in the nineteenth century, arising in the context of descriptive and diagnostic social sciences of human behaviour. It was only adopted into political theory, as a result of a political process of struggle, about 100 years later in the 1970s. When it arrived, gender was itself a highly political concept, signalling a rearrangement of the scope, terms and politics of political theory itself. Gender theorists at that point conceived of their work within political theory as a further engagement of feminism with 'malestream' thought, that is, theorisations of politics written by men and reflecting their assumptions and interests. The feminist stance towards the discipline, and towards its traditionalist practitioners, was critical and transformative.[1]

To understand this important development in political theory, however, we will need to examine the concepts of sex and sexuality as well. Moreover, it will also be necessary to bear in mind that gender, woman and women's lives are all feminist concepts, but that within feminism itself they are *not all the same thing*. Finally, to make matters even more interesting, political theory is now engaged with theorisations of gender drawn from very recent developments, such as cultural studies, media studies, multiculturalism, post-structuralism and post-modernisms. These ideas and interests are not necessarily aligned with all, or indeed any, of contemporary feminisms in terms of subject matter or inspiration. On the whole, though, there is a tremendous debt in this area to feminist thought.

While strong claims can be made for understanding gender in feminist frame, this is to some extent a matter of acknowledging a conceptual development in history, rather than stating a necessary truth about the concept. Political theory itself records any number of historical encounters in which specific movements have defined and deployed philosophical concepts, which have then been dropped or redefined as political circumstances changed. 'Monarch', 'republic', 'citizen', 'equality', 'right' and 'obligation' are obvious examples. Gender is another concept in political theory recording and consolidating a political engagement, that of feminism with malestream thought, but its own conceptual genesis predates contemporary feminisms, and its future is open to other interpretative moves and political movements.

1 Sex and the single political theorist

Political theorists in the malestream canon have certainly noticed sex, taking sex as the two 'opposite' sexes – male and female – and considering them reproductively. Or rather, when the subject of reproducing the community arises, women appear as wives and mothers (in that order), and men appear in relation to them as husbands and fathers within 'the family'. This is not necessarily just any family, as it could be a royal family (in theorists of patriarchal, hereditary monarchy). At the other end of the class spectrum the family arrangements of slaves, household servants, unpropertied workers (on or off the land) are rarely explicitly theorised. Rather traditional political theory most usually characterises a subject or citizen of a certain class and status, whose sex only emerges as explicitly male when reproductive issues eventually arise. Otherwise the subject or citizen has an abstract quality in relation to sex, and specifically to femaleness, in that this supposedly generic 'man' is always singular (that is, never pregnant) and occupies a public status that presumes certain background institutions, typically but not exclusively the family.[2]

Background institutions are not wholly forgotten or excluded, of course. Sexual, reproductive and 'family' circumstances are generally theorised as natural and therefore inevitable and unchanging. Nonetheless, they are, somewhat paradoxically, also theorised as subject to the protection and supervision of the 'properly' political processes that constitute the foreground of political theory. Theories that naturalise relationships and institutions always provoke a certain tension, because they also *necessarily* invoke a concept of unnaturalness and a need for regularisation. If heterosexual marriage and patriarchal families are so completely natural, why then theorise them at all? In political theory they are theorised not only in relation to 'public man' the subject or citizen as background, but also as a potential political problem within foreground concerns. One of the political responsibilities of 'public man' is the orderly maintenance of 'natural' reproductive arrangements in the 'family' and heterosexual relationships in patriarchal marriages, even when these are (rather disingenuously) claimed to be 'private' and somehow protected from state 'interference'.

Political theorists have in general been complicit with the backgrounding and naturalising of sexual, reproductive and 'family' arrangements. There are, of course, exceptions, and it is worth exploring one in particular in order to raise the issue of bodily differences and the question of the validity of generalisations in relation to sex. Plato's dramatic dialogue *The Republic* (c. 380–370 bc) is the sole malestream work that raises female sexual difference as an issue in relation to citizenship roles that were almost universally limited to men. In this work, leadership (or 'guardianship') is conceived as membership of a class of warriors and rulers constrained to serve the best interests of the community. They are explicitly divorced from the more usual self- and family-centred concerns which all too often tempt those who exercise public power into material corruption at community expense. The 'dialogue' actually recounts dramatic yet conversational interchanges between Socrates (as a character) and other named male individuals, and the build-up given by Socrates to the introduction of such a controversial topic is considerable. He assumes that his audience will find the idea of female warriors and rulers ridiculous and absurd, which indeed they do (449a–457b).

This episode in political theory has been notorious, rather than influential, and in particular it has not been much revived by feminist commentators. In *The Republic* Socrates does not involve himself in any detailed discussion of the bodily characteristics that are generally taken to constitute the femaleness and maleness that the notion of two 'opposite' sexes is generally taken to reflect. The male audience is happy in their idea that men are physically and intellectually more suited to martial valour and wise rulership through their bodily capacities than women, whereas women are more suited to domestic concerns and child-bearing through their bodily capacities than men. The argument put forward by Socrates, in contrast, is based on exceptions to that generalisation, which the male audience is forced to admit. These include an admission that some men are better than some women at supposedly female-only pursuits, and an acknowledgement that the barriers to martial training for females are culturally rather than physically determined, and therefore malleable. Quite why Plato the author wants to make Socrates the character propound this line of argument is never explained. Feminists have been understandably unhappy with the presumed validity of the generalisations about woman, however embedded in dialogical concerns, and with the overall absence of interest in the history of female oppression and of vision with respect to women's lives.[3]

What Socrates does not do in *The Republic* is to explore the supposed basis of the sexual distinction between males and females in the first place to any significant degree. He deals with bodily difference by noting that women bear children and men mount women. This rather brutal account of sexual difference enables him to argue that it really does not bear on any other activities in society such that *all* women or *all* men are suitable or unsuitable for any task or tasks. He thus theorises a panoply of individual differences in relation to social activities that must be sorted out in every single case. This has the advantage of respecting any particular individual's personal qualities, without first establishing what must *necessarily* be true of them as a man or as a woman, or what is *likely* to be true of them (to which generalisations there could, with argument, be exceptions). Whether Socrates has produced a defensible theorisation of the human subject in relation to life cycle and occupational issues, or whether he is merely another reflection of malestream inattention to the body, and in particular to the female body (for example, wombs/parturition, breasts/lactation), are interesting points of current debate.

2 Sexual behaviour and the panopticon of science[4]

Gender was coined as a term, not in political theory, but in nineteenth-century social science. The context then was the incorporation of the 'study of man' into the current framework of science, involving factual observation of regularities, careful recording of data, inductive procedures of theory-formation, deductive formulation of predictions and a search for causal factors of explanation. As with the industrial technologies that developed in conjunction with the progress of the natural sciences, so there were policy-orientated and therapeutic practices that developed from the social sciences. These ranged from bureaucratised teacher training and mass education to social work and psychoanalysis, as new 'knowledges' were conceptualised and operationalised. Sexual behaviour became a subject of study (in fields that came to be known as psychology, psychoanalysis, sociology and anthropology) and a concept was needed to indicate that biological sex itself did not produce uniform patterns of behaviour in individuals. Rather, individuals progressed through a process of development that originated in maleness or femaleness, but either arrived at corresponding masculine and feminine forms of behaviour, or did not.

Forms of behaviour that were thought to correspond correctly to maleness were, unsurprisingly, those that tended towards physical and intellectual aggression, unemotional individualism and competitive achievement, sexual promiscuity and risk-taking (among other similar human attributes). Those behaviours that were thought to correspond to femaleness were, of course, presumed to reflect an opposite: physical weakness and dependency, emotional excess and co-operative social strategies, sexual constancy and security-consciousness (again, among other similar characteristics). Moreover correctly corresponding behaviours in early gender theory were not limited to individualised expressions of masculinity and femininity, as just described, but also to the presumed biological relationship of the two sexes to the reproductive process. Desire and behaviour between the sexes (and in a negative way, within each of the two sexes) was also theorised in terms of gender, that is, masculine men and feminine women were theorised as desiring each other sexually within a reproductive relationship, or within courtship rituals and choices reflecting this supposed imperative.

Thus gender as a concept presumed that biological sex issued forth in corresponding behaviours related both to rather generalised strategies in social behaviour (for example, independence and aggression versus dependence and co-operation) and to specifically sexual activity (for example, heterosexual courtship and reproductive marriage). For the policy-orientated and therapeutic practices that flowed from this laboriously observed (if not newly discovered) scientific knowledge, the concept of unsuccessful, incomplete or abnormal behaviours was crucially important by definition, because policies and therapies must conceptualise the problems they aim to solve. It follows that these problems must be intensely observed in order to discover their causes, and strategies must be developed to deal with their consequences, both individually and socially.

Within the social science of human sexology, masculine women and feminine men were defined conceptually, located, observed, recorded and studied. Homosexual behaviour was similarly studied and made individually and socially problematic. Linkages between 'inverted' gender (masculine women and feminine men) were theorised, but rather unsatisfactorily: homosexual men did not always seem to exhibit any uniformity of pairing behaviour between feminine men (unless such 'inverts' were defined tautologously as 'feminine' in virtue of same-sex attraction). In so far as masculine women and lesbians were investigated, which was considerably less, much the same kind of incongruity arose. Attempts to map same-sex relationships back on to assumptions that sexual relationships require the attraction of 'opposites' generally tended to fail. In sum, gender came to stand for the behavioural aspects of sex and sexuality, whether in correct correspondence with 'reproductive biology' or in deviance from it in diverse but problematic ways.

Between societies these behaviours could be similarly tracked and classified, subject to cultural and historical differences that social scientists were trained to factor out. A naturalised conception of opposite sexes and reproductive heterosexuality was clearly the basis from which the concept of gender emerged, and it did so precisely because it enabled social scientists to project the presumed truths of biological science forward into hitherto unsystematic studies of human behaviour, given that humans were in their bodily construction, and deepest identities, necessarily of two 'opposite' kinds.

3 Sexual politics and political theory

Political theory has reflected methodological assumptions in common intellectual currency. These, of course, have been different, at different times. Plato's dialogues reflect a particular way of doing philosophy, and a number of assumptions about how truth is produced, and what it is for. Other theorists have employed rather different assumptions, reflecting other views about truth, and what political difference its circulation could make (for example, Hobbes's 'science of politics'). Moreover political theorists have often had more or less overt political agendas themselves, and have been in touch with political movements that they hoped to influence, and which influenced them. These movements may have been highly elitist or radically egalitarian, or anything moderate and moderating in between.

Political theorists thus typically endeavour to link the most abstract questions of method applicable to human affairs with truths that are communicable to their contemporaries and even translatable, at times, into actions and institutions. The attempted incorporation and ultimate acceptance (at least in some circles) of gender as an important, perhaps even fundamental concept in political theory, has involved similar considerations. That is, a link between feminism as a political movement, and feminist political theorists, has been fundamental in this process. Moreover feminists in political theory have arguably contributed independently to a reconceptualisation of gender, sexuality and sex itself, with far-reaching consequences for the social sciences and, indeed, for the way that biological science conceptualises the human life form, and others.

Feminism, as a theory of women's oppression, and a practice of resistance to male domination, brought women's lives, woman and gender to political theory. This was not an easy process, as the canon of authors, the register of concepts and the discursive presumptions – about 'man' and 'his' social relationships, and about who is writing for whom about what kind of things – were regarded as, if not fixed, at least very stable. Indeed, by the 1950s and 1960s it was suggested that perhaps this stability in political theory reflected a decline because the world had less need for political theory itself. Ideological battles were said by some to be over, and liberal consensus declared to be ascendant. Feminists were not the only ones to disturb this latter-day tranquillity, but disturb it they did. Battling to get women's concerns recognised as theoretically significant, and woman validated as an object of theoretical interest, feminists launched the gendering of political theory.

This involved more than introducing woman as an idea and empirical referent, precisely because this introduction challenged the former universality of 'man' as the human individual. This was a double challenge: 'man' was revealed to incorporate masculine presumptions concerning social behaviour and bodily configurations; woman introduced whole new areas to political theory that had formerly been treated as pre-political, non-political or anti-political. These included reproductive roles, family structures, sexual relationships, domestic spaces and numerous moral or religious or cultural issues as they bore on women's lives. These had generally been unnoticed, discounted or naturalised by male political theorists. Whether there is any way of salvaging an unsexed conception of the human individual as a foundational concept in political theory, or any point in doing so, is currently an area of debate within, as well as outside, contemporary feminisms. Similarly, whether there are any aspects of women's lives (or anyone's life) that are, or should be, excluded or protected from politics, is again a debatable question.

It is clear, however, that feminist work has considerably developed and enhanced the concept of gender in interesting and complex ways within political theory, and in the disciplines on which it draws. Working through this development requires rigorous attention to what gender adds to conceptions of sex and sexuality. In so far as gender slips back towards the supposed simplicities of males and females as 'opposite' sexes, it fails to add value to those notions, and detracts from the work that the concept should be doing. Gender as a synonym for sex is clearly redundant, and reductive strategies to push it that way produce confusion. Rather than reinscribe conventional understandings of sex and sexuality in political theory, theories of gender must *locate* sex and sexuality in relevant ways. Or, in other words, beware of the current tendency to substitute gender for sex just to the side of the boxes where you are supposed to tick M or F.[5]

4 Three theories of gender

While there is a case to be made that three theories of gender have emerged chronologically, it is certainly true that all three exist at present, are utilised, and are useful. It is probably better to view them that way than as evolutionary steps in a literature towards something superior, with possible reverse extinctions. I shall try to indicate something of the strengths of each theory as I go, by suggesting the kinds of problems that each could address, and the characteristic kinds of conceptualisations that a theorist would employ. Perhaps rather against the grain of canonical conceptions of political theory, I have chosen this somewhat authorless way of presenting ideas. However, I hope in this way to keep a clear analytical focus, and to provide a framework through which to follow what particular authors are saying. I would not claim that any set of authors exemplifies any one of my theories, the way that I have set them out, nor that anyone's work would be better if this happened. Most authors provide discussions that employ at least one of my three theories at some stage. Nonetheless I have given some reading for each theory that is particularly relevant to the area, either as background or as analysis. My hope is that readers (and authors) will get a clearer picture of what they mean by gender at different points in any discussion, and not fall into the trap of letting this useful term slip to mean just 'biological sex'.

4(a) *Behavioural theories of gender*[6]
In these theories gender stands for behavioural aspects of sex and sexuality, understood at first in a biological context of presumed reproductive instincts located in individuals, who are of two profoundly different types, namely, male and female. Individuals of these two types then exhibit a range of 'normally' corresponding individualised behaviours, as masculine men and feminine women, or other-directed behaviours, as heterosexuals (of two types, males and females), desiring biological opposites and reproductive mates. This further entails exhibiting non-sexual behaviours in relations with other individuals of the same sex, given the impossibility of biological mating. Where individual behaviours deviate from this 'normality', whether individually as personality-types or in interpersonal relations, this is then deemed scientifically and therapeutically problematic, and causes are hypothesised, mechanisms described, and tests conducted.

The strength of these theories is precisely that they are behavioural, and that observations can be accumulated and regularities postulated. This would not have been possible if the relationship between biological sex and behaviour (both as sexed individual, and within interpersonal sexuality) was presumed to be fixed. If that were the case, then certain processes could never be observed, because they could never exist. Here the theories become more complex and developmental as they move out of the biological and into the sociological and psychoanalytic realms. Theorisations include individual processes of psychosexual development and socialised forms of education, such that boys become boys, girls become girls, men men and women women. Political theory became gendered, that is, concerned with individual sexed behaviour and with sexual relationships of all kinds, as central both to the very notions of the human individual and political society.

Unsurprisingly there have been a number of protests, and protest movements, reacting to the claims of deviancy and abnormality that were openly stated or covertly implied in the study of gender. Feminisms and gay movements struggled against the stigmatising and demeaning classificatory schemes within gender studies, while simultaneously enriching and realigning the scope and content of the research conducted. While these critiques revealed that classification schemes and research results were in general very close reflections of the assumptions and prejudices of the researchers and of dominant groups in their respective societies, the approach still has a certain conceptual and descriptive validity.

4(b) *Power theories of gender*[7]

As a theory of women's oppression, feminism is by definition concerned with power. The framework sketched above was already, if not always explicitly, imbued with a further dimension, that of power-relations. This included both structural power in terms of institutions and micro-power in terms of interpersonal relations. In this theoretical framework gender works not merely to reveal the role of institutions and agency in individual behaviours and relationships, but to analyse and evaluate the power-relations that are characteristically in place as sexed individuals and sexual relationships are produced in societies according to certain regularities. Feminist analysis and commentary revealed the extent to which individuals that ('successfully') became conventionally masculine/heterosexual then accumulated advantages at the expense of those who were produced as female/homosexual. Theories of patriarchy reflect this linkage between the characteristic ways that masculine/heterosexual men are produced as power-wielding individuals, and as intimidatory ideals, in relation to women's lives and any usual concept of woman.

While patriarchy is literally 'rule of the fathers', the term has been successively refined and rechristened as fratriarchy and viriarchy to denote the homosocial relationships among masculine/heterosexual men through which economic and emotional resources are monopolised, against the participation and influence of women. Theorisations of this kind have been criticised for over-generalisation about power-relations, neglecting the competitive power-relations within masculine/heterosexual power structures, and for devaluing, dismissing or denying the extent to which women can, to their advantage, gain entry to power-relations as they currently exist. The former point has been addressed by work that theorises dominant and non-dominant masculinities, particularly non-heterosexual ones. The latter point has been aired by feminists keen to promote equality of opportunity and individual achievement for women in contemporary conditions, even at the possible expense of an all-encompassing female solidarity.

These debates within feminism have raised very traditional issues in political theory: what is the good society? What are the appropriate strategies for realising it? How are individual rights and present entitlements balanced against the possibilities for collective change? How can change benefit excluded and oppressed groups? Without a theory of gender, the relevance of sex and sexuality to these questions would not be visible, and without a power-theory of gender, the link between contemporary political debates and movements, and the literature of political theory, would not be available.

Much of conventional political theory has been descriptive and naturalising, telling us what must be the case about 'man and society', such that we can understand why relations of political power in society are necessary, and then see which principles and institutions are most advisable within realistic bounds of possible change. Power theories of gender imply a new agenda for political change, driven by political theory. This is one that bears on very basic questions of individual identity, fulfilment and protection. Theorisations suggesting that politics is about 'who gets what' or about 'individuals choosing life-plans' now seem rather bland and simplistic.

Once the individual that political theory conceptualises becomes much more complicated and differentiated, and more thoroughly embedded in complex and constitutive relationships and bodily configurations, then power relationships become much more varied and problematic. This opens the way to radical revisions of political theory, rather than just critique, however thorough, of existing frameworks. Once sexed behaviour and sexual relationships are released from biological or psychoanalytic reductionism, it follows that gender describes and empowers 'differences' that far exceed the limited and limiting vocabulary of conventional wisdom: male/female, straight/gay, masculine/feminine.

Gender politics liberated 'difference' in a way that affects everyone (as opposed to race/ethnicity, multiculturalism, and any number of other rather more sociological categories that might not *seem* to affect every human individual). However, gender, because of its origins in sex and sexuality, also *seems* to license a constant reduction of 'difference' back to the supposed basics of sex and sexuality. Is there a hierarchy within 'differences'? Are sex and sexuality more central to human political identities than, for example, race/ethnicity or religion? If not, what concerns then allow or circumscribe an intelligible and predictable politics of identity? Political theory currently reflects this tension in its theorisations, much as practical politics reflects the ways that people battle it out. Feminism faced up to these questions when confronted with 'women of colour', who famously refused the generalisations about woman that white women had offered. Any identity politics faces these issues, and political theory is one area in which such debates take place.

4(c) *Performative theories of gender*[8]

The 'linguistic turn' in post-structuralist philosophy has been extremely influential across the social sciences and humanities, and particularly so in gender studies. Feminists had already addressed categorial questions about the relation between women's lives and the category woman, both in terms of the way that social institutions produce women and in terms of the ways that female- or feminine-identified categories are defined in relation to, or as the 'other' of, male- and masculine-identified ones. Feminists had charted the way that these categories are represented visually and in other non-textual ways, particularly in popular culture. It was a small but revolutionary step from these studies to a dramatic reversal of the sex-gender story.

Rather than presuming, however variably and malleably, the supposed biological baseline of male/female difference, and seeing behavioural gender and gendered power-relations as in some sense following on from sex differences embedded in the body, a performative theory of gender reversed direction. Very simply, gender was no longer viewed as an aspect of sex, but rather our very idea of sex was said to be an aspect of gender. Gender was said to be a categorial structure of binaries, arranged hierarchically, such that concepts of sexual difference and sexualities were produced, including the apparently natural biology of reproductive sex. That is, conceptual binaries male/female, man/ woman, masculine/feminine, rational/irrational, strong/weak, active/passive, physical/emotional, and so on, exist within language. From that language we construct and create realities of all kinds, including supposed 'natural' or 'biological' facts as sexual difference. The hierarchical binaries through which core identities are constructed are then mapped back on to bodies, enforcing their identification as male or female, irrespective of inter-chromosomal and other deviations from a norm that biological and psychological sciences themselves create. On this view 'nature' does not create anything; rather, humans have concepts of nature that explain, often with political import, what is fixed and inevitable about the world.

Gender is thus a 'performative', that is, a category that seems to name as a reality that which it constructs itself in and through the performances that are its only existence. Or in other words, there is nothing natural or biological that gives us men and women. Men and women are constructed conceptually through hierarchical conceptual binaries that make such social and physical identifications as possible as they are. These performances are so thoroughly learned through processes of citation and repetition that they generally seem natural to the subjects who perform them. Human subjects are thus stylised and scripted, naturalised and inscribed, such that concepts of voluntary action and agency exist always and already within this apparent core of personal identity.

While this kind of theorisation is counter-intuitive, there are clues to its validity that we can recognise. One is the extent to which supposedly naturalised realities have to be regularised, enforced and produced through social processes involving education, medicine and commercialisation. This includes all manner of goods and services that seem to be directed at men and women, but actually as performances constitute human subjects in these guises. Personal consumption of men's and women's items, on this view, does not reflect identities and differences that have the universal and natural importance that they are said to have. Rather these patterns of consumption cite a socially constructed and culturally malleable pattern of hierarchical binaries, as subjects are 'educated' and 'disciplined' into gendered groups to consume them.[9]

Conceiving of gender as a constantly changing, yet relentlessly naturalising, system of hierarchical binaries, allows for an almost infinite differentiation between ways of being men and women, and ways of being sexual. In this way niche markets create new kinds of consuming subjects, who come to feel their 'inner' identities as natural. The work in gay studies on the origin and development of the homosexual subject, as well as feminist work on 'drag' and other subversions of femininity, have been influential in revealing the extent to which gender as a performative allows for 'playful and erotic games' that we all come to understand.[10] These occur within the performances through which gender, as an open-ended and inherently diversifying system, pervades an increasingly sexualised and concomitantly commercialised society.

5 Gender and political theory

Gender is arguably the biggest thing to hit political theory since democracy. Equally arguably, gender is a conceptualisation that has arisen within the globalised thrust of democratic political change. This movement has not only expanded the categories of persons deemed worthy to share in ruling and being ruled, it has also expanded the scope of state power to determine rights and obligations, to protect and regulate all kinds of activities, and to promote and distribute material welfare. As mentioned above, the emancipation of women from restricted civil liberties and reduced material welfare is proceeding, and this has brought considerations of sex (specifically as femaleness) into political theory from a new perspective. It has also raised corresponding issues concerning men, along with matters related to children and 'family' roles, including reproductive heterosexuality. This has effectively and irrevocably politicised an apparently natural order of things. Something of the same considerations apply to sexualities alternative to reproductive heterosexuality, further loosening the grip of naturalising accounts that validate behaviours for some, and criminalise or demean the behaviours of others.

Concepts of sex and sexuality are linked to behaviour via theories of gender, of which I have outlined three. These do the additional work of raising a description or categorisation into an issue. Behavioural theories of gender map the distance between behaviours (both sexed and sexual) and the presumed fixities of reproductive biology or psychoanalytical development. Power theories of gender track the disparities of power and resources between behavioural groups (from masculine/heterosexual men on down) as society reproduces them through educational and disciplinary processes. Performative theories of gender present the binary and hierarchical character of the concepts through which the lived experience of sex and sexuality is constructed, including the supposed 'natural' truths of reproductive biology.[11]

Performative theories of gender are most effective in linking gendered theory to further theories of 'difference', typically involving race/ethnicity, cultural markers and multiculturalism, religious and linguistic identities, and so on. They have the effect of removing the claims of any one characteristic, even the bodily characteristics we demarcate as sex, from any clear prioritisation over any other characteristic. This defuses debates as to which identity, or which form of oppression or discrimination, is more significant or hurtful or pressing, because that form of identity is more intrinsic, natural, unchangeable, inevitable or foundational to the human person. Prioritisation must come through a clearly political process, and cannot, on this view, be factored into 'natural' hierarchies and binaries.

This move could facilitate an interesting rainbow of coalition politics, and a clearer alignment of political theory with all sections of any given community than canonical texts have allowed. On the other hand, the extent to which more traditional and foundational conceptualisations of 'difference' have a more immediate appeal, and thus a long-term future, is undeniable, given the way that political organisation and conceptual discussion tend to proceed along familiar, well-trodden paths, perhaps for very good reasons. Ultimately gender could dissolve into one aspect of the 'politics of difference', among others.[12] Alternatively, the universality of sex and sexuality, and their persistent connection to power relations in society, suggest that the concept of gender will attain a permanent and salient position in the political theory of the future.

Notes

1 For standard works on the engagement of feminist with 'malestream' theory, see S.M. Okin, *Women in Social and Political Thought* (Princeton, NJ, Princeton University Press, 1979); G. Lloyd, *The Man of Reason: 'Male' and 'Female' in Western Philosophy* (London, Methuen, 1984); J. Grimshaw, *Feminist Philosophers: Women's Perspectives on Philosophical Traditions* (Brighton, Wheatsheaf Books, 1986); E. Kennedy and S. Mendus, *Women in Western Political Philosophy* (Brighton, Wheatsheaf Books, 1987); A. Nye, *Feminist Theory and the Philosophies of Men* (New York, Routledge, 1989); M. Gatens, *Feminism and Philosophy* (Cambridge, Polity Press, 1991); D. Coole, *Women in Political Theory: From Ancient Misogyny to Contemporary Feminism* (Brighton, Harvester Press/Wheatsheaf Books, 1992, 2nd edn); R. Prokhovnik, *Rational Woman: A Feminist Critique of Dichotomy* (London and New York, Routledge, 1999).

2 The classical account of this analysis is C. Pateman, *The Sexual Contract* (Cambridge, Polity Press, 1988).

3 See the discussions in J. Annas, *An Introduction to Plato's Republic* (Oxford, Clarendon Press, 1981), pp. 183–5; and in N. Pappas, *Plato and the Republic* (New York, Routledge, 1995), pp. 101–6.

4 For helpful background discussions, see J. Lorber, *Paradoxes of Gender* (New Haven, CT, and London, Yale University Press, 1994), esp. pt 1, pp. 13–119; J. Grant, *Fundamental Feminism* (New York and London, Routledge, 1993), pp. 160–88; T. Carrigan, B. Connell and J. Lee, 'Toward a New Sociology o Masculinity', in H. Brod (ed.), *The Making of Masculinities: The New Men's Studies* (Winchester, MA, and Hemel Hempstead, Allen and Unwin, 1987), pp. 65–89; R.W. Connell, *Gender* (Cambridge, Polity Press, 2002), pp. 1–11, 28–52.

5 For a discussion of these issues, see T. Carver, 'A Political Theory of Gender: Perspectives on the "universal subject"', in V. Randall and G. Waylen (eds), *Gender, Politics and the State* (London, Routledge, 1998), pp. 18–24.

6 See, for example, S. Firestone, *The Dialectic of Sex: The Case for Feminist Revolution* (London, Cape, 1971); N. Chodorow, *The Reproduction of Mothering: Psychoanalysis and the Sociology of Gender* (Berkeley, CA, University of California Press, 1978).

7 See, for example, S. Walby, *Theorizing Patriarchy* (Oxford, Blackwell, 1990); J. Hearn, *The Gender of Oppression: Men, Masculinity and the Critique of Marxism* (Brighton, Wheatsheaf, 1987).

8 See, pre-eminently, J. Butler, *Gender Trouble: Feminism and the Subversion of Identity* (London, Routledge, 1990); for a very recent exposition of this position in a political theory context, see R.C. Synder, *Citizen-Soldiers and Manly Warriors: Military Service and Gender in the Civic Republican Tradition* (Lanham, MD, Rowman and Littlefield, 2000), pp. 3–7, 138–47.

9 See D.T. Evans, *Sexual Citizenship: The Material Construction of Sexualities* (London, Routledge, 1993), pp. 36–64.

10 See J. Weeks, *Sexuality and its Discontents: Meaning, Myths and Modern Sexualities* (London, Routledge and Kegan Paul, 1985), pp. 211–45; see also Butler, *Gender Trouble*, pp. 128–41.

11 For the classic feminist critique of scientific certainties in biology and reproduction, see D. Haraway, *Simians, Cyborgs, and Women: The Reinvention of Nature* (London, Free Association, 1991).

12 For an interesting set of chapters that explore this theme, see G. Bottomley, M. de Lepervanche and J. Martin (eds), *Gender/Class/Culture/Ethnicity* (Sydney, Allen and Unwin, 1991).

15

Green political theory

Andrew Vincent

Introduction

One of the deep attractions of green political theory is its claim to be focused on the very survival of the whole natural ecosystem of the planet. In consequence, it also addresses the conditions for our biological continuance as a species. From our own species' perspective, green theory could thus be said to be articulating the conditions whereby further meaningful human life is possible. Exactly how we address these conditions is not just a question of choice in a plural framework of values. Environmental conditions are far too important for such a response. Thus, green political theory often claims, with some justification, to be markedly different to most political theory to date. It carries a health warning. This whole perspective gives green political theory a unique signature. The purpose of this chapter is to analyse this unique signature with particular reference to political theory. The key element of this signature is 'nature'. Green political theory conceives of itself as 'green', 'environmental' or 'ecological' *because of* its key focus on nature. Nature is seen as a crucial entity in its own right – of which we are just a very minor part. Thus, green theory is not a conventional theory, disinterestedly examining the value status of the non-human world. If this more conventional philosophical path were its sole brief, there would be no purpose in overtly labelling itself green, ecological or environmental. Nature, qua green, *is* the key theme. The underlying issue of this essay therefore concerns the relation between nature and political theory. If green theory does articulate the conditions of ecological and biological survival and flourishing, then politics must be imbricated, in the sense that *how* humans act politically has a crucial impact on nature and, thus, indirectly upon our survival as a species. It follows that the character of politics itself would need to be adapted to the imperatives of green political theory. Green theory articulates a politics which is responsive to nature and therefore the conditions for human continuance. The same point would hold for green political economy.

The first section of the chapter, briefly and non-controversially, identifies the underlying notion of political theory employed by most greens, examines two perspectives on green political theory and locates common green preoccupations. Second, the argument then turns to the history of the concept of nature. Third, having analysed the conceptual and historical dimensions of the concept of nature, the discussion shifts to a critical appraisal of the claims of green political theory. The chapter concludes on a sceptical argument which suggests that green political theory suffers from a deep internal tension arising from its focus on nature.

1 Green political theory

First, a dominant perspective on political theory, in the Anglo-American context, over the last thirty years, has been the normative view. John Plamenatz defined this as 'systematic thinking about the purposes of government'.[1] This is not conceived as a descriptive exercise, qua political science. It seeks to *evaluate* rather than *explain*. However, this conception of theory embodies a number of sub-approaches. The main normative foundational contenders are utilitarianism, consequentialism, Aristotelianism and deontology – with many subtle overlappings and variations.[2] It is within this general normative perspective that green theorists tend to utilise the term 'political theory'. Yet, green political theory works in an idiosyncratic manner. Unlike the bulk of normative theory to date, which has been largely focused on the very human purposes of government, justice, equality or rights, the green agenda characteristically tries to extend beyond human concerns.

Turning to the second issue of this first section: prima facie there are broadly two green normative political theory positions. The first identifies a wholly unique conception of political theory. This is the *radical* ecocentric perspective of writers such as Arne Naess, Bill Devall, Warwick Fox and Robyn Eckersely.[3] The central philosophical axiom of this perspective is 'that there is no firm ontological divide in the field of existence'.[4] An inclusive monistic conception of nature is adopted. The most well-known example of this is the Gaia hypothesis which reads the whole earth as a single organism.[5] The ecocentric value perspective has developed on two lines. The first is intrinsic value theory, which sees nature as an end in itself.[6] Crucially, intrinsic value does not require human recognition for it to exist. Nature has objective 'value-imparting characteristics'. The second ecocentric perspective bypasses value theory. It argues that what is required is not so much ethics as a psychological change in 'ecological sensibility'. The real issue is therefore psychology and ontology, not ethics. Ecological ethics derives from a mature and developed psychology.[7] Overall, for radicals, political theory can never be the same discipline again.[8]

The second dimension of green theory is underpinned by variants of *anthropocentric* argument. It is important to be sensitive here to gradations within anthropocentrism. Anthropocentric arguments stress that human beings are the sole criterion of value. The value of nature is instrumental in character. However there are many subtle variations within this approach.[9] It is important to draw an initial distinction between a deep and pliant anthropocentrism.[10] Deep anthropocentrism is indifferent to nature and is largely outside the domain of green theory. Pliant anthropocentrism stresses co-dependency with nature, although still filtered through human interests. The 'pliant' perspective leaves traditional normative theory largely unchanged. However new issues and questions are mapped onto the older normative concerns. Green political theory thus takes conventional issues of justice, freedom, equality, citizenship or rights and then adds a green dimension, emphasising co-dependency with nature. This perspective is embodied in the *reformist* ideas of writers such as R.E. Goodin, John Dryzek and John Barry. In reformism there is a belief that green aims can be achieved through coalitions within existing institutional structures.[11]

The third issue of this section focuses on 'linking themes' in *all* green theories. Despite the above variance of views, there are four formal themes affirmed by green theories of most shades – although the reformists and radicals tend to configure these themes differently. First, all assert the interdependence or intermeshing of the human species with nature. This is the *signature* of green political theory. One broad implication of this is that human beings are linked with nature.[12] In consequence, there is a tendency to be sceptical about the supreme moral position of human beings. Minimally, value extends beyond human beings. Second, green theories usually think in terms of greater wholes, such as nature, of which we are, in some manner, a part or co-dependent. Third, there is a more sensitised awareness of nature than found in all other conceptions of political theory. Fourth, there is an anxiety about what industrial civilisation is actually doing to nature.

If we focus on the above themes, then the above two green perspectives can be restated with more precision. First, for ecocentric theory we are wholly intermeshed with nature, however, the bulk of contemporary political theory is seen to be premised on a separation between humanity and nature. The supposition often underpinning the separation is that human persons are morally fundamental. Human persons are regarded as morally (not physically) distinct from their natural environment.[13] Kantian understanding of human agency and autonomy provides a classical rendering of this point. Kantian freedom, rationality and morality are wholly distinct from 'natural causation'. The rational agent exists autonomously as an end in herself and stands morally apart from the natural world. Natural objects, or nature in general, can always be treated as a means to an end. The human person is the only entity which can be considered morally as an end in itself.[14]

In reformist theory there is still an underlying unease about the position of human persons, but it is held less stringently. Reformists adhere to the view that one must accept a more realistic anthropocentrism. This is neatly summarised in Robert Goodin's point that one can be human centred without being human instrumental.[15] Further, naturalness, itself, can be a source of value. Goodin suggests, for example, that nature's independence is crucial to its meaning.[16] He remains, though, agnostic over the metaphysical load which might be attached to this 'independence'. John Dryzek also suggests that the notion of ecological rationality is embedded in an anthropocentric life-support system. He notes that 'the human life-support capacity of natural systems is the generalisable interest par excellence, standing as it does in logical antecedence to competing normative principles such as utility maximisation or rights protection'.[17] Ecological rationality is essentially 'the capability of ecosystems consistently and effectively to provide the good of human life support'.[18] It is important to emphasise here that it is only humans who are involved in the rational ecological dialogue. This is a pliant anthropocentrism mediated through an ecological rationality.[19] In sum, despite the anthropocentric focus of reformists, it is still a modified focus, which stresses the need to maintain a stable relation between humanity and nature.

The second issue concerns 'inclusive wholes'. There are greater wholes which provide value in more traditional political theory, for example, the community, nation, culture, state or race, but all these 'wholes' still focus exclusively on human beings (individually or collectively). The crucial aspect of green theory is that it focuses systematically on even broader wholes – the biosphere, ecosphere or nature. For ecocentric theories, this demands a wholly different ontological perspective. As Arne Naess argues, individual human agents should be considered as mere 'knots in the biospherical net' and not as 'separate actors'.[20] The self is viewed as a developing process within a more inclusive whole; it is, in effect, a locus of identification and the more comprehensive the identification, the broader the self.[21] In consequence, the diminishment of the river, forest, mountain or ecosystem becomes my diminishment. In this context, the widest self would be the whole of nature. In the reformist view, a via media is again sought. Reformists see their theory as a 'halfway house' between the ecocentric and deep anthropocentric positions. As indicated, humans are still intermeshed with the greater whole of nature, but *not* completely. It is only humans who can become conscious of this interdependence. It is therefore important, for Goodin, that 'just as you cannot reduce the value of nature wholly to natural values (as the deep ecologists might attempt), neither can you reduce the value of nature wholly to human values (as the shallowest ecologists wish)'. Value *is* always 'in relation to us', but this is not same as only having value 'for us'. Consequently, 'saying that things can have value only in relation to us is very different from saying that the value of nature reduces to purely human interests'.[22] Some features of nature exist independently from us, and, for reformists such as Goodin, nature as a whole can have value-imparting characteristics. Thus, green theory 'links the value of things to some naturally occurring properties of the objects themselves'.[23]

Third, it would be a truism to say that the majority of political theories to date have not been preoccupied with nature. However, nature, particularly humanity qua nature, *is* the central focus of all green theories. This is not to say that traditional political theories are not adaptable to green problems, but to date this has not been their overriding concern. This is a relatively uncontroversial point, shared by both radicals and reformists, with the one proviso that reformists see adequate moral resources within traditional moral and political theories – in Goodin's case in consequentialist utilitarianism, in Dryzek in Habermasian communicative ethics and in Barry in a form of neo-naturalistic ethics – whereas radicals see the need for a new ontology.

Fourth, most contemporary political theories assume that some form of industrial growth is unproblematic. However, the problem of industrialism has figured prominently in green debates. As Jonathan Porritt noted 'by industrialism, I mean adherence to the belief that human needs can only be met through *permanent* expansion of the process of production and consumption – regardless of the damage done to the planet, to the rights of future generations . . . The often unspoken values of industrialism are premised on the notion that material gain is quite simply more important to more people than anything else'.[24] In fact, industrial development is often considered desirable. This is the complete opposite to green theory. There are admittedly long-standing debates within green theory about sustainable and unsustainable industrialism, however, this is still premised on the point that *something* is amiss in the modus operandi of industrial culture. Ecocentric theories have been particularly concerned to either modify industrialism or to find a radical economic alternative to it. Reformists have been more concerned to use traditional or more orthodox tools of law and state policy to control industrialism.

However, do green ideas fundamentally change the character of political theorising? The radical response to this question is that mainstream political theory is rooted in certain beliefs which are totally antithetical to environmental concerns. As Robyn Eckersley comments, 'environmental philosophers have exposed a number of significant blind spots in modern political theory'. For Eckersley, these are not just trifling issues which can be rectified by minor adjustments. These blind spots concern, for example, our whole relation with the 'non-human world'. They are, in other words, fundamental issues which address our very survival as a species, in relation to nature. We require therefore a radically new perspective, which moves away from the myopia of traditional theory.[25] For Eckersley, these fundamental issues have rarely been given the time of day in contemporary political theory. Inter-human relations take absolute priority in mainstream political theory. The state, sovereignty, justice, equality, rights and freedom are seen to be focused unremittingly on humanity, as indifferent to nature. Humans decide on whether or not to allot values to the non-human. The crucial issue here is that it is human *decisions* and human *interests* which are crucial to mainstream political theory. The non-human is merely a backdrop to the drama of human affairs. For Eckersley, the ecocentric root and branch questioning of this whole perspective should give rise to 'a genuinely new constellation of ideas', as opposed to a mild adjustment.[26] The reformist response is, however, more nuanced than the ecocentric, partly because it tries to find a *via media* between the radical perspective and an indifferent deep anthropocentrism. Ecocentric theory is seen to be rooted in unacceptable metaphysical beliefs. Deep anthropocentrism is also unacceptable, due to its potential indifference to nature. Reformists therefore present a case for a green theory supplementing a more traditional conception of theory. John Barry's notion of 'critical anthropocentrism' catches the drift of this reformist position. It focuses on 'the place nature has within some particular human good or interest'.[27] It is ecologically based, but not ecologically centred.

In conclusion, despite sharing concerns, ecocentric political theory does imply a wholly new 'constellation of ideas' which transforms the whole of political theory. The new focus would be on the absolute priority of nature. For reformists, however, green political theory needs conversely to work with contemporary political theory, arguing for a green supplementation of traditional questions of justice, the state, citizenship or rights.

2 Nature

Rather than tackle the minutiae of the above reformist/radical debate, I want to refocus the discussion on a point which is distinctive in both green positions. Both perspectives, despite their manifest differences, are premised on the significance of nature. This is a controversial point, since radicals and reformist read nature differently. My contention would still be that nature remains central to both. This is what I referred to earlier as the unique 'signature' of green theory. The concept of nature enables us to identify something as *green* political theory. Nature is a fundamental datum on which the edifice of green political theory rests, whether in a co-dependent or monistic form. This is not a concept which has to necessarily bear any heavy metaphysical load. Minimally one expects every green theory to be concerned about nature. Yet, what is precisely meant by the term 'nature'? This question can be approached conceptually and historically.

First, the concept of nature implies a *source* or *principle of action* that makes something behave in a certain way. Any discussion of the nature of human beings would usually have this denotation. This is, in fact, the older sense of the term. It is an idea familiar from Greek philosophers to the present. However, there is a second conceptual sense of nature that refers to the *sum total* of things and events. This sense of the 'sum total' can also imply two different ideas: first, it can signify those things which are distinct from human action, intention or artifice. Another way of putting this is – nature refers to things which are driven by patterns of causation distinct from human action. The bulk of our own organic life is in fact driven by this kind of causation – the facts of death or indigestion, for example, are not under our control, only their timing or occasion. Nature is the sum of what is *not* the result of human action. Ironically, this idea has been attractive for ecocentric theories. For example, when deep ecologists speak of wilderness, it is usually nature untouched by human action. It is the wild mountain or river system without any 'unnatural' human presence. The aesthetic of wilderness experience is premised upon this 'pristine' untouched quality. The irony here is that most ecocentric theories appear to work with a monistic metaphysics which consistently denies 'dualisms', particularly dualisms which prioritise humans. Humans are envisaged as mere temporary 'knots' in the 'biospherical net', rapidly unravelling and slipping back into the organic soup. Yet, paradoxically, the insistence on wilderness implies that humans are in someway distinct from nature. Thus, ecocentric theories, from the opposite end to deep anthropocentric theories, make a subtle contribution to a new dualism between humans and nature. In this case, humans are villains, qua ecocentrism, rather then heroes, qua deep anthropocentrism.[28]

The second broad sense of 'sum total' addresses the issue that humans are as much part of nature as any river system. Thus, the sum total includes humans and *all* their actions. In one sense, an aspect of this argument is grasped by some ecocentric theories, which accept that humans are omnivorous, and thus hunting animals for personal consumption is 'natural'. This view is premised on the point that human action is natural. Humans are part of the natural order. However, it is also important to note that this latter argument has unpredictable extensions. To follow out its logic more rigorously would include all human activity in industry, economics, culture and politics within the ambit of 'nature'. This, in turn, raises a further issue, namely, that environmental degradation, as a result of human actions, could also be considered natural. If humans are an evolutionary species, then all human activities are natural, even if some are extremely risky for species survival. It may be natural for us to overreach ourselves as a species and perish. It has happened to countless other species. In summary, the concept of nature is deceptive. This point is reinforced if we turn to a brief history of the concept of nature.

The historical argument sees nature as a contingent concept. In ancient Greek thought nature was intimately related to intelligence or soul. Greek thinkers would have been genuinely puzzled by later dualistic conceptions of mind and nature. Another dimension of this intelligence in nature is teleology. A design or purpose is implicit in nature. This idea precedes Aristotle and Plato in the ancient world. Cities, temples, gardens and the like are designed and will decay without an artisan, craftsman or designer. Analogously, for the ancient world, nature in general implies a purposeful intelligent ordering.[29] This idea of nature as a designed and purposeful order was influential in medieval Christian thought. Two views derived from this Christian perspective: the first advocated stewardship and care for God's created order, the second arose within the ambit of the fall. In the latter, a *contemptus mundi* and fear of a corruption implicit in nature affected the whole argument. In sixteenth- and seventeenth-century European thought the concept of nature changed again. It came to be viewed as largely devoid of intelligence, rationality or purpose. It was, in effect, analogous to a machine. In thinkers such as Descartes, Galileo, Bacon and Kepler dualisms arose with a vengeance – body and mind or nature and mind. For Galileo, for example, what was true in nature was measurable and quantitative. In the nineteenth and twentieth centuries the most decisive idea to affect the conception of nature was evolutionary theory. Evolutionary theory emphasised that nature had an immensely complex and mutable history (of which we are part), and that nature was a process and not a mechanism (mechanisms being finished and completed things). Evolution also emphasised the point that nature was not necessarily benign. Humans were essentially a primate species who had, for a contingent brief moment, successfully adapted. There was nothing very special about us, except that our organic brains had evolved in a quite unique way and we possessed some limited grasp of our situation. The upshot of this brief conceptual and historical excursus is that the concept of nature is both mutable and contested. It *cannot* be simply deployed as a source of value or as a way of differentiating green theory from other perspectives, without further explanation.[30]

This conclusion has a bearing on another question: in what sense can politics ever be considered natural? Green discussions of this question usually differentiate green politics as something uniquely natural. Either green politics is conducive to a harmonious relation with nature, or, the communal arrangements are, quite literally, natural. These can be called the *intrinsic* and *instrumental* uses of 'natural' qua politics. The intrinsic view suggests that certain types of politics or morality *are* natural in themselves.[31] Thus, there can be a natural morality or politics, in an ecological sense. This argument relies on the idea that there is a non-contested objective natural order to which we can refer. This view is characteristic of radical approaches. The instrumental view argues that certain conceptions of politics are more *conducive* to a natural order, in so far as they facilitate a more symbiotic and sensitive way of living with nature. This position is more characteristic of the reformist perspective. However, the upshot of both these views is that there are certain forms of social and political arrangements which are either harmonious with or functional for the natural environment. Consequently, it is possible to identify a natural sense of rationality, democracy, citizenship or justice. However, given that nature is contested, what effect does this have on green argument?

3 Critique of green values

The problem with green argument is the ambiguity concerning nature. Deep anthropocentrism ignores *any* co-dependence with nature. The opposite problem is encountered in radical ecocentrism. It prioritises a monistic conception of nature. For ecocentric theory *everything* has the equal right to subsist. The ethical community includes landscapes and river systems. Ecocentrism consequently advocates biospherical egalitarianism. However, what reformists try to do is recognise that value extends beyond humans, but not so far as to ignore humans as valuers. The language of interests, qua nature's interests, is still a human language. In speaking of nature's interests we inevitably anthropomorphise nature, however it still remains independent, to a degree. Yet, what does nature mean here?

In my own reading, the 'problem of nature' is truly sensed by reformist writers, far more so than radicals. Reformists link an awareness that human interests are crucial with the point that we are relational co-dependent beings. We filter nature through our interests, but, we are still intimately related to an independent nature. Yet, this position has its own problems, namely, how does one account for both the link between humans and nature, in tandem with their separateness?

The strategy for dealing with this issue was originally canvassed by the social ecologist Murray Bookchin. It involves a subtle blending between nature as *distinct* and nature as *integral* to us. To achieve this blending, Bookchin distinguishes between 'First Nature' (as the product of biological evolution) and 'Second Nature' (society and culture as human artefact).[32] First Nature, for Bookchin, embodies a dim sense of purpose. Yet, it is only in humanity that nature is rendered self-conscious.[33] This is 'Second Nature'. Green theory, for Bookchin, *is* nature in human consciousness (qua Second Nature) addressing itself. As Bookchin put it, somewhat fancifully, in green theory, nature appears to be 'writing its own natural philosophy and ethics'.[34] Second Nature, qua green theory, reveals how a society ought be organised. Second Nature has 'built in' imperatives. Humanity *is* self-conscious nature; we therefore have responsibilities to direct evolutionary processes. This involves fostering a diverse and complex biosphere, it also implies new concepts of urbanism, decentralised authority, liberating technology and new types of community. Bookchin refers to this Second Nature as the 'new animism'. As we evolve, we see ourselves as 'nature rendered self-conscious and intelligent'. In social ecology we co-operate with the implicit teleology of nature.[35]

A more restrained and less teleological argument can be found in other thinkers. Barry, for example, articulates the point that we are biological as well as cultural products. As he comments, '"we" are adapted to "our" culture, which in turn is, at least temporarily adapted to its environment'. Directly echoing Bookchin, he speaks of the 'first level of our nature' which is premised upon our biological constitution. He distinguishes this from our 'second nature' which is focused on 'the centrality of culture in the determination of human nature'. For Barry, as for Bookchin, 'culture is our species-specific mode of expressing our nature . . . As it is continuous with our nature as social beings, human culture does not represent a radical separation from nature, but can be viewed as our "second nature"'. In this context, Barry defines morality and politics in 'relational terms' – relational meaning rooted in a community of humans, the community being co-dependent with nature.[36] Ethics is therefore viewed in the context of a form of *communitarian naturalism*.[37] It accepts our favouritism for our own species as quite rational, yet, as evolutionary creatures we can also criticise our own conduct, adapt and modify our activities (thus Barry's 'critical anthropocentrism'). Inevitably, in this reading, our interests move outside our own immediate species. The ethical standing of nature is itself natural. Culture 'can thus be seen as a collective capacity of humans to adapt to the particular and contingent conditions of their collective existence, including, most importantly, the environments with which they interact and upon'.[38]

The same distinction, between first and second nature, can be found in other thinkers who favour a reformist agenda. Thus, Andrew Brennan's distinction between relative and absolute notions of the natural, or Mary Midgely's distinction between open and closed instincts (closed are biologically fixed, whereas open instincts indicate tendencies to certain types of behaviour which are consciously modifiable), express a parallel thesis.[39]

There are, however, problems with this naturalistic argument. The first concerns the roots of natural morality in local communities. John Barry is adamant that naturally based ecological democracy, justice and the like, have universal significance.[40] Yet, if it is in our (second) nature to live in local communities, how do we get from this communitarian 'natural difference' to a global naturalistic ethic? The term 'natural' seems to be working extremely hard here and in contradictory ways. Second, it is not at all clear why authoritarian, tribal or many other types of political community cannot be natural. Third, it is not apparent why the conception of 'first nature' cannot explain culture or second nature.

Another reformist approach to the question of value is taken by Goodin. He draws a firm distinction between *agency* and *value*. Value 'provides the unified moral vision running through all the central substantive planks in the green political programme'.[41] For Goodin, the core green values are all 'consequentialist at root'.[42] Agency, however, only advises on how to bring values into practice. Thus, the 'green theory of agency is a theory about how best to pursue the Good'. Thus, importantly for Goodin, one can agree on values, without agreeing on the agency. There is no necessity whatsoever to adopt a particular lifestyle to be green.[43]

There are major problems with Goodin's distinction. First, can means (agency) and ends (values) be so firmly separated? Green's characteristically are concerned with how people live. Goodin is clearly out of step here with the movement. Second, values do usually give rise to policies and agency. The connection between agency and value is culturally prevalent – whether correct or not. Third, many individuals do respond to ecological issues by adopting lifestyle changes – which they perceive to be in their own long-term interest. Fourth, Goodin's value theory has no particular agency implications. Nothing that Goodin says rules out authoritarian agency. Goodin's value theory could just as well be linked with fascist ecology. Fifth, a related point, is that Goodin's consequentialist utilitarianism is potentially fickle. As Brian Barry remarks succinctly, many greens are 'quite right to reject Goodin's proposed substitute for the quite straightforward reason that it makes the case for the preservation of the natural environment depend upon what people actually want'.[44] If someone says that there is a utility in chopping down trees (as many logging groups across the world do argue), then nothing significant can be said against it from Goodin's perspective. If the consequence is massive profits and employment, then it could be regarded as a consequential good. Utilitarian calculus, because of its second order nature, is notoriously capricious. Sixth, Goodin's agnosticism over the 'value-imparting quality' of nature is problematic. For Goodin, the value is not there at the behest of human consciousness and the 'value-imparting quality' (whatever it is) reacts with the cogniser. To admit this takes the edge off his dismissal of ecocentrism. Despite separating humans and nature, Goodin also suggests that humans are part of nature and that his argument is not so much a defence of nature, as of human modesty in dealing with nature. As if this was not puzzling enough, he then raises the question whether the separation between humans and nature *is* morally significant at all.[45] This admission takes his whole value argument full circle. This is not an uncommon dilemma for reformists.

Nature, in all the above green accounts, appears to be a contingent resource, lacking coherence. It might be argued, in response to this, why should not green theory be motivated by the question: what status should be given to the non-human environment in terms of policy? Why should there be a problem with nature at all? There is no decisive answer to this question, yet the following points should be noted. First, the critic would not deny here that many green theorists – for example, the whole ecocentric dimension – have been fixated on nature. Second, *all* dimensions of the green political theory do focus on the importance of nature, in one shape or another. There is no reason to call oneself green, if nature is insignificant. It would, however, be a truism that distinct dimensions of green theory work with differing understandings of nature. Third, there is nothing to stop any theorist pondering the value of the non-human world – even those utterly indifferent to nature. However, one might hesitate, with good reason, to say that this was *green* theory, as commonly understood. Thus, I would still contend therefore that nature is the crucial category of a political theory that claims to be green as opposed to one that merely addresses green issues.

Conclusion

The crucial question is, who or what defines nature? If culture in general is reduced to nature, then there appears to be nothing, logically, that could tell us definitively what nature is. If, on the other hand, nature is a cultural and historically mutable concept, then our economic, religious, scientific and philosophic discourses continuously anthropomorphise the 'natural'. We filter this 'something' through our interests. The 'something' remains noumenal. Even calling something 'first' or 'second' nature performs this filtering task. We cannot know outside of the 'webs of significance' that we weave. Speaking of 'nature's interests' brings this 'something' into our cognitive domain. As such, either there is no way categorically to know what is outside human production and human culture, or, if we claim that we are wholly natural, then we *still* could not know the natural because *everything* becomes natural. The status of nature per se thus becomes baffling. Intermediate positions, like pliant anthropocentrism, try to resolve the conundrum by relabelling, which, in substance, simply restates the paradox in new terminology. Therefore, we do not really know, in green terms, what is being damaged or degraded. We do not know what nature is. Nature is clearly integral (definitionally) to green theory, but nature remains incoherent and contested. If green political theory is premised on nature and we have no coherent or uncontested understanding of nature, then it follows that green political theory is teetering on incoherence.

Notes

1 J. Plamenatz, 'The Use of Political Theory', *Political Studies*, 8 (1960), p. 37. D. Miller roughly follows this in defining political theory as 'systematic reflection on the nature and purposes of government', D. Miller (ed.), *The Blackwell Encyclopaedia of Political Thought* (Oxford, Blackwell, 1987), p. 383.

2 Subsequently, other subtle normative variants – communitarianism, feminism, rational choice and republicanism – have also moved into the forefront of political theory debate.

3 R. Eckersley, *Environmentalism and Political Theory* (London, UCL Press, 1992); A. Naess, *Ecology, Community and Lifestyle*, tr. D. Rothenberg (Cambridge, Cambridge University Press, 1990); B. Devall and G. Sessions, *Deep Ecology: Living as if Nature Mattered* (Salt Lake City, UT, Gibbs M. Smith Inc., 1985). There are though differences between these writers.

4 Warwick Fox quoted in R. Sylvan, 'A Critique of Deep Ecology', *Radical Philosophy*, 40 and 41 (1984–85), p. 103.

5 The general inspiration for this type of argument came initially from the North American writer, Aldo Leopold's, *A Sand County Almanac*, and later from the philosopher Arne Naess. For Leopold, a thing is right when it tends to preserve the integrity, stability and beauty of the biotic community. As Leopold stated 'a land ethic changes the role of Homo Sapiens from conqueror of the land . . . to plain member and citizen of it', Leopold quoted in D. Scherer and T. Attig (eds), *Ethics and the Environment* (New York, Prentice Hall, 1983), p. 7.

6 Entities which are ends in themselves have interests in sustaining themselves and a good of their own. An entity having a good of its own is morally considerable.

7 As John Rodman has commented, 'It is worth asking whether the ceaseless struggle to extend morality and legality may now be more a part of the problem than its solution', J. Rodman 'The Liberation of Nature', *Inquiry*, 20 (1977), pp. 103–4. This latter judgement is open to the charge that requiring a change in 'ecological sensibility' is still indirectly making a moral claim. There is some truth to this point. However, in response, it could be said that the whole order of priority has changed, namely, the 'ecological sensibility' argument is suggesting that moral action is a result of a prior change in human psychology. Moral sensibility is the *result* of a mature psychology, it is not the result of being convinced by moral argument or obeying moral imperatives. The sensibility argument is suggesting that one cannot expect any moral behaviour from anyone unless you are dealing with psychologies which are mature enough to actually *be* that way.

8 The ecocentric position (deep ecology) is described by two of its proponents as a search 'for a more objective consciousness and state of being through an active deep questioning and meditative process and way of life', see Devall and Sessions, *Deep Ecology*, p. 66.

9 There is, in fact, a great deal more complexity within all these green approaches, which cannot be dealt with here. For an attempt at a more comprehensive typology, see A. Vincent, 'The Character of Ecology', *Environmental Politics*, 2:2 (1993), pp. 248–76; also see A. Vincent, *Modern Political Ideologies* (Oxford, Blackwell, 1995, 2nd edn), pp. 215–21.

10 Many environmental writers, like John Rodman, Warwick Fox, Max Oelschlaeger, Richard Sylvan, John Passmore and Robyn Eckersley, also subdivide the above pliant anthropocentric concerns into 'conservation' and 'preservationism'.

11 J. Barry, *Rethinking Green Politics* (London, Sage, 1999); J. Dryzek, *Rational Ecology: Environment and Political Economy* (Oxford, Blackwell, 1987) and R.E. Goodin, *Green Political Theory* (Cambridge, Polity Press, 1992). Again, it is important to stress that there are marked differences between these reformist writers.

12 There are loose parallels here with communitarian arguments, particularly critical conceptions of the autonomous self considered separately from the community. The ecological self, for example, is quite clearly encumbered, although the encumbrance is nature.

13 This is not therefore a denial of our *physical* dependence on our natural surroundings.

14 It is important to note here that this does not imply that Kantian agents can treat nature simply as they like.

15 Goodin, *Green Political Theory*, p. 45.

16 A 'restored bit of nature is necessarily not as valuable as something similar that has been "touched by human hands"', Goodin, *Green Political Theory*, p. 41. See also B. McKibben's, *The End of Nature* (London, Penguin, 1990). McKibben suggests that 'Nature's independence *is* its meaning; without it there is nothing but us', p. 54.

17 Dryzek, *Rational Ecology*, p. 204.

18 Dryzek, *Rational Ecology*, p. 36.

19 John Barry tries to expand upon Dryzek's view of ecological rationality in his work.

20 See A. Naess, 'The Shallow and the Deep, Long-range Ecology Movement. A Summary', *Inquiry*, 16 (1973), p. 263.

21 The self is thus, for Naess, 'as comprehensive as the totality of its identifications', see Naess, 'The Shallow', pp. 263–4, also Naess, *Ecology, Community and Lifestyle*, p. 261.

22 Goodin, *Green Political Theory*, pp. 44–5.

23 Goodin, *Green Political Theory*, pp. 25–6.

24 J. Porritt in E. Goldsmith and N. Hildyard (eds), *Green Britain or Industrial Wasteland* (Cambridge, Polity Press, 1986), pp. 344–5 (original emphasis).

25 As Christopher Stone noted ' A radical new conception of man's relationship to the rest of nature would not only be a step towards solving the material planetary problems: there are strong reason for such a changed consciousness from the point of making us far better humans', C. Stone, *Should Trees Have Standing? Towards Legal Rights for Natural Objects* (Los Altos, CA, Kaufman, 1974), p. 48.

26 Eckersley, *Environmentalism and Political Theory*, pp. 2–3.

27 Barry, *Rethinking Green Politics*, p. 35.

28 There is another ecocentric way round this dualism, namely, to regard humans as still part of monistic nature, yet, we should be considered as equivalent to a troublesome virus. Thus, we might take up the view of Earth First!, and other such eco-warriors, in regarding human beings as a natural pestilence which nature will eventually eradicate to maintain ecological balance.

29 See C. Glacken, *Traces on the Rhodian Shore* (Berkeley, CA, University of California Press, 1967), p. 147.

30 It is also important to ask, in the same sceptical vein, whether the term nature is coterminous with the term environment? When ecocentric theorists speak of nature or the environment, then mountains and wildernesses make a quick appearance. In fact, most animals including humans, have usually lived on savannahs or coastal plains, where food sources are easier to come by. To push the point further, for most humans, at the present moment, the environment *means* an urban or constructed one. This is natural to us. The incisive point here is that the natural environment for most animals is *not* a mountain wilderness. The ecocentric notion of the natural environment is bizarrely idiosyncratic, although it has precise equivalents in romantic pantheistic theories from the late eighteenth and nineteenth centuries. Further, for the majority of human animals the environment is urbanised. Why then have Green theories not taken on this pervasive conception of the environment and the natural? The answer is complex, but must in part be due to the fact that Green theories to date have not really articulated a coherent concept of nature.

31 The characteristic doctrine arguing this is the ecocentric idea of bioregionalism, see K. Sale, *Dwellers in the Land: The Bioregional Vision* (San Francisco, CA, Sierra Book Club, 1985).

32 This has direct choes of earlier discussions, from the late nineteenth century over natural and social evolution, as in Herbert Spencer or L.T. Hobhouse.

33 Compare with Goodin's comment that we are the only creatures with a 'sufficiently sophisticated consciousness for this purpose', Goodin, *Green Political Theory*, p. 45.

34 M. Bookchin, 'Towards a Philosophy of Nature', in M. Tobias (ed.) *Deep Ecology* (San Diego, CA, Avant Books, 1985), p. 229. This also links up with Bookchin's central thesis that domination of nature follows from social domination.

35 For Bookchin 'The truth or falsity of nature philosophy lies in the truth or falsity of its unfolding in reality', Bookchin 'Towards a Philosophy of Nature', p. 228.

36 See Barry, *Rethinking Green Politics*, p. 46.

37 It is worth briefly underscoring this term 'communitarian naturalism', since it will be subject to criticism in the penultimate section of the discussion.

38 John Barry, *Rethinking Green Politics*, p. 50.

39 A. Brennan, *Thinking about Nature* (London, Routledge, 1988). For Brennan, 'humans, like all other natural creatures, grow and develop by interacting with their various environments (social and natural)', p. 184; M. Midgely, *Beast and Man: The Roots of Human Nature* (London, Routledge, 1995). Goodin implicitly recognises this distinction in his discussion of the problem of 'faking' nature, see Goodin, *Green Political Theory*, pp. 35–6.

40 '[I]it is a basic moral fact of life that under normal circumstances relations between "human beings" regardless of cultural membership, are or ought to be founded upon a set of moral considerations', Barry, *Rethinking Green Politics*, p. 56.

41 Goodin, *Green Political Theory*, p. 15.

42 Goodin, *Green Political Theory*, p. 120.

43 For Goodin, therefore, 'we should turn a blind eye to some of the crazier views (views about personal life-styles, transformations of consciousness)', Goodin, *Green Political Theory*, see pp. 16, 17.

44 See Barry, *Justice as Impartiality* (Oxford, Clarendon, 1995), p. 22.

45 Goodin, *Green Political Theory*, pp. 46, 52.

16
International justice

David Boucher

Introduction

Is justice intra-national or international, localised or globalised, communitarian or cosmopolitan, universal or particular, in its scope? Do richer countries have a duty to help poorer countries and, if so, is this duty a matter of charity or justice, or both? Answers to these questions are often dependent upon an answer to a prior question: are state boundaries morally arbitrary and, if so, do we have a responsibility to help the less well off beyond these borders? A whole range of positions are taken which often cut across the cosmopolitan–communitarian divide favoured by such theorists who work within the field of international relations as Chris Brown, Janna Thompson, Charles Jones and Peter Sutch.[1]

Cosmopolitanism points to the justification of our moral principles as having a universal basis. For the cosmopolitan the existing social arrangements have no special status as the source of our value. The type of universal principles required is generated by three different sources of cosmopolitanism: Kantianism, utilitarianism and Marxism. Although utilitarianism is an entirely different moral theory from that of Kant, it is nevertheless cosmopolitan. Jeremy Bentham is, of course, the classic utilitarian. His theory is clearly cosmopolitan in that values are universal, and not the product of various particularistic communities. Each individual feels pleasure and pain and this is the basis of human values. Individuals have a basic duty to increase the happiness of humankind in general. The institutions of the family and state, for example, have claims on our duty because they promote the maximisation of the general happiness and not because they have priority over utility. Similarly, governments have a duty to promote the happiness of humankind even if this somehow damages the interests of its own citizens. The principle of the greatest happiness has to be the guide to what is right and wrong. In so far as international law is conducive to the general happiness it should be encouraged, and in so far as war is detrimental to the general happiness it should be discouraged. Nothing in Bentham's view has intrinsic value, except pleasure: everything, including the existence of states, has to be judged on their consequences.[2]

The central feature of communitarianism is that the source of value derives from the community, and that communities themselves are ethically significant. Individuals derive their meaning in life from, and are constituted by, the political communities they inhabit. Such theorists as Frost and Brown call themselves constitutive theorists in order to get away from the connotation that communitarianism has of giving priority to the nation or state, but also in order to jettison the metaphysics associated with Hegelianism. Brown, like Frost, relies on Hegel for his account of the development of individuality. Brown quite explicitly rejects Hegelian metaphysics and presents us with what he calls a 'demythologised' version.[3] Through the family, the individual develops a personality and sense of belonging in the world based on unconditional love. Taking responsibility for one's projects in the context of civil society, and participating in the world of private property, the market and the institutions which sustain them, constitutes a further stage in the development of consciousness. This stage, however, places individuals in competition, and in civil society they experience the law as an external imposition and constraint. More consciously developed individuals come to internalise the law and appreciate others as fellow citizens and not competitors. The rationale of the modern ethical state, based on the principles of the rule of law and the separation of the powers, is to bring about this transformation in consciousness.

Rather than as polar opposites the various versions of cosmopolitanism and communitarianism in international relations are best conceived as occupying places on a scale, the ends of which are not absolute zero and infinity, but a universalism or cosmopolitanism which is not completely devoid of communitarianism or particularism, and a particularism which accommodates universalism. Neither is insensitive to the concerns of the other. One of the best syntheses is that of Onora O'Neill whose concerns are cosmopolitan-based duty rather than rights. This enables her better to incorporate the particularist special obligation virtue ethics which motivate communitarians. This chapter, therefore, surveys the cosmopolitan and communitarian positions before turning to her synthesis of the two.

1 Cosmopolitanism/universalism

The seminal starting point in discussions of distributive international justice which transcends state borders, and denies the nation as an ethically relevant factor in such considerations, is the position of Peter Singer.[4] Singer's argument implicitly covers both humanitarian aid, typically generated by a sense of solidarity when natural disasters dramatically threaten lives, and what is called development aid, which contributes towards programmes of self-sustainment such as establishing irrigation systems, sinking wells, transforming farming practices and so on. The programmes are less visible than emergency aid, but of more importance in the long run.

As a utilitarian, the alleviation of harm and suffering is crucial to his line of reasoning, although he denies that his argument relies upon utilitarianism. He starts with the assumption that suffering and death caused by a lack of food, shelter and medical care are bad, and that if it is in our power to prevent it from happening without sacrificing something of comparable moral significance then we ought to do it. The principle requires us only to prevent what is bad, not to promote that which is good. Even in a modified form, which requires us only to prevent very bad things from happening without having to sacrifice any-thing of moral significance, the consequences are deceptively far reaching. There are two momentous implications. First, distance and proximity are not morally relevant factors: 'If we accept any principle of impartiality, universal-izability, equality, or whatever, we cannot discriminate against someone merely because he is far away from us'.[5] Second, it makes no significant moral differ-ence whether I alone, or millions of other people, are in the same position to prevent the harm, which in Singer's examples are saving a drowning child or helping Bengali famine victims. Put starkly, neither geography nor numbers lessen our obligation to prevent the harm. This means that giving money to, say, the Bengali relief fund is a matter of duty rather than charity, and that the act is not supererogatory, that is something that is good to do, but not morally reprehensible if I fail to do it.

How much are we obliged to give, and is it a matter of duty rather than char-ity? On the strong version, we should help others up to the level of marginal utility, that is the point at which by giving more we would cause a comparable amount of harm to ourselves or our dependants. On the moderate version, where we are required to prevent bad things happening without sacrificing anything of moral significance, we would still witness a considerable transfor-mation in society because expenditure upon trivia, which the consumer society encourages, would be morally indefensible.

Both the strong and the moderate versions require us when saving lives is at issue to invoke a standard of *absolute* poverty, where the lack of food and resources lead to malnutrition and death, or when life is threatened by the com-paratively rare occurrence of extreme famine and natural disaster. If, however, we are to take a more relaxed standard than *absolute* poverty, where not only life itself, but the quality of life should be a concern, then we invoke some notion of *relative* poverty, where, for example, eastern Europeans are well-off in compar-ison with Africans, but poor in comparison with western Europeans. It is a stan-dard that does not signify any particular level of suffering or death.[6] The strong version of Singer's case, the one that he prefers, would in fact commit us to relieving relative poverty to the point where we are almost as poor as the recip-ients. Even the weaker version, in his opinion, would lead to a significant shift of resources.

The argument, however, lacks a time dimension, and suffers from an inabil-ity to assess comparative benefits and costs. The cost of the *QE2* was indeed immense when compared with the suffering that may have been relieved at the same cost. The jobs provided, the additional allied businesses that relied upon the venture, and the multiplier effect in the European economy may well mean that in the long run more has been given to charity through governments and individual contributions by prolonging the life of the ship building industry than if it had been allowed to sink into decline.

More fundamentally, Hare's objections to intuitive morality apply to Singer's type of argument. Singer is not offering a moral theory as such, but presenting us with something that it is said everyone would agree to, and if we agree to it, then we must agree to something else because the principle is the same. Singer gives the example of saving a drowning child at the expense of getting one's trousers muddy, and extends the obligation felt in this situation to saving a starving Bengali 10,000 miles away.[7] What is presupposed is, first, that something that it is said everyone would agree to, ought to be agreed to, and second, that the principles really are the same. This would entail a scrupulous examination of what the principle is, but it gives us no reason why we should accept it, and not reject both judgements.[8]

Garret Hardin raises a different kind of objection. Can it be morally right to redistribute resources if the benefits are far from evident? Redistributing benefits may have an affect on what is distributed. Hardin argues that the world is like a lifeboat unable to take all those who want to be saved. Some people are in it and others are in the water wanting to get in. If access is not restricted everyone will sink, and no one will benefit.[9] This is a metaphor, but like all metaphors may be misleading. What Hardin denies is the right of the poor to a share of the resources of richer countries, and he casts doubt on the moral efficacy of charitable redistribution. What he assumes is that the benefit is fixed and if spread too thinly will cease to be a benefit. Again, the time factor needs to be considered. The world does not have a fixed capacity, nor can we predict the effect of redistribution on population growth, nor the effect of population growth on economic sustainability. There is in fact much evidence to suggest that once a society has developed sufficiently to provide adequate food, basic health care and security in old age, increasing population trends level out or decline.[10] Indeed, poverty may increase populations on the principle that one extra mouth to feed equals two extra hands. In addition, if the benefit can be diminished by being spread too thin, it can also be increased by being spread wisely. His argument is based on 'the law of diminishing returns' which states that when there are small increases in a factor of production, other factors remaining constant, say, adding labourers to a fixed acreage of land, the resulting increases in output will after a certain point progressively get smaller. However, this consideration has to be balanced against the law of marginal utility. The additional amount of benefit I receive from each additional unit of value diminishes to the point where negative utility may be achieved. The amount of utility I get from, say, each additional ice cream diminishes until I make myself sick. What is of negative benefit to me will on someone else's utility curve produce positive benefits. For example, if I give my fifth ice cream in a relatively short period to someone who is starving the utility derived from it by the other person is much greater than mine.

Hardin's position denies the efficacy of both charity and duties of justice. The distinction between duty and charity which was made by Peter Singer is applied differently by Gordon Graham. Graham contends that the recognition that everyone in the world has basic rights to the necessities of life can generate nothing more than imperfect obligations, that is, claims upon everyone, but upon no one in particular. The right to social justice requires and assumes a government or state as the distributor, capable of enforcing contributions and deterring free-riding, but at the international level no such authority exists. Basic needs are best met out of a sense of charity rather than as a matter of redistributive justice which stops at the borders of the state.[11]

Brian Barry extends Singer's and Hardin's distinction further in suggesting that acting from considerations of justice is different from, but not incompatible with acting out of a sense of humanity. Accepting Singer's argument, Barry contends that we have an obligation to give humanitarian aid to the poor, but on the question of how much he suggests that no hard and fast rule can be determined.[12]

Humanitarian obligation is not derived from justice, but this does not mean that it is an act of generosity or that it should be left to the discretion of the individual. The principles relating to humanity are goal based in that they are concerned with the well-being of individuals and have to do with questions of welfare, freedom from poverty and disease, and provision for satisfying basic needs. In Barry's view, the duty of humanity is a matter of doing good. A humanitarian tax may be levied and distributed through international agencies to promote goal-orientated projects. Humanitarian redistribution would as now be earmarked for specific use and its receipt would be conditional. The control of the resources would be in the hands of international bodies such as the International Monetary Fund or the World Bank.

On considerations of justice, however, the 'distribution of control of resources would actually be shifted'.[13] In other words, the transfer of resources would not depend upon the use made of them. Humanitarian aid may justifiably have strings attached in order to attain the desirable state of affairs it is designed to bring about. By contrast, justice is not concerned with these things at all. Justice relates to a set of wholly different principles which have to do with power. It is partly about who is entitled to what. Barry's point is effectively this: it makes little sense to argue about what a state should do with its own resources, for example, how it should distribute various benefits to the poor, until it is determined what those resources are. In Barry's argument, they include a right to a share of the income from the world's natural resources.[14] If we have a basically just international distribution, then the need for humanitarian aid is reduced to responding to extraordinary problems relating to epidemics, famine, droughts, floods and earthquakes.

The principles of international justice have to do with resources in the broadest sense, including non-material resources which incorporate issues of rights

– such as acting without interference from others, limiting the actions of others and regulating changes to the non-human environment. Justice, then, has to do with the distribution of control over material resources and the principles governing how control ought to be allocated. At this level of abstraction the principles of allocation are supplemented with the principle of equal liberty which relates to control over non-material resources. The fortuitous allocation of natural resources throughout the world is morally arbitrary, and the populations of the various countries can hardly be held responsible for their good or bad fortune, and the benefits or miseries which ensue.[15] The assumption is that benefits from favourable natural resource allocation are 'unearned' and that people have no exclusive right to the benefits they obtain from them.

The principle of the strong powers exploiting the weak by laying claim to their resources has been somewhat weakened by various conventions and United Nations resolutions to the effect that states have absolute sovereign control over their natural resources. This morality of the lottery is preferable to the morality of control and exploitation. However, it is less acceptable to seeing the world's natural resources as the common possession of the world's population as a whole. International justice, Barry contends, is not a matter of charity. The redistribution of resources raised through an international resources tax is a matter of entitlement. Therefore, it must be transferred unconditionally to the recipient countries. By contrast, Rawls dismisses out of hand the relevance of the arbitrariness of resource distribution to international justice. A country's fortunes, he contends, are due more to its political culture and the virtues of its people than to natural resources.[16]

Charles Beitz and Thomas Pogge postulate a form of cosmopolitanism that does not depend upon the idea of a universal political community of humankind. They are concerned to emphasise the interdependence of states, and the effects that each has upon others, many of which have moral significance. Given these effects can be both good and bad, there is a need for some form of co-operation and regulation. They subscribe to the Kantian point that just institutions must be established among all those whose actions can impact upon each other. Beitz's argument for applying the Rawlsian difference principle to the international context is essentially that the extensive global system of trade, or complex interdependence, which is part of the conventional wisdom of international relations, constitutes a worldwide co-operative scheme in which every country is implicated.[17] Rawls himself denies that the world constitutes a common co-operative enterprise, sufficient to qualify for considerations of distributive justice in the same way as bounded communities. Because there is no global society engaged in a co-operative enterprise, there is no co-operative surplus for which principles of distribution must be found. Although, more recently, Rawls has conceded that there is a case for the just distribution of basic liberties, and agrees with the aims of neo-Rawlsian cosmopolitans, such as Beitz and Pogge,[18] of attaining liberal institutions, securing human rights and providing for basic needs in accordance with what he calls a 'duty of assistance', he does not agree with the principles they present for redistributive justice.[19]

Beitz distinguishes between a resource distribution principle, which applies when states are self-sufficient and where inequalities arise from uneven resources, and a global distribution principle. The latter arises when there are flows of goods and services from one country to another leading to co-operative surpluses for which an international difference principle may be invoked. Beyond the duty of assistance, which responds to gross injustices and inequalities, Rawls cannot see the appeal of the global principle because it posits no determinate target and is essentially open-ended. Its consequences, he suggests, would be unwelcome because it would be unacceptable to subsidise choices.[20] If two liberal or decent countries of equal resources choose different paths of development, the one industrialisation and increased real saving, while the other prefers more traditional ways of living, why when vast inequalities of wealth appear should the former subsidise the latter through taxation?

Rawls's duty to assist does have a target and a cut off point. The target is burdened societies that are too poor to develop their own just institutions and equality of liberty, and the purpose of assistance to provide primary goods for basic needs is to raise a people to the point of establishing such institutions and to become capable of making their own choices. Such assistance need not take the form of redistributive justice, and it should not be assumed that giving money, although this is essential, will redress fundamental political and social injustices. In this respect change, is more likely if assistance is tied to respect for basic human rights. Rawls's criticism of Beitz is equally applicable to Steiner's argument for international distributive justice. Steiner deduces two different types of rights from the fundamental right to equal freedom. The first is the right to self-ownership, and the second to an equal share of natural resource values, the value being calculated by subtracting the value added by 'labour embodying improvements'. Steiner is elaborating upon the notoriously ambiguous Lockean proviso to leave as much and as good for everyone when appropriating land. Steiner contends that 'the equality of each person's land-value entitlement is necessarily *global* in scope'.[21] In his view, we not only have a duty to desist from inflicting bodily harm on foreigners because of the principle of everyone's self-ownership, but also have a duty to pay their land value entitlement. The essential difference is this: Beitz, Pogge and Steiner wish to establish principles for equality of liberties, but in addition to Rawls press for a just distribution of resources.

2 Communitarianism/particularism

The later Rawls, because of his emphasis upon a political liberal conception of justice, has increasingly been allied to a communitarian or particularist position in which the elements of universalism derive from the principles which regulate communities or peoples. He can no longer be accused of having a view of the person as unencumbered or pre-social. For Rawls's theory personality depends upon both the formation and pursuit of a conception of the good, and on being embedded in the political culture of liberal democracy, or at least a well ordered hierarchical society that respects human rights, which are 'a special class of urgent rights'.[22]

He arrives at what these rights are by deploying the methods of ideal theory. International relations, for Rawls, rest on a second contract between what he calls 'peoples', or at least their representatives. Rawls is quite explicit about the fact that his Law of Peoples is an extension of a liberal conception of justice for domestic regimes. Rawls calls the result of his ideal theorising a realistic utopia, in that it takes people as they are, but develops laws and institutions that are as they may become. The resulting Law of Peoples applies not only to relations among liberal well ordered regimes, but also to decent hierarchical well ordered peoples, who, although not liberal, uphold human rights and respect basic liberties. They are not liberal because they support a comprehensive doctrine, whether it be political or religious, and those who do not adhere to it fail to enjoy the full range of citizenship rights, but do enjoy a basic minimum, including the security of acceptance of the rule of law.

A political conception of justice has recourse to those ideas which are immanent, or latent, in a democratic society's public political culture. The human rights endorsed by Rawls's political conception of justice operate on a different plane from those that arise from and are supported by comprehensive doctrines. This is something that Charles Taylor endorses in believing that there can be an overlapping consensus on basic human rights, but the reasons for valuing them may derive from very different comprehensive doctrines.[23]

Rawls specifies what these human rights are: they are not parochial or peculiarly liberal, nor do they depend upon any comprehensive doctrine or philosophical theory of human nature. His conception of human rights is very like that put forward by the British Idealists over a century ago. They are those rights that have come to be recognised as essential for social co-operation, and for promoting the common good. In fact they are universal, subscribed to by decent peoples all over the world, and ought to be by those who do not. Rawls places the responsibility for sustaining human rights firmly in the hands of governments. They are rights relating to basic needs such as the right to life, and to the means of subsistence and security, including the protection of ethnic minorities against genocide and ethnic cleansing, and to freedom from slavery. In addition, he advocates basic political rights such as liberty of conscience, equality before the law, and the right to personal property.[24] Human rights fulfil three roles: they are the necessary conditions of the decency of a society's institutions and legal system; upholding them averts any question of justifying foreign intervention in a people's domestic affairs, such as trade sanctions or military force; and, they circumscribe the limits of reasonable pluralism among peoples.[25]

Others give even greater emphasis to the ethical significance of a particular community or nation. It is quite common among those who deny the ethical significance of a cosmopolitan community to argue that much closer ties of kinship or group solidarity generate the obligations we have to others. Both Walzer and Miller, for example, argue that there is no consensus that the needs of other humans, simply in their capacity as humans, impose any obligations of justice upon us, indeed there is insufficient consensus on what counts as a need. Typical of writers from the British Idealists to Walzer and Rorty, Miller does not see compassion exhausted by an enhanced sense of justice towards one's compatriots, one's family or co-religionists. On the contrary, it is equally as likely that as long as conflicting demands are not imposed our caring for outsiders will strengthen rather than diminish.[26] Walzer makes a distinction between maximal and minimal morality, the latter residing in the former. Minimal morality is universal only to the extent that it is widely endorsed, not because it constitutes an objective reality. It is essentially the shared sum of overlapping outcomes which different moral codes have in common, without any suggestion that they have a common source. Maximal morality is embedded deeply in communities and is relative to one's cultural surroundings. Walzer claims that distributive justice is inextricably tied to the shared meanings of a community because it has to do with the allocation of social goods such as food, wealth, education and health care provision, whose meanings differ considerably from one community to another. All discussion of social justice, Walzer claims, 'will be idiomatic in its language, particularist in its cultural reference . . . historically dependent and factually detailed'.[27]

Justice can be determined in a particular society by interpreting for its members the shared meanings of the goods distributed among themselves. Once the shared meaning of a good is ascertained, criteria for its distribution follow as a matter of course. Barry calls Walzer's theory conventionalism.[28] If we were to take the globe as our site of justice we would have to invent the shared meanings for this imagined community.[29] Ironically, this is the very accusation that Dworkin levels at Walzer in relation to interpreting the meanings of American Society. With regard to health care, for example, Walzer is accused of inventing what Americans think. Far from the democratic socialism attributed by Walzer to Americans, they favour only a basic minimum and emergency treatment as a welfare provision.[30] Furthermore, the absence of shared meanings at the global level is just as much a feature of the domestic scene as it is of the international, and if justice were to hinge on such a consensus of meanings, then there is no place for it inside or outside of state borders.

On the question of whether current resource distributions constitute international injustice, Walzer wants to rely for the criterion upon culpable harm being perpetrated by past interventions, rather than upon a universal principle of redistributive justice. External responsibility for internal ills, arising from such actions as political control of trade, imperial wars, and the like, constitute international injustices which may require large-scale redistribution of resources. Where serious suffering and inequality exist, but which is not the consequence of some form of intervention, similar redistributions may be necessary, but they would not be a matter of justice. Justice does not, in Walzer's view and in harmony with Gordon Graham, exhaust morality, and ordinary principles of humane treatment and compassion may impel us to act out of charity rather than justice.[31]

Walzer, does not, however, want to abandon completely the idea of minimum universal standards of human rights based upon a thin universalism. In *Spheres of Justice* Walzer clearly denies the existence of universal principles of justice. Walzer refuses to ground our ordinary notions of justice in such fundamental principles as equal treatment, desert or inalienable rights. By the time he wrote 'Interpretation and Social Criticism' (1988) and 'Nation and Universe' (1989), Walzer appeared to have change his mind in suggesting that killing, torture and deception were universally unacceptable, and evident universal consensus on such issues constitutes a minimal code of justice.[32] However, he had already posited something like a minimum code of morality in *Just and Unjust Wars* (1977) some years earlier when he claimed that part of what we mean by being human is to have a right to life and liberty, whether natural or invented. They are features of our moral landscape.[33] He claims not to create a new morality regarding just war, but to identify the shared meanings that are globally acknowledged.

Walzer distinguishes between the covering law type of universalism, which gives priority to a way of life as uniquely right, and which can be used as the basis for imperialist arguments, and reiterative universalism, which accepts that subject to minimal universal constraints there are many different and valuable ways of life that have equal rights to flourish in their respective locations, and deserve equal respect to our own. These universal elements are learnt through diverse experiences, but he denies that there is a common substance. They are overlapping sets of values which have family resemblances, but which are nevertheless products of the particularity of historical moral worlds. This is the point that Walzer is making when he argues that maximal morality, the type embedded in our societies and social practices, precedes universal minimal morality, which is in fact abstracted from the former.[34]

This minimum international morality amounts to the principles of self-determination (non-intervention), non-aggression and pluralism (the accommodation of tribalism within borders). Walzer's fundamental point is that the international community regards infringements of territorial and political sovereignty as self-evidently wrong. Sovereign integrity is ensured by the internationally accepted right of non-intervention which is analogous to the moral right of the individual to self-determination. Any infringements would therefore require extra-ordinary circumstances and special justifications. Given that the rationale of a state in his view is the protection of individual rights, particularly human rights, only gross infringements on a significant scale, for example genocide, would justify intervention if there are 'reasonable expectations of success'.[35] In such circumstances, a state falls significantly below what the idea of statehood requires, and breaches the trust endowed upon it by its citizens in some form of social contract. Walzer's argument brings clearly into relief the fundamental clash between the settled norms of sovereignty and those of human rights: the first prioritise the state and its moral relevance, and the second the individual whose moral status is often in conflict with that of the state.[36]

3 Overcoming universalism versus particularism – O'Neill

There are many arguments which link human rights with basic needs, and affirm an obligation to help the poor based upon these rights. Onora O'Neill, however, wants to move away from such associations posited by, among others, Henry Shue and Alan Gerwith. She wants to maintain that helping those in need is a matter of virtue and obligation but not of right or *recht*. She is critical of communitarians because their particularism and norm-orientated practical reason are relativistic and cannot provide the principles for international justice in an obviously interdependent world. Cosmopolitans or universalists are defective because they begin by assuming idealised starting points 'satisfied only by hypothetical agents whose cognitive and volitional capacities human beings lack'.[37]

O'Neill has argued that modern writers on ethics have tended to sever the traditional connection between justice and virtue. She associates cosmopolitans, or universalists, with arguing the case for justice, and communitarians with propounding a constitutive and embedded view of the virtues. What is crucial for her is the distinction between perfect and imperfect obligations. O'Neill's distinction rests upon the idea that perfect obligations are those which have determinate correlative rights and right-holders, whereas imperfect obligations differ in structure in that they have no correlative rights attached to them. In her view, this feature makes them no less obligatory. Those theories that make rights the fundamental ethical category, and which therefore rely heavily upon the notion of acts of recipience, find it difficult to justify as good or obligatory other act-types which cannot be claimed as of right. Thus the virtue of charity is deemed supererogatory, that is beyond what is regarded obligatory, and therefore in the realm of discretion, because it has no correlative right attached to it. The virtue of charity has, therefore, almost become a pejorative term in the vocabulary of rights based ethical theorists. O'Neill argues that such theorists, including Rawls, have tended to assume that all obligations have correlative rights.

O'Neill's response to such views is to acknowledge that it is not feasible to rely on the social virtues to discharge the functions of social justice. It is a justifiable fear that unless rights to certain goods and services can be established then the weak and vulnerable are thrown onto the mercy of the good will of others which is all too often absent. She acknowledges that it is necessary to have institutions which establish rights and responsibilities in order to protect the vulnerable from systematic and gratuitous injury. To show that social virtues, such as charitableness, compassion, pity and generosity of spirit, cannot in themselves adequately protect the vulnerable and cannot therefore take the place of social justice, does not make them redundant. There may still be a whole range of required and necessary action that is not itself a matter of justice or claimable as a right.[38]

Justice is a matter of perfect obligation. Its requirements fall upon everyone and are matched by correlative rights. Virtues, by contrast, are a matter of imperfect obligation. Their requirements fall upon everyone, but specify no one as their recipients. Can principles of virtue, like principles of justice, also be inclusive or are they always embedded in situations? As with justice there must be certain principles of virtue which connect, or act as a manifold, for the different spheres of activity in which an agent moves in the world: 'The spheres of action must be linked not only by public institutions that co-ordinate or subordinate them, but by continuities of character which support continuities of activity, including feeling, relationships and community'.[39] Without some consistency of character in different situations, life would be erratic and unpredictable, and the basis for trust and sustainable relationships would be eroded. O'Neill's point is that virtues are inextricably related to justice and must be embodied not only in individuals but also in institutions, traditions and the common culture of social groups. Institutions established on principles of justice cannot be sustained for long if they operate in a culture of corruption. The virtues of justice such as fairness, reciprocal respect, truthfulness, probity and fidelity are essential to the maintenance of just institutions both domestically and internationally.

Conclusion

In conclusion, then, there is as great a variety of responses to the question of international distributive justice from the perspective of special rights and obligations generated by communal ties of patriotism or nationality, as there are universalist claims. Where they differ, in general, is not in denying universal claims, but in suggesting that these claims have their basis and source in the thick morality, to use Walzer's words, of embedded communities. The particularist and the universalist is just as likely, however, to have the same goal of expanding the moral community to encompass the whole world, without resorting to an institutional cosmopolitanism. We are talking about differences in degree, and not in kind, depending upon from which end of the continuum one begins. For instance, Beitz, Barry and O'Neill are perfectly aware that our sense of justice and obligation does not extend very far beyond the borders of our states as things currently stand. They are concerned to show, on the basis of universal principles, how we have such obligations to others beyond our borders, and how, given existing institutional arrangements, they may be modified better to fulfil those obligations. What is particularly interesting about O'Neill's argument is that she readily acknowledges that the development of institutions to eliminate as far as possible avoidable systematic and gratuitous injury can very rarely come about *de novo*. Conceptions of reform and the will to make changes more often than not build upon current institutions and traditions. It is a matter of modifying what is to hand, redesigning parts rather than the whole, and re-establishing relations that have become disengaged. The purpose is to shape institutions in such a way that they better embody abstract principles of justice.[40]

The cosmopolitan who takes the individual as the subject of a universal moral law, what Beitz calls moral or ethical cosmopolitanism, is not thereby committed to an institutional cosmopolitanism.[41] The key idea here as Pogge suggests 'is that every human being has a global stature as an ultimate unit of moral concern'.[42] The idea of a global moral community of humanity does not logically preclude the division of the world into smaller administratively manageable units, in whatever political form may be deemed most appropriate; states, federations, empires. Typically in the modern era that unit has been the sovereign state often coinciding with a desire on the part of a community for national self-determination. The point that the Natural Law theorist and modern cosmopolitans such as Barry and Goodin, and cosmopolitan Marxists would want to make is that the division is not absolute and that states are merely more or less convenient administrative apparatuses to sustain the purported common good of the communities they serve. Together these states in co-operation with each other serve the common good of humanity. In such a view there is an overlaying of responsibilities, laws, rights and obligations, and at some point a conflict of duties may arise between one's obligations as a citizen and as a person. Kant's cosmopolitanism, for instance, is fully cognisant of the existence of a primordial community of humankind and of the impracticality of a world state. The best that could be hoped for was a peaceful federation of states. A modern Kantian ethical cosmopolitan, such as O'Neill, acknowledges that nationality and other forms of community have an importance, and securing a national state may be instrumental in achieving justice for some, as for example looks to be the case with the Kurds. Yet the achievement of a national state may be just as likely to be the instrument of injustice to others, as the nationality problem in the former Soviet Union testifies.[43]

Notes

1 C. Brown, *International Relations Theory* (London, Harvester Wheatsheaf, 1992); J. Thompson, *Justice and World Order* (London, Routledge, 1992); C. Jones, *Global Justice: Defending Cosmopolitanism* (Oxford, Oxford University Press, 1999); P. Sutch, *Ethics and International Justice* (London, Routledge, 2001).

2 Brown, *International Relations Theory*, pp. 23–51.

3 C. Brown (ed.), *Political Restructuring in Europe* (London, Routledge, 1994), p. 173; M. Frost, *Ethics in International Relatons: A Constitutive Theory* (Cambridge, Cambridge University Press, 1996).

4 P. Singer, 'Famine, Affluence and Morality', *Philosophy and Public Affairs*, 1 (1971), pp. 229–243: P. Singer, 'The Singer Solution to World Poverty', *New York Times*, 5 September 1999.

5 Singer, 'Famine, Affluence and Morality', p. 232.

6 G. Graham, *Ethics and International Relations* (Oxford, Blackwell, 1997), p. 136.

7 Singer, ' Famine, Affluence and Morality', pp. 231–2.

8 R.M Hare, *Essays on Political Morality* (Oxford, Clarendon Press, 1989), p. 3.

9 G. Hardin, 'Lifeboat Ethics: The Case Against Helping the Poor', *Psychology Today*, 8 (1974), pp. 38–43.

10 N. Dower, 'World Poverty', in P. Singer (ed.), *A Companion to Ethics* (Oxford, Blackwell, 1993), pp. 273–84.

11 Graham, *Ethics and International Relations*, pp. 152–5.

12 B. Barry, 'Humanity and Justice in Global Perspective', in B. Barry, *Liberty and Justice* (Oxford, Clarendon Press, 1991), pp. 186–7.

13 Barry, 'Humanity and Justice in Global Perspective', p. 207.

14 Cf. H. Shue, 'Morality, Politics and Humanitarian Assistance', in B. Nichols and G. Loescher (eds), *The Moral Nation: Humanitarianism and U.S. Foreign Policy Today* (Notre Dame, University of Notre Dame Press, 1989), pp. 14–16, and Jones, *Global Justice*, p. 13.

15 C. Beitz, *Political Theory and International Relations* (Princeton, NJ, Princeton University Press, 1979), pp. 136–43.

16 J. Rawls, *The Law of Peoples* (Cambridge, MA, Harvard University Press, 1999), p. 117.

17 Beitz, *Political Theory and International Relations*, p. 149.

18 Beitz, *Political Theory and International Relations*, and T. Pogge, Cosmopolitanism and Sovereignty', in *Political Restructuring in Europe*, ed. C. Brown (London, Routledge, 1994).

19 Rawls, *The Law of Peoples*, p. 116.

20 Rawls, *The Law of Peoples*, p. 117.

21 H. Steiner, 'Territorial Justice', in S. Caney, D. George and P. Jones (eds), *National Rights, International Obligations* (Boulder, CO, Westview Press, 1996), p. 45 (original emphasis).

22 Rawls, *The Law of Peoples*, p. 79.

23 C. Taylor, 'Conditions of an Unforced Consensus on Human Rights', in J. Bauer and D.A. Bell (eds), *The East Asian Challenge for Human Rights* (Cambridge, Cambridge University Press, 1999), p. 124.

24 Rawls, *The Law of Peoples*, pp. 65 and 79.

25 Rawls, *The Law of Peoples*, p. 80.

26 D. Miller, 'The Ethical Significance of Nationality', *Ethics*, 98 (1988), pp. 661–2.

27 M. Walzer, *Spheres of Justice: A Defence of Pluralism and Equality* (Oxford, Blackwell, 1983), pp. 21–2.

28 B. Barry, 'Spherical Justice and Global Injustice', in D. Miller and M. Walzer (eds), *Pluralism, Justice and Equality* (Oxford, Oxford University Press, 1995), p. 75.

29 Walzer, *Spheres of Justice*, pp. 29–30.

30 M. Walzer and R. Dworkin (1983), '*Spheres of Justice*, an Exchange', *New York Review of Books*, 21 July 1983, pp. 43–6.

31 M. Walzer 'Response', in D. Miller and M. Walzer (eds) *Pluralism, Justice and Equality* (Oxford, Oxford University Press, 1995), pp. 292–3.

32 M. Walzer, 'Interpretation and Social Criticism', in S.M. McMurrin (ed.) *The Tanner Lectures on Human Values* (Salt Lake City, UT, University of Utah Press, 1988), and M. Walzer, 'Nation and Universe', in G.B. Petersen (ed.) *The Tanner Lectures on Human Values* (Salt Lake City, UT, University of Utah Press, 1989).

33 M. Walzer, *Just and Unjust Wars* (first published 1977) (New York, Basic Books, 1992, 2nd edn), p. 54.
34 M. Walzer, *Thick and Thin* (Notre Dame, University of Notre Dame Press, 1994), p. 13.
35 Walzer, *Just and Unjust Wars*, p. 107.
36 Frost, *Ethics in International Relations*.
37 O. O'Neill, 'Abstraction, Idealization and Ideology in Ethics', in J. Evans (ed.), *Moral Philosophy and Contemporary Problems* (Cambridge, Cambridge University Press, 1987). For a very good critical appraisal of O'Neill's position see Sutch, *Ethics, Justice and International Relations*, pp. 85–113.
38 O. O'Neill, *Towards Justice and Virtue: A Constructivist Account of Practical Reasoning* (Cambridge, Cambridge University Press, 1996), p. 190.
39 O'Neill, *Towards Justice and Virtue*, p. 172.
40 O'Neill, *Towards Justice and Virtue*, pp. 182–3.
41 C. Beitz, 'Cosmopolitan Liberalism and the States System', in C. Brown (ed.) *Political Restructuring in Europe* (London, Routledge, 1994), pp. 124–5.
42 Pogge, 'Cosmopolitanism and Sovereignty', p. 90.
43 O'Neill, *Towards Justice and Virtue*, pp. 78–9.

17
Just war

Anthony Coates

Introduction

The idea of the just war is in danger of becoming one of the political clichés of the new century. From an object of neglect and indifference it has been transformed into the dominant image of war in the post-cold war age. Moral distaste for war and things military, widely felt during an era of superpower rivalry and nuclear confrontation, has given way (in some circles at least) to enthusiastic moral approval of the use of force for an avowed humanitarian purpose. Even a seasoned observer of war like the military historian John Keegan appears infected with the new spirit: 'The world community needs, more than it has ever done, skilful and disciplined warriors who are ready to put themselves at the service of its authority. Such warriors must properly be seen as the protectors of civilisation not its enemies.'[1] In the 'New World Order' the moral rehabilitation of war gathers pace.

This development might be expected to meet with the enthusiastic approval of just war theorists. After all, rescuing war from the clutches of realists, pacifists and assorted moral sceptics has been the primary aim of the just war tradition throughout its long history. The idea of the moral determination of war, once so hotly contested, now seems widely, if not universally, accepted. Yet this transformation is not without its dangers. It poses a threat not just to the theory of just war – compromising its critical force and utility – but also to the practice that the theory seeks to shape or influence.

Classically and, it seems, authentically, just war theory is aimed more at the restraint of war than it is at its justification. Upholding the moral primacy of peace over war, it begins from a moral presumption against war. Now, not for the first time in the tradition's long history, that primacy and that presumption are in danger of being reversed, with the idea of just war as moral restraint and inhibition giving way to the idea of just war as moral justification and empowerment. In this more positive and bellicose form, the idea of just war threatens to become part of the problem of war rather than part of its solution.

1 The ambiguity of the just war tradition

The phenomenon is neither new nor accidental. 'For the past 3,000 years', writes F.H. Russell, 'just war theories have had the dual purpose of restraining and justifying violence, essentially a self-contradictory exercise.'[2] Restraint or justification? In its inherent ambiguity lies the central dilemma of just war thinking. Without restraint war cannot be justified and yet, it seems, the more war is justified the less restrained it becomes. As realists have frequently observed, the attempt to subject war to moral regulation leads, all too easily, to its escalation rather than its limitation. Paradoxically, the biggest threat to the moral containment of war may come from morality itself. The more war is informed with moral purpose, the less limited it becomes – the more eagerly is it sought and the more intensely is it fought. In such a destructive enterprise as war we may have more to fear from a surfeit of morality than we have from any deficit.

Must we choose, therefore, between the restraint and the justification of war, as Russell implies and realists argue? Is the restraint and justification of war 'essentially a self-contradictory exercise'? Are we to conclude, with the realist, that the surest way of limiting war is to eschew morality altogether? However tempting it may be, such a conclusion is less than compelling, for the restraints placed on war by the amoral pragmatism of the realist are themselves far from secure. Those limits spring from realism's understanding of the instrumental nature of war, according to which a war fought as a means to the attainment of finite, specific goals – as an instrument of policy – is likely to remain limited in conception and execution. However this realist concept of limited war is inherently unstable.

In the first place, the idea of limitation articulated here is quite distinct from moral limitation. Ends and means may be 'limited' in the realist sense and yet be at odds with moral principle. Second, policy goals may not remain limited, as realists themselves readily admit. 'If policy is grand and powerful', wrote Clausewitz, 'so also will be the war, and this may be carried to the point at which war attains to its absolute form.'[3] Third, even if the goals of policy do remain limited, there is no guarantee that they will be pursued by limited means. In short, total war is alien neither to the theory nor to the practice of realism.

Realism, therefore, is no solution to the problem of the restraint of war. Neither is pacifism. By washing its hands of war, pacifism leaves the way open to its unbridled prosecution. The solution lies not in a rejection of the very idea of just war, but in a conception of just war that recognises its threat as well as its promise.

2 Two concepts of just war

The real choice is between two radically different concepts of just war, with opposing logical structures and divergent effects. It is not a choice between restraint and justification, but between two different forms of justification: one 'negative', restrictive and inhibiting, the other 'positive', expansive and empowering. In the 'negative' concept restraint and justification work together. War is justified in such a way as to strengthen moral inhibitions over the use of force and to reinforce the moral containment of war. In the 'positive' concept justification works against restraint, energising war and acting as a form of moral empowerment. It is not, therefore, the justification of war, as such, that needs to be rejected, but a form of justification that undermines the essential restraining role of just war theory. The ambiguity of just war thinking stems from this struggle between the logic of restraint and the logic of empowerment.

The concept of just war as restraint is based on a moral presumption against war. The claim that just war theory, in its classical and authentic form, starts from such a presumption is contested by some just war thinkers. For example, James Turner Johnson (the most prominent contemporary historian of the just war tradition) argues that a negative presumption is part of a modern distortion of just war theory.[4] It is the result of a radical scepticism about war that has more in common with pacifism than it has with just war theory. According to Johnson, the classical view of war itself is a neutral one. It is the moral presumption in favour of justice that determines whether the response to war is a negative or a positive one.

There is reason to be wary of regarding war with the kind of moral equanimity that this neutral view of war seems to encourage. Of course, to question the neutrality of war is not to regard war as an intrinsic moral evil. Johnson's concern to dissociate just war thinking from pacifism is understandable. To retain any intellectual integrity the just war tradition must uphold the potential moral use of war, a use that pacifism is at pains to deny. However, upholding that instrumentality seems wholly consistent with the retention of a moral presumption against war, a presumption that perhaps reveals the shared past (and continuing, though limited, affinity) of the just war and pacifist traditions.

In the western world at least, the idea of just war as moral restraint appears to have its source in the writings of medieval theologians and philosophers. Though notions of the just war are discernible in Greek and Roman thought, both ancient cultures were too indebted to war and military values to develop the idea of just war as restraint. The Heraclitean view that 'war is the father of all things' was as much a cultural principle as it was a philosophical one.[5] As a result, the justification of war came too easily to Greek (or Roman) thinkers. The pacifist tendencies of early Christianity, however, established a moral presumption against war that survived the later renunciation of pacifism itself.

Unlike their pacifist predecessors, Christian thinkers like Augustine (354–430) and Aquinas (1224–74) were prepared to defend the potential moral instrumentality of war. At the same time, the fundamental orientation of their thinking about war remained a negative one, as evidenced by the question with which Aquinas begins his moral analysis of war: 'Is warfare always sinful?'[6] This was, and remains, an ethical conception of war imbued with an abiding moral scepticism. In this way of thinking there is always something anomalous about war. Morally speaking, war is the exception rather than the norm. The presumption is that war is not justified though, in certain extreme (but none the less real) circumstances, that presumption (like any moral presumption) may be overcome.

To say that, in certain circumstances, the negative moral presumption may be overcome is only partially true. In a fundamental sense, that presumption is never overcome but continues to guide the course of the just war in its 'negative' form. The 'positive' concept, on the other hand, may admit a negative moral presumption as a point of departure, but that initial phase is quickly transformed into an affirmation of war. In this case the moral presumption against war really is 'overcome'. The initial moral struggle against war is resolved once and for all; a negative presumption changes into a positive moral preference, even, in extreme but not uncommon cases, into a real lust for war. By contrast, the 'negative' idea of just war not only starts from a moral presumption against war, it is grounded in such a presumption, and the structure and dynamics of the theory are such as to keep that presumption to the fore at all times.

The restraining role of just war theory is not limited to the identification and proscription of unjust wars. This 'negative' concept of the just war is as much concerned with maintaining a moral hold on wars that are perceived to be just as it is with the moral exclusion of manifestly unjust wars. Indeed, in this self-critical form of just war reasoning, the dividing line between just and unjust wars is not nearly as clear-cut as some, more positive, conceptions of just war would have us believe. The danger of concentrating on the distinction between just and unjust wars is that it may deflect moral attention away from those wars that have been identified as 'just' with the result that the application of the idea of just war comes to have an empowering rather than restraining effect. In such instances the early (in fact, premature) delivery of a 'just war' verdict seems designed to quell moral doubts about a war, to silence or forestall moral criticism, to marshal support or to clear a path for war. Thereby, an instrument of moral criticism is in danger of being transformed into a tool of political propaganda.

In the 'negative' concept of just war the persistence of a moral presumption against war manifests itself in a keen, actively sustained, awareness of the physical evil of war. Both the just recourse to war (*ius ad bellum*) and the just conduct of war (*ius in bello*) depend on it. Failure to realise the cost of war in human suffering distorts moral judgement and undermines the moral response to war. Addressing just belligerents, Augustine wrote, 'Let every one, therefore, who reflects with pain upon such great evils, upon such horror and cruelty, acknowledge that this is misery.'[7] That acknowledgement is often lacking in a belligerent whose moral imagination has been fired by the justice or the moral grandeur of his cause. In its 'positive' form the idea of just war can generate an ethic of hardness that makes the 'just warrior' impervious to suffering, whether of himself or of others. By contrast, maintaining a sympathetic awareness of the real horror of war is a mark and a condition of the just war in its 'negative' sense.

It is not just the physical evil of war that warrants a continuing moral presumption against it. From this 'negative' standpoint, no real war is free of moral ambiguity. Assumptions of moral purity are both misplaced and dangerous. No war, however 'just', is without moral deficiency and the potential for moral catastrophe. As noted earlier, this approach stops short of regarding war as an intrinsic moral evil, in which it is impossible to participate without committing injustice. Such a view of war underpins pacifism, not just war theory. Rather, it is a question of recognizing the real moral poverty of war and its potential moral evil, of guarding against the moral pitfalls in which any war must abound and the moral degradation that is the common, if not inevitable, accompaniment of war.

Unlike its 'positive' rival, therefore, the concept of just war as restraint does not 'idealise' war. On the contrary it keeps the physical and moral costs of war clearly and constantly in view. In this regard it remains faithful to Augustine's counsel of moral realism: 'Take off the cloak of vain opinion, and let such evil deeds be examined naked. Let them be weighed naked and judged naked.'[8] When war is viewed in this way, the adoption of a posture of moral neutrality towards it seems misplaced. Given its brutal and brutalising nature, nothing less than a moral presumption against war will do.

3 The structure of just war theory

The complex structure of just war theory, properly understood, embodies its 'negative' or restraining role. Ostensibly, the mechanisms of restraint in just war theory are the various principles or criteria that the theory articulates and upholds. Traditionally, two broad areas of ethical concern and ethical limitation have been identified: one preceding the outbreak of war – the matter of recourse to war – and one following the outbreak of war – the matter of the conduct of war. Though there is no absolute agreement among just war theorists about their number, nature, or manner of application, the following criteria are now commonly acknowledged: in respect of the recourse to war (*ius ad bellum*), legitimate authority, just cause, right intention, proportionality, prospects of success, and last resort; in respect of the conduct of war (*ius in bello*), proportionality and discrimination (or noncombatant immunity).

The ambiguity of just war thinking is evident in the manner in which these criteria are understood and deployed for, depending on their interpretation, they can serve as instruments either of moral empowerment or of moral restraint.

3(a) *Just recourse*
The role allotted to the criteria of just recourse is a matter of considerable import and potential controversy. In some versions of just war theory (even more so in instances of practice or application) their role seems, predominantly, one of moral endorsement. Often, the individual criteria are understood and applied

discretely or separately, in the manner of a checklist that, successfully completed, sets the moral seal of approval on the war in question. One theorist writes:

> [T]hese principles have no more than a checklist status when it comes to theory application. The leader who is thinking about going to war checks off whether there is a just cause leading to war and then moves on to the other principles in the *of* [*ad bellum*] portion of the theory . . . The necessary and sufficient condition [for war] is achieved when a positive answer favoring war has been arrived at for each and every one of the criteria.[9]

Conceived in this way, the application of the criteria appears more like a form of moral therapy than one of moral criticism. It seems designed to resolve doubt and assuage anxiety, to overcome moral resistance to war (as if a moral barrier to war already existed). In such an understanding moral restraint and inhibition readily give way to moral endorsement and empowerment. The negative moral presumption, which should remain a permanent feature of any authentic just war, has been transformed in this justificatory version into a positive presumption in favour of war. In this way, the criteria that ought to act as restraints on war become, instead, the moral catalysts of war. A war that has passed these moral tests is a war invested with a newfound (and dangerous) moral energy and vigour.

From the 'negative' standpoint, just war criteria are understood differently. They are not fixed moral counters to be applied externally to the business of war, but analytical concepts, formed as much in the light of the 'facts' as in the light of abstract principles, designed to unearth moral complexities and to raise moral issues that are unlikely to surface spontaneously. The more dogmatic the criteria are in conception the less effective they are likely to be in this regard. Criteria need to remain open, or receptive, to the complex realities they seek to illuminate and regulate.

They need, too, to be seen in dynamic interaction. The deficiency of the checklist approach is its failure to focus on the interrelation between the several criteria. Instead it treats them singly and apart (mechanically not organically), as if they were wholly discrete and independent of one another. The effect of this approach is further to diminish the restraining power of the criteria, which derives in large measure from their interactive force.

For example, the manner in which just cause is conceived will greatly affect the application of last resort. In the Gulf war of 1990–91 the prospects of a non-violent, diplomatic solution to the crisis always appeared dim, given the historical parallel drawn from the outset by Prime Minister Thatcher and President Bush between Saddam Hussein and Adolf Hitler.[10] A similar phenomenon was evident in the moral posture adopted by western leaders towards Serbia in the Kosovo war. The initial moral characterisation of the conflict left the parties with little room for subsequent political and diplomatic manoeuvring.

The fact is that some concepts of just cause are more reconciliatory than others, some are more confrontational than others – sometimes so confrontational that an important criterion like last resort is rendered largely redundant or unworkable. Interaction works both ways but, whether towards restraint or empowerment, the manner in which one criterion is understood will have a powerful impact on the way in which other criteria are understood and applied.

In the 'negative' concept of just war the criteria are viewed, not as moral validators, but as moral hurdles or obstacles, designed to inhibit recourse to war.[11] The aim is to raise the moral threshold of war, to strengthen moral resistance to war. The need for such strengthening is often acutely felt. The moral presumption against war that this concept of just war upholds owes much to the perception that, far from there being any natural or spontaneous resistance to war, a strong presumption in favour of war often exists. The last thing needed is moral reinforcement or encouragement of that presumption. In this negative tradition the idea of the moral abnormality of war goes hand in hand with the recognition of a pervasive and widespread disposition to war.[12]

One of the commonest forms of moral empowerment (and causes of loss of restraint) stems from a drastic reduction in the criteria of moral assessment, involving either the simple omission, or the severe weakening, of important criteria. More specifically, it is the tendency of just cause to monopolise the moral assessment of war (to the extent that just recourse is often simply equated with just cause) that undermines moral restraint. This can be seen to apply regardless of the actual content of just cause. The distinction between 'negative' and 'positive' just war concepts should not be confused with the conventional distinction between 'defensive' and 'offensive' war. It cuts across that distinction. The present argument runs counter to the common assumption that a war of self-defence is inherently limited or that an offensive war is naturally expansive. So-called 'defensive' wars can be conceived and fought 'positively,' just as 'offensive' wars (armed humanitarian intervention for example) can be conceived and fought 'negatively'.

In its 'positive' form just cause is understood in stark (even Manichaean) terms. A clear moral divide – a moral chasm – is seen to exist between potential or actual belligerents. The idea that adversaries inhabit the same moral universe – a key concept in the 'negative' theory of just war – is alien to this positive approach. Here absolute good is ranged against absolute evil. The conception of the conflict veers towards the apocalyptic. Given what is thought to be at stake, morally speaking, this is hardly surprising. The struggle with Evil brooks no compromise and, in any case, such a demonic, or pathological, adversary is thought to be beyond all rational-instrumental appeal.

This inflated moral characterisation of war is not uncommon; no doubt in part a reflection of the high propaganda value attached to this moralistic form of political rhetoric. For example, speaking of the conflict with Iraq in 1990–91, President Bush declared, 'For me it boils down to a very moral case of good versus evil, black versus white'.[13] In the President's view the Gulf war was a 'just war' in that unequivocal sense. Justice belonged entirely to one side and injustice to the other. In the mind of the President, it seems, this is what a just war entails. Many would agree with him.

In the current 'war against terrorism', President George W. Bush appears to share his father's (and, ironically, Osama bin Laden's) absolutist view. This is a war dubbed immodestly (but, as an indicator of underlying moral assumptions, revealingly) 'Operation Infinite Justice' (a jihad, or holy war, in all but name). According to the President, the war 'will be a monumental struggle of good versus evil [in which] good will prevail'.[14] The idea of the 'just war' articulated by the President is without any sense of moral ambiguity, moral self-criticism, or moral self-doubt. It is portrayed as a struggle, not between civilisations but, much more grandiosely and exultantly, between Civilisation and Barbarism, a struggle that embraces the global community, a struggle that knows only friends or enemies. No neutral, no intermediate, no politically and morally nuanced, positions are recognised. 'Either you are with us or you are with the terrorists', insists the President (as if to be critical about aspects of American foreign policy, or to voice concerns about some of the means employed in the counter-terrorist war, is automatically to side with terrorism).[15]

The problem with the absolutist, or unilateralist, conception of just cause is twofold. In the first place, it does scant justice to the ethical realities and complexities of international politics. By contrast, in the 'negative' theory the criterion of just cause is approached with a moral caution and a healthy scepticism that flow from the recognition that the moral boundaries of international politics are always blurred. The idea of absolute or unilateral justice ill accords with this more complex appraisal of the sources of international conflict. The just war is not the struggle between Good and Evil that the 'positive' concept takes it to be. Such an exclusive moral vision of the world flies in the face of a moral reality where justice and injustice are, more often than not, shared. Consequently, what the 'negative' concept of just war upholds is a bilateral or comparative understanding of just cause that makes explicit the shared, or mixed, nature of justice and injustice among potential belligerents.

Second, and more urgent, the absolutist rendering of just cause threatens the restraint of war. The permissive and perilous implications of an undue regard for just cause are captured clearly, though unwittingly, in the advice given by Bernard of Clairvaux to those about to embark on the Second Crusade: 'O mighty soldiers, O men of war, you have a cause for which you can fight without danger to your souls.' Here the sheer moral allure of the cause silences moral doubt and releases moral inhibitions. The sense of the moral threat inherent in war, on the preservation of which the moral restraint of war crucially depends, is dulled. Moral defences are swept aside by the force of the moral impulse itself. Nothing does more to undermine the just war (from within) than this insidious idea of a war that can be fought 'without danger to the soul'. It is anathema to the 'negative' concept of just war. Despite common and persistent assumptions to the contrary, no cause, however 'just,' carries with it the power of moral absolution. A 'just cause' is no guarantee of the justice of war. On the contrary, the more inflated the cause, the greater the potential for the moral corruption of war.

The magnification of just cause in the minds of potential belligerents undermines the restraining power of the other criteria of just recourse. In the case of legitimate authority, for example, the right to war is readily assumed by those who are convinced (or who claim to be convinced) of the moral, or historical, importance of their cause. In the modern revolutionary tradition, or in the practice of contemporary terrorism, for example, the perceived justice of the cause is invariably seen as sufficient authorisation for the use of force by self-appointed, often miniscule, minorities. In such cases, moral or ideological conviction is able to withstand the counter pressure of an adverse, even hostile, public without apparent moral qualm or effort. The same can be seen to apply to the assumption of the right to war by states (particularly in the case of wars of intervention) without prior legal or institutional international sanction. In both cases the principals claim to be acting on behalf of the very communities that withhold their support or voice their opposition. The inflated moral claims made for war help to overcome, or suppress, the problems (and the hurdles) that are meant to be raised by the criterion of legitimate authority.

Traditionally, right intention is about the moral disposition that is brought to war. Though relatively neglected in modern times, it was perhaps the key to a just war for classical writers like Augustine and Aquinas. They realised that the moral containment of war depended ultimately upon the moral habits and dispositions of the parties involved. The greatest obstacle to the moral containment of war is the 'lust for war' that commonly takes hold of belligerents, even (perhaps especially) those engaged in the pursuit of 'just' wars. It would be unsafe to assume, as exponents of the 'positive' concept of just war tend to assume, that all that is required to fulfil the criterion of right intention are strength of moral conviction and unity of moral purpose. A 'moral' disposition, in itself, is no guarantee of right intention. A moral disposition that is vindictive and triumphalist is a recipe for unjust war (and unjust peace). There is no lust for war to compare with a moral lust for war.

The criterion of proportionality suffers just as badly. So elevated is the conception of just cause that no war, however destructive its potential impact, can appear disproportionate and, therefore, unjust. 'Better wipe out Ireland in one year's civil war', wrote Patrick Pearse, the leader of the 1916 Easter Rising, 'than let England slowly bleed her to death'.[16] The higher the goal of war, the more tolerant of war prospective belligerents become. Indeed, the apparent disproportionality of war, far from engendering doubt about the recourse to war, can strengthen moral resolve. A war that is apocalyptic in its conception demands the symmetry of great destructive force. 'How close could we look into a bright future', wrote Che Guevara, 'should two, three or many Vietnams flourish throughout the world with their share of deaths and their immense tragedies.'[17] As many apologists of the First World War argued, there is no price that is too high to pay for 'a war to end all wars'.[18] Indeed, the higher its price, the more just war seems.

As noted previously, this immoderate version of just cause has an equally destructive impact on the criterion of last resort. The absolute and unilateral conception of just cause diminishes the prospects of (or, in more extreme cases, rules out completely) nonviolent – political or diplomatic – means of resolving conflict, the very means that the criterion of last resort is intended to advance. The view, attributed to Hamas,[19] that a negotiated settlement is 'the path of shame' is widely shared by those who uphold such an uncompromising version of just cause. A negotiated peace with the 'Great Satan,' or with any adversary that is thought to be utterly beyond the moral pale, would constitute a betrayal of the most fundamental kind (not least of those who have already sacrificed their lives for the cause).

Moreover, as Aron observes, the more elevated the ends of war the more war begins to acquire its own intrinsic, and not simply instrumental, value.[20] In the end, war may be invested with such creative, or redemptive, power that it comes to be seen as a thing of first, rather than of last, resort, a unique source of communal and personal fulfilment. Milovan Djilas wrote that

> Wars and rebellions are a vital proving ground for leaders, ideas, and nations. Wars and rebellions are an imperative: to renounce war when it is time for war means to renounce one's own inner nature. In opting for war, we came to understand who we were. Only in armed conflict could we affirm ourselves and force the enemy to understand us and grant us recognition. That affirmation, that self-realization – of the self and of the nation – took place on July 13, 1941 [the day the partisan war commenced].[21]

From this inflated, moral or ideological, perspective, there really is no substitute for war. There is a good to be had in war that cannot be had in peace. In this way the moral primacy of peace over war, which the criterion of last resort is meant to uphold, is decisively reversed.

In the 'negative' concept of just war just cause is not allowed to silence the other criteria of recourse. Far from making them redundant, the bilateral or comparative understanding of just cause invokes and strengthens them. The more complex and contested nature of the moral claim underlines the need to establish – not assume – legitimate authority. The recognition that justice and injustice are, to a degree, shared by potential belligerents cultivates right intention and diminishes the triumphalism and the vindictiveness that flow from a sense of moral certitude and moral exclusiveness. When war is stripped of its false grandeur, its proportionality can no longer be taken for granted: the more limited the end the more disproportionate a means war seems. The impetus to war is checked, as moral divisions become more blurred and moral enthusiasm wanes. The moderation of just cause strengthens the moral imperative to seek, creatively and imaginatively, a solution to the conflict that stops short of war. At the same time, the acknowledgement that justice and injustice are not absolute or unilateral – that potential belligerents have mutual rights, duties and interests – enhances the prospects of finding such a solution.

3(b) *Just conduct*

The interaction between the moral categories of just recourse and just conduct underlines the need to conceive just war theory as a whole, and not as a set of discrete principles that operate independently of one another. Though there are criteria that apply specifically to the conduct of war (proportionality and discrimination), the force of those criteria is greatly affected by the way in which the prior criteria of just recourse are understood and applied. In war ends and means work together: the 'justice' of the means will reflect the 'justice' of the ends (and vice versa). Just as it did with the criteria of recourse, the 'positive' concept of just cause tends to undermine the criteria of just conduct. The more inflated and one-sided the belligerents' sense of the justice of their cause, the more unjust their conduct of war seems likely to become.

The absolute, or unilateral, concept of just cause leads to the 'demonisation' of an adversary, and to the dehumanisation of both sides (an agent of Good being just as inhuman, or unreal, as an agent of Evil). It suppresses that fundamental moral equality and moral solidarity between belligerents, on the recognition of which the just conduct of war ultimately rests. As a result, proportionality and discrimination are irreparably damaged. Both the economical and the discriminate use of force begin to lose their moral attraction in the face of an enemy absolutely conceived. At the extreme, but not hypothetical, end of the 'positive' spectrum of just war thinking, a war of annihilation may seem an entirely appropriate moral response to the presence of an absolute moral evil.

'[O]ne has duties only towards one's equals', wrote Nietzsche.[22] However dubious this might seem as a general proposition (particularly, in its Nietzschean sense), its moral and psychological force in time of war often seems compelling. Moral community among belligerents is the underlying principle of the just conduct of war. The more inclined we are to distance ourselves from an adversary, the less likely we are to treat him with the respect that just conduct demands. The debilitating impact on the moral conduct of war of a sense of fundamental difference and superiority and, conversely, the moderating effect of a vestigial sense of community, have been frequently observed in the history of warfare.

The contrast between the conduct of war on the Eastern and Western Fronts in the Second World War is instructive in this regard. While the relatively 'civilised' conduct of war on the Western Front may indicate that some rudimentary sense of community or solidarity among belligerents remained intact despite hostilities, the 'barbaric' conduct of war in the East owed much to the moral and ideological gulf that divided belligerents from the start. Given the moral contempt that both sets of belligerents had for one another (a result of the systematic suppression of any sense of common humanity), the inclination to conduct the war proportionately and discriminately was bound to be lacking. In this 'battle of ideologies' (or *Weltanschauungkrieg*) a quite contrary inclination was at work, to devastating effect.[23]

The absolute understanding of just cause erodes the distinction between combatant and non-combatant on which the principle of discrimination rests. A war fought to vindicate a particular 'civilisation' or 'way of life' (let alone a war fought on behalf of 'Civilisation' in some absolute and universal sense) is not easily contained. Such 'countervalue' warfare seems unlimited in its prevailing tendency. The threat that justifies the use of force is not simply the threat posed by 'combatants,' in the conventional and limited sense of those directly engaged in war-making, but the threat posed by an entire society, nation, race, class, religion, or culture. From this perspective the status of 'combatant' extends to all those who belong to the category in question and, therefore, so does the liability to attack. The 'friend or foe' mentality that so often accompanies this grandiose approach to war is blind to the careful distinctions that any serious application of the principle of discrimination demands. Such crude categorisation seems designed to evade the constraints on war imposed by that principle. 'Those who are not with us are against us.' To be classed as the 'enemy' – to lose one's right of immunity from attack – it is no longer necessary to be party to some hostile act of war. The refusal to take sides may be considered offence enough.

The very disposition cultivated by this all too moral war jeopardises its just conduct. In extreme cases an excess of zeal engenders the reckless and the ruthless conduct of war in equal measure. The readiness to sacrifice oneself and others becomes the test of moral authenticity and commitment to the cause. An inverse logic, whereby the sense of the justice or moral worth of a war increases with its destructive force, strengthens the movement towards total war. 'A lot of killing', Conquest notes, 'seems to convince people of the seriousness, and thus the justifiability, of a cause.'[24] In this intensely, morbidly, moral world, the more vicious and deadly its conduct the greater the moral aura attached to war. Virtue and crime become indistinguishable. The readiness to violate basic moral norms becomes the measure of moral worth. One commentator, struggling to make sense of the thinking behind the attack on the World Trade Center, surmised: 'It rests on a perverted syllogism: only a great cause would justify killing at random; I have killed at random, therefore my cause is great.'[25]

In contrast to the permissive tendencies of its 'positive' counterpart, the 'negative' concept of just war strengthens the criteria of just conduct. The limitations inherent in the justification of recourse to war exert a restraining influence upon the conduct of war. The modest definition of just cause invites a proportionate use of force that is also an economical use of force. The bilateral or comparative understanding of justice, that recognises the moral equality and the rights and interests of an adversary, encourages both the proportionate and the discriminate use of force. No enemy is beyond the moral pale. Therefore, no enemy is without rights (and no belligerent without reciprocal duties). The moral preference for non-violent resolution of conflict, embodied in the *ius ad bellum* criterion of last resort, continues to inform and guide the conduct of war. As a result, war is fought in a restrained way with a view to peace and the ultimate reconciliation of adversaries. The idea of peace as victory, that animates the 'positive' concept of just war and that encourages belligerents to prosecute total war, is here replaced by the idea of peace as community. Just conduct rests on the recognition of a moral tie and a common good that unite adversaries even in the midst of war. The aim is not to vanquish but to unite (or reunite) in just order. That aim makes the limited conduct of war a political as well as a moral necessity.

Conclusion

For practical as well as theoretical reasons, the argument has focused on the ambiguity of the just war tradition. That ambiguity is of particular concern in the new 'cosmopolitan' age, when war is being invested with a heightened moral purpose. It would be dangerous to assume that such investment solves the problem of war. Far from solving the problem, it may add to it. The just war is a double-edged sword that can make things worse as well as better. Contemporary 'just' wars, fought for proclaimed humanitarian goals, are in danger of veering towards the 'positive' end of the just war spectrum. In doing so, they pose a substantial threat to the moral limitation of war. The moral restraint of war requires that the moral impulse itself be kept very firmly in check. The 'negative' concept of just war seems better equipped to meet that requirement than its 'positive' rival.

Notes

1 J. Keegan, *A History of Warfare* (London, Hutchinson, 1993), p. 391.
2 F.H. Russell, *The Just War in the Middle Ages* (Cambridge, Cambridge University Press, 1975), p. 308.
3 C. von Clausewitz, *On War* (London, Penguin Books, 1982), p. 403.
4 J.T. Johnson, *Morality and Contemporary Warfare* (New Haven, CT, and London, Yale University Press, 1999).
5 M. Austin, 'Attitudes to Warfare', in S. Hornblower and A. Spawforth (eds), *The Oxford Companion to Classical Civilization* (Oxford, Oxford University Press, 1998), pp. 773–4.
6 P.E. Sigmund (ed.), *St Thomas Aquinas on Politics and Ethics* (New York, Norton, 1988), p. 64.
7 St Augustine, *The City of God*, ed. and tr. R.W. Dyson, XIX, 7 (Cambridge, Cambridge University Press, 1998), p. 929.
8 St Augustine, *The City of God*, III, 14, p. 111.
9 N. Fotion, 'Reactions to War: Pacifism, Realism, and Just War Theory', in A. Valls (ed.), *Ethics in International Affairs* (Lanham, MD, Rowman and Littlefield, 2000), p. 28.
10 See A. Coates, 'Just War in the Persian Gulf?', in A. Valls (ed.), *Ethics in International Affairs* (Lanham, MD, Rowman and Littlefield, 2000), pp. 33–47.
11 Even 'moral hurdles' does not do justice to the concept of just war as restraint. The problem is that, once surmounted, 'hurdles' are left behind. Here criteria are seen to exercise a more enduring and dynamic influence.

12 This theme is treated more extensively by A. Coates in *The Ethics of War* (Manchester, Manchester University Press, 1997), see esp. ch. 2.

13 Quoted in S.J. Wayne, 'President Bush Goes to War', in S.A. Renshon (ed.), *The Political Psychology of War* (Pittsburgh, PA, University of Pittsburgh Press, 1993), p. 40.

14 *The Times*, 13 September 2001, p. 1.

15 Speech to the Joint Session of Congress (20 September 2001), *The Times*, 22 September 2001, p. 16.

16 P.H. Pearse, *Political Writings and Speeches* (Dublin, Talbott Press, 1952), p. 188.

17 J. Gerassi (ed.), *Venceremos! The Speeches and Writings of Ernesto Che Guevara* (London, Weidenfeld and Nicolson, 1968), p. 423.

18 See A. Marrin, *The Last Crusade* (Durham, NC, Duke University Press, 1974).

19 A. Taheri, *Holy Terror* (London, Sphere, 1987), p. 8.

20 R. Aron, *Peace and War* (London, Weidenfeld and Nicolson, 1966), p. 593.

21 M. Djilas, *Wartime* (London, Secker and Warburg, 1980), p. 22.

22 F. Nietzsche, *Beyond Good and Evil* (London, Penguin Books, 1973), s. 260.

23 See the work of O. Bartov, for example, *Hitler's Army* (Oxford, Oxford University Press, 1991).

24 R. Conquest, *The Great Terror* (London, Macmillan, 1968), p. xiii.

25 M. Colvin, 'Suicide Terrorists Find a New Way to Marry into Death', *Sunday Times*, 16 September 2001, p. 21.

Bibliography

Anderson, B., *Imagined Communities* (London, Verso, 1991).

Annas, J., *An Introduction to Plato's Republic* (Oxford, Clarendon Press, 1981).

Appiah, K.A., 'Multicultural Misunderstanding', *New York Review of Books*, 44, 9 October (1997).

Arendt, H., *The Human Condition* (Chicago, University of Chicago Press, 1958).

Arendt, H., *The Origins of Totalitarianism* (first published 1948) (London, Harvest, 1976).

Armstrong, C., 'Philosophical Interpretation in the Work of Michael Walzer', *Politics*, 20:2, May (2000).

Arneson, R., 'Against Rawlsian Equality of Opportunity', *Philosophical Studies*, 93 (1999).

Aron, R., *Peace and War* (London, Weidenfeld and Nicolson, 1966).

Arrow, K., *Social Choice and Individual Values* (New Haven, CT, Yale University Press, 1963, 2nd edn).

Atkinson, A.B., *Public Economics in Action: The Basic Income/Flat Tax Proposal* (Oxford, Oxford University Press, 1995).

Austin, J.L., *Sense and Sensibilia* (Oxford, Oxford University Press, 1962).

Austin, M., 'Attitudes to Warfare', in S. Hornblower and A. Spawforth (eds), *The Oxford Companion to Classical Civilization* (Oxford, Oxford University Press, 1998).

Badhwar, N., 'Moral Agency, Commitment and Impartiality', *Social Philosophy and Policy*, 13 (1996).

Barrett M. and Phillips, A., (eds), *Destablising Theory* (Cambridge, Polity Press, 1992).

Barry, B., 'Equal Opportunity and Moral Arbitrariness', in N. Bowie (ed.), *Equal Opportunity* (Boulder, CO, Westview, 1988).

Barry, B., *Theories of Justice: A Treatise on Social Justice, Vol. I* (Hemel Hempstead, Harvester Wheatsheaf, 1989).

Barry, B., 'Humanity and Justice in Global Perspective', in B. Barry, *Liberty and Justice* (Oxford, Clarendon Press, 1991).

Barry, B., 'Spherical Justice and Global Injustice', in D. Miller and M. Walzer (eds), *Pluralism, Justice and Equality*, (Oxford, Oxford University Press, 1995).

Barry, B., *Justice as Impartiality* (Oxford, Oxford University Press, 1995).

Barry, J., *Rethinking Green Politics* (London, Sage 1999).

Barry, B., *Culture and Equality: An Egalitarian Critique of Multiculturalism* (Cambridge, Polity Press, 2001).

Bartov, O., *Hitler's Army* (Oxford, Oxford University Press, 1991).

Bauman, Z., *Globalization: The Human Consequences* (Cambridge, Polity Press, 1998).

Baumann, G., *The Multicultural Riddle* (London, Routledge, 1999).

Beccaria, C., *On Crime and Punishment and Other Writings*, ed. R. Bellamy (Cambridge, Cambridge University Press, 1995).

Beitz, C., *Political Theory and International Relations* (Princeton, NJ, Princeton University Press, 1979).

Beitz, C., 'Cosmopolitan Liberalism and the States System', in Chris Brown (ed.) *Political Restructuring in Europe* (London, Routledge, 1994).

Bell, D., *Communitarianism and its Critics* (Oxford, Clarendon Press, 1993).

Bellamy, R. and Ross, A., *A Textual Introduction to Social and Political Theory* (Manchester, Manchester University Press, 1996).

Benhabib, S., *Situating the Self: Gender, Community and Postmodernism in Contemporary Ethics* (Cambridge, Polity Press, 1992).

Berlin, I., 'Two Concepts of Liberty', in I. Berlin, *Four Essays on Liberty* (Oxford, Oxford University Press, 1969).

Blair, T., Preface, *A New Contract for Welfare* (CSS), Cm 3805 (London, Stationery Office, 1998).

Bobbio, N., 'The Great Dichotomy: Public/Private', in N. Bobbio, *Democracy and Dictatorship* (Minneapolis, MN, University of Minnesota Press, 1989).

Bookchin, M., 'Towards a Philosophy of Nature', in M. Tobias (ed.), *Deep Ecology* (San Diego, CA, Avant Books, 1985).

Boonin-Vail, D., *Thomas Hobbes and the Science of Moral Virtue* (Cambridge, Cambridge University Press, 1994).

Bottomley, G., de Lepervanche, M. and Martin, J. (eds), *Gender/Class/Culture/ Ethnicity* (Sydney, Allen and Unwin, 1991).

Brennan, A., *Thinking About Nature* (London, Routledge, 1988).

Breuer, M. Faist, T. and Jordan, B., 'Collective Action, Migration and Welfare States', *International Sociology*, 10:4 (1995).

Brink, D., 'The Separateness of Persons, Distributive Norms and Moral Theory', in R. Frey and C. Morris (eds), *Value, Welfare and Morality* (Cambridge, Cambridge University Press, 1993).

Brink, D., 'Rational Egoism and the Separateness of Persons', in J. Dancy (ed.), *Reading Parfit* (Oxford, Blackwell, 1997).

Brown, C., *International Relations Theory* (London, Harvester Wheatsheaf, 1992).

Brown, C. (ed.), *Political Restructuring in Europe* (London, Routledge, 1994).

Brown, G., 'Why Labour is still Loyal to the Poor', *Guardian*, 2 August 1997.

Brueckner, J.K., 'Property-Value Maximisation and Efficiency', *Joural of Urban Economics*, 14 (1983).

Bubeck, D., *Care, Gender and Justice* (Oxford, Clarendon Press, 1995).

Buchanan, J. and Tullock, G., *The Calculus of Consent* (Ann Arbor, MI, University of Michigan Press, 1962).

Buchanan, J.M., 'An Economic Theory of Clubs', *Economica*, 32 (1965).

Buchanan J.M. and Goetz, C.J., 'Efficiency Limits of Fiscal Mobility: An Assessment of the Tiebout Model', *Journal of Public Economics*, 1 (1972).

Butler, J., *Gender Trouble: Feminism and the Subversion of Identity* (London, Routledge, 1990).

Campbell, B., *Goliath: Britain's Dangerous Places* (London, Methuen, 1993).

Canovan, M., 'Patriotism is not Enough', *British Journal of Political Science*, 30:3 (2000).

Carrigan, T., Connell, B. and Lee, J., 'Toward a New Sociology of Masculinity', in H. Brod (ed.), *The Making of Masculinities: The New Men's Studies* (Winchester, MA, and Hemel Hempstead, Allen and Unwin, 1987).

Carter, I., *A Measure of Freedom* (Oxford, Oxford University Press, 1999).

Carver, T., 'A Political Theory of Gender: Perspectives on the "universal subject"', in V. Randall and G. Waylen (eds), *Gender, Politics and the State* (London, Routledge, 1998).

Castel, R., 'From Dangerous to Risk', in G. Burchell, C. Cordon and P. Miller (eds), *The Foucault Effect: Studies in Governmentality* (London, Harvester, 1991).

Checkland, S.G. and Checkland, E.O.A. (eds), *The Poor Law Report of 1834* (Harmondsworth, Penguin, 1974).

Chodorow, N., *The Reproduction of Mothering: Psychoanalysis and the Sociology of Gender* (Berkeley, CA, University of California Press, 1978).

Christman, J. (ed.), *The Inner Citadel: Essays on Individual Autonomy* (Oxford, Oxford University Press, 1989).

Christman, J., 'Liberalism and Individual Positive Freedom', *Ethics*, 101 (1991).

Clausewitz, C. von, *On War* (London, Penguin Books, 1982).

Coates, A., *The Ethics of War* (Manchester, Manchester University Press, 1997).

Coates, A., 'Just War in the Persian Gulf?', in A. Valls (ed.), *Ethics in International Affairs* (Lanham, MD, Rowman and Littlefield, 2000).

Cohen, G.A., 'Capitalism, Freedom and the Proletariat', in D. Miller (ed.), *Liberty*, (Oxford, Oxford University Press, 1991).

Cohen, G.A., *Self-Ownership, Freedom and Equality* (Cambridge, Cambridge University Press, 1995).

Cohen, J., 'Democracy and Liberty', in J. Elster (ed.), *Deliberative Democracy* (Cambridge, Cambridge University Press, 1998).

Colvin, M., 'Suicide Terrorists Find a New Way to Marry into Death', *Sunday Times*, 16 September 2001.

Connell, R.W., *Gender* (Cambridge, Polity Press, 2002).

Connolly, W.E., *The Terms of Political Discourse* (Oxford, Blackwell, 1974).

Conquest, R., *The Great Terror* (London, Macmillan, 1968).

Coole, D., *Women in Political Theory: From Ancient Misogyny to Contemporary Feminism* (Brighton, Harvester Press/Wheatsheaf Books, 1992, 2nd edn).

Coole, D., 'Cartographic Convulsions: Public and Private Reconsidered', *Political Theory*, 28:3 (2000).

Costa, P., *Il progetto giuridico* (Milano, Giuffré, 1974).

Cox, R.H. 'From Safety Nets to Trampolines: Labour-Market Activation in the Netherlands and Denmark', *Governance: An International Journal of Politics and Administration*, 11:4 (1998).

Cox, R.H. *The Consequences of Welfare Reform: How Conceptions of Social Rights are Changing* (Norman, OK, Department of Political Science, University of Oklahoma, 1999).

Cullis, J. and Jones, P., *Public Finance and Public Choice: Analytical Perspectives* (London, McGraw Hill, 1994).

Dagger, R., 'Membership, Fair Play, and Political Obligation', *Political Studies*, 48 (2000).

Dahl, R., *A Preface to Democratic Theory* (Chicago, University of Chicago Press, 1956).

Dahl, R., *On Democracy* (New Haven, CT, Yale University Press, 1988).

Dahl, R., *Democracy and its Critics* (New Haven, CT, Yale University Press, 1989).

De Giorgi, A., *Zero Tolleranza. Strategie e pratiche della società di controllo* (Roma, Derive Approdi, 2000).

Department of Social Security, *A New Contract for Welfare*, Cm.3805 (London, Stationery Office, 1998).

Devall B., and G. Sessions, *Deep Ecology: Living as if Nature Mattered* (Salt Lake City, UT, Gibbs M. Smith Inc., 1985).

Devlin, P., *The Enforcement of Morals* (Oxford, Oxford University Press, 1965).

Djilas, M., *Wartime* (London, Secker and Warburg, 1980).

Dower, N., 'World Poverty', in P. Singer (ed.), *A Companion to Ethics* (Oxford, Blackwell, 1993).

Dryzek, J., *Rational Ecology: Environment and Political Economy* (Oxford, Blackwell, 1987).

Dunn, J. (ed.), *Democracy: The Unfinished Journey* (Oxford, Oxford University Press, 1992).

Dworkin, R., 'Justice and Rights' (first published 1973), reprinted in R. Dworkin's *Taking Rights Seriously* (Cambridge, MA, Harvard University Press, 1978).

Dworkin, R., *Law's Empire* (Cambridge, MA, Harvard University Press, 1986.

Eckersley, R., *Environmentalism and Political Theory* (London, UCL Press, 1992).

Eisenstein, Z., *The Radical Future of Liberal Feminism* (New York, Longman, 1981).

Elshtain, J.B., *Public Man, Private Woman: Women in Social and Political Thought* (Oxford, Martin Robertson, 1981).

Erikson, E. and Weigärd, J., 'The End of Citizenship? New Roles Challenging the Political Order', in C. McKinnon and I. Hampsher-Monk (eds), *The Demands of Citizenship* (London, Continuum, 2000).

Esping-Andersen, G., *Welfare States in Transition: National Adaptations in Global Economies* (London, Sage, 1996).

Esping-Andersen, G., 'The Jobs-Equality Trade-Off', paper presented to the summer school on Welfare States in Transition, European University Institute, Florence, 8 July 1999.

Etzioni, A., *The Spirit of Community: Rights, Responsibilities and the Communiarian Agenda* (London, Fontana, 1995).

Etzioni, A., *The New Golden Rule: Community and Morality in a Democratic Society* (London, Profile Books, 1997).

Etzioni, A, *The Limits of Privacy* (New York, Basic Books, 1999).

Etzioni, A., *The Third Way to a Good Society* (London, Demos, 2000).

Evans, D.T., *Sexual Citizenship: The Material Construction of Sexualities* (London, Routledge, 1993).

Evason E. and Woods, R., 'Poverty, Deregulation of Labour Markets and Benefit Fraud', *Social Policy and Administration*, 29:1 (1995).

Ewald, F., 'Insurance and Risk', in G. Burchell, C. Cordon and P. Miller (eds), *The Foucault Effect: Studies in Governmentality* (London, Harvester, 1991).

Firestone, S., *The Dialectic of Sex: The Case for Feminist Revolution* (London, Cape, 1971).

Fishkin, J., *Justice, Equal Opportunity, and the Family* (New Haven, CT, Yale University Press, 1983).

Flew, A., *The Politics of Procrustes* (London, Temple Smith, 1981).

Floud, J., 'Report', *British Journal of Criminology*, 22:3 (1982).

Floud, J. and Young, W., *Dangerousness and Criminal Justice*, Cambridge Studies in Criminology XLVII, ed. Sir L. Radzinowicz (London, Heinemann, 1981).

Foldvary, F., *Public Goods and Private Communities: The Market Provision of Social Services* (Aldershot, Edward Elgar, 1994).

Forst, R., *Contexts of Justice* (Berkeley, CA, University of California Press, 2002).

Foster, H., 'Postmodernism: A Preface', in H. Foster (ed.), *Postmodern Culture* (London, Pluto Press, 1985).

Fotion, N., 'Reactions to War: Pacifism, Realism, and Just War Theory', in A. Valls (ed.), *Ethics in International Affairs* (Lanham, MD, Rowman and Littlefield, 2000).

Foucault, M., *Discipline and Punishment: The Birth of the Prison* (Harmondsworth, Penguin, 1977).

Fraser, N., 'Rethinking the Public Sphere: A Contribution to the Critique of Actually Existing Democracy', in C. Calhoun (ed.), *Habermas and the Public Sphere*, (Cambridge, MA, MIT Press, 1992).

Frazer, E., *The Problems of Communitarian Politics* (Oxford, Oxford University Press, 1999).

Friedan, B., *The Feminine Mystique* (Harmondsworth, Penguin, 1963).

Friedman, M. and Friedman, R., *Free to Choose* (Harmondsworth, Penguin, 1980).

Frost, M., *Ethics in International Relations: A Constitutive Theory* (Cambridge, Cambridge University Press, 1996).

Galbraith, J.K., *The Culture of Contentment* (Harmondsworth, Penguin, 1993).

Gallie, W.B., 'Essentially Contested Concepts', *Proceedings of the Aristotelian Society*, 56 (1956).

Garland, D., 'The Limits of the Sovereign State. Strategies of Crime Control in Contemporary Society', *British Journal of Criminology*, 4 (1987).

Gatens, M., *Feminism and Philosophy* (Cambridge, Polity Press, 1991).

Gellner, E., *Culture, Identity,and Politics* (Cambridge, Cambridge University Press, 1987).

Gerassi, J. (ed.), *Venceremos! The Speeches and Writings of Ernesto Che Guevara* (London, Weidenfeld and Nicolson, 1968).

Giddens, A., *The Third Way: The Renewal of Social Democracy* (Cambridge, Polity Press, 1998).

Gilbert, M., *Living Together: Rationality, Sociality and Obligation* (New York, Rowman and Littlefield, 1996).

Gilligan, C., *In a Different Voice: Psychological Theory and Women's Development* (Cambridge, MA, Harvard University Press, 1982).

Glacken, C., *Traces on the Rhodian Shore* (Berkeley, CA, University of California Press, 1967).

Gloz, P., *Manifest für eine neue europäische Linke* (Berlin, Wolf Jobst Siedler, 1985).

Goldsmith E. and Hildyard, N. (eds), *Green Britain or Industrial Wasteland* (Cambridge, Polity Press, 1986).

Goodin, R., *Green Political Theory* (Cambridge, Polity Press, 1992).

Goodin, R., *Motivating Political Morality* (Oxford, Blackwell, 1992).

Goodin R., Headley, B., Muffels, R. and Dirven, H.K., *The Real Worlds of Welfare Capitalism* (Cambridge, Cambridge University Press, 1999).

Graham, G., *Ethics and International Relations* (Oxford, Blackwell, 1997).

Graham, K., 'Being Some Body', in B. Brecher, J. Halliday and K. Kolinská (eds.), *Nationalism and Racism in the Liberal Order* (Aldershot, Ashgate, 1998).

Graham, K., 'Are all Preferences Nosy?', *Res Publica*, 6 (2000).

Graham, K., 'Collective Responsibility', in T. van den Beld (ed.), *Moral Responsibility and Ontology* (Dordrecht, Kluwer, 2000).

Graham, K., *Practical Reasoning in a Social World: How We Act Together* (Cambridge, Cambridge University Press, 2002).

Grant, J., *Fundamental Feminism* (New York and London, Routledge, 1993).

Gray, T., *Freedom* (London, Macmillan, 1991).

Green, K., *The Woman of Reason. Feminism, Humanism and Political Thought* (Cambridge, Polity Press, 1995).

Grimshaw, J., *Feminist Philosophers: Women's Perspectives on Philosophical Traditions* (Brighton, Wheatsheaf Books, 1986).

Habermas, J., *The Theory of Communicative Action, Volume One – Reason and the Rationalisation of Society*, tr. T. McCarthy (Boston, MA, Beacon Press, 1984).

Habermas, J., *The Theory of Communicative Action, Volume Two – Lifeworld and System: A Critique of Functionalist Reason*, tr. T. McCarthy (Boston, MA, Beacon Press, 1987).

Habermas, J., *The Structural Transformation of the Public Sphere*, tr. T. Burger (Cambridge, MA, MIT Press, 1989).

Habermas, J., 'Citizenship and National Identity', in J. Habermas, *Between Facts and Norms Contributions to a Discourse Theory of Law and Democracy*, tr. W. Rehg (first published 1990) (Cambridge, Polity Press, 1996).

Habermas, J., *Between Facts and Norms. Contributions to a Discourse Theory of Law and Democracy*, tr. W. Rehg (Cambridge, Polity Press, 1996).

Hamowy, R., 'Law and the Liberal Society', *Journal of Libertarian Studies*, 2 (1987).

Haraway, D., *Simians, Cyborgs, and Women: The Reinvention of Nature* (London, Free Association, 1991).

Hardin, G., 'Lifeboat Ethics: The Case Against Helping the Poor', *Psychology Today*, 8 (1974).

Hare, R.M., *Essays on Political Morality* (Oxford, Clarendon Press, 1989).

Harrington, J., *The Commonwealth of Oceana* (Cambridge, Cambridge University Press, 1992).

Harrison R., *Democracy* (London, Routledge 1993).

Hart, H.L.A., *Punishment and Responsibility: Essays in the Philosophy of Law* (Oxford, Clarendon Press, 1968).

Hart, H.L.A., 'Rawls on Liberty and its Priority', in N. Daniels (ed.), *Reading Rawls* (Oxford, Blackwell, 1975).

Hart, H.L.A., 'Social Solidarity and the Enforcement of Morals' (first published 1968), in H.L.A. Hart, *Essays in Jurisprudence and Philosophy* (Oxford, Clarendon Press, 1983).

Hayek, F. von, *The Road to Serfdom* (London, Routledge, 1944).

Hayek, F. von, *The Constitution of Liberty* (London, Routledge and Kegan Paul, 1960).

Hayek, F. von, *The Political Order of a Free People* (London, Routledge, 1979).

Hearn, J., *The Gender of Oppression: Men, Masculinity and the Critique of Marxism* (Brighton, Wheatsheaf, 1987).

Held, D., *Democracy and the Global Order* (Cambridge, Polity Press, 1995).

Held, D., *Models of Democracy* (Cambridge, Polity Press, 1996, 2nd edn).

Helly D. and Reverby, S. (eds), *Gendered Domains: Rethinking Public and Private in Women's History* (Ithaca, NY, Cornell University Press, 1997).

Hemerijck, A., 'Prospects for Effective Social Citizenship in an Age of Structural Inactivity', in C. Crouch, K. Eder and D. Tambini (eds), *Citizenship, Markets and the State* (Oxford, Oxford University Press, 2000).

Herman, B., *The Practice of Moral Judgement* (Cambridge, MA, Harvard University Press, 1993).

Hirsch, F., *The Social Limits to Growth* (London, Routledge and Kegan Paul, 1977).

HM Treasury, *Pre-Budget Report* (London, Stationery Office, 2000).

Hobbes, T., *Leviathan*, ed. R. Tuck (Cambridge, Cambridge University Press, 1996).

Hobbes, T., *On the Citizen*, eds R. Tuck and M. Silverthrone (Cambridge, Cambridge University Press, 1998).

Hobhouse, L.T., *Elements of Social Justice* (London, Allen and Unwin, 1922).

Hobsbawm, E., *Nations and Nationalism since 1780* (Cambridge, Cambridge University Press, 1990).

Home Office, *Fairer, Faster and Firmer – A Modern Approach to Immigration and Asylum*, Cm 4018 (London, Stationery Office, 1998).

Honneth, A., *The Struggle for Recognition: The Moral Grammar of Social Conflict* (Cambridge, Polity Press, 1995).

Horton, J., *Political Obligation* (Atlantic Highlands, NJ, Humanities Press International, 1992).

Hume, L.J., *Bentham and Bureaucracy* (Cambridge, Cambridge University Press, 1981).

Ignatieff, M., 'Why "Community" Is a Dishonest Word', *Observer*, 3 May 1992.

Ingram, A., 'Constitutional Patriotism', *Philosophy and Social Criticism*, 22:6 (1996).

Isaac, J., 'A New Guarantee on Earth: Hannah Arendt on Human Dignity and the Politics of Human Rights', *American Political Science Review*, 90:1 (1996).

Iversen, T. and Wren, A., 'Equality, Employment and Budgetary Restraint: The Trilemma of the Service Economy', *World Politics*, 50 (1998).

Jaggar, A., 'Love and Knowledge: Emotion in Feminist Epistemology', in S. Kemp and J. Squires (eds), *Feminisms* (Oxford, Oxford University Press, 1997).

Johnson, J.T., *Morality and Contemporary Warfare* (New Haven, CT, and London, Yale University Press, 1999).

Jones, C., *Global Justice: Defending Cosmopolitanism* (Oxford, Oxford University Press, 1999).

Jordan, B., *A Theory of Poverty and Social Exclusion* (Cambridge, Polity Press, 1996).

Jordan, B., *The New Politics of Welfare: Social Justice in a Global Context* (London, Sage, 1998).

Jordan, B. and Jordan, C., *Social Work and the Third Way: Tough Love as Social Policy* (London, Sage, 2000).

Jordan, B. and Travers, A., 'The Informal Economy – a Case Study in Unrestrained Competition', *Social Policy and Administration*, 32:3 (1998).

Jordan, B., Agulnik, P., Burbidge, D. and Duffin, S., *Stumbling Towards Basic Income* (London, Citizens Income Study Centre, 2000).

Jordan, B., James, S., Kay, H. and Redley, M., *Trapped in Poverty? Labour-Market Decisions in Low-Income Households* (London, Routledge, 1992).

Kant, I., *Groundwork of the Metaphysic of Morals (The Moral Law)*, tr. H.J. Paton (London, Unwin Hyman, 1948).

Kant, I., 'Perpetual Peace', in *Kant's Political Writings*, ed. H. Reiss (Cambridge, Cambridge University Press, 1970).

Kant, I., 'The Metaphysics of Morals', in *Kant's Political Writings*, ed. H. Reiss (Cambridge: Cambridge University Press, 1970).

Kearney, R., *Postnationalist Ireland* (London, Routledge, 1997).

Keegan, J., *A History of Warfare* (London, Hutchinson, 1993).

Kemshall, H., *Reviewing Risk: A Review of Research on the Assessment and Management of Risk and Dangerousness: Implications for Policy and Practice in the Probation Service* (Croydon, Report for the Home Office, Research and Statistics Directorate, 1996).

Kennedy, E. and Mendus, S., *Women in Western Political Philosophy* (Brighton, Wheatsheaf Books, 1987).

Kiss, E., 'Democracy and the Politics of Recognition', in I. Shapiro and C. Hacker-Cordón (eds), *Democracy's Edges* (Cambridge, Cambridge University Press, 1999).

Kramer, M.H., *The Quality of Freedom* (Oxford, Oxford University Press, 2003).

Kristjánsson, K., *Social Freedom: The Responsibility View* (Cambridge, Cambridge University Press, 1996).

Kukathas, C., 'Liberalism, Communitarianism and Political Community', *Social Philosophy and Policy*, 13 (1996).

Kymlicka, W., *Liberalism, Community and Culture* (Oxford, Oxford University Press, 1989).

Kymlicka, W., *Multicultural Citizenship: A Liberal Theory of Minority Rights* (Oxford, Clarendon Press, 1995).

Kymlicka, W., *Contemporary Political Philosophy* (Oxford, Oxford University Press, 2001, 2nd edn).

Kymlicka, W. and Norman, W., 'Return of the Citizen: A Survey of Recent Work on Citizenship Theory', *Ethics*, 104:2 (1994).

Landes, J., 'The Public and the Private Sphere: A Feminist Reconsideration', in J. Landes (ed.), *Feminism: The Public and the Private* (Oxford, Oxford University Press, 1998).

Larmore, C., 'The Idea of a Life Plan', in E.F. Paul, F.D. Miller, F. Dycus and P. Jeffrey (eds), *Human Flourishing* (Cambridge, Cambridge University Press, 1999).

Leonard, M., 'Informal Economic Activity: Strategies of Households and Communities', paper presented at 4th ESA Conference, 'Will Europe Work?', Amsterdam, 18–21 August 1999.

Lewis, T., 'On Using the Concept of Hypothetical Consent', *Canadian Journal of Political Science*, 22 (1989).

Lister, R., *Citizenship: Feminist Perspectives* (Basingstoke, Macmillan, 1997).

Lister, R., 'From Equality to Social Inclusion: New Labour and the Welfare State', *Critical Social Policy*, 18:55 (1998).

Lloyd, G., *The Man of Reason: 'Male' and 'Female' in Western Philosophy* (London, Methuen, 1984).

Locke, J., *Two Treatises of Government* (first published 1690), ed. P. Laslett (Cambridge, Cambridge University Press, 1970, 2nd edn).

Locke, J., *A Letter Concerning Toleration in Focus*, eds J. Horton and S. Mendus (London, Routledge, 1991).

Lorber, J., *Paradoxes of Gender* (New Haven, CT, and London, Yale University Press, 1994).

MacCallum, G.C. jr, 'Negative and Positive Freedom', *Philosophical Review*, 76 (1967), reprinted in D. Miller (ed.), *Liberty* (Oxford, Oxford University Press, 1991).

MacIntyre, A., *After Virtue: A Study in Moral Theory* (London, Duckworth, 1981).

MacKinnon, C., *Toward a Feminist Theory of the State* (Cambridge, MA, Harvard University Press, 1989).

Malthus, T., *An Essay in the Principle of Population as It Affects the Improvement of Society* (London, J. Johnson, 1798).

Markell, P., 'Making Affect Safe for Democracy? – On "Constitutional Patriotism"' *Political Theory*, 28:1 (2000).

Marrin, A., *The Last Crusade* (Durham, NC, Duke University Press, 1974).

Marske, C.E., *Communities of Fate: Readings in the Social Organization of Risk* (Lanham, VA, University Press of America, 1991).

Martin, R., *A System of Rights* (Oxford, Clarendon Press, 1993).

Martison, R., 'What Works? – Questions and Answers about Prison Reform', *The Public Interest*, 35 (1974).

McKibben, B., *The End of Nature* (London, Penguin, 1990).

McMahon, C., *Authority and Democracy* (Princeton, NJ, Princeton University Press, 1994).

Mead, L.M., *Beyond Entitlement: The Social Obligations of Citizenship* (New York, Free Press, 1986).

Midgely, M., *Beast and Man: The Roots of Human Nature* (London, Routledge, 1995).

Miller, D., 'Constraints on Freedom', *Ethics*, 94 (1983).

Miller, D., *The Blackwell Encyclopaedia of Political Thought* (Oxford, Blackwell, 1987).

Miller, D., 'The Ethical Significance of Nationality', *Ethics*, 98 (1988).

Miller, D., 'Deliberative Democracy and Social Choice', *Political Studies*, 40 (1992).

Miller, D., *On Nationality* (Oxford, Oxford University Press, 1995).

Miller, D., *Principles of Social Justice* (Cambridge, MA, Harvard University Press, 1999).

Miller, D. (ed.), *Citizenship and National Identity* (Cambridge, Polity Press, 2000).

Mueller, D., *Public Choice II* (Cambridge, Cambridge University Press, 1989).

Mulhall S., and Swift, A., *Liberals and Communitarians* (Oxford, Blackwell 1992).

Munoz-Darde, V., 'Is the Family to be Abolished Then?', *Proceedings of the Aristotelian Society*, 72 (1998).

Myers, G.M., 'Optimality, Free Mobility and the Regional Authority in a Federation', *Journal of Public Economics*, 43 (1990).

Naess, A., 'The Shallow and the Deep, Long-range Ecology Movement: A Summary', *Inquiry*, 16 (1973).

Naess, A., *Ecology, Community and Lifestyle*, tr. D. Rothenberg (Cambridge, Cambridge University Press, 1990).

Nietzsche, F., *Beyond Good and Evil* (London, Penguin Books, 1973).

Nozick, R., *Anarchy, State, and Utopia* (New York, Basic Books, 1974).

Nye, A., *Feminist Theory and the Philosophies of Men* (New York, Routledge, 1989).

O'Brien, M., *The Politics of Reproduction* (London, Routledge and Kegan Paul, 1983).

O'Neill, O., 'Abstraction, Idealization and Ideology in Ethics', in J. Evans (ed.), *Moral Philosophy and Contemporary Problems* (Cambridge, Cambridge University Press, 1987).

O'Neill, O., *Towards Justice and Virtue: A Constructivist Account of Practical Reasoning* (Cambridge, Cambridge University Press, 1996).

O'Neill, O., 'Women's Rights: Whose Obligations?', in *Bounds of Justice* (Cambridge, Cambridge University Press, 2000).

Oates, W.E., *Fiscal Federalism* (New York, Harcourt Brace Jovanovich, 1972).

Oates, W.E., 'Searching for Leviathan: An Empirical Study', *American Economic Review*, 75 (1985).

Offe, C., *Modernity and the State: East, West* (Cambridge: Polity Press, 1996).

Okin, S.M., *Women in Social and Political Thought* (Princeton, NJ, Princeton University Press, 1979.

Okin, S.M., *Gender, Justice and the Family* (New York, Basic Books, 1989).

Okin, S.M., 'Gender, the Public and the Private', in A. Phillips (ed.), *Feminism and Politics* (Oxford, Oxford University Press, 1998).

Oppenheim, F., *Dimensions of Freedom: An Analysis* (New York, St. Martin's Press, 1961).

Oppenheim, F., *Political Concepts: A Reconstruction* (Oxford, Blackwell, 1981).

Outhwaite, W., *Habermas – a Critical Introduction* (Cambridge, Polity Press, 1994).

P6, 'Can the Obligations in Welfare-to-Work Schemes be Morally Justified?' (Glasgow, Department of Government, University of Strathclyde, 2000).

Pappas, N., *Plato and the Republic* (New York, Routledge, 1995).

Parekh, B., *Rethinking Multiculturalism* (London, Macmillan, 2000).

Pateman, C., 'Feminist Critiques of the Public/Private Dichotomy', in S. Benn and G. Gaus (eds), *Public and Private in Social Life* (London, Croom Helm, 1983).

Pateman, C., *The Sexual Contract* (Cambridge, Polity Press, 1988).

Pateman, C., *The Disorder of Women* (Stanford, CA, Stanford University Press, 1989).

Pateman C., and Brennan, T., 'Mere Auxiliaries to the Commonwealth: Women and the Origins of Liberalism', *Political Studies*, 27 (1979).

Pearse, P., *Political Writings and Speeches* (Dublin, Talbott Press, 1952).

Pettit, P., *Republicanism: A Theory of Freedom and Government* (Oxford, Oxford University Press, 1997).

Pettit, P., 'Contestatory Democracy', in I. Shapiro and C. Hacker-Cordón (eds), *Democracy's Value* (Cambridge, Cambridge University Press, 1999).

Pettit, P., *Republicanism: A Theory of Freedom and Government* (Oxford, Oxford University Press, 1999, 2nd edn).

Phillips, A., 'Universal Pretensions in Political Thought', in A. Phillips and M. Barrett (eds), *Destablizing Theory* (Cambridge, Polity Press, 1992).

Phillips, A., *Democracy and Difference* (Cambridge, Polity Press, 1993).

Plamenatz, J., 'The Use of Political Theory', *Political Studies*, 8 (1960).

Plato, *Five Dialogues*, tr. G.M.A. Grube (Indianapolis, IN, Hackett, 1981).

Pogge, T., *Realizing Rawls* (Ithaca, NY, Cornell University Press, 1989).

Pogge, T, 'Cosmopolitanism and Sovereignty', in C. Brown (ed.), *Political Restructuring in Europe*, (London, Routledge, 1994).

Poole, R., 'Liberalism, nationalism and identity', in B. Brecher, J. Halliday and K. Kolinská (eds), *Nationalism and Racism in the Liberal Order* (Aldershot, Ashgate, 1998).

Prokhovnik, R., *Rational Woman: A Feminist Critique of Dichotomy* (London and New York, Routledge, 1999).

Przeworski, A., 'Minimalist Conception of Democracy: A Defense', in I. Shapiro and C. Hacker-Cordón (eds), *Democracy's Value* (Cambridge, Cambridge University Press, 1999).

Rawls, J., 'Two Concepts of Rules', *Philosophical Review*, 54 (1955).

Rawls, J., *A Theory of Justice* (Oxford, Oxford University Press, 1972).

Rawls, J., *Political Liberalism* (New York, Columbia University Press, 1993).

Rawls, J., *A Theory of Justice* (Cambridge, MA, Harvard University Press, 1999).

Rawls, J., 'Constitutional Liberty and the Concept of Justice' (first published 1963), in J. Rawls (S. Freeman (ed.)), *Collected Papers* (Cambridge, MA, Harvard University Press, 1999).

Rawls, J., *The Law of Peoples* (Cambridge MA and London, Harvard University Press, 1999).

Raz, J., *The Authority of Law* (Oxford, Clarendon Press, 1979).

Raz, J., 'On The Nature of Rights', *Mind*, 93 (1984).

Raz, J., *The Morality of Freedom* (Oxford, Oxford University Press, 1986).

Raz, J., *Ethics in the Public Domain* (Oxford, Oxford University Press, 1994).

Raz, J., 'Multiculturalism: A Liberal Perspective', *Dissent*, Winter (1994).

Riker, W., *Liberalism against Populism* (San Francisco, CA, Freeman and Co., 1982).

Roche, B., 'Migration in a Global Economy', speech to the Institute for Public Policy Research Conference, 8 September 2000.

Rodman, J., 'The Liberation of Nature', *Inquiry*, 20 (1977).

Rousseau, J.-J., *The Social Contract and Other Later Political Writings*, tr. V. Gourevitch (Cambridge, Cambridge University Press, 1998).

Rowlingson, K., Whyley, C., Newburn, T. and Berthoud, R., *Social Security Fraud* (London, HMSO, 1997).

Ruddick, S., *Maternal Thinking: Towards a Politics of Peace* (Boston, MA, Beacon Press, 1989).

Rusche, G. and Kirchheimer, O., *Punishment and Social Structure* (New York, Russell and Russell, 1968).

Russell, F.H., *The Just War in the Middle Ages* (Cambridge, Cambridge University Press, 1975).

Sale, K., *Dwellers in the Land: The Bioregional Vision* (San Francisco, CA, Sierra Book Club, 1985).

Salt, J., 'Labour-Market Recruitment to the UK', paper given at a Home Office Conference, Bridging the Information Gaps: Research in Asylum and Immigration in the UK, National Liberal Club, London, 21 March 2001.

Sandel, M., *Liberalism and the Limits of Justice* (Cambridge, Cambridge University Press, 1982).

Scanlon, T., 'Contractualism and Utilitarianism', in B. Williams and A. Sen (eds), *Utilitarianism and Beyond* (Cambridge, Cambridge University Press, 1982).

Scanlon, T.M., *What We Owe to Each Other* (Cambridge, MA, Belknap Press, 1998).

Scherer D., and Attig, T. (eds), *Ethics and the Environment* (New York, Prentice Hall, 1983).

Scott, A., 'Globalization: Social Process or Political Rhetoric?', in A. Scott (ed.), *The Limits of Globalization* (London: Routledge, 1997).

Scott, J., *Weapons of the Weak: Everyday Forms of Peasant Resistance* (New Haven, CT, Yale University Press, 1985).

Scott, J., 'Deconstructing Equality-Versus-Difference: Or, the Uses of Poststructuralist Theory for Feminism', in D.T. Meyers (ed.), *Feminist Social Thought: A Reader* (New York and London, Routledge, 1997).

Searle, J.R., *The Construction of Social Reality* (Harmondsworth, Penguin, 1995).

Seglow, J., 'Universals and Particulars: The Case of Liberal Cultural Nationalism', *Political Studies*, 46 (1998).

Seglow, J., 'Liberalism and the Politics of Recognition', in M. Evans (ed.), *The Edinburgh Companion to Contemporary Liberalism* (Edinburgh, Edinburgh University Press, 2001).

Sen, A., *Inequality Reexamined* (Oxford, Oxford University Press, 1992).

Shanley, M.L. and Narayan, U., *Reconstructing Political Theory* (Cambridge, Polity Press, 1997).

Shaw, C.D. and McKay, H.D., *Juvenile Delinquency and Urban Areas* (Chicago, University of Chicago Press, 1942).

Sher, G., 'Qualifications, Fairness, and Desert', in N. Bowie (ed.). *Equal Opportunity* (Boulder, CO, Westview Press, 1988).

Shklar, J. 'Political Theory and the Rule of Law', in A.C. Hutchinson and P. Monahan (eds), *The Rule of Law: Ideal or Ideology?* (Toronto, Carswell, 1987).

Shue, H., 'Morality, Politics and Humanitarian Assistance', in B. Nichols and G. Loescher (eds), *The Moral Nation: Humanitarianism and U.S. Foreign Policy Today* (Notre Dame, University of Notre Dame Press, 1989).

Sigmund, P.E. (ed), *St Thomas Aquinas on Politics and Ethics* (New York, Norton, 1988).

Simmons, A.J., *Moral Principles and Political Obligations* (Princeton, NJ, Princeton University Press, 1979).

Singer, P., 'Famine, Affluence and Morality', *Philosophy and Public Affairs*, 1 (1971).

Singer, P., 'The Singer Solution to World Poverty', *New York Times*, 5 September 1999.

Skinner, Q., *Liberty before Liberalism* (Cambridge, Cambridge University Press, 1998).

Smith, A., *Nationalism and Modernity* (London, Routledge, 1998).

Spruyt, H., *The Nation State and its Competitors* (Princeton, NJ, Princeton University Press, 1995).

Squires, J., 'Feminist Visions of Political Citizenship', in C. McKinnon and I. Hampsher-Monk (eds), *The Demands of Citizenship* (London, Continuum, 2000).

St Augustine, *The City of God*, ed. and tr. R.W. Dyson (Cambridge, Cambridge University Press, 1998).

Stark, C., 'Hypothetical Consent and Justification', *Journal of Philosophy*, 97 (2000).

Starrett, D.A., *Foundations of Public Economics* (Cambridge, Cambridge University Press, 1988).

Steinberger, P., 'Public and Private', *Political Studies*, 42 (1999).

Steiner, H., *An Essay on Rights* (Oxford, Blackwell, 1994).

Steiner, H., 'Territorial Justice', in S. Caney, D. George and P. Jones (eds), *National Rights, International Obligations* (Boulder, CO, Westview Press, 1996).

Steiner, H., 'Freedom and Bivalence', in I. Carter and M. Ricciardi (eds), *Freedom, Power and Political Morality: Essays for Felix Oppenheim* (London, Palgrave, 2001).

Stone, C., *Should Trees Have Standing? Towards Legal Rights for Natural Objects* (Los Altos, CA, Kaufman, 1974).

Sugden, R., 'The Metric of Opportunity', *Economics and Philosophy*, 14 (1998).

Sumner, L.W., 'Positive Sexism', *Social Philosophy and Policy*, 5 (1987).

Sutch, P., *Ethics and International Justice* (London, Routledge, 2001).

Sutherland, E.H., *Criminology* (Philadelphia, PA, Lippincott, 1924).

Sylvan, R., 'A Critique of Deep Ecology'. *Radical Philosophy*, 40 and 41 (1984–85).

Synder, R.C., *Citizen-Soldiers and Manly Warriors: Military Service and Gender in the Civic Republican Tradition* (Lanham, MD, Rowman and Littlefield, 2000).

Taheri, A., *Holy Terror* (London, Sphere, 1987).

Tamir, Y., *Liberal Nationalism* (Princeton, NJ, Princeton University Press, 1993).

Taylor, C., *Philosophy and the Human Sciences* (Cambridge, Cambridge University Press, 1985).

Taylor, C., 'Cross Purposes: The Liberal-Communitarian Debate', in N. Rosenblum (ed.), *Liberalism and the Modern Life* (Cambridge, MA, Harvard University Press, 1989).

Taylor, C., *Sources of Self* (Cambridge, Cambridge University Press, 1989).

Taylor, C., 'What's Wrong with Negative Liberty', in A. Ryan (ed.), *The Idea of Freedom* (London, Oxford University Press), reprinted in D. Miller (ed.), *Liberty* (Oxford, Oxford University Press, 1991).

Taylor, C., 'The Politics of Recognition', in A. Gutman (ed.), *Multiculturalism: Examining 'The Politics of Recognition'* (Princeton, NJ, University Press, 1994, 2nd edn).

Taylor, C., 'Conditions of an Unforced Consensus on Human Rights', in J. Bauer and D.A. Bell (eds), *The East Asian Challenge For Human Rights* (Cambridge, Cambridge University Press, 1999).

Thompson, E.P., *The Making of the English Working Class* (Harmondsworth, Penguin, 1965).

Thompson, J., *Justice and World Order* (London, Routledge, 1992).

Tiebout, C., 'A Pure Theory of Local Expenditures', *Journal of Political Economy*, 64 (1956).

Tomasi, J., 'Kymlicka, Liberalism and Respect for Cultural Minorities', *Ethics*, 105 (1995).

Tronto, J., *Moral Boundaries: The Political Argument for an Ethic of Care* (New York, Routledge, 1993).

Tully, J., *Strange Multiplicity: Constitutionalism in an Age of Diversity* (Cambridge, Cambridge University Press, 1995).

Turner, T., 'Anthropology and Multiculturalism: What Is Anthropology that Multiculturalism Should Be Mindful of It?', *Cultural Anthropology*, 8 (1993).

Van Parijs, P., *Real Freedom for All: What (If Anything) Can Justify Capitalism?* (Oxford, Clarendon Press, 1995).

Vincent, A., 'The Character of Ecology', *Environmental Politics*, 2:2 (1993).

Vincent, A., *Modern Political Ideologies* (Oxford, Blackwell, 1995, 2nd edn).

Vincent, A. and Plant, R., *Philosophy, Politics and Citizenship: The Life and Thought of the British Idealists* (Oxford, Blackwell, 1984).

Viroli, M., *For Love of Country – an Essay on Patriotism and Nationalism* (Oxford, Clarendon Press, 1995).

Voet, R., *Feminism and Citizenship* (London, Sage, 1998).

Wacquant, L., *Les prisons de la misère* (Paris, Raisons d'Agir, 1999).

Walby, S., *Theorizing Patriarchy* (Oxford, Blackwell, 1990).

Waldron, J., 'Introduction', in J. Waldron (ed.), *Theories of Rights* (Oxford, Oxford University Press, 1984).

Waldron, J., 'A Right to Do Wrong', *Liberal Rights: Collected Papers 1981–1991* (Cambridge, Cambridge University Press, 1993).

Waldron, J., 'Can Communal Goods be Human Rights?', *Liberal Rights: Collected Papers 1981–1991* (Cambridge, Cambridge University Press, 1993).

Waldron, J., 'Liberal Rights: Two Sides of the Coin', *Liberal Rights: Collected Papers 1981–1991* (Cambridge, Cambridge University Press, 1993).

Waldron, J., 'Rights in Conflict', *Liberal Rights: Collected Papers 1981–1991* (Cambridge, Cambridge University Press, 1993).

Waldron, J., 'Special Ties and Natural Duties', *Philosophy and Public Affairs*, 22 (1993).

Walker, B., 'Plural Cultures, Contested Territories: A Critique of Kymlicka', *Canadian Journal of Political Science*, 30 (1997).

Walzer, M., *Spheres of Justice: A Defence of Pluralism and Equality* (Oxford, Basil Blackwell, 1983).

Walzer, M., 'Interpretation and Social Criticism', in S.M. McMurrin (ed.), *The Tanner Lectures on Human Values* (Salt Lake City, UT, University of Utah Press, 1988).

Walzer, M., 'Nation and Universe', in G.B. Petersen (ed.), *The Tanner Lectures on Human Values* (Salt Lake City, UT, University of Utah Press, 1989).

Walzer, M., *Just and Unjust Wars* (first published 1977) (New York, Basic Books, 1992, 2nd edn).

Walzer, M., *Thick and Thin* (Notre Dame, University of Notre Dame Press, 1994).

Walzer, M., 'Response', in D. Miller and M. Walzer (eds), *Pluralism, Justice and Equality* (Oxford, Oxford University Press, 1995).

Walzer, M. and Dworkin, R. (1983), '*Spheres of Justice*, an Exchange', *New York Review of Books*, 21 July 1983.

Wayne, S.J., 'President Bush Goes To War', in S.A. Renshon (ed.), *The Political Psychology of War* (Pittsburgh, PA, University of Pittsburgh Press, 1993).

Weale, A., *Democracy* (London, Macmillan, 1999).

Weber, M., *Economy and Society*, eds G. Roth and C. Wittich (New York, Bedminster Press, 1968).

Weber, M., *Max Weber: Essays in Sociology*, eds H. Gerth and C. Wright Mills (London, Routledge, 1991).

Weeks, J., *Sexuality and its Discontents: Meaning, Myths and Modern Sexualities* (London, Routledge and Kegan Paul, 1985).

Weintraub, J., 'The Theory and Politics of the Public/Private Distinction', in J. Weintraub and K. Kumar (eds), *Public and Private in Thought and Practice: Perspectives on a Grand Dichotomy* (Chicago, University of Chicago Press, 1997).

Weldon, T.D., *The Vocabulary of Politics* (Harmondsworth, Penguin, 1953).

Wildasin, D.E., *Urban Public Finance* (Chicago, Harcourt Press, 1986).

Williams, B., 'The Idea of Equality', in B. Williams, *Problems of the Self* (Cambridge, Cambridge University Press, 1973).

Willoughby, W., *Social Justice* (New York, Knopf, 1900).

Wilson J.Q., *Thinking About Crime* (New York, Vintage, 1971).

Wilson, J.Q. and Kelling, G., 'Broken Windows: The Police and Neighborhood Safety', *Atlantic Monthly*, March (1982).

Wilson, W.J., *The Truly Disadvantaged* (Chicago, University of Chicago Press, 1987).

Yeatman, A., *Postmodern Revisionings of the Political* (New York, Routledge, 1994).

Young, I.M., *Justice and the Politics of Difference* (Princeton, NJ, Princeton University Press, 1990).

Young, I.M., 'Impartiality and the Civic Public', in J. Landes (ed.), *Feminism: The Public and the Private* (Oxford, Oxford University Press, 1998).

Index

Alexander the Great 95
Anderson, B. 57
Appiah, K.A. 159
Aquinas, St Thomas 213–14, 219
Arendt, H. 55–6
Aristotle
    on legitimacy 95–6, 97–9 *passim*
    The Politics 95–6
    on public versus private 132–3
Aron, R. 220
Arrow, K. 109
Augustine, St
    on legitimacy 96
    on just war 213–14, 219

Bacon, F. 188
Barry, B.
    on green political theory 184, 187,
        190–1
    on international justice 200–1,
        204
    on multiculturalism 161–4
    on Rawls, J. 31
    on Walzer, M. 204–5
Bauman, Z. 65–6 *passim*
Beccaria, C. 67, 71
Beitz, C. 201
Bentham, J. 80, 196
Berlin, I. 5–9 *passim*
Bookchin, M. 190
Brennan, A. 191
Brown, C. 196–7 *passim*
Buchanan, J. 110

Canovan, M. 58
Carter, I. 15n.6, 15n.18
Castel, R. 69
Christman, J. 8
Cicero 127
Clausewitz, L. von 212
Clemenceau, G. 56
Cohen, G.A. 15n.16
Cohen, J. 111–12
communitarianism *see* community
community 145–54
    and collective agency 146–9
    defined 145–9
    and the distinctness of persons
        151–3
    identification and dissociation
        149–50
    Kukathas, C. on 154n.2
    McMahon, C. on 154n.2
    Mulhall, S. and Swift, A. on 154n.2
    Nozick, R. on 151–3 *passim*
    Poole, R. on 149
    Rawls, J. on 151
    Raz, J. on 146
    Sandel, M. on 146
    Taylor, C. on 145–6
consent 41–4
    tacit 42
contract 41–4
    and punishment 67–8, 71
Coole, D. 136, 140–1
cosmopolitanism *see* international justice
crime *see* punishment

Dahl, R. 107–10, 112
democracy 105–16
    Arrow, K. on 109
    Buchanan, J. and Tullock, G. on 110
    Cohen, J. on 111–12
    contestory 114–15
    Dahl, R. on 107–10, 112
    deliberative model of 111–14
    interest-aggregating model of 107–11
    Miller, D. on 109, 113
    minimal view of 105–7
    Owen, D. on 130n.15
    Pettit, P. on 114–15
    Przeworski, A. on 105–6
    Riker, W. on 109–10
Descartes, R. 188
Devall, B. 183
Djilas, M. 220
domination 93–5, 120
Dreyfus, A. 56
Dryzek, J. 184–5
duties
    Hobbes, T. on 97
    imperfect 24
    international 198
    and rights 18, 21
    see also obligations

Eckersely, R. 183, 186–7
ecology *see* green political theory
Eisenstein, Z. 135
Elshtain, J.B. 138–9
environment *see* green political theory
equality
    and gender 32
    of opportunity 28–38 *passim*
    Rawls, J. on 28–38
Etzioni, A. 77, 84

families 31–2
feminism
    Coole, D. on 136, 140–1
    Eisenstein, Z. on 135
    Elshtain, J.B. on 138–9
    Friedan, B. on 138
    Okin, S.M. on 135–8 *passim*
    Pateman, C. on 136–40 *passim*
    Phillips, A. on 141–2

Young, I.M. on 138–9
    see also gender; public and private
Foucault, M. 68
Fox, W. 183
freedom 4–14
    Cohen, G.A. on 15n.16
    constraints on 11–14
    deprivation of 68
    Hayek, F. von on 12–13, 126–7
    Herman, B. on 27n.13
    Humbold, W. von 7–8
    internal constraints on 12
    and libertarianism 12–14
    Locke, J. on 11
    Mill, J.S. on 7–8
    natural social obstacles to 11–12
    negative and positive 5–9
    Oppenheim, F. on 15n.7
    Rawls, J. on 33–5
    Raz, J. on 165
    republican 8–9
    right to equal 17
    Rousseau, J.-J. on 5–6
    socialists and 12
    Steiner, H. on 12–14
    Taylor, C. on 14n.4
    triadic relation 9–11
    Weber, M. on 100
Friedan, B. 138
Frost, M. 197

Galileo, G. 188
Garland, D. 65
Gellner, E. 66
gender 169–80
    behavioural theories of 175–6
    equality and 32
    family and 170
    Hobbes, T. on 173
    homosexuality and 173, 176
    malestream and 170–80 *passim*
    performative theories of 178–9
    Plato on 170–1
    power theories of 176–7
    sexual behaviour and 172–3
    sexual politics and 173–4
    social science and 172–3
    see also feminism

Gewirth, A. 206
Giddens, A. 82
globalisation 65–6, 78–9
Gloz, P. 74
Goodin, R.E. 53–4, 184–6, 191–2
Graham, G. 200
Green, T.H. 78
green political theory 182–93
  and anthropocentrism 183–4
  Barry, B. on 191
  Barry, J. on 184, 187, 190–1
  Bookchin, M. on 190
  communitarian naturalism 190
  concept of nature 187–9
  critiques of 189–92
  deep anthropocentrism 184
  Devall, B. on 183
  Dryzek, J. on 184–5
  Eckersely, R. on 183, 186–7
  ecocentrism on 183–4 *passim*
  first and second nature 190
  Fox, W. on 183
  Gaia hypothesis 183
  Galileo on nature 188–9
  Goodin, R.E. on 184–6, 191–2
  inclusive wholes 185
  Naess, A. on 183, 185
  pliant anthropocentrism 184
  Porritt, J. on 186
Guevara, C. 219

Habermas, J. 63n.26
  on nationalism 60–1
  on public and private 139
Hardin, G. 199–200
Hare, R.M. 199
Harrington, J. 127
Hart, H.L.A. 67, 71
Hayek, F. von
  on freedom 12–13, 126–7
  on punishment 124
  on rights 123
  The Road to Serfdom 122–3
  on the rule of law 121–7
  and tyranny of the majority 127
  on welfare 128
Held, D. 115
Herman, B. 27n.13

Hobbes, T.
  on civil science 96, 173
  on the Fool 97–103 *passim*
  and law 120–1
  and legitimacy 96–103 *passim*
  and obligations 41–4, 97
Humboldt, W. von 7–8

immigration 79–81, 161
Ingram, A. 61
international justice 196–208
  Barry, B. on 200–1, 204
  Beitz, C. on 201–2
  Bentham, J. on 196
  Brown, C. on 196–7 *passim*
  cosmopolitanism/universalism
    197–202
  Frost, M. on 197
  Gewirth, A. on 206
  Graham, G. on 200
  Hardin, G. on 199–200
  Hare, R.M. on 199
  Jones, C. on 196
  Kant, I. on 196
  Miller, D. on 204
  O'Neill, O. on 197, 206–7
  and particularlism 206
  Pogge, T. on 201–2
  Rawls, J. on 201–3, 206
  Shue, H. on 206
  Singer, P. on 197–200
  Steiner, H. on 202
  Sutch, P. on 196
  Thompson, J. on 196
  Walzer, M. on 204–5

Johnson, J.T. 213
Jones, C. 196
just war 211–23
  Aquinas, St Thomas on 213–14, 219
  Aron, R. on 220
  Augustine, St on 213–14, 219
  defined 212–5
  Djilas, M. on 220
  Guevara, C. on 219
  ius ad bellum 214
  ius in bello 214
  Johnson, J.T. on 213

and just conduct 214, 221–3
and just recourse 214–20
Osama bin Laden and 218
Pearse, P. on 219
Russell, F.H. on 212
justice
    Kantian duties of 17
    social justice 28–38
    theories of social justice 84–6

Kant, I.
    on agency and autonomy 184
    and the categorical imperative 17,
        24–6
    and duties of justice 17–26 *passim*
    and international justice 196
Kearney, R. 57–8
Kelling, G. 70–1
Kepler, J. 188
Kramer, M.H. 15n.6
Kukathas, C. 154n.2
Kymlicka, W.
    on culture 158–60
    on immigration 161
    Liberalism, Community and Culture
        156
    Multicultural Citizenship 158–60
    on public and private 132

law
    and law-making 120, 127–9
    rule-like nature of 120–7
    see law, rule of
law, rule of 118–29
    arbitrary rule 119–20, 124–5
    Hayek, F. von on 121–7
    Hobbes, T. on 120–1
    and law-making 120, 127–9
    legislative process 127–9
    and multiculturalism 128–9
    rechtsstaat 121
    and republicanism 127–9
    res publica 127
    and rights 129
    and rules 120–7
    Shklar, J. on 118
    Skinner, Q. and Pettit, P. on 127
    versus rule of persons 119

legitimacy 93–103
    Aristotle on 95–6, 97–9 *passim*
    Augustine, St on 96
    Hobbes, T. on 96–103 *passim*
    Locke, J. on 99–101
    Rawls, J. on 102–3
    Rousseau J-J. on 100–1
    Weber, M. on 93–5
libertarianism 82–3
    and freedom 12–14
    and punishment 71–4
liberty *see* freedom
Locke, J.
    on freedom 11
    and social contract 71
    on legitimacy 99–101
    on national sovereignty 54
    on obligations 41–4

MacCallum, G. 9–11 *passim*
Machiavelli, N. 127
McKinnon, C. 121
McMahon, C. 154n.2
Midgely, M. 191
Mill, J.S.
    on freedom 7–8
    on public and private 138
    on welfare 78
Miller, D. 58–9, 109, 113
    on international justice 204
    on multiculturalism 160–1
Mulhall, S. 154n.2
multiculturalism 53, 128–9, 156–66
    Appiah, K.A. on 159
    Barry, B. on 161–4
    and immigration 161
    Kymlicka, W. on 156, 158–60
    Miller, D. on 160–1
    Parekh, B. on 160–1
    and the politics of recognition 160–6
    and rights 157–8
    Tamir, Y. on 160–1
    Tully, J. on 160–1
    Young, I.M. on 160–1, 162
Munoz-Dardé, V. 32

Naess, A. 183, 185
nationalism 52–62

Anderson, B. on 57
Arendt, H. on 55–6
Canovan, M. on 58
civic 55
and economic sovereignty 79–81
ethnic nationalism 55–6
Habermas, J. on 60–1
Ingram, A. on 61
the Jacobin tradition 56
Kearney, R. on 57–8
liberal nationalism 58–9
Miller, D. 58–9
patriotism 59–61
post-nationalism 57
Viroli, M. on 60–1
nation-states *see* nationalism
New World Order 211
Nietzsche, F. 221
Nozick, R. 151–3 *passim*

O'Neill, O. 18–24, 197, 206–7
obligations 41–9
and allegiance 53–4
and apartheid 45
and benefits 44–6
and consent theory 41–4
Hobbes, T. on 41–4
Locke, J. on 41–4
moral versus general grounds for
47
Rawls, J. on 50nn.4–5, 50n.6
Simmons, A.J. on 50n.5
and voluntariness 47–8
and voting 42
see also duties
Offe, C. 66
Okin, S. M. 135–8 *passim*
Oppenheim, F. 15n.7
Owen, D. 130n.15

Parekh, B. 160–1
Pateman, C. 136–40 *passim*
Pearse, P. 219
Pettit, P. 114–15, 127
Phillips, A. 141–2
Plamenatz, J. 183
Plato
    Crito 41, 44

on gender 170–1
The Republic 170–1
Pogge, T. 201
Poole, R. 149
Porritt, J. 186
private sphere *see* public and private
Przeworski, A. 105–6
public and private 131–42
Aristotle on 132–3
Coole, D. on 136, 140–1
defined 131–3
Eisenstein, Z. on 135
Elshtain, J.B. on 138–9
feminist critiques of 132–42
four approaches to 136–7
Friedan, B. on 138
Habermas, J. on 139
Kymlicka, W. on 132
Mill, J.S. on 138
Okin, S. M. on 135–8 *passim*
Pateman, C. on 136–40 *passim*
Phillips, A. on 141–2
Young, I.M. on 138–9
public sphere *see* public and private
public–private split *see* public and private
punishment 65–75
and actuarial criminal policy 71–4
and social groups 71–4
Bauman, Z. on 65–6 *passim*
Beccaria, C. on 67
Castel, R. on 69
and character 68–9
and deprivation of liberty 68
disintegration theory 71
Foucault, M. on 68
Garland, D. on 65
Gloz, P. on 74
Hart, H.L.A. on 67
Hayek, F. von on 124
insurance strategy 72
Kelling, G. on 70–1
and libertarianism 71–4
and penitence 68
and poverty 65–7, 69
Rawls, J. on 67
and rehabilitation 68–70
and risk distribution 71–4
and social contract 67–8, 71

and social control 65–9 *passim*
and Thatcher, M. 73
Wacquant, L. on 65
Weber, M. on 66
and welfare 69
Wilson, J.Q. on 70–1
and zero tolerance 70–1

Rawls, J.
    A Theory of Justice 29–30, 38
    on allegiance 53–4
    on Barry, B. 31
    the difference principle 29–30,
        33–6
    on equality 28–38
    on families 31–2
    individual and community 151
    on international justice 201–3, 206
    The Law of Peoples 203
    on legitimacy 102–3
    on obligations 50n.4–5, 50n.6
    Political Liberalism 35, 38
    principles of justice 29–30
    on the priority of liberty 33–4
    on punishment 67
    on welfare 77–81 *passim*
Raz, J. 17, 20, 146, 165
rights 16–26
    the basis/content distinction 18
    content of 17–18
    context sensitivity 19
    and criminality 65, 67
    and duties 18, 21
    Hayek, F. von on 123
    interest-based (IB) approach 16–26
    and Kantian duties of justice 17–26
        passim
    multicultural 157–8
    non-interference and 17–19 *passim*,
        27n.13
    O'Neill, O. on 18–24
    prima facie 18–19
    Raz, J. on 17, 20
    Rechtsstaat 121
    rights-respecting institutions 20
    rule of law 129
    Taylor, C. on 203
    universal versus special 20

Waldron, J. on 17–24
    welfare 17–21 *passim*
Riker, W. 109–10
Rorty, R. 204
Rousseau, J-J.
    on freedom 5–6
    on legitimacy 100–1
    and national sovereignty 54
    on political community 111
rule of law *see* law, rule of
Rushdie, S. 163
Russell, F.H. 212

Sandel, M. 146
Schumpeter, J. 105–6
self-ownership 67–8
Sen, A. 15n.15
Sher, G. 37
Shklar, J. 118
Shue, H. 206
Simmons, A.J. 50n.5
Singer, P. 197–200
Skinner, Q. 127
social exclusion 81–4
    see also welfare
Socrates 41–4 *passim*
Steiner, H. 12–14, 202
Sutch, P. 196
Swift, A. 154n.2

Tamir, Y. 160–1
Taylor, C.
    on community 145–6
    on freedom 14n.4
    and the politics of recognition
        160–6
    on rights 203
Thatcher, M. 73
Thompson, J. 196
Tullock, G. 110
Tully, J. 160–1

United Nations Declaration of Human
    Rights 21

Van Parijs, P. 77, 85–6
Viroli, M. 60–1
Voltaire 54

voluntariness 47–8

Wacquant, L. 65
Waldron, J. 17–24
Walzer, M.
    Barry, B. on 204
    and international justice 204–5
    Just and Unjust Wars 205
    Spheres of Justice 205
    on welfare 78
Weber, M.
    and freedom 100
    on legitimacy and domination
        93–5
    on punishment 66

welfare 77–89
    communities of choice 77–81, 84–5
    Etzioni, A. on 84
    Green, T.H. on 78
    Mill, J.S. on 78
    neo-Hegelians on 78
    Rawls, J. on 77–81 *passim*
    and social exclusion 81–4
    and socially reproductive work 87–8
    Walzer, M. on 78
Wilson, J.Q. 70–1

Young, I.M. 138–9, 160–2

zero tolerance 70–1